N

MANTLE OF HEROISM

MANTLE OF HEROISM

Tarawa and the Struggle for the Gilberts, November 1943

Michael B. Graham
Foreword by Ken Hechler

PRESIDIO

Published by Presidio Press
505 B San Marin Dr., Suite 300
Novato, CA 94945-1340

Library of Congress Cataloging-in-Publication Data

Graham, Michael B., 1961-
    Mantle of heroism : Tarawa and the battle for the Gilberts /
Michael B. Graham.
        p. cm.
    Includes bibliographical references and index.
    ISBN 0-89141-496-7
    1. Tarawa, Battle of, 1943. 2. World War, 1939–1945—Campaigns–
–Kiribati.   I. Title.
D774.T37G73 1993
940.54'26—dc20   93-7008
                                                          CIP

Photographs courtesy of The National Archives

Typography by ProImage
Printed in the United States of America

"There had to be a Tarawa . . . What the Marines accomplished there set a standard for future amphibious operations. It was much more than a successful battle. . . .

"Tarawa, without question, was one of the most crucial and difficult battles participated in by Marines. Seldom has the mantle of heroism fallen over so many shoulders in so short a period of time. The valor displayed there will be sung in the Corps for years and years to come.

"God grant us today and in the future the courage, the intelligence and the will to win which the Marines displayed at Tarawa. . . ."

Lt. Gen. Leo D. Hermle
U.S. Marine Corps, 1953

Contents

MAPS

Author's Note

The study of Operation Galvanic, the American invasion of Tarawa and the Gilbert Islands during World War II, has been my passion since 1977 when I found a dusty copy of Robert Sherrod's incomparable *Tawara: The Story of a Battle*. I recall the shadows that passed over the faces of my granddads when I shared with them this bargain book discovery. They were both veterans, and it struck me that both had curiously deep, apparently personal, impressions of Tarawa, although neither had been there. One served in the navy in the Marianas and the Philippines, and at Okinawa, in landing craft. The other served in the army, and earned bronze arrowheads for the landings at Morocco, Sicily, Salerno, Anzio, and southern France, and for the Rhine crossing. Even my dad, a Vietnam war veteran who spent ten years in the navy, revealed a silently respectful perception of Tarawa, having heard about it from World War II veterans whom he encountered in the fifties and sixties. In these three men in my family, when I uttered the syllables TAR-uh-wuh, dreadful images were conjured up that I did not then comprehend. Precisely because of their dark reactions, in spite of them, I resolved to learn all that I could about this singularly haunting American military experience.

Now as I write this preface to *Mantle of Heroism,* it is one year before Galvanic's fiftieth anniversary in 1993. In promoting the project I suggested that it would be appropriate to note the occasion by publishing a narrative history of the campaign. I pointed out that there had been but one account, however brief, that had covered the American undertakings against the Japanese in the Gilberts in their entirety. That had been in 1978 when there appeared *Storm Over the Gilberts,* a quick read written by the prolific journalist and historian Edwin P. Hoyt.

To be sure, Mr. Sherrod's *Tarawa* had set the tone for writing about the Gilberts. There had been other notable accomplishments with respect to the battle for Tarawa, but so dramatic and compelling was the fighting there, so graphic the eyewitness reporting of correspondents, that critical supporting land, sea, and air actions had been all but ignored. Quite simply, the conquest of the Gilberts was so far overshadowed by its costliest component that the larger story of the campaign has been all but forgotten. The product of Hoyt's labor had dealt with the perspectives of the opposing naval forces to the exclusion of just about all other facets of the campaign; there was a need, then, for a new approach.

But when I began ten or more years ago to consult the popular literature as well as the official sources on the Gilberts campaign, it was some time before I fully realized that the story of Galvanic was more than that Tarawa produced the worst casualties in twentieth century U.S. military history, proportional to the number of troops engaged. Indeed, by 1982, I had read everything available about the campaign, and it seemed to me that writing on the subject had reached a dead end. After delving deeper into the archives, however, I began to see and understand the angle that the whole of the campaign was more than the appalling sum total of the dead and wounded at Tarawa. It was only then that the idea of this narrative and its form really began to jell.

The first draft was completed two days before Iraq invaded Kuwait. I continued the work for nine months thereafter, when I could steal a few hours after duty as a U.S. government foreign affairs officer specializing in the Middle East and South Asia. The day after Kuwait fell, the State Department began pulling together what came to be called the Kuwait/Gulf War Task Force. Thanks to the recommendation of my supervising officer, Janet Wilgus, I was assigned to the team handling the press and public affairs angle of the crisis. In fact, the war in the Gulf delayed the appearance of this volume but in the process improved my grasp of the fragile nature of crisis communications and information through intimate association.

In fielding inquiries, I quickly discovered myself being drawn into a moving human story, rather than merely passively observing the emerging horror of another twentieth-century conflict. As family and friends across the country began shipping out, I became fascinated by what kinds of people were really involved, what kinds of families they came from, and how they reacted together when in harm's way in the Gulf. But if this experience revealed something about myself that I did not previously know was there, it is also part of another story. Suffice it to say, as a result of my experience during the crisis, I promised myself that I would remain in touch with the thoughts and fears that ran through my mind during those ominous days leading up to and through the herculean buildup to the allied coalition's counteroffensive in January and February.

Thus as I resumed research on Operation Galvanic, I consulted the wartime literature of correspondents and official public affairs and information officers who had written copiously on the campaign that would prove so critical to the end of Japan's gamble to control Asia and the Pacific. With a new eye I turned to the immediacy of the works of Sherrod, Zurlinden, Lucas, Shaffer, Richardson, Johnston, Hannah, and others, all of whom had lived through the Gilberts campaign and written about it.

Afterward I could not help but be pleased with the transformation I saw occur in *Mantle of Heroism*. Where before I had looked down at a dry military narrative that spoke to me only of dual superfiring turrets, units of fire, assault waves, and bomb tonnage, now there also was the story of people: men of the American armed forces, the Japanese enemy they fought, and the civilians who were caught up in the bloody Central Pacific confusion in 1943.

Therefore the work at hand is principally a narrative of the island fighting in the Gilberts, but not exclusively; the import of Tarawa in particular is intelligible only when set in the context of the Gilberts and the Central Pacific campaign in all its aspects. This history, then, is conceived as a systematic narrative of the American fighting forces involved in the multifaceted operation to seize and occupy the Gilberts, especially as it has not been reported heretofore. A narrative of this scope obviously must be governed by a principle of selectivity. In my conception of telling the story of the Gilberts, Tarawa is the center of the circle: The more influenced the persons and events are by Tarawa, the more detailed the treatment; the more peripheral, the less detailed.

Selectivity is by definition hazardous. I aimed to be as inclusive as practical; omissions of people or events indicate no negative judgment.

Though I would love to have tried, if all persons and events that played a part in the Gilberts campaign had been included, this book would have reached unreasonable proportions. As for deep background, such as the intricate science of calculating tides, it did not seem necessary or desirable to repeat everything already recorded in official studies. Rather, persons and events have been included to the extent that they help to illustrate the principal developments and characteristics of this unique, large-scale amphibious operation. To accomplish these purposes, I decided to follow a chronological order more or less, making chapter divisions according to the natural phases in the operation.

This narrative is neither a complete nor official history of Operation Galvanic in all its dimensions, but it lays the foundation for that larger objective. It is a synthesis based primarily on the achievements of writers and historians specializing in the American war with Japan; many of these people were present for the campaign. Thus in researching this subject, I relied upon the official histories as well as all the monographs, battle studies, biographies, and memoirs that have appeared since the war. I am privileged to have known men who were there, and I have tried to encapsulate in their words a sense of what it was like for the soldiers, sailors, coast guardsmen, airmen, and marines. Some of the material herein, then, is new and essentially offers a freshly enhanced perspective for looking at this particular campaign.

I benefited not only from personal encounters with participants but also to one degree or another from the guidance and resources of the Army War College, Marine Corps Headquarters and Historical Center, U.S. Information Agency, Naval Historical Center and Archives, Office of the Chief of Military History, U.S. Army Military History Institute, the Pentagon Library, the Library of Congress, National Defense University, and National Archives. I devoured all the official and unofficial information ever published on the subject of the campaign. Avid readers of the naval and military history of the Pacific war who read this narrative will immediately recognize many primary sources.

Although thanks are due to many people, it is impossible to credit everyone to whom I own some recognition for their contributions. Those who helped directly or indirectly over the years are just too numerous to mention in total. Nevertheless, among those who provided assistance, it is a distinct pleasure to acknowledge the generous contribution of The Honorable Dr. Ken Hechler: Secretary of State of the great state of West Virginia, professor, World War II U.S. Army combat historian, author, adviser to presidents, congressman—truly a hillbilly for the ages. Secretary Hechler was the first to read the entire manuscript, and his foreword speaks for itself. Few transplanted mountaineers such as myself ever had a finer role model. Deep gratitude also to my agent, Mr. David Stewart Hull, president of Hull House Literary Agency, for his kindness, counsel, and enthusiasm. I must also express my appreciation to a magnificent editor, Ms. Joan Griffin, of Presidio Press. Without her keen eye I would most certainly have made many an error. Finally, as always, I owe a great deal of gratitude for the patience and forbearance of my wife, Tina. I am deeply grateful to them all.

Michael Bryan Graham
Owings, Maryland, and
Arlington, Virginia

Foreword

Those who fought at Tarawa and elsewhere in the Gilbert Islands are fortunate that the author decided to chronicle their exploits. Too many writers of military history get bogged down in the bewildering details of units, or of minor actions. To be able to distinguish the forest from the trees is a rare art. In this volume, Michael Graham has achieved a tour de force.

Graham's training as a journalist enables him to get his priorities straight. It also produces a highly readable account. In addition, he displays a keen sensitivity toward the individual soldiers, sailors, coast guardsmen, airmen, and marines who bore the brunt of the battle. It is easy for a journalist to fall into the trap of producing a potboiler that is superficial in tone, but this volume is characterized by depth and careful research.

Journalists before Michael Graham have produced outstanding military histories. As a combat historian in World War II, Brig. Gen. S. L. A. Marshall headed up the U.S Army's historical coverage in the European theater of operations. His career as a military commentator for the *Detroit News* was eclipsed by the many volumes he produced on such subjects as the battles for Bastogne, Kwajalein, and Makin. General Marshall's techniques of combat interviewing and his lucid, dramatic writing have been emulated by the research and interviews with which Michael Graham has been able to humanize the official records of Operation Galvanic.

It is obvious that the author has worked long and hard on this book. He has combed through all the published and unpublished sources over a period exceeding ten years. Ordinarily, this would lead to an attempt to parade the results of this exhaustive research. Fortunately for the reader, Graham has resisted this temptation. He has attacked his subject with the kind of sustained delight that bespeaks countless hours of research. The result is a labor of love that excites the reader to the kind of admiration usually reserved for marathon runners who break into a fresh sprint when they enter the stadium.

Some of us who have served as combat historians feel that smelling the smoke of battle is necessary to produce a genuine military history. Of course, writers such as Shelby Foote do pretty well long after the surrender at Appomattox. Michael Graham does not profess to be a novelist, yet he writes like one. Furthermore, his journalism background has been enhanced by U.S. government foreign affairs service. This volume then has the great advantage of informed perspective on the chain of events that occurred about half a century ago.

Mantle of Heroism, the title of this volume, comes from an unusually graphic sentence by a marine general. Although some future debunker may discover that this great phrase emanated from the pen of an enlightened public relations man, nevertheless it is a colorfully accurate characterization of the battles described herein.

Having fought in the European theater of operations, I have always been amazed that we could mount the type of successful offensive we did in the Central Pacific so quickly after the disaster at Pearl Harbor. The major priority in World War II was obviously in Europe, commanding the most in combat troops and their armament. This volume unfolds the dramatic story of how the strategic planning of combined arms, coupled with the indomitable fighting spirit of American troops, not only won the battle for Tarawa and the Gilberts, but also paved the way for subsequent island victories on the road to Tokyo.

In writing *The Bridge at Remagen*, I learned a great deal about the fighting spirit of American citizen-soldiers in my interviews with both high-ranking German officers and men in the front lines. They all commented on the speed, determination, and initiative of American combat troops, as well as their ability to take quick advantage of opportunities in the heat of battle. Michael Graham ably demonstrates that these same traits served Americans well during the Tarawa and Gilberts operations.

This foreword is being written too close to the ending of hostilities in Operation Desert Storm to draw definitive conclusions and comparisons with the battles the author describes. However, to draw

Michael Graham out on this theme, I asked him to set down his personal observations on the subject. His answer, written only a couple of weeks after the fighting stopped in Kuwait and Iraq, is worth repeating:

> In terms of the "AirLand Battle" doctrine of the various services in the Gulf War—employing combined operations both swiftly and massively; relying on global strategical and tactical mobility, deception, and violent air power to overwhelm strong emplacements; breaching of obstacles by infantry forces; and pushing strong armored forces through those units—there occurred a revolution in doctrinal procedure and tactical execution not unlike the Gilberts experience.
>
> The marines who took Kuwait City in 100 hours, the wild race of U.S. "mech" infantry across southern Iraq, and the awe-inspiring VII Corps drive into the Iraqi flank ossified the term *blitzkrieg* and ushered in *hyperwar*. Similarly, the marines who took Tarawa in 76 hours, the soldiers at Makin, and the carrier operations in support of Galvanic also provided the first textbook example of an untried doctrinal procedure and tactical execution—modern amphibious warfare.

The above, spur-of-the-moment statement, written on March 21, 1991, will I believe stand the test of time. So also will this volume.

KEN HECHLER
Secretary of State of West Virginia
Author,
The Bridge at Remagen and *Working with Truman: A Personal Memoir of the White House Years.*

Introduction

OPERATION GALVANIC:
THE BATTLE FOR THE GILBERT ISLANDS
NOVEMBER–DECEMBER 1943

Shortly before dawn on Sunday, November 20, 1943, in the seas of the northern and central Gilbert Islands, 108,000 men stirred among the greatest gathering of warships yet assembled in the Allied war against Japan. From dozens of troop-carrying transports soldiers, sailors, marines, and coast guardsmen boarded landing craft. From the heaving decks of eighteen carriers the greatest number of naval aircraft ever assembled for a single operation rose into the sky. In this action, RAdm. Raymond A. Spruance, the commander in chief, Central Pacific, uncoiled Galvanic, one of the costliest actions of World War II.

The scope of the operation was epic. The naval air forces alone amounted to nearly a thousand planes; army, navy, and marine land-based fighters, bombers, and reconnaissance aircraft numbered another two hundred. That Sunday morning, the first of thirty-five thousand troops—an American marine amphibious corps, accompanied by six thousand vehicles and many thousands of tons of supplies and equipment—began landing on the Japanese-held islands of Makin and Tarawa. They were preceded by a naval and air bombardment, the destructive power of which was unprecedented in the history of war. On the islands, protected by the strongest fortifications encountered anywhere by any nation in the war, were the Japanese forces.

What follows, then, is the story of the fighting for the Gilberts and the events leading up to that bitter battle.

The Prelude

PART ONE

Chapter One

August 1943. A new plane landed on the deck of the American light carrier *Independence* steaming off the coast of Oahu. The plane, a Grumman F6F Hellcat fighter, had a ceiling of 37,500 feet and a range of 1,530 miles with drop tanks, and could carry one thousand-pound bomb under each wing. The Hellcat could fly, climb, and dive faster than the Mitsubishi A6M Zero, the infamous Japanese fighter it was designed to counter. The Hellcat was also more maneuverable and more heavily armored, and had superior firepower.

With the Hellcat, the Avenger torpedo bomber, and the Dauntless dive-bomber, the United States would take its first decisive steps toward the Japanese home islands. But Japan lay five thousand miles from Hawaii, and the path the navy would have to take was blocked by hundreds of Japanese-held islands in the Central Pacific, many studded with air bases. The new planes and the new carriers that would take them into battle first had to be introduced to the fleet. The Central Pacific seemed the ideal place to use the new forces.

Admiral Ernest J. King, the tough commander in chief of the U.S. Navy (COMINCH), produced the means in April. "We have to start somewhere," he had told RAdm. Raymond A. Spruance, chief of staff of the U.S. Pacific Fleet. "We've retaken Guadalcanal from the Japanese in the South Pacific and pushed them out of Papua New Guinea. The British are about to launch an attack in Burma. We need to go on the offensive in the Central Pacific. We should start in the Marshalls."

Spruance returned to Hawaii and informed his boss, Adm. Chester W. Nimitz, commander in chief of the U.S. Pacific Fleet (CINCPAC), that Admiral King wanted action in the Central Pacific. "Are we ready?" asked Nimitz. "Can we take the Marshalls?"

Neither Nimitz nor Spruance was sure. They assigned the war plans staff of CINCPAC the job of finding out. In July Spruance reported back to Nimitz that Japanese fortifications in the Marshall Islands were too strong for the limited American forces then available to attack at this time. He recommended that America's resurgent naval and ground forces first seize the Gilbert Islands, which the fleet strategists suspected were not so heavily defended. Then airfields could be built so that land-based air forces could reconnoiter and soften up the Marshalls prior to an invasion.

Thus did Admiral King in Washington trigger the beginning of Operation Galvanic, the code name of the first major American amphibious operation of the war in the Pacific. The original plan was to capture two island groups in the Gilbert Islands and nearby Nauru. The demands of the operation would be overwhelming. The attack would be staged from Pearl Harbor, 2,100 miles away, and would require not only the largest assembly of warships yet accomplished in World War II but would also constitute the longest voyage of an invasion fleet in the history of warfare.

Although it was believed that the Gilberts would be easier to take than the Marshalls, the Americans would still face a significant dual challenge when Galvanic was launched in November. The naval forces would have to be strong enough to support the Gilberts invasion and at the same time be prepared to fight the vaunted Kido Butai, the Main Striking Force of the Japanese Combined Fleet based at Truk in the Caroline Islands.

The Gilbert Islands, now the independent nation of Kiribati (pronounced KEE-ree-bahss), lay across the equator, extending more than 400 miles from southeast to northwest and covering 200,000 square miles of ocean. The Gilbert Islands include sixteen lesser island groups, on two of which Japanese troops could be found in strength: Tarawa (TAR-uh-wuh) and Makin (MUG-rin). Another island group, Abemama, supported the southernmost Japanese radio listening post in the South Seas. The northernmost island group, Makin, which the planners expected to ignore, was only 250 miles south of the eastern Marshalls, where the Japanese had major air bases at Mili and Jaluit. To the west, 380 miles from Tarawa, squats Nauru, which the Japanese had transformed into another major air base. The nearest American airfield was in the Ellice Islands, at Funafuti, 700 miles south of Tarawa.

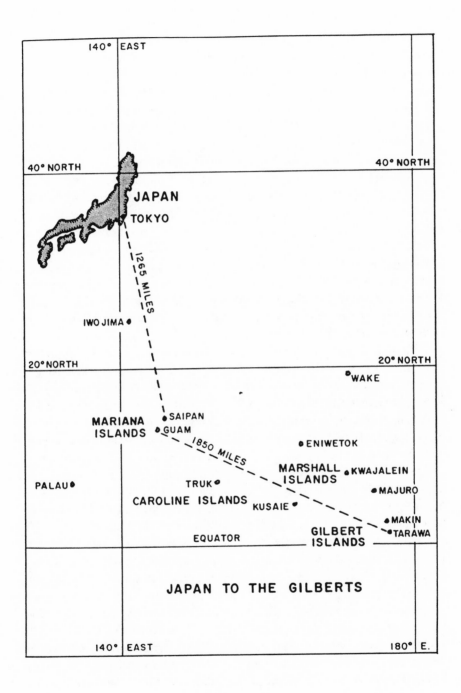

JAPAN TO THE GILBERTS

Although Admiral King thought that American forces were strong enough to go into action in the Central Pacific—certainly they could capture the Gilberts and Nauru, he believed—nearly everyone at CINCPAC was apprehensive. All the advantages the Americans had enjoyed in the South Pacific, such as naval mobility, the Japanese now would enjoy in the Central Pacific. Furthermore, American possessions east of Hawaii supported only air bases. These islands did not have the anchorage capacity to support a major fleet operation such as Galvanic. Therefore the naval and ground forces would have to sortie from elsewhere. In the end, some would depart from as far away as San Diego and San Francisco. Most, however, would steam from Pearl Harbor and the New Hebrides.

"With our paucity of carriers—and with the urgency to get started on our return march to the westward—it was essential we seize Tarawa," said Nimitz, "first, so that we could use it as an unsinkable carrier in our operation against the Marshalls, and second, to eliminate Tarawa as a threat to our important line of communications between our West Coast and Australia and New Zealand."

The Joint Chiefs of Staff (JCS) set November 15, 1943, as the target date for the Gilberts invasion. As soon as Tarawa, Nauru, and Abemama were seized, navy Seabees would develop the Japanese airfields and establish other air bases for land-based army and marine fighters and army Seventh Air Force heavy B-24 Liberator bombers. Ten weeks later, by January 30, 1944, the Marshalls would be attacked.

Nimitz would use the new U.S. Fifth Fleet to carry out Galvanic. This powerful naval force would be enormous. It included six attack carriers; five light carriers; seven escort carriers; a dozen battleships; fifteen cruisers; sixty-five destroyers; thirty-three large amphibious transports; twenty-nine tank landing ships (LSTs); twenty-eight miscellaneous support ships, such as cargo carriers, oilers, tugs, and tenders; and hundreds of smaller landing and assault craft. The fleet would carry 35,000 army and marine assault and garrison troops, 117,000 tons of cargo, and 6,000 vehicles. Finally, RAdm. Charles A. Lockwood, commander in chief, submarines, Pacific (COMSUBPAC), would provide ten submarines for Galvanic.

The Fifth Fleet, with its nucleus of fast carrier forces, was under the overall command of Spruance. Like Nimitz he also favored an attack on the Gilberts first. Spruance concluded, "Without them we held no positions close enough to the Marshalls to enable us to obtain the amount of photographic reconnaissance required for the capture of the Marshalls. A further reason for the capture of the Gilberts was the need for land-based air strength to wear down enemy positions in the Marshalls prior to Operation Flintlock—the invasion of the Marshalls that was to follow Galvanic—and to cooperate with our carrier attacks during the initial assault in eliminating Japanese air strength throughout the entire island group."

On August 23 RAdm. Charles A. "Baldy" Pownall began the preliminaries to the autumn action. Task Force 15, a small armada of three carriers, one battleship, two cruisers, several destroyers, and a tanker, sortied from Pearl Harbor under his command. Ostensibly Nimitz sent them to attack the Japanese airfield and installations on Marcus Island, an isolated outpost of just 740 acres. Marcus lay 1,200 miles southeast of the Japanese home islands and 650 miles west of Wake. A mere 700 miles from sprawling enemy air bases in the Bonin and Marianas chains, Marcus was deep in Japanese waters and too strongly defended until now to risk attack by American forces.

In reality, however, not much in the way of destruction was expected of the hit-and-run raid. It was devised primarily to provide the untried and inexperienced fast carrier forces with a live training mission. CINCPAC was curious how the new aircraft carriers would perform as strategic weapons, which the young carrier captains then joining the fleet passionately argued they were. Nimitz decided that the time had come to test the growing naval air power at his disposal. Marcus, a largely unheard-of speck in the Pacific, would serve nicely for that test.

All three carriers and their crews assigned to the raid were new and passed to Rear Admiral Pownall's command after he had spent a year as commander of naval air forces on the West Coast. Pownall had served with distinction in World War I. An expert in mechanical engineering, he was best known in the fleet for his scientific work as the former chief of the engine section in the naval Bureau of Aeronautics. Among his accomplishments in that job was his management of a project that had eliminated carbon monoxide poisoning as a danger to pilots.

Triangular-shaped Marcus Island, which the Japanese call Minami-Tori-Shima, was little more than an airfield surrounded by sea. Its three runways were paved with crushed coral and paralleled the short coastlines. The island had been left alone since VAdm. William F. "Bull" Halsey had conducted a startling raid in March 1942, more than eighteen months before, with the carrier *Enterprise*. Since then the Japanese had increased the island's defenses and installations four times over. Now the airfield was a key stepping-stone in the Japanese line of communications from the home islands to the huge naval and air base at Truk and all points beyond.

The carrier planes began launching before sunrise 130 miles northeast of Marcus. By 0605 they were over the target. The combined air attacks by the Dauntlesses and Avengers, protected by the new Hellcat fighters, caught the Japanese completely by surprise. Lights were burning in buildings and Japanese air controllers on duty in the airfield tower were not in the least suspicious when approaching planes appeared with running lights burning brightly. They had no reason to think that the aircraft were anything but friendly. They did not even have time to second-guess themselves and hit the air raid warning as a precaution before the thunder of two-thousand-pound bombs crashing all around them confirmed the worst.

Lieutenant Commander Richard Upson in his Avenger was the first to sight Marcus. "There it is, boys!" he shouted into his radio. "There it is!" Upson, the torpedo squadron leader, fired the first shots that marked a revolution in American sea power—the affirmation of the task force and the carrier attack battle group. It had been his idea for the American planes to switch on their running lights.

By 0700 fully 30 percent of the Japanese installations on Marcus were already damaged. The raid lasted nine hours. Six strikes totaling 275 combat sorties were made. Several torpedo bombers were destroyed on the ground and the airfield was badly damaged. Not one Japanese plane got into the air. Eighty percent of the buildings, aircraft hangars, storage depots, and antiaircraft (AA) and coastal artillery positions had been knocked out. In addition, the airfield had been rendered temporarily unusable, throwing the Tokyo air defense system into panic and confusion.

In contrast, American losses were surprisingly light. Only three Hellcats and one Avenger were lost. As the last fighters left Marcus for the carriers, a cloud of smoke eight thousand feet high towered over the island. Under the headline "Island Raid Gives Japs the Jitters," *Stars and Stripes,* the newspaper of the U.S. armed forces, speculated, "The attack on Marcus appears to be the first blow in a possible offensive opening in a direct invasion route to Japan."

There is no question that the raid shocked the Japanese. Radio Tokyo warned, "The Americans could have raided the mainland if they had wanted to. The Japanese people must solidify their defense against the enemy."

The fast carrier force had passed its first test. But it was just the beginning. The raid on Marcus merely established the pattern for future action in the Pacific. Two weeks later, Pownall, leading another carrier battle group of new ships, would again be in action against a far more important target.

Chapter Two

With the advent of the task force concept in 1943, the rebirth of American sea power in the Pacific was nearly complete.

"Paradoxical as it may sound," said VAdm. Frederick J. Horne, deputy chief of naval operations at the time, "the fleet as such no longer exists— that is, as an operational unit. Missions in modern warfare are now generally accomplished by task forces. In these the cruiser plays an essential part. But the ideal task force is built around the aircraft carrier, and, since the carrier is relatively inferior in armament, it is necessary that someone run interference for her. The cruiser is the ideal type for flexibility, speed, and armament."

Yet even as CINCPAC planned Operation Galvanic to seize the initiative in the Central Pacific and the fast carrier forces began to flex their muscle in hit-and-run raids, the Japanese were formulating their own plans. Fleet Admiral Meinichi Koga, commander in chief of the Imperial Combined Fleet, suspected that the Americans would move in strength somewhere before the end of the year, especially after the surprise September 1 raid on Minami-Tori-Shima. Koga planned for a major showdown in the South or Central Pacific.

It had been that way since May 1943. Then Koga had succeeded to command of the Combined Fleet after the brilliant naval strategist Fleet Adm. Isoroku Yamamoto died when his plane was ambushed by American fighters and shot down. The new navy commander in chief, who had been a disciple of the naval air theories advanced by Yamamoto and had accepted them without reservation, was a heavy man with a "samurai belly," and was known for the large size of his head. He was very much aware of the difficulties he had inherited from his legendary predecessor. "Our enemy is preparing to seek final victory in developing his means of offensive and in preparing plans for the strategic application of new weapons," said Koga to his staff. "There was only one Yamamoto and no one is able to replace him. His loss is an insupportable blow to us."

Now, during meetings at Truk, Koga listened to VAdm. Ryusonuke Kusaka, commanding the defense of the South and southwest Pacific, who reported on the campaigns in these areas. That Gen. Douglas A. MacArthur and Adm. William Halsey were both attacking "with utmost speed and drive" was bad news indeed; even worse were their obvious intentions of heading for Rabaul. "Halsey, in particular," Kusaka told the Combined Fleet commander, "is making dangerous progress."

After months of stormy discussion among the naval leaders since the death of Admiral Yamamoto in April, Japanese options were declining. Allied grand strategy seemed to be overtaking them. In the south, MacArthur's forces were making the main drive across the northern coast of Papua New Guinea; this was the route that Admiral Yamamoto had called, in a report to the Naval General Staff, "a saber pressed against our belly." In the southeast, Halsey's forces were leapfrogging through the Solomons and were headed into the Rabaul area, drawing off the Japanese forces that could be used against MacArthur.

Either of these complementary advances could become the main line of attack if one or the other of the offensives faltered, warned Kusaka. Clearly the Americans were approaching their goal in the South Pacific. For the Combined Fleet it was immensely distressing that of all the enemy commanders it was Halsey—the American whom the Japanese despised most for his highly publicized racial slurs—who seemed destined to reach the major Japanese naval and air base at Rabaul. Halsey's Third Fleet had been specially reinforced for the offensive, with high priority in ships, troops, air support, supplies, and equipment.

In all, Halsey and MacArthur together had under their command 250,000 American and Australian troops in some fifteen divisions and attached units, including the I and III Amphibious Corps and U.S. Sixth Army. They were supported by 700 Third Fleet ships and landing craft and 1,000 aircraft, including Maj. Gen. George C. Kenney's U.S. Fifth Air Force, which Radio Tokyo called "The Beast." Indeed the strategic balance could only be expected to worsen. Imperial General Headquarters (IGH) predicted that Allied increases in the South Pacific before the end of the year would be monumental. Then, it was estimated,

MacArthur and Halsey would have perhaps 400,000 to 500,000 troops and 1,500 planes. All the while, Nimitz could not be expected to sit on his hands; his strength would also grow at Pearl Harbor.

It had been five months earlier, in May 1943, that the matter of a comprehensive plan for strategic defense in the Pacific had been considered by the Combined Fleet planning staff. On that occasion Koga had sat at the head of a conference table at Truk, flanked by aides and advisers, among them Vice Admirals Kusaka and Nobutake Kondo. The plan proposed by Kusaka and approved by IGH in Tokyo had called for major reinforcement of the South and Central Pacific with as many aircraft as possible. The Second Fleet would be brought up to full strength at Truk. Only then was it believed that American offensives in the Solomons, Central Pacific, and eastern New Guinea could be checked.

Troop reinforcements would be sent to strengthen the Gilberts and Marshalls. In the event that the Americans attacked either of these island groups, aircraft would be transferred from the Bismarcks and Truk to the Marshalls. The Combined Fleet at Truk, supported by submarines, would sortie as soon as it was notified of an American movement toward the Central Pacific. But heavy losses in operations against MacArthur and Halsey had continued throughout the summer, and the need for a new strategy was again apparent.

Just two years before, there had been no necessity for a plan. Up to June 1942 Japanese victory had seemed so certain that there appeared no need for island fortifications. The Rising Sun was aloft everywhere. French Indochina had been subjugated before the war with the Allies even started. Great tracts of coastal China and all of Manchuria had been carved up as long ago as 1931. The war was not even six months old when the colonies of Western Europe and the United States began falling into Japanese hands. Guam fell in a day. Wake, reinforced at the last minute, held out a little longer. Then, in spring 1942, in just five months, Japan's victorious legions conquered the Philippines, the East Indies, and Southeast Asia up to the Indian frontier; then, as a horrified world gasped in disbelief, it drove the American and British fleets from the sea in a succession of stunning naval victories. After the intoxicating collapse of Singapore, all that prevented Japanese mastery of the Pacific was a war-weary Australia and an enfeebled United States. Indeed what need had Japan for a strategic defense?

But Admiral Yamamoto did not invade Hawaii. He had wanted to, but the army demurred, gambling that the Allies would sue for peace. As time passed, the war situation rapidly changed. The IGH became obsessed with neutralizing Australia. In January and February, even after the U.S. Navy had reorganized itself around its carriers and conducted raids on the Marshalls and Gilberts, little attention had been paid to the Central Pacific flank. But the United States staged a miraculous recovery, and suddenly Japan's vast possessions in the Pacific became a liability. Still, little work was done on fortifications.

Then, in August 1942, the pendulum of war began to swing against Japan with the invasion of Guadalcanal. Simultaneously there occurred the most spectacular commando operation of the Pacific war, when 220 elite U.S. Marine Corps "Raiders" under Lt. Col. Evans F. Carlson and Maj. James Roosevelt, President Franklin Roosevelt's son, landed by submarine at Makin in the Gilberts. It was a bloody two-day prelude to future Allied operations. Planners learned just how fanatically the Japanese intended to defend even the smallest, most isolated flyspeck of sand in the Pacific.

At Makin the Raiders had sixty-six casualties, of which thirty-seven were killed. The Japanese garrison, estimated at a hundred, fought to the last man—to the death. The long-term results of the raid were catastrophic. Much like army Brig. Gen. James H. Doolittle's daring air raid on the home islands in spring 1942 had shocked the Japanese into undertaking the Midway operation, Carlson's commando raid shocked the Japanese into striking south from the Marshalls. They seized and fortified the rest of the Gilberts as well as nearby Ocean and Nauru islands.

Over the next year thousands of Japanese naval troops and Korean "volunteer" laborers were shipped to these islands to build fortifications. Enormous quantities of concrete and steel were ordered; so much work was planned that a then staggering $1.7 million was allocated for air base construction in the Gilberts alone in 1943. Concrete and steel were made to go further by engineers—nearly all the bunkers and blockhouses in the Gilberts were reinforced by crushed coral and thick coconut logs. So prodigious was the work and so great the demand for material and equipment that parts of the old British fortifications at Singapore were cannibalized for the Central Pacific. By summer 1943, although the construction work was not finished, the fortifications, especially in the Gilberts, were already a frightening reality.

But with heavy losses in the Solomons fighting, Koga concluded that a more realistic plan was necessary than that upon which the frantic work had been carried out in the Gilberts. He drew two circles, one within the other. The inner circle represented the area of resources and possessions controlled by Japan and considered vital to the war effort—the Carolines, Marianas, and Philippines. The outer circle—the Marshalls, Gilberts, Solomons, and New Guinea—represented the area that was expendable. This zone would be defended only with what could be spared from elsewhere. No further major efforts would be made on possessions in the outer circle unless an opportunity arose to fight a decisive naval battle.

During the first week of September Koga issued the "New Operational Policy." It was centered on the Yogaki plan, or "waylaying attack," a strategy to wait for the enemy fleet to enter Japanese waters and then fight a decisive naval engagement. Koga had a dozen air bases in the potential battle areas, including facilities in the Marshalls, Gilberts, Solomons, Carolines, and New Britain. His land-based air forces in these islands could help his carrier fleet destroy the Americans when they came forward. The Japanese also possessed three large naval anchorages in the South and Central Pacific, one at Truk in the Caroline Islands, one at Kwajalein in the Marshall Islands, and another at Rabaul on the northeast coast of New Britain.

The best opportunity to bring the elusive American navy to battle would occur if Nimitz appeared in the Central Pacific in force. If the Americans invaded the Marshalls to seize a forward fleet anchorage and the air bases there, or attacked the Gilberts, Koga would put the Yogaki plan into effect. The strategy for a possible battle in the Gilberts was drawn up on September 8. Rear Admiral Keiji Shibasaki, who recently had been named commander of the Gilberts and Nauru, already had eight thousand naval infantry and support troops. Five thousand of these were based at Tarawa and the rest were dug in on Makin, Ocean, and Nauru islands. Scouts were based on other islands.

But Koga intended to make the Gilberts even stronger with whatever resources could be spared from the strengthening of the inner area. He planned to send elements of VAdm. Masashi Kobayashi's Fourth Fleet amphibious force, under RAdm. Matsu Matsanaga at Kwajalein, to reinforce the Gilberts with twenty-five hundred Imperial marines. He also called on naval Comdr. Goro Matsuura, commander of the 22d Air Flotilla at Truk, using bases throughout the Marshalls, to support the plan by attacking the American carrier forces all around the forward edge of the battle area when they appeared.

Meanwhile, under RAdm. Takeo Takagi, commanding the Japanese Sixth Fleet, large I-type fleet submarines from Rabaul and Truk and small RO-type coastal patrol submarines in the Marshalls would move up and begin scouting north to south in the vicinity of the Marshalls and Gilberts. When the enemy appeared the submarines would concentrate their attacks against naval forces.

The Second Fleet, or Scouting Force, with its heavy cruisers and numerous destroyers under Kondo, would advance and operate in the area north of Nauru to lure the American fleet westward. After the American carriers had been led westward, land-based naval air forces of the Eleventh Air Fleet based at Rabaul would weaken the advancing enemy fleet. The Second Fleet would move up to the eastern Marshalls around Mili and continue operations. If necessary a squadron of destroyers would depart Rabaul to assist. Planes of the Third Air Fleet, then in training, would join in the defense of the Gilberts, regardless of the level of preparedness they had attained.

"Your Cruiser Scouting Force will not only support the defense of Nauru," Koga told Admiral Kondo, "but the enemy will be forced to send his carrier fleet westward in order to shield any landings in the Gilberts. We can then begin the Yogaki plan and eliminate the American carriers."

To achieve this, Koga depended on the Kido Butai. In September, the Main Striking Force included 3 carriers with nearly 200 combat aircraft, the superbattleships *Yamato* and *Musashi* with their monstrous 18-inch guns, and 2 battleships and a destroyer squadron from the First Fleet. On the island air bases of the Marshalls, Gilberts, Carolines, and elsewhere, Koga had another 150 land-based planes. Further, the Naval General Staff of IGH could be expected to transfer some of the more than 2,000 planes in the general strategic reserve in the home islands to the Combined Fleet if an opportunity occurred to fight a decisive naval battle. Also available was the Third Fleet, which had a combined strength of 3 carriers with 150 aircraft, 2 battleships, 11 heavy cruisers, 3 light cruisers, and scores of destroyers. Kobayashi's

Fourth Fleet could contribute 2 light cruisers, 4 destroyers, and 6 submarines. Finally, Takagi's Sixth Fleet included 24 submarines.

"It was not," said VAdm. Shigeru Fukudome, chief of staff of the Combined Fleet, "a plan of any positive action to draw the American fleet into a decisive action, but rather to wait until the American fleet came up; and Admiral Koga felt sure that they were bound to come up if he only waited." Nevertheless, not since the battle for Midway had the Japanese had such a strong force available for action. Koga reasoned that with enough time to prepare he would be as ready as the steadily deteriorating condition of Japan's strategic situation would allow. He was certain that the Yogaki plan could defeat the U.S. Pacific Fleet wherever it appeared.

Unfortunately for Koga, time was the last thing that CINCPAC intended to give him. No sooner had the ink dried on the Yogaki plan, or the New Operational Policy, than Rear Admiral Pownall and the American fast carrier forces struck the Gilberts with all the fury of a hurricane.

Chapter Three

The two-day hit-and-run air raid on the Gilberts, which began September 18, 1943, resembled the attack on Marcus—but it was also something more. The first operation had been a tune-up for what was to come. When Rear Admiral Pownall's TF 15 appeared out of the east in the Gilberts on the night of September 17, the carrier chiefs were still learning their craft. This time, however, there also was every expectation that a heavy blow was about to be lowered on the Japanese. Admiral Nimitz had told Pownall, "We have to decrease enemy pressure on our holdings in the Ellice Islands."

The fast carrier forces were to test Japanese defenses and soften them up as much as possible. They were also to gather as much information about the Japanese positions in the island group as they could. The Gilberts, two thousand miles southeast of Marcus, had not been hit by navy planes since Vice Admiral Halsey's task force had visited them and the Marshalls in January and February 1942 prior to the *Enterprise* raid on Marcus. The only other important American action in the group had been the daring submarine-launched commando attack on Makin by Carlson's Raiders thirteen months earlier.

Since the Gilberts were to be invaded in November, Nimitz and Rear Admiral Spruance were not at first interested in sending a carrier strike force against them at this time. However, lack of information about the islands convinced them that there was more to gain than to lose in hitting them. Marine Maj. Gen. Holland M. Smith, for one, whose troops of the V Amphibious Corps would assault the Gilberts, was skeptical. He feared that the fast carrier operations would tip the American hand in the Central Pacific. He was not alone.

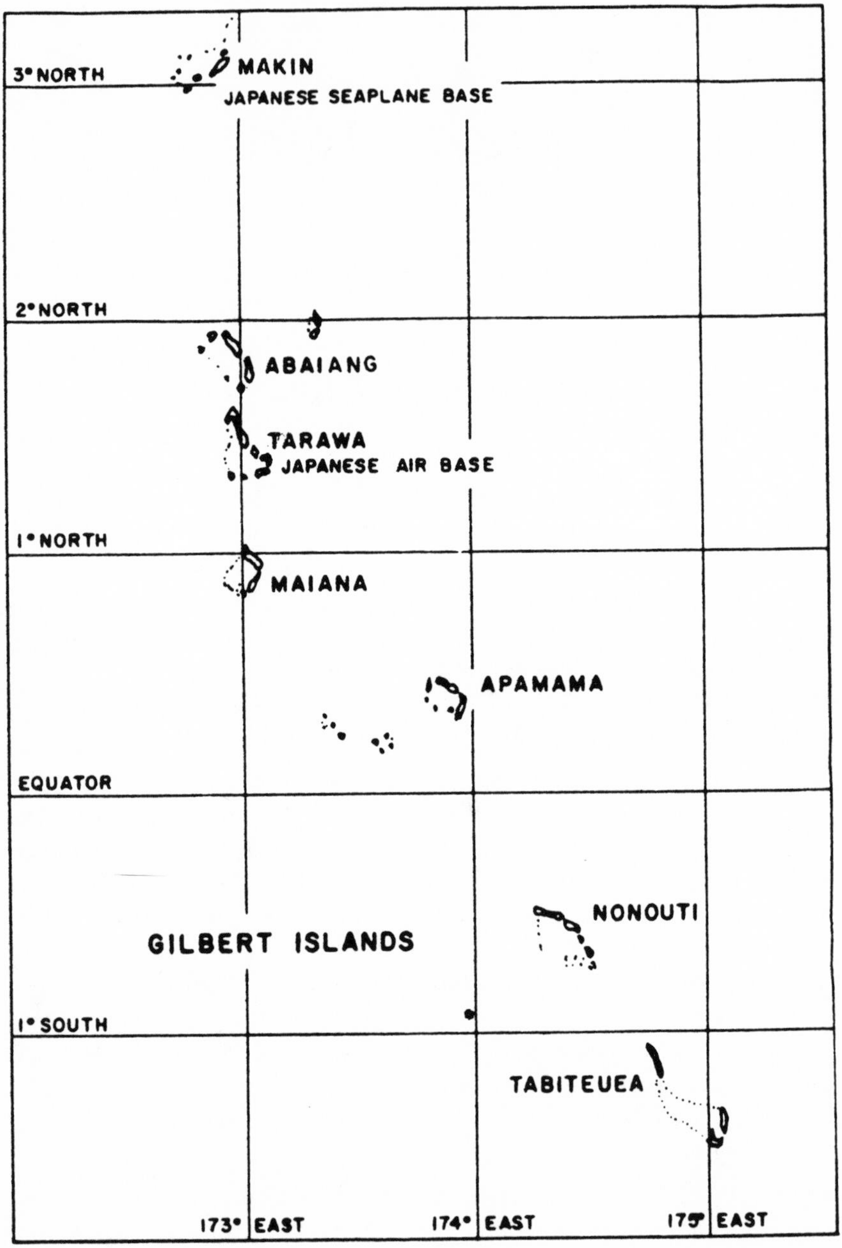

3° NORTH

MAKIN
JAPANESE SEAPLANE BASE

2° NORTH

ABAIANG

TARAWA
JAPANESE AIR BASE

1° NORTH

MAIANA

APAMAMA

EQUATOR

NONOUTI

GILBERT ISLANDS

1° SOUTH

TABITEUEA

173° EAST   174° EAST   175° EAST

Many officers at CINCPAC, chief among them "The Gun Club"—
the influential group of battleship and other surface commanders
who still resisted the far-reaching implications of naval air power—
branded the carrier captains and air admirals prima donnas who were
endangering the war effort. In part, the battleship men were worried
that their own influence in the fleet was waning. They envied the
degree of operational independence the fast carrier forces were suddenly enjoying. They argued that the time spent on hit-and-run raids
by small carrier battle groups would be better used in training for a
general fleet engagement.

Spruance supported this view. He was deeply troubled by the prospects
of a violent Japanese reaction to the raids. But Nimitz, though he privately
agreed with Spruance, thought differently. In order to keep peace among
the naval high command in the Pacific, he felt that he had to give the
carrier chiefs their chance. Because there were more targets involved
in the Gilberts operation than at Marcus, this raid would prove more
difficult. There would surely be problems of coordination. The potential
for Japanese counterattacks also was proportionally greater. There was
no question that the raid on the Gilberts was an important event, fraught
with all kinds of unimaginable dangers.

The naval air enthusiasts were elated. The success at Marcus had
stirred their ambition and determination to decisively influence Allied grand strategy in the Pacific. They pined for a free hand, and the
coming raid was another opportunity. Their pleasure, however, was
mixed. Between the Marcus and Gilberts raids, with the carriers back
in their berths at Pearl Harbor, their pilots unwinding and crews preparing for further action, "Baldy" Pownall was rewarded with the newly
created position of commander, fast carrier forces, Pacific. No one had
been more surprised than he.

Nevertheless, the proponents of air power were less than enthusiastic. Pownall may have been qualified as a pilot, they complained,
but he was first and foremost a student of the old peacetime navy—
a cautious commander who never went beyond the limits of the absolute minimum. To the carrier chiefs' way of thinking, extreme caution negated the incredible destructive power of the fast carrier forces.
Caution in command of carriers, they argued, was at best a gross misuse
of their striking power and at worst a recipe for disaster. But Nimitz,
who had made a name for himself in submarines and had no carrier

experience, was committed to keeping the peace in the fleet as best he could. Although he was prepared to give the fast carrier forces a degree of operational autonomy, he was not ready to turn the air admirals entirely loose. Hence the appointment of Pownall to operational command of the carrier forces.

The top target for TF 15 was Betio (pronounced BAY-she-oh), the principal island of Tarawa Atoll in the central Gilberts. Twenty-two miles long, Tarawa had nine large islands, numerous small ones, and a large lagoon. Consequently, the Japanese had turned it into their most important forward air base in the South Seas. Just to be on the safe side, therefore, it was arranged, much to the chagrin of the carrier captains, to give the fast carrier forces some help. Heavy and medium bombers of the army's Seventh Air Force, based in Hawaii and staging through newly acquired American bases in the Ellice Islands, and others of the Thirteenth Air Force at Guadalcanal would strengthen the attack.

In fact, the first B-24 strikes in the region had occurred nine months earlier. Long before the Joint Chiefs of Staff in Washington had settled upon the Central Pacific as the next theater of operations against Japan, bombers of the Seventh Air Force had begun harassing the Gilberts as well as nearby Nauru. In the Ellices, an airfield had been developed at Funafuti, seven hundred miles southeast of Tarawa, and the first elements of the 11th Bombardment Group were moved up from Canton Island. The B-24s made their first practice run against Tarawa on January 23. Three of the big four-engine bombers made a combined reconnaissance and bombing attack and discovered the airfield on Betio. Another mission on February 17 discovered the seaplane base at Makin.

The first major strike, however, did not occur until April 20. Logistical difficulties had kept pushing it back, but it finally got away—twenty-two Liberators, with army Maj. Gen. Willis H. Hale, commander of the Seventh Air Force, leading the attack in person. The Japanese sent up a dozen Zeros; one B-24 was shot down—the first Seventh Air Force loss in combat in the Gilberts—and several others were damaged. The bombers dropped nearly thirty tons of high explosives on Nauru. They damaged the Japanese airfield and hit the important phosphate factory.

The attack on Nauru was the first clue that RAdm. Tomanari Saichiro, then in command of the South Seas area and based at Tarawa, had that the Americans had built an airfield near enough to strike the Gilberts. A Japanese bomber followed the B-24s home to Funafuti, and Saichiro decided to hit back. On April 21 he sent a dozen twin-engine bombers against the American base at dawn and scored results. Two of the valuable B-24s were destroyed on the ground and six others were damaged in the raid; six American airmen were killed and a dozen injured.

Two days later Hale retaliated. Twelve Liberators droned over Tarawa with moderate success. The result: The airfield on Betio was back in service overnight. From then on, owing to the lack of American air bases, the vast distances involved, and strong Japanese resistance, B-24 missions occurred infrequently. Only sixty-two more combat sorties were made in the entire Central Pacific until September.

Psychologically, the results were worrisome to CINCPAC, and the effect was not lost on the navy. What was happening was no secret—the Japanese were getting stronger every day. Good reconnaissance photos had been taken on each Seventh Air Force mission since the first raid in January. Island defenses, especially at Tarawa and Nauru, were steadily becoming impregnable. Notwithstanding climbing ship sinkings by American submarines, Japanese supplies and reinforcements were getting through and their strength was increasing. They apparently intended to fight very hard for the Central Pacific. All this helped convince Nimitz and Spruance that the Gilberts had to be taken before the Marshalls.

By the time that TF 15 was ready to raid the Gilberts in September, things were improving somewhat. The marines had seized Nukufetau and Nanomea islands, the latter just 525 miles southeast of Tarawa, and the army built airfields on them. This made it possible for the B-24s to mount heavier bombing missions. The same day that the carrier planes struck the Gilberts, two dozen B-24s of the 11th and 30th Heavy Bombardment Groups attacked Tarawa just before dawn. Meanwhile, fourteen Thirteenth Air Force B-24s from Guadalcanal bombed Nauru. In the afternoon twenty-eight Liberators combined photo-reconnaissance and bombing missions over Tarawa, Abemama, Makin, and Nauru.

The effects were mixed. Although the raids served to hamper enemy air movements, the land-based bombers attacked with poor results. The airfield at Nauru was neutralized only for the duration of the operation by the carriers. Betio, which is less than 290 acres—about the size of New York City's Central Park—was attacked from as high as 20,000 feet and even less damage was done. Some bombers failed to find the targets. Thus began the air assault of the Gilberts on September 18.

That morning TF 15 carriers *Princeton, Lexington,* and *Belleau Wood* turned into the wind and were in launching position two hours before dawn, just a hundred miles east of Tarawa. They would strike Betio as well as Butaritari, the southernmost island at Makin, and Abemama, the island group seventy-five miles south of Tarawa. The tactical objective of the attacks for the aircrews was to annihilate Japanese installations, combat strength—gun positions and planes in particular—and shipping in the Gilberts.

A searchlight on *Lexington* signaled "launch planes" in order to preserve radio silence. The first wave took off at 0330, roaring down *Princeton's* flight deck and rising slowly into the night sky. The planes circled and climbed in the dark, organizing for the flight to the target. They headed for Makin, a hundred miles north of Tarawa. Pownall had settled on a sunrise strike against Makin as part of the opening phase of the attack, partially for the purpose of knocking out the Japanese long-range seaplanes based there. The Emily seaplanes could search up to seven hundred miles from their base. If the Hellcats could knock out this threat early, the chance of the Japanese locating TF 15 would be reduced and the raid could proceed with less danger to the carriers.

It was a beautiful tropical morning, with low-lying, billowy clouds from two thousand to eight thousand feet in the sky. Visibility was good up to six miles. A few minutes before 0500 the first wave of blue and silver planes—two Avenger torpedo bombers with two Hellcat fighter escorts from *Princeton*—arrived over Makin from the southeast. It was still too dark to attack, so they circled offshore until sunrise. Then they maneuvered into formation over the lagoon and dived. The AA fire was light. One of the Hellcats made four passes over the large wharf area and strafed it. The other attacked the seaplanes, which were moored in the center of the lagoon. Three strafing runs with incendiary bullets set the seaplanes afire. The Avengers dropped four five-hundred-pound bombs on the wharf. All four planes returned to TF 15.

Meanwhile, the launch for the first strike on Tarawa was set for 0445. The darkness encountered by the planes at Makin led Pownall to push takeoff back to 0500. Among the up and alert Japanese, the morning routine, which normally would have included the organization of labor parties to repair the damage from the predawn raid by B-24s, was canceled when word arrived of the attack on Makin. Thereafter aircrews attempted to get their planes into the air so that they would not be destroyed on the ground. But all this was interrupted when less than an hour later twenty-two planes from *Princeton* and *Belleau Wood* appeared over Tarawa at seven thousand feet just as four bombers were taking off from the airfield.

Wave after wave of American planes streamed across the lagoon and hurled their deadly warheads upon the frantic enemy. Each crew had targets selected for them in advance by combat intelligence analysts working from Seventh Air Force reconnaissance photos, and they separated into attack groups to concentrate on their specific objectives. The sky was dotted with black puffs of AA fire and the lacing of machine-gun tracer. A great many things happened in a very short time—in all just twenty minutes. The planes attacked again and again with killing blows. First went the strafing fighters, then torpedo bombers and dive-bombers.

When they had gone, Tarawa presented an unforgettable scene. The principal island of Betio was a mass of fire from one end to the other. The surface of the water in the lagoon for a large distance around the end of the Burns-Philp trading company's pier was blazing from hundreds of gallons of burning fuel oil. Elsewhere in the lagoon a terrific explosion had fairly lifted into the air the small interisland freighter *Saida Maru,* a veteran of the South Seas. Her back broken by a thousand-pound bomb dropped from a Dauntless dive-bomber, she settled stern first on the bottom in shallow water with her load of critical construction material.

"The island is a sea of flames," wrote a Japanese artilleryman at Tarawa. "Seven of our medium attack bombers were destroyed and a great number of our guns damaged. Moreover, shell dumps, ammunition dumps, various storehouses and barracks on Bairiki [the island east of Betio] were destroyed. A great number of men were killed and wounded." Similarly, at Makin one of the bombs dropped near On Chong's wharf scored a direct hit on an air raid shelter, killing thirty men.

In the midst of the turmoil at Tarawa, the crew of a torpedo patrol boat tried to get underway and head for the north. As she moved she became a target for numerous planes and was repeatedly strafed until, badly crippled, she was run aground on a neighboring island under withering machine-gun fire and bombs. In all, eight Japanese planes were destroyed and two damaged on the ground. The four bombers caught taking off as the attack began escaped and disappeared to the southwest toward Nauru.

By the time Pownall called off the attacks at 1822 and TF 15 retired to the south for the night, the carriers had made seven strikes totaling approximately three hundred sorties against Tarawa, Makin, and Abemama. Eighty-four tons of bombs had been dropped, nearly all on Tarawa. Half the eighteen Japanese planes based at Tarawa and three seaplanes at Makin were destroyed. Several wandering enemy bombers northwest of Makin were shot down by *Lexington*'s combat air patrol (CAP). Three torpedo patrol boats and a freighter were sunk. Considerable quantities of fuel and ammunition were destroyed, buildings were demolished, and vitally important photoreconnaissance was achieved.

One of the air victories on this day belonged to Lt. Thad T. Coleman, Jr. Piloting one of the new Hellcats, he made a remarkable kill that was recorded in a series of photographs taken by the gun camera fitted to his fighter. Coleman found a big four-engine Emily floatplane, a model only recently introduced to the Combined Fleet, flying patrol east of the Gilberts. The Japanese plane was spotted off the fighter's starboard quarter at an altitude of eight thousand feet. Coleman raked the patrol bomber with his six .50-caliber machine guns, and soon the outer and inboard starboard engines burst into flames. Fire enveloped the cockpit and fuselage and the Emily spun into the ocean and exploded. In all, the air action had lasted just five minutes.

The next day twenty B-24s from Canton were sent against Tarawa again. But the airfield on Betio had been repaired overnight and put back in service in less than twenty-four hours. Air reinforcements had flown in from the Marshalls, and eighteen Japanese fighters of the 755th Naval Air Group intercepted the American bombers. The B-24s fought through the fighter screen and six Zeros were destroyed and four seriously damaged. However, the enemy fighters managed to separate the bombers from their groups and their attacks achieved only moderate success.

The two-day combined naval and army air raid on the Gilberts cost the Americans five planes, including three Hellcats, one Avenger, and a badly damaged B-24 that crash-landed upon its return to Nanomea. But, coupled with the success at Marcus, the principle of the carrier battle group or task force had been soundly demonstrated. It was clear that the war in the Pacific would be a very different one from here on.

The final chapter of the raid on the Gilberts, however, was not written until several days later. Maddened by the destruction wrought upon their fortress, the enemy defenders of Tarawa rounded up the two dozen Allied prisoners of war (POWs) and civilians remaining in the islands. Most had been picked up in the months following Carlson's raid when the Japanese had swept into the Gilberts in force. Only the French Catholic missionaries had not been imprisoned. The POWs were Australian, British, and New Zealand soldiers, seamen, coast watchers, and civilians, men who had either been captured or had stubbornly refused to leave the islands when the Japanese came. They had since been pressed into service as laborers. When the American planes attacked, these unfortunate men had been crushing coral near the pier, and with each explosion on the island they had waved and cheered. The Japanese determined that in their animated joy the POWs had been signaling the planes in code. All of them were executed.

No sooner had a long-range reconnaissance plane—launched from a Japanese submarine west of Hawaii—flashed word to Truk that an American carrier battle group had departed Pearl Harbor than Admiral Koga had the Combined Fleet on the move in the Central Pacific. The Second and Third Fleet elements of the formidable Kido Butai left Truk on September 18 even as American TF 15 and heavy bombers were pounding the Japanese-held islands of Makin, Tarawa, Abemama, and Nauru. This large Japanese force of 3 carriers and 175 aircraft, 2 battleships, 7 heavy cruisers, 3 light cruisers, and a destroyer squadron—in all, far more powerful than TF 15—rushed toward the eastern Marshalls.

Koga had every hope of meeting the unsuspecting American warships in a major fleet action. He determined that the eastern Marshalls was the best location from which to stage an ambush. The Japanese fleet arrived at Eniwetok on September 20. But when Koga failed to find the American task force (then racing home to Hawaii), he took his ships back to Truk.

This swift sortie of the Kido Butai badly shook CINCPAC. Naval intelligence analysts who had broken the Japanese naval codes were able to listen to the enemy radio communications. They had followed the movement of the Japanese with great concern and kept Rear Admiral Pownall fully informed of their whereabouts up to the minute. But never again would such a small, vulnerable American carrier task force operate alone. More of the new fleet carriers had arrived at Hawaii. After conferring with his staff, Admiral Nimitz strengthened American striking power for the next hit-and-run raid. When Rear Admirals Alfred E. Montgomery, Van H. Ragsdale, and Arthur Radford steamed from Pearl Harbor on October 3 for the third "training" mission in five weeks of the fast carrier forces, they commanded an astounding six flattops—*Essex, Lexington, Yorktown, Independence, Belleau Wood,* and *Cowpens*—carrying among them 375 aircraft.

Veteran *Time-Life* war correspondent Robert Sherrod had only just arrived at Pearl Harbor aboard a navy PB2Y Catalina seaplane from San Francisco when he learned of the important mission: "My God, I said, are they going to invade the Jap-held islands so soon?" He was not disappointed. "It was a carrier-based raid on Wake Island, which could not fail to be a good story, because (1) it was the largest carrier task force ever assembled and (2) Wake Island was a place Americans would never forget." Indeed Wake was the tiny island that had been so heroically defended by Maj. James Devereux and his band of marines in December 1941.

No one was certain what kind of Japanese reaction there would be when the navy planes swept in. The air admirals believed that the carriers could take care of themselves. The twenty-seven-thousand-ton fleet carriers *Essex, Lexington,* and *Yorktown* each mounted seventeen quad 40mm Bofors and sixty-five rapid-firing dual 20mm AA guns. For added heavy protection, they each had six 5-inch guns, capable of firing a devastating fifteen proximity-fused AA shells a minute up to ten miles away. Meanwhile, the eleven-thousand-ton light carriers *Independence, Belleau Wood,* and *Cowpens* each had two quad 40mm and nine 20mm guns. The carrier chiefs took great comfort in the fact that the AA flak capacity of the battle group alone was infinitely more dangerous than what the naval aircrews could possibly encounter over Wake.

Nevertheless, it was apparent that the Combined Fleet was itching for a fight and might sortie everything it had—exactly what Rear

Admiral Spruance and The Gun Club feared most. After Koga's swift sortie as a result of the Gilberts raid, Nimitz was not inclined to take unnecessary chances. Therefore, in addition to the six carriers under his command at Wake, Montgomery had at his disposal seven cruisers and twenty-five destroyers, making up a fast, powerful task force nearly as strong in air power as the Kido Butai.

Everything possible had been done to prepare for the worst. Long-range patrol bombers had made numerous reconnaissance flights over Wake in order to pinpoint Japanese installations and AA gun emplacements for the fast carriers. A squadron of B-24s manned by navy crews from Midway would add their weight to the assault. A "lifeguard," the submarine *Skate*, commanded by Lt. Comdr. Eugene B. McKinney, of Eugene, Oregon, would be patrolling the area to perform rescue duty for downed fliers. Montgomery also planned to move his cruisers in close to Wake for a naval bombardment.

The fast carrier group—designated TF 14 for this raid—arrived on station unobserved by the Japanese. However, after the first wave of 180 planes launched before dawn on October 5 and approached the target, enemy radar picked them up. Twenty-seven Zeros and 7 bombers were airborne and waiting. It was the strongest resistance the new Hellcat fighters had faced. They performed better than anyone had hoped they could. Two Hellcat squadrons flying escort for the Dauntlesses, Avengers, and new Helldiver dive-bombers shot down the entire Japanese interceptor force. It was another stunning demonstration of the superiority of the new navy fighters. This not only set the tone for the remainder of the raid but also for the remainder of World War II in the Pacific.

With opposition in the air eliminated, the bombers roared in. They struck hard at installations, airfield revetments, and heavy AA gun positions. Japanese bombers revving and lined up on the runways were strafed and bombed. None succeeded in getting into the air. Only three American bombers were lost to flak. In the afternoon two Japanese flights of six Zeros and six bombers each flew into the maelstrom from the Marshalls. They registered on the radar of the carrier battle group, and Hellcats on CAP decimated their ranks.

Some Japanese air reinforcements survived and landed on Wake's pitted airfield, littered with twisted, burning wrecks from previous bombing strikes. But by nightfall victory was nearly complete. With the threat from the air reduced, the cruisers moved in and contributed to the destruction with their 8-inch guns. The carrier planes had flown a record 740 sorties. But losses were higher than in all the previous hit-and-run raids combined. Eleven American planes had been shot down.

During the night most of the Japanese planes that had survived the day's violent action fled south and returned to the Marshalls. The next morning, unlike in previous operations, the fast carrier force struck again. By the time they were finished they were opposed only by light AA fire. Wake had been rendered temporarily defenseless against air attack. Altogether, in two days of intense battle, not counting the heavy raids by B-24s, the TF 14 carriers flew eleven hundred missions— more combat sorties than had been flown by all land- and carrier-based air forces in the Central Pacific since January. The aircrews claimed sixty-five Japanese planes shot down or destroyed on the ground. An oil tanker and several small picket craft were sunk. Twelve American planes were shot down and fourteen others were lost to damage or mishaps, such as crash landings or lost overboard.

The friendly air losses were somewhat offset by the stunning life-guard performance of Lieutenant Commander McKinney and the crew of *Skate*. But however gallant was their heroic achievement, it had not been without jeopardy. Much of the submarine's rescue duty was undertaken within six miles of shore and under shellfire from Japanese coastal batteries. In addition, *Skate*'s executive officer was fatally wounded when a Zero dived unseen out of the haze at dawn on October 6 and strafed the boat.

The next day the submarine escaped a dive-bombing attack and further shelling while rescuing four downed fliers from *Lexington*. In all, *Skate* spent five days rescuing six fliers around Wake. After departing the area, the grateful captain of *Lexington* hailed *Skate* with the message: "Anything in *Lexington* is yours for the asking. If it is too big to carry away, we will cut it up in small parts." Thereafter a submarine on lifeguard duty was an essential feature of Allied carrier operations.

CINCPAC had no idea that the attack on Wake had been a rather close call. Japanese naval intelligence specialists, using information acquired from radio listening posts in the Marshalls and Abemama in the Gilberts, had alerted Admiral Koga of the impending attack. The chief of the Combined Fleet hoped that this was the opportunity for which he had been waiting. Anxious to fight the decisive battle, he interpreted the American raid on Wake, as well as the few ships seen in Pearl Harbor on October 17 by the crew of a long-range scout plane, as indications that Nimitz was going all-out to seize Wake. Koga did not intend to miss this chance, as he had done when TF 15 hit the Gilberts the previous month.

The Japanese fleet commander again rushed the Kido Butai to Eniwetok in the Marshalls. The Combined Fleet elements that left Truk on October 17 were even more powerful than the large force that had rushed forward in September when TF 15 struck Makin, Tarawa, and Abemama. The same 3 carriers with 180 aircraft were in the vanguard, but this time they were accompanied by 6 battleships, 8 heavy cruisers, 3 light cruisers, and 2 destroyer squadrons—again more powerful overall than the American raiding force.

Koga had every hope that an American invasion fleet would appear at Wake or in the Marshalls. The Kido Butai arrived at Eniwetok on October 20. The warships remained a few days while scores of scout planes searched fruitlessly for the U.S. fleet. Koga then sailed three hundred miles north toward Wake and searched some more before returning once again empty-handed to Truk on October 24. The elusive American carriers (then safely home at Pearl Harbor) had escaped yet again.

But even as Koga was engaged in this game of hide-and-seek, the October sortie of the Kido Butai had gone entirely unnoticed by CINCPAC. The Japanese had maintained strict radio silence. Naval intelligence analysts in Hawaii who recorded and deciphered the Japanese naval codes were blissfully unaware that the Combined Fleet had even sailed. All the while they had been reporting that the Kido Butai was still buttoned up at Truk.

As the Combined Fleet steamed into the lagoon at Truk on October 26, Koga received word that the Americans appeared ready to launch a major operation in the South Pacific. There was very little guessing to be done. The ultimate objective would be the neutralization of Rabaul. Koga knew what he had to do.

After the Yogaki plan for action in the Central Pacific had been drawn up in September, IGH had gone to work on a complementary plan for the South Pacific as well. Operation RO, Admiral Koga was told, "consists merely of a whittling-down campaign against the enemy which relies upon the momentary use of crucial battle forces when conditions are favorable." In mid-October the planes of the First Air Fleet were to transfer from their carriers to land bases centered around Rabaul in the South Pacific. Koga did not like the fact that the operation would temporarily incapacitate the Combined Fleet. However, if it offered the slightest chance of slowing down Admiral Halsey's seemingly irresistible advance, he was prepared to go forward with it.

In the last week of October the Japanese reluctantly stripped the Kido Butai of its main striking power and on November 1 sent the fleet's carrier aircraft to reinforce Rabaul. As the enemy planes departed Truk, Halsey's forces were invading the jungle island of Bougainville, just two hundred miles southeast of Rabaul. Believing that yet another opportunity for a naval battle was developing, Koga not only sent his elite carrier air wings to Rabaul but also shifted his naval surface strength southward. The heavy cruiser force of the powerful Second Fleet steamed for Rabaul.

More often than not entirely overlooked in histories of the Pacific war, Operation RO was an all-or-nothing gamble of historic proportions. Unknown to anyone at the time, least of all Koga, it was to have far-reaching effects on the forthcoming American invasion of the Central Pacific.

At Wake, as had occurred only weeks before at Tarawa, the Japanese garrison assembled the Allied captives they held. The unfortunates were one hundred American civilian construction workers. They had been kept on Wake when the rest of the POWs, more than a thousand Americans, were sent to Japan in December 1941 after the island fell. As the intensity and accuracy of the American air attacks had grown, the Japanese accused the civilians of aiding the raids by means of clandestine radio contact with the carriers. On the night of October 7, the day after the fast carrier force had gone, the Americans were lined up on a beach and machine-gunned to death. They were buried in a common mass grave, their fate unknown until the end of the war.

Chapter Four

At Pearl Harbor, as the fast carrier forces delivered devastating blows against Japanese-held islands, planning for the impending action in the Central Pacific had continued apace. Admiral Nimitz leaned back on the leather sofa at CINCPAC headquarters. He was listening to his chief of staff, Rear Admiral Spruance. There had been plenty of discussions regarding the invasion of the Gilberts, as the bustle in the Hawaiian Islands indicated. Everyone understood that the decisions regarding the invasion would have a decisive effect on the course of the war. At least one of the American naval leaders realized this from the start. "This will only be the beginning," he had said in spring when COMINCH ordered him to commence planning. That man was Admiral Chester W. Nimitz.

Now in autumn of 1943 the Allies were embarking upon truly momentous days in the massive struggle with the Japanese empire. In the South Pacific, where nearly a half million Allied troops were fighting, the Japanese had suffered their biggest and bloodiest defeat: Guadalcanal, over which desperate battle raged for six months, had fallen, and as many as thirty thousand Japanese soldiers, sailors, and airmen had been killed, wounded, or captured, and nearly seven hundred planes destroyed. Scores of Japanese and Allied warships had been sunk in frightful naval battles.

In New Guinea, the largest island in the Pacific, General MacArthur was making unprecedented gains on numerous fronts. In the north Pacific, the Japanese had been driven from the Aleutians. In China, India, and Burma, they continued to hang on grimly against increasing Allied military might. Throughout the Pacific, American submarines had sunk nearly two million tons of merchant shipping. And now

CINCPAC was sharpening plans for yet another terrible blow—Operation Galvanic, the commencement of an all-out invasion of the Central Pacific.

The American plan of action had been created under confusing and cautious conditions. The one man most directly affected by its ponderous provisions and intangibles would be Spruance, in command of the powerful new U.S. Fifth Fleet. The difficult job of trying to plan ahead—to prepare both the Gilbert Islands offensive and what to do in the event that the Japanese Combined Fleet sortied—had been given to Spruance, known affectionately by his Naval Academy classmates as "Sprew." Officially, however, he was known as COMCENPAC (commander in chief, Central Pacific). When he was promoted to the post, he was told by Admiral Nimitz: "Spruance, you are lucky."

Nonetheless, his task was mind-boggling. In preparing Galvanic, Spruance had to consider all sorts of unanswerable mysteries. What would happen if the enemy fleet intervened so quickly that the invasion forces were caught off balance, as had happened in August 1942 by the unexpected Japanese reaction to the invasion of Guadalcanal? Which troops—soldiers and marines—would be assigned which objectives? Which islands in the Gilberts chain would be attacked? Who would command the amphibious forces? Who would command the ground forces? Who would command the air forces? And how would they all be integrated toward one ultimate goal? These were the initial and most important fundamental questions. They all had to be answered clearly if Japanese strength was to be overcome in the Central Pacific.

Until the great Allied conference in Washington in May 1943, no detailed plan for the war in the Pacific had ever been agreed on. Various military authorities in the United States and Britain had been preoccupied with the war against Germany and Italy. Although in the United States there was tremendous interest in finishing off Japan, even while continuing to fight in Europe, little progress had been made in setting down an overall strategy. The army and navy each had their own and very different ideas. They agreed only on one thing: Japan should be defeated as quickly as possible. Otherwise, they warned, the war in the Pacific might last until 1946.

The army, with General MacArthur heavily engaged in the southwest Pacific and obsessed with the notion of returning to the Philippines, had no trouble at all arriving at a plan. Returning to the Philippines had been taken for granted by MacArthur, and he had always known exactly how he would do it. In March 1943 he bluntly informed the Joint Chiefs of his plans for 1943, naming the islands he intended to occupy and build airfields on.

It was a staggering agenda: In his victory plan MacArthur contemplated fighting along the northern coast of New Guinea, jumping across the Dampier Strait to New Britain, continuing the battle up the Solomons ladder to New Ireland, and culminating the year in a massive Allied assault on Rabaul—with its 135,000 Japanese defenders and five fully operational airfields. But, above all, MacArthur wanted to be named supreme allied commander in the Pacific, with responsibility for directing the entire Allied war effort against Japan. The general envisioned for himself a role similar to that of the still to be named Allied commander in chief in Europe. As his aides calmly laid down his plans to the JCS, American and Australian forces had not yet completely secured eastern New Guinea, where Japanese forces were still fighting desperately.

The navy considered MacArthur's plans impractical. Admiral King flatly refused to turn over command of the fleet to a soldier in a theater dominated by blue water. Thus by spring the navy was preparing plans of its own. COMINCH recommended command in the Pacific remain divided between Admiral Nimitz and General MacArthur. King also issued a broad "Strategic Plan for the Defeat of Japan," which advocated a two-pronged attack, with Nimitz driving across the Central Pacific—not to the Philippines but to China. The Philippines, King suggested, should be bypassed. Moreover, MacArthur's forces should undertake only those operations that would support the Central Pacific drive and secure its flank.

MacArthur of course was displeased by the navy plan. His forces, in the south, would have a sphere of responsibility clearly subordinate to Nimitz and the navy. He worried about the Philippines remaining in Japanese hands. Above all, however, he feared that his fame might evaporate if he were relegated to a supporting role in the war in the Pacific. "Operations in the Central Pacific," he declared, "would of course complement the main drive"—meaning his own—"but should not receive a higher priority in resources than the Southwest Pacific theater."

Nevertheless, the JCS felt compelled to compromise as a result of the competing plans. The subject was of pressing concern because Allied military might was becoming so great that something had to be done to use it effectively. As the navy saw matters, MacArthur was challenging not only the navy role in the Pacific but also the prewar American plans for war against Japan (which had not foreseen the use of Australia as a base of operations). If Allied grand strategy in the Pacific were changed to accommodate the general, a huge influx of men and material would be necessary.

MacArthur demanded that in order for his plan to succeed he must have twenty-three infantry divisions, forty-five groups of aircraft, and the bulk of the new U.S. Pacific Fleet. The JCS feared that this would delay—and could conceivably jeopardize—the outcome of the war against Germany. It seemed clear that MacArthur either did not comprehend the immense logistical efforts that would be required for his plans or, more likely, he understood them perfectly well and believed that nothing was more important than retaking the Philippines. But in the view of the JCS the price was preposterously high.

When the discussion ended the JCS left no doubt in the minds of the various American high commands in the Pacific what they wanted. United States strategy as envisioned by the compromise meant the quartering of one million men in the Pacific and an additional 1.5 million tons of shipping—costly drains on the all-out effort against Germany, but with every prospect of victory over Japan at a minimum of time. The plan for the defeat of Japan, from which Operation Galvanic emerged, called for a swift thrust into the enemy's inner ring of island possessions—"an amphibious blitzkrieg"—that would carry American land, sea, and air forces into the Central Pacific and from there to the Japanese home islands themselves. MacArthur would continue his operations toward the eventual recapture of the Philippines—with smaller forces than he had wanted. But, above all, the decisions reached in Washington meant that Admiral King's determination to have action in the Central Pacific had been realized.

In mid-September, between the hit-and-run raids by the fast carrier forces on the Gilberts and Wake, the various command elements began gathering and organizing in Hawaii. The plans for Galvanic were published and distributed. The operation appeared straightforward enough. Two reinforced divisions of marines and soldiers would attack, seize, and develop as bases for future operations the islands of Tarawa in the Gilberts group and nearby Nauru. A smaller reconnaissance force would seize Abemama. The navy would isolate the Gilberts area from Japanese naval and air forces. The campaign had to be wrapped up quickly, for all of the shipping would be needed for the Marshalls invasion, scheduled to occur right behind Galvanic.

Among the commanders assigned to Galvanic were men who had practically written the book on amphibious warfare. By now the United States had gained experience in the invasions of Guadalcanal and elsewhere in the Solomons, of North Africa, and most recently of Sicily and Italy. Nearly every potential problem in the Gilberts, these men believed, had been worked out and compensated for in advance.

Yet the invasion of the Gilberts would be different. Primarily, the targets were all incredibly small and encircled by coral barrier reefs. These factors troubled the planners most. Difficulties were compounded by the critical shortage of shipping available. When it was determined that not enough shipping was on hand to take all the objectives at once, Nauru was dropped from the list with Admiral King's permission. It was replaced with Makin, which was much closer to the main objective of Tarawa and was defended by a vastly smaller Japanese force. It was apparent to all that the landings at Tarawa would require a frontal assault against heavy fortifications. Yet in both cases it was privately hoped that the marine and army units could accomplish the conquests of Makin and Tarawa in a matter of hours. In the end, before the Gilberts were cleared of Japanese, it took a week.

The amphibious command structure was the most complicated so far in the war:

(1) Rear Admiral Spruance, the victor of the battle for Midway, would be in overall command. He would accompany the forces assigned to the capture of Tarawa, where the heaviest Japanese resistance was expected.

(2) Rear Admiral Richmond Kelly Turner, who had directed amphibious forces in the South Pacific under Halsey, would command the 5th Amphibious Force as well as the Northern Attack Force assigned to seize Makin in the northern Gilberts.

(3) Rear Admiral Harry W. Hill, fresh from command of a battleship division in the South Pacific, would command the Southern Attack Force, which would seize Tarawa and Abemama. He

had commanded a cruiser in the U-boat–plagued North Atlantic in 1942.

(4) Marine Maj. Gen. Holland M. Smith, generally regarded as the father of modern amphibious warfare, would command the assault units under the designation V Amphibious Corps. In matters of amphibious warfare, Smith was as farseeing and influential as Yamamoto had been with respect to naval air power. The ground forces that the marine general would command included:

    (a) For Tarawa, the battle-tested 2d Marine Division, Reinforced, under Maj. Gen. Julian C. Smith.

    (b) For Makin, elements of the army's untried 27th Infantry Division, commanded by Maj. Gen. Ralph C. Smith.

    (c) For Abemama, the V Amphibious Corps Reconnaissance Company under Capt. James L. Jones, whose marine scouts would land from the submarine *Nautilus*.

Major General Holland Smith, sixty-three years old, of Hatchechubee, Alabama, was known for his acerbic temper, which had dogged him since 1906 as a second lieutenant in the Philippines and earned him the sobriquet "Howlin' Mad." This was his first campaign in the Pacific war. When it came to his beloved marines he was as blindly devoted as Admiral Turner was to the navy; Turner's unflattering if revealing moniker was "Terrible Turner." Galvanic was only the first of many campaigns for the two men who would engineer the American amphibious war in the Pacific and whose relations were always anything but congenial.

In June "Howlin' Mad" Smith, then in command of American amphibious training for the Pacific, had accepted Nimitz's invitation to command the Central Pacific ground forces in the coming offensive. Two months later he arrived at Pearl Harbor and was greeted by Turner, who although he was an admiral would actually be in nominal command of all troops assigned to Galvanic. Later in the war the command structure would be better clarified and reflect a reasonable line of authority, but for the invasion of the Gilberts, Smith was officially a notch below Turner. This did nothing to improve the view each had of the other's role in the operation.

Planning conditions for Galvanic were not the best. Both assault divisions were widely separated not only by the philosophical chasms of different branches of military service but by geography: The 2d Marine Division, re-forming after the battle for Guadalcanal, was based around Wellington, New Zealand, southeast of Australia. The 27th Infantry Division was based at its permanent camp on Oahu in the Hawaiian Islands. In view of geography and the fact that the V Amphibious Corps was undergoing organization at the time, the enormous burden of planning for the assault fell to the staff of the two divisions. "Sometimes," recalled Lt. Comdr. Patrick J. Grogan, who would be the navy beachmaster at Tarawa, "the planning rooms reminded you of a giant toy factory, with hundreds of little boats, tanks, LVTs, artillery and sometimes toy soldiers."

On August 5 the 2d Marine Division had received COMCENPAC's order to prepare for Tarawa, and immediately the staff began to produce an outline. It was called Operation Longsuit, which everyone soon forgot. The invasion of Tarawa, unlike the invasion of Normandy (Operation Overlord) or the invasion of North Africa (Torch), for example, was like Iwo Jima and the other horrendous battles of the Pacific in that it was never really referred to as anything except the name of its chief objective. The principal island of Betio, upon which the main blow of Galvanic would fall, was known to the assault troops by its code name Helen.

Affectionately called by his troops "Uncle Julian" or "General Julian," Maj. Gen. Julian Smith, fifty-eight years old, of Elkton, Maryland, had overall responsibility for planning the marine landing at Tarawa. With thirty-three years of service in the Corps, he had commanded the 5th Marines in 1940–41 and before World War I had seen action in Cuba, the Canal Zone, Veracruz, and Hispaniola. More recently he had been chief of staff at Marine Corps headquarters at Quantico and a U.S. naval observer in Britain. Smith had taken command of the 2d Marine Division in May 1943. At least one marine officer thought Smith looked like "the guy next door who spent Saturday night baby-sitting with his grandchildren."

While half the 2d Marine Division were veterans, the 27th Infantry Division never had been in combat. The division, a formation of the New York National Guard, had been activated in October 1940 and placed on garrison duty in Hawaii since March 1942. Major General Ralph Smith, forty-nine years old, of Omaha, Nebraska, was regarded as the leading American expert on the French army. Before the war he had studied, and later lectured, at France's Ecole Superieure de la Guerre, or War College, in Paris. A World War I veteran, by 1943 he was regarded in army circles as a distinguished tactician and somewhat an intellectual. He had taken over the 27th Division almost exactly one year prior to the invasion of the Gilberts. He, too, had served in wartime staff positions—first as chief of military intelligence for the General Staff in Washington, then as assistant commander of the 76th Infantry Division—before getting his first combat command. In contrast to "Howlin' Mad" Smith, the army Smith was "breezy" in nature.

From August until late October, then, these men, with the various naval and air commanders, directed the planning for the assault phases of Galvanic—the largest and most sweeping operation yet undertaken by the United States in the Pacific in World War II.

Chapter Five

The greatest air battles fought in the Pacific since Midway and Guadalcanal—perhaps the Combined Fleet's last real chance to fend off the inevitable—broke the back of Japanese air power and affirmed the beginning of the end of the war. The hit-and-run raids on Rabaul by American fast carrier forces and heavy land-based air forces that took place during the first two weeks of November 1943 would prove as important as the battle for Midway, though it was not known then. The raids dwarfed the surprise attack on Pearl Harbor nearly two years earlier in combat intensity and, more importantly, in long-term results. Unlike American naval and air forces after Pearl Harbor, there would be no resurrection of Japanese forces. After Rabaul, Japanese naval air power was for all intents and purposes finished as a strategic asset.

Operation RO was daring and desperate—reflective of an empire whose military forces were strained beyond their capacity to resist the world's largest industrial power. The Combined Fleet had not recovered from its cumulative losses suffered thus far in the war, particularly from the battles for the Coral Sea, Midway, and Guadalcanal. The carrier air power that Admiral Koga sent to Rabaul—in fact, practically everything that could fly—represented all that was left of the vaunted naval air forces that had swept unchallenged to victory in 1941–42.

From October 27 to November 1, in great formations, 82 fighters, 45 dive-bombers, 40 torpedo bombers, and 6 reconnaissance aircraft—in all, 173 carrier aircraft—left Truk for Rabaul. The heavy air reinforcements gave Admiral Kusaka nearly 400 naval and military aircraft at Rabaul—enough, it was hoped, to devastate Admiral Halsey's forces that landed on Bougainville on November 1. Koga also concentrated the bulk of his surface forces at Rabaul. Admiral Takeo Kurita arrived with a fleet of 8 cruisers and 4 destroyers.

But it was all for naught. On November 2 Allied photoreconnaissance planes discovered 240 Japanese aircraft at Rabaul and the beginning of the unprecedented buildup of major naval and air forces. General Kenney, commander of the U.S. Fifth Air Force, hurriedly assembled a massive strike of 160 B-25 bombers and P-38 fighters. They were intercepted over the target by 150 Japanese fighters. General Mac-Arthur, under whose command the attack was generated, reported, "Our fighter cover engaged the attacking Japanese planes and our medium bombers went in at masthead height. The harbor was swept practically clean, nearly every ship there being heavily hit or sunk with 1,000-pound bombs."

In reality, although hits and near misses were reported by nearly all planes, Japanese damage was confined to the loss of three cargo ships, a minesweeper, and two harbor craft, and damage to a ten-thousand-ton oil tanker. Forty-five American pilots and crewmen were lost when eight bombers and nine fighters were shot down. Two dozen other planes were so badly damaged that they cracked up on landing at their bases or were later cannibalized.

About twenty Japanese planes had been shot down and as many, including ten valuable air-search reconnaissance floatplanes, were destroyed on the ground or in the harbor. But this major Allied air assault on Rabaul confirmed the threat represented by the transfer of enemy air forces from their carriers at Truk. Fifth Air Force crews reported that the enemy fighter and AA opposition were the most dangerous they had encountered in the South Pacific, and their losses proved it.

Meanwhile, the Japanese 5th Cruiser Division under VAdm. Sentaro Omori sortied from Rabaul and was defeated forty miles from Empress Augusta Bay while attempting to attack Admiral Halsey's transports off Bougainville. In a ninety-minute naval battle at night, American radar-directed gunfire sank the cruiser *Sendai* and a destroyer. The heavy cruisers *Myoko* and *Haguro,* in the center of the Japanese battle line, collided and were damaged. The next morning, of sixty-seven Japanese aircraft that attacked the American warships, seventeen were shot down. Despite the fury of the combined naval and air engagement, not one American ship was damaged.

On the morning of November 5 an enormous swarm of American aircraft, 107 in all, appeared out of the southeast. The air groups attached to the carriers *Saratoga* and *Princeton,* two AA cruisers, and ten destroyers under RAdm. Frederick P. Sherman had been supporting the marines at Bougainville with strikes on the Japanese airfields fifty miles northwest at Buin and Kahili and farther north at Buka. But when Halsey learned from air reconnaissance and the thin line of submarines that watched the approaches to Rabaul of the impending arrival of Kurita's fleet, he decided to go after them in a bold fast carrier raid. He hoped to catch them unaware while they were refueling at Simpson Harbor. Halsey later said of his decision, "I never expected to see those two carriers again."

The surrounding Japanese airfields had been under attack for weeks by American land-based air forces in the Solomons and the Fifth Air Force. After steaming through the night at twenty-seven knots, TF 38 arrived on station in the Solomon Sea and launched every combat plane aboard the carriers. Swarms of navy and marine land-based fighters flew CAP over the carrier battle group. *Saratoga*'s planes of Air Group 22 formed the first echelon, followed by *Princeton*'s Air Group 23. With perfect visibility and a seven-knot wind, they attacked, sweeping over Rabaul at 0900.

One hundred Japanese fighters and bombers scrambled and came up to meet them. Some thirty men-of-war, chief among them the cruisers and destroyers from Truk, and scores of noncombatant vessels frantically attempted to cast off fuel lines and get underway. They zigzagged wildly through the main channel in a vain effort to reach open sea. The fighter escort of fifty-five Hellcats went after the enemy CAP. The dive-bombers and torpedo bombers plunged through the intense AA fire and bored in on the heavy concentration of warships that congested Simpson Harbor.

Commander H. H. Caldwell, commander of Air Group 22 from *Saratoga,* was piloting an Avenger torpedo plane when he and his crew were jumped by eight Zeros. Airman Paul Barnett, of Corpus Christi, Texas, was killed by machine-gun fire while photographing a head-on attack by one of the Japanese planes. Weapons specialist Kenneth Bratton, of Mississippi, in the turret of the same plane, was wounded. Teaming with a Hellcat, Caldwell and his crew fought off all the enemy planes, downing three, damaging two, and chasing off the others.

The first attack ended by 0915. All that could be seen of the harbor were towering columns of smoke and burning ships and installations. Of the seventy Japanese fighters that rose to meet the raid, twenty-four were shot down and twenty-two others were listed as "probables." A squadron of B-24s and fifty-eight fighters of the Fifth Air Force followed in the afternoon and bombed and strafed the wharf area.

The scene later at Kurita's headquarters was grim. Staff officers exchanged information and damage reports. The Japanese cruiser force had been devastated.

Takao had taken a torpedo hit, developed a serious leak, and as a result was listing heavily. She would have capsized except for excellent damage control.

Atago had escaped any torpedo hits but had suffered varying degrees of damage from several near misses by armor-piercing (AP) bombs.

The light cruisers *Noshiro* and *Agano* took the worst poundings of any of the big ships in the harbor. Each had been hit by heavy bombs that penetrated the decks and exploded within their hulls, leaving both ships no longer battleworthy.

Maya had taken a bomb hit that penetrated the deck and exploded in the main engine room, causing much destruction.

Mogami had suffered bomb hits and was also severely damaged.

Two destroyers, *Fujinami* and *Wakatsuki*, had been damaged.

Ashore the bombing also had taken its toll. All five naval and military airfields around Rabaul, the heart of the Japanese air defense system for the South Pacific, had been strafed and bombed. Runways had been cratered and could be made usable after quick repairs, but many of the aircraft crowding the fields had been damaged or destroyed. Some of the major air installations, such as revetments and armament depots, had also been damaged by bombs, and many of the ground crews had been killed or wounded. Casualties among AA gun crews had been especially heavy.

The long-term results were tremendous. Four of Kurita's cruisers were so damaged as to be nonoperational for months to come. They would be scattered from Rabaul to Tokyo for repairs before they could steam into battle again. *Myoko* and *Haguro*, which had been damaged by American naval gunfire and collision off Bougainville, would require extensive repairs; yet another cruiser, *Tone*, was in dry dock undergoing periodic maintenance. In contrast, ten American carrier aircraft had been shot down.

But the tremendous attrition of Japanese air forces did not end there. On November 8 *Princeton* and *Saratoga* were located by Japanese search planes 240 miles northeast of Rabaul and attacked by one hundred aircraft. They survived undamaged, and another two dozen Japanese planes were lost.

Three days later another American carrier task force—*Essex, Bunker Hill,* and *Independence,* composing the southern group of carriers for the Gilberts invasion under Rear Admiral Montgomery—arrived in the area. They teamed up with *Princeton* and *Saratoga* for renewed air attacks on Rabaul by five carriers. The sight that greeted the vanguard of the squadrons on November 11 was exactly what they had not wanted to see. The crews had been to innumerable briefings, but heavy rainsqualls covered half of Simpson Harbor and beyond the main channel, making identification of likely targets difficult. Numerous cruisers and destroyers maneuvered frantically to find cover in the poor weather. Nevertheless, 185 American aircraft attacked en masse and their firepower was moderately effective. A light cruiser and two destroyers were damaged.

When Montgomery's air groups came in later, rainsqualls still covered the battle area. But despite poor weather and furious Japanese CAP, the raids continued until noon. In a plodding Dauntless dive-bomber, Lt. William L. Gerner of Bombing Squadron 17 from *Bunker Hill* scored a thousand-pound AP bomb hit on *Agano.* He pulled out of the steep dive between two volcanoes on the peninsula flanking the harbor just as two Zeros jumped him. His rear gunner, Airman S. E. Wallace, shot down both of them with his powerful twin .30-caliber machine guns.

By noon the destroyer *Suzunami* had been sunk, succumbing to a hail of bombs that struck her amidship as she tried vainly to clear the harbor. Three other destroyers—*Umikaze, Naganami,* and *Urakaze*—and two cruisers—*Agano* and *Yubari*—had been damaged. *Agano* was so badly stricken that she would later have to be towed to Truk. Even before forty B-24s from the Solomons followed up the raid in the afternoon, another thirty-five Japanese fighters had been shot down. The storm was not over yet.

Chapter Six

A twin-engine Kawanishi H6K combined medium high-level and heavy torpedo patrol bomber, known by its Allied code name Mavis, passed near the American carrier group after noon. It had followed an enemy air group from Rabaul. The monstrous seaplane was packed full of radio gear and was crewed by men with years of training and experience. Radio direction finding (RDF) equipment searched for the signals of Allied radio transmissions. Once an enemy force was found, they would close on it and chart its location with great care, always remaining well outside AA fire or easy fighter interception range.

The Mavis had twenty-four hours of endurance, but it was slow and practically defenseless if forced to fight back against an interceptor. "We have located the Yankee navy," the crews who flew the lumbering patrol planes joked. "Honor our memory by visiting our spirits at Yasukuni Shrine" (the Shinto monument to Japanese war dead located near the Imperial Palace in Tokyo). But on this occasion the navigator noted the large enemy formation and plotted the coordinates as southeast of Rabaul.

Within minutes, the information was received at Rabaul. For the next half hour, ground crews readied aircraft, and flight crews were given urgent briefings at the five airfields around the anchorage at Rabaul on the northeast coast of New Britain. The airmen were anxious, no less than their American counterparts whose ships were low on fuel. This was the opportunity for which the Japanese air forces had been concentrating at Rabaul—all the while suffering horribly from American air attacks. What could be salvaged of Operation RO was about to be put to the test.

The slow Kates lifted off first, pushed by their reliable single Nakajima

NK1B Sakae-11 air-cooled radial engines. Each takeoff was difficult for the torpedo bombers. They were fully loaded with 1,764-pound warheads. The airfields were so heavily cratered that air controllers were challenged to find operational runways for them. They were followed by Aichi 99 Val dive-bombers with their single Mitsubishi Kinsei radial engines and five-hundred-pound fuselage-mounted AP bombs. Much swifter navy Zero and army Nate and Oscar fighters launched last and would overtake the slower bombers. Once off the ground the strike force headed east, organizing into V formations before heading southeast and passing Cape St. George on New Ireland as slow turns took them toward the center of the Solomon Sea.

Several hundred miles away at Guadalcanal, the radio intelligence–gathering apparatus of COMAIRSOLS (commander, air, Solomons)—which often heard more of Japanese communications than did most enemy receiving stations—was working overtime. Technicians listened in on radio transmissions between enemy aircraft and controllers as the strike formed up. The specialists determined the strength of the raid as best they could and sent an urgent warning broadcast.

The message was relayed to scattered Allied communications stations in the Solomons, and before long was received by the combat intelligence center (CIC) aboard the fleet carrier *Essex*. Radar picked up the incoming air formations. A staff officer brought the message immediately to Montgomery. The "Talk Between Ships" system (TBS) crackled and Montgomery's staff officer for air operations gave a voice alert: "Bogies closing from three-three-six degrees true, distance seventy miles, altitude fifteen and twenty-two thousand feet."

The main carrier battle group was steaming northwest directly toward the oncoming Japanese strike, launching planes for another raid on Rabaul. Montgomery stopped launching and altered course. The carriers *Essex, Bunker Hill,* and *Independence* fell into line, steaming in the center of a rough ring maintained by nine destroyers. The Japanese knew exactly where the carrier group was as a result of the constant information they received from their circling seaplanes whose crews tracked the ships.

Sherman's smaller carrier group of *Princeton* and *Saratoga,* operating far to the north, had been steaming at full speed all morning, launching and landing planes in almost a dead calm. The screening destroyers had burned up their fuel, and the battle group retired at reduced speed to Espiritu Santo—to get beyond range of the Japanese aircraft.

Not nearly so vulnerable, Montgomery put his carrier group's fighters and COMAIRSOLS' land-based cover on station to intercept the incoming raid. "Do not launch any more planes," he ordered. "Send those already in the air to strike." Their mission was to locate and engage the Japanese planes before they could reach the carrier group. For both sides, the fundamental task was to battle through opposing fighter screens: the Japanese through Hellcats and Corsairs in order to get at the carriers, the Americans through swarms of Zeros and Hamps in order to get at the enemy bombers. What followed, beginning at 1330, was the culmination of the heaviest land-based air assault yet launched against carriers in World War II.

The Kates, Vals, and twin-engine Mitsubishi OB-01 Bettys were escorted by army and navy fighters; after organizing for their final approach, they changed course slightly east, heading directly for the point of the carrier battle group's course track. With heavy armament slung beneath their fuselages, the bombers were highly vulnerable to interception. Nevertheless, the Vals among them had the ability to perform as slow fighters and stood at least a chance of survival on their own, even in the face of determined fighter opposition. The Kates and Bettys had no chance at all if intercepted. Still, the crews of the carrier planes were the elite of Japanese naval air strength, better paid and trained than any of their land-based counterparts from either the navy or army. Now it was time to make good on their preferential treatment.

The numerous waves of aircraft flew southeast at maximum speed, their crews nervously watching the sky and sea for any sight of the enemy during the long overseas flight. Then they heard the word "Contact!" The banter of Zero pilots filled their ears as the American fighter screen was engaged with shouts of "BANZAI!"

Nervous men in the CIC on each ship bent low over the tracking board, watching the radar plot as the incoming raid was charted. The radar picture enabled not only the battle group commander but all his ship commanders to follow the action. At first nothing could be seen except the blips of Japanese and American aircraft converging across the Solomon Sea from the northwest and southeast.

As the Japanese planes began to swing east, having pinpointed the enemy carrier battle group, they maneuvered to encircle the American ships, then concentrate against them from all directions. The accuracy of the threat assessment improved as the Japanese closed the range. Technicians aboard *Essex* adjusted their charts as radar tracked the Japanese aircraft.

"Radar indicates *many* bogies to the northwest," the plotting officer reported to the bridge. "Bearing has changed to three-four-five true. Distance is four-five miles. Speed one-eight-oh."

Twenty-odd intercepting Hellcat fighters of Air Group 17 from *Bunker Hill* were the first on station. Each had an auxiliary gas tank. The CAP— navy and marine Corsairs from the Solomons—circled over the fast-moving battle group. The aircraft that had been spotted on the flight decks for immediate takeoff against Rabaul were moved at once to the hangars. If the Japanese raid penetrated the interceptors, clearing the decks would minimize the danger of fire and explosion if the carriers were hit.

Warned that a major air battle was likely in minutes, the Dauntlesses and Avengers that already had launched or were preparing to land upon returning from Rabaul were prudently vacating the area. They would remain out of harm's way even if it meant having to ditch or land at far-off fields in the Solomons. The carriers were racing east now at twenty-seven knots to increase the distance the Japanese aircraft would have to cover from their bases and then back to Rabaul. Thousands of American servicemen waited.

Lieutenant Commander Thomas Blackburn and the Hellcats of his Fighting 17th had been flying protective cover over the carriers as the bombers from the earlier raids on Rabaul returned when the commander of the air group (CAG), Comdr. M. P. Bagdanovitch, quickly vectored him out to intercept the Japanese. Since then he had been accumulating information relayed to him from the radar plot. He now had confirmation of four Japanese formations, but what he saw was shocking. Under normal circumstances air operations staff aboard the ships would have heard the intercept commander shout "tally-ho" when he sighted the enemy aircraft. This time they were startled to hear Lieutenant Commander Blackburn exclaim, "KEE-RIHST! There are millions of them out here."

The CIC plotting staff exchanged mixed expressions of relief and worry. The Japanese strike had been intercepted just twenty minutes from the carriers, and they knew that each mile northwest meant a greater chance that the thin-skinned flattops would survive. Now came the real test. Battle plans for the interception of a massive enemy air attack before it reached its targets at sea had been formulated throughout the previous three months and practiced at Marcus and Wake, and near the Gilberts. It had worked every time.

Now it was the real thing.

Over the fighter net Lieutenant Commander Blackburn shouted, "Let's go to work!"

"Contact!" The CAG aboard the flagship grabbed the interphone. "Enemy raid intercepted by our fighters. Bearing three-four-five true. Range four-five miles. Speed one-eight-oh."

Montgomery brought his carriers around to reduce the size of the targets available to the Japanese planes. On a single command, the formation of ships made a sharp turn. The radar screens revealed that the American interceptor force had run into a cloud of enemy aircraft— far more than a hundred. Radar-directed AA fire controllers were trained northwest and eleven skippers waited for the word from The Flag.

"Numerous incoming bandits, estimate count one-zero-zero plus," announced CIC. "Distance two-seven miles. Radar indicates raid has broken up into three, possibly four, groups. One is closing rapidly. Bearing three-four-zero true."

On the bridge of *Essex,* staff turned their binoculars on a large group of enemy planes approaching in V formation—Val dive-bombers. Montgomery issued his orders through the chief gunnery officer: "Man your guns and blast those bastards!" Five-inch guns firing proximity-fused AA shells opened up first, and were soon joined by the smaller ordnance of 3-inch guns. The shells exploded in the air near the aircraft, leaving a sudden fiery red ball followed by an ugly black puff cloud. It soon became apparent that more than 125 Japanese aircraft were headed for the American ships.

"Watch out for dive-bombers coming in on you!" warned Montgomery. The Vals continued on, straight and level. They carried five-hundred-pound AP bombs, which would be released automatically by a toggle switch in the cockpit. When they arrived over a target, the pilots would dip the noses down and the aircraft would dive on a carrier at two hundred miles per hour.

"Knock off firing on our own planes," ordered Montgomery. But the air over the battle group was a fury of confusion. Nearly two hundred Japanese and American aircraft were tangling in the sky. Japanese fighters and bombers were blasted out of the air every few seconds, it seemed. The fighter screen had done amazingly well, but scores of Japanese bombers still roared in on their targets with a closing speed of 180 miles per hour. The rapid fire of 40mm pom-pom guns joined the fray.

The identity and distribution of targets were nearly impossible to determine. In several cases more than one Hellcat and numerous AA guns went after the same target, nearly always ensuring its destruction. As bombs dropped and torpedo planes boxed in ships below the AA belt, the battle group began a radical series of maneuvers. Hellcat pilots used the explosions of AA fire as a means of makeshift fighter direction, flying right into the thick maelstrom of air bursts that they knew indicated elusive enemy aircraft.

Bunker Hill, with Japanese aircraft converging on it from all directions—dead ahead, dead astern, and on both beams—had been unable to clear her decks entirely. Several fully loaded Dauntlesses had been caught warming up on the flight deck, spotted for takeoff when the battle commenced. In the midst of the wild air melee, acting on their own initiative, their rear-seat gunners augmented the AA firepower with their rear-mounted, twin .30-caliber machine guns.

Lieutenant George M. Blair of the Fighting 9th swung in on the tail of a Kate making its torpedo bombing run. He fired short bursts into its stern until his guns jammed. Not breaking off the hard-to-come-by contact, he climbed directly over his unfortunate adversary and dropped his auxiliary fuel tank. With freakish success, the unlikely missile struck the Japanese plane, set it afire, and knocked it flaming into the sea.

Suddenly the two-hour battle was over. Despite the furious confrontation and the immense size of the Japanese attack, not one ship had been hit. The only damage was superficial—from strafing and misdirected friendly AA fire. By sunset the land-based CAP had returned to the airfields in the Solomons. Montgomery called off the planned afternoon strike on Rabaul and headed for Espiritu Santo, elated that he had beaten off the Japanese air attack and kept his carriers intact.

Although the Japanese aircrews would report accounts of wild success—of American carriers and cruisers burning—the air admirals and carrier chiefs knew who had won the fight. Montgomery's battle group and the carrier and land-based CAP had shot down seventy-six Japanese planes—60 percent of the attacking force—before the enemy had been forced to break off combat. Only three American planes had been lost. Fewer than ten of the attackers returned to Rabaul undamaged. The Fighting 9th of *Essex* alone was given credit for downing forty-one planes, which, when added to the fourteen the squadron had claimed over Rabaul in the morning, gave it a record fifty-five kills in one day.

In just the first two weeks of November, then, on the eve of the greatest Allied offensive yet undertaken in the Pacific, all but one of the 11 cruisers that Admiral Kurita's powerful Second Fleet had deployed in September had been put out of action. Equally important, the naval air strength that Admiral Koga had concentrated at Rabaul had been ravaged; 121 planes, or roughly two-thirds of the entire force, had been lost in huge air battles. The carrier aircraft and their invaluable crews had been hard hit. Of the 192 highly trained carrier flight crews dispatched from Truk to Rabaul, 86 had been lost. Koga, with great disappointment, recalled the survivors to Truk on November 12.

"Consequently," said Vice Admiral Fukudome, Japanese "fleet air strength was almost completely lost, and although the Gilberts fight appeared to be the last chance for a decisive fight, the fact that the fleet's air strength had been so badly depleted enabled us to send only very small air support to Tarawa and Makin. The almost complete loss of carrier planes was a mortal blow to the fleet since it would require six months for replacement. In the interim, any fighting with carrier forces was rendered impossible."

With Japanese air power at Rabaul and Truk now crippled, the possibility of a dramatic air intervention over the Gilberts was eliminated. Operation Galvanic, the first major American amphibious operation in the Central Pacific, had begun in the South Pacific.

Chapter Seven

Rear Admiral Keiji Shibasaki arrived at Betio in August. The tiny island is eighty miles north of the equator. It lies at the southwestern end of Tarawa Atoll in the center of the Gilberts chain, a coral archipelago branching off the eastern Marshalls like the offshoot of a vine. Tarawa is, in fact, a triangular-shaped group of thirty-eight long, narrow, coconut-studded islands practically surrounded by a forbidding coral barrier reef. Its large, dreamy lagoon has one major pass to deep water. Its eastern and southern legs are eighteen and twelve miles long, respectively.

Betio, the largest island at Tarawa, was the principal fortified island of the Gilberts. The island closely resembles a bird, complete with tail and beak. The total length is thirty-eight hundred yards, just short of two miles. The width varies from five hundred yards from the beak and across the crown to six hundred yards from the bird's belly to its back, then gradually tapers off to a point on the tail. Altogether the island is so small that it must be grossly exaggerated in order to appear on a standard map of the Pacific.

Yet Shibasaki had been sent to defend the island—to hold it as long as possible against the American assault that was expected within the year. His responsibility included the Gilberts as well as nearby Nauru and Ocean islands. Tarawa was originally part of the South Seas area command, only 535 miles southeast of Kwajalein. But by the time of Vice Admiral Kusaka's reorganization of Japanese defenses in May, the Gilberts already had been detached from the Fourth Fleet and made an independent command. Located on a line running almost directly southeast from the Caroline Islands, almost exactly halfway between

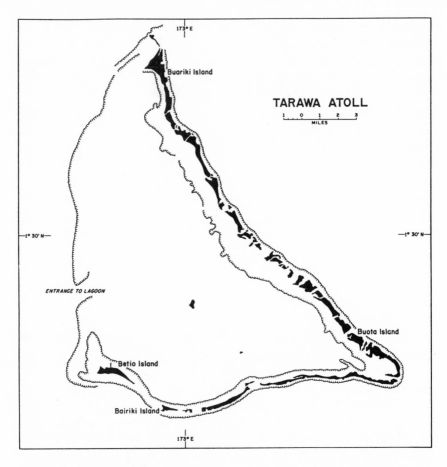

Truk and the Fiji Islands, Tarawa marked the limit of Japanese expansion in the South Seas and their front line of defense in the Central Pacific.

Upon his arrival Shibasaki had made an in-depth inspection of his command area. What he saw impressed him. Rear Admiral Tomanari Saichiro, who had been in command of all naval and air forces in the Gilberts since February 1943, had overseen completion of the swift buildup of Japanese strength following the surprise assault by Carlson's Raiders on Makin in August 1942, and there now seemed to be not one square foot of Betio that was undefended. Saichiro had turned the island into a veritable fortress, but the work had taken its toll.

To his men, the wiry, little admiral had seemed tireless in his quest to prepare the Gilberts for battle. But he was in poor health and appeared a physical wreck. That summer Saichiro had asked a visiting admiral from Tokyo for reinforcements. Instead, to his embarrassment, he got as his successor the youthful and confident Shibasaki, who arrived fit and full of vigor. The disappointed Saichiro had wanted desperately to command the garrison in battle, but now he would return with honor to Japan for much needed rest and recuperation.

Before Carlson's raid there had been nothing more than a lookout station in the Gilberts. In all, less than a hundred Japanese combat troops and service personnel had been in the island group. But within a month the 6th Yokosuka Tokusetsu Butai, or Special Naval Landing Force (SNLF), followed with fifteen hundred naval infantry. In addition, four companies of the 43d and 62d Naval Guard Forces were dispatched to Nauru and Ocean islands.

Saichiro was primarily a naval engineer and construction specialist, and his orders had been to develop the Gilberts' defenses and build the airfield at Tarawa. That had been in winter. In fall when Rear Admiral Shibasaki arrived, the airfield had been in commission eight months. It was built as a triangle with two runways and a taxi strip. The major runway was four thousand feet long and paralleled the southern, or oceanside, beaches along the bird-shaped island's back.

The airfield supported a detachment of the 755th Naval Air Group made up of twelve Zeros, six twin-engine Bettys that could be used either as high-level or torpedo bombers with equal effectiveness, and four hundred airmen. Planes of the 755th based in the Marshalls had been among those that had participated in the invasion of Wake Island in December 1941 and damaged the American aircraft carrier *Enterprise* in February 1942 when Admiral Halsey raided the Marshalls and Gilberts for the first time.

The buildup had not slackened once under Saichiro. He had directed preparations for the American attack with unusual foresight. With his arrival, IGH decided that the importance of the Gilberts required special attention. The command was renamed the 3d Konkyochitai, or Special Base Force. This placed it on an echelon equal to that of Kwajalein in the Marshalls and guaranteed it a greater share of men and material. This was likely to increase in the near future, for with the fall of Guadalcanal it was hoped some of the troops then preparing for the Solomons could be diverted to the Central Pacific. Saichiro reported directly to Rear Admiral Kobayashi at Truk. He was given every indication that when other forces became available they would also be sent to Tarawa.

When Rear Admiral Shibasaki took over command of the Gilberts, however, all the reinforcements that would be sent were already in place. He had a solid core of battle-hardened troops in the 7th Sasebo SNLF, about 1,500 formidable men under Capt. Takeo Sugai, who had preceded Shibasaki to Tarawa by a few months. Koga had ordered the crack unit moved from Rabaul where it was then attached to the Second Fleet and reorganizing after the fighting for Guadalcanal. The men began arriving in mid-May. The Sasebo naval infantry was the strongest force at Tarawa.

Other units already in place in the Gilberts included the 6th SNLF, 1,100 men strong; the 111th Pioneers, a combat engineer unit corresponding to the American Seabees, 1,250 men strong; and a Fourth Fleet naval construction battalion, about 1,000 men strong, of whom more than half were unreliable Korean "volunteers." At Makin, nearly 300 troops of the 6th SNLF were dug in, supported by about 500 airmen, engineers, and Korean laborers of the 111th Pioneers and Fourth Fleet construction unit. About 2,500 other troops were based at Nauru and Ocean islands.

It has become part of the myth of Tarawa that Rear Admiral Shibasaki was only a fighting admiral. In fact, he was more. Like Tomanari Saichiro, the new commander at Tarawa was one of the very few senior officers of the Imperial navy who were master engineers capable of supervising construction on the scale envisaged for Tarawa. Shibasaki had graduated from the University of Tokyo with qualifications in military, naval, and structural engineering. Such accomplishments had led to his selection for the Gilberts command. But Shibasaki was also a fighting admiral who had been doing just that—and winning—on other fronts for some time. Disappointed as Saichiro was, his successor reflected the evolution of the Gilberts from a backwater of the war to the front lines.

Though Shibasaki had missed the first B-24 raids on Tarawa, which had taken place in April, he felt the sting of the growing American strength in the Central Pacific from his first day in command when he learned what already had been lost. On May 18, for example, a major reinforcement—twelve hundred combat troops of the 6th Konkyochitai and four powerful 8-inch naval artillery pieces—had sailed from Kwajalein

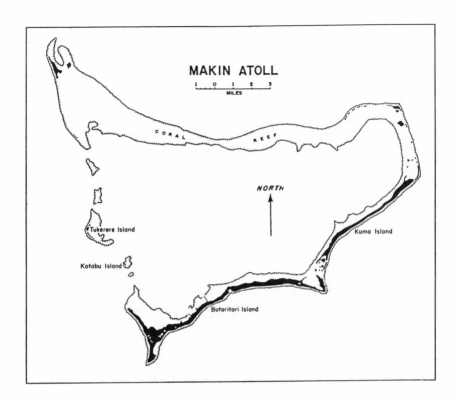

MAKIN ATOLL

in the fifty-four-hundred-ton auxiliary cruiser *Bangkok Maru* and another cargo ship bound for Tarawa. It never reached the Gilberts.

Unknown to the Combined Fleet, COMSUBPAC learned of the convoy from a radio message decrypted by American naval intelligence in Hawaii. They learned of the convoy's special cargo and were determined to keep the big naval guns from reaching the Gilberts. COMSUBPAC ordered the submarine *Pollack,* then patrolling in the Marshalls under Comdr. B. E. Lewellen, of Savannah, Missouri, to waylay the convoy.

Two days later, as the convoy approached Jaluit, just 350 miles north of Tarawa, *Pollack* closed in and launched a spread of four torpedoes. *Bangkok Maru*'s stern was blown off and she sank quickly. The unfortunate auxiliary cruiser had not been carrying the Tarawa-bound guns, but had been transporting the 6th Konkyochitai detachment. Two-thirds of the combat troops were rescued, but the vessel went down with nearly all the unit's equipment. COMSUBPAC was sorely disappointed that the 8-inch guns reached Betio, but as it would turn out the trade-off of twelve hundred enemy naval infantry for four big guns on Betio was a plus. Japanese patrol craft took the survivors to Jaluit, where they remained until the end of the war. Their loss was a terrible blow for the Gilberts' defenders.

During the summer, however, Japanese strength in the Gilberts had continued to grow. Fourteen tanks arrived in July. Rear Admiral Shibasaki resolved, too, upon his arrival to continue the development of fortifications. Whole tracts of the coral reef were dynamited and cut with hand tools to provide rubble to strengthen the concrete used in constructing bunkers and pillboxes. From experience in the Solomons, the combat troops had learned to build shelters capable of withstanding the heaviest high-explosive blasts from naval gunfire and air bombardment. Whole companies of naval infantry were employed in clearing neighboring islands of their coconut groves. The trees were mowed down so their tough timbers could be used to reinforce bunkers and fortifications and extend the seawall that nearly surrounded Betio.

By midsummer, nearly all that the U.S. Marines would face in November was in place, and it was truly staggering. Off the beaches, antiboat obstacles, such as mined concrete tetrahedrons, dragon's teeth, coral cairns, and barbed-wire and log barricades, were arranged in such a way that landing craft would be diverted into lanes covered by artillery. Along the edge of the island, a few feet from the water's edge, a seawall three to five feet high, built mostly of coconut logs and steel wired and spiked together, presented yet another barricade to an attacker.

Constructed behind the seawall, sited to fire over it or through ports, was a system of 13mm and 7.7mm machine-gun emplacements, some with the dual capability of AA or infantry fire. Others were covered by coconut logs, coral sand and concrete, and, occasionally, armor plating. They were connected by revetted trenches with rifle ports, command posts, and convenient ammunition dumps. At the corners of the island and at various other points along the shore, there were sited fourteen coast defense guns ranging in size from 3- and 5-inch pieces to the supremely dangerous 8-inch naval guns. Although all the large gun emplacements had bombproof shelters for crews, underground storage vaults for ammunition, and precision fire control systems, the 8-inch batteries were easily the most heavily protected emplacements on the island.

Along the coast and inland of the beach, twenty-five field guns, ranging from 37mm to 75mm split trail mountain guns, were positioned to fire anywhere on the island. They were in covered emplacements, mostly in dugouts well protected from shrapnel blasts by thick coverings of coconut logs, crushed coral, and sand. They were immune to all but direct hits from the largest naval guns. Additional firepower included a phalanx of 13mm, 90mm, and 120mm AA guns and the tanks with their 37mm cannon, several of which had their gun turrets dug in hull down and immobilized as steel pillboxes.

The system of bombproof shelters, perhaps the most extensive encountered anywhere in the war, covered barracks and headquarters areas as well as the beaches. They were built of coconut logs strengthened by angle irons, and their roofs, six feet and more thick, were so constructed of sand, logs, and corrugated iron that only direct hits by large-caliber AP or delayed-action high-explosive (HE) shells could penetrate them. Many were partitioned inside so that defenders were protected from explosives hurled through the apertures. For such a small area, transport was in abundance. One hundred motor vehicles, including cars, trucks, and motorcycles with sidecars, had been shipped to the island. In addition, the troops had a thousand bicycles.

Saichiro had organized an unholy welcome for an attacker, and Shibasaki had strengthened it. He believed the island was impregnable. Never in the history of warfare had a more powerful or deadly means of resistance been prepared. The official U.S. Army history of Operation Galvanic concluded that, with the possible exception of Iwo Jima, Tarawa's beaches "were better protected against a landing force than any encountered in any theater of operations throughout the Second World War."

Shibasaki ordered the garrison "to defend to the last man all vital areas and destroy the enemy at the water's edge. In a battle where the enemy is superior, it is necessary to lure him within range of our fixed defense installations, and then, using all our strength, destroy him." Finally, he confidently told his troops, "Even with a million men in a hundred years, the Americans could not take Tarawa."

At Pearl Harbor, Lt. Comdr. Fred A. Connaway, of Helena, Arkansas, looked up from his perch atop the conning tower of the submarine *Sculpin* on the morning of November 5. The tropical trade winds pushed dirty smoke from the navy yard shops out to sea. Immense clouds towered over the majestic Koolau mountain range. The submarine skipper awaited a special passenger. He was anxious to get underway.

Corvina, under Comdr. Roderick S. Rooney, had departed Pearl Harbor the day before. Together, the two submarines would take station off Truk as a prelude to Operation Galvanic. *Searaven* and *Apogon* would also be in the area. Truk had four main entrances and each would be guarded by an American submarine. If the Kido Butai sortied to aid the Japanese defense of the Gilberts, the submarines would report the enemy movement, then attack. In all, between Truk and the Gilberts, nearly a dozen submarines would support the operation.

At last Capt. John P. Cromwell, of Henry, Illinois, emerged from the nearby headquarters of COMSUBPAC. He had stopped by the office of VAdm. Charles Lockwood to bid farewell and receive last-minute instructions. COMSUBPAC briefed him a final time on the huge operation about to be undertaken in the Gilberts.

"Stand by to get underway," Commander Connaway told the officer of the deck (OOD). He climbed down the ladder to the main deck to meet the senior naval officer, who would travel aboard *Sculpin* as commander of Submarine Division 42. In the event that the Kido Butai sortied, Captain Cromwell would organize the submarines into a wolf pack—the first such tactical grouping of American submarines in the war. He would be assisted in his job by information obtained from the deciphering of Japanese naval communications. Cromwell stepped aboard, saluted the colors, and shook hands with Commander Connaway.

"Take in all lines," shouted the OOD through a bullhorn. Cromwell went below and the skipper took the con.

"Engines ahead one-third," ordered Connaway after *Sculpin* had backed into the main channel and started toward the harbor entrance. A searchlight from the navy yard tower flashed.

"Message from COMSUBPAC," said the signalman standing on the bridge beside Connaway. "It reads, 'Good hunting.'"

"Acknowledge, and tell him 'Thank you.'"

The antisubmarine warfare (ASW) net strung across the harbor gate was lowered, and *Sculpin* passed through the barrier. Connaway shaped a course to the southwest and the Central Pacific.

Chapter Eight

Meanwhile, the first concrete major U.S. offensive against Japan had been taking shape. Major General Holland Smith approved the 2d Marine Division's plan for Tarawa on September 14. It had been drafted by the unit's superb chief of staff, redheaded Col. Merrit A. Edson, of Washington, D.C., and thirty-nine-year-old Col. David M. Shoup, the division's former crack operations officer from Covington, Indiana.

Colonel Edson, or "Red Mike," as he was known, was at forty-six years old one of the youngest senior staff officers in the marines—and one of the toughest. He was a leader who had experienced combat. From the time Edson landed at Tulagi in August 1942 in command of the famed 1st Marine Raider Battalion—Carlson had the 2d Raiders—he had been known for his soft-spoken and thoughtful courage. He was credited with having saved the day at Guadalcanal. In the midst of the first ferocious fighting there, when the Japanese were on the brink of breaking through the marine lines, Edson had exposed himself under heavy fire to stem the Japanese offensive. With communications knocked out and Japanese infiltrators among the thin American positions, he moved among his men, shouting, "Rally to Red Mike." The Raiders held and the Japanese attack was beaten off. The action, for which Congress awarded Edson the Medal of Honor, became a classic in the legend and lore of the Corps.

Colonel Dave Shoup was equally tough. He also had fought at Guadalcanal, and had earlier led troops in Central America and China. He had been promoted to command of the assault troops for the capture of Tarawa during the rehearsals at Efate, when the commander of the 2d Marines suffered a heart attack. Shoup was something of a paradox in the Corps—a rough, profane leader of men who enjoyed writing poetry. Brigadier General Leo "Dutch" Hermle, of Coronado, California—who would become the only general, albeit briefly, to land at Tarawa on D day and then repeat the feat more than a year later at Iwo Jima—was the assistant division commander.

At Tarawa, the 2d Division would storm ashore on Betio's northern or lagoon beaches. Landing conditions on the southern beaches facing the ocean were better, and "General Julian" at one point suggested making the landing there. The lagoon beaches, with a deep indentation at the western end of the island and the long Burns-Philp pier jutting out across the reef, would give the Japanese excellent opportunities for placing enfilading fire on the marines. But it soon became apparent that the lagoon would probably permit an amphibious assault at less cost. The beaches on the northern coast were wider and more regularly formed, although Japanese firepower and fortifications were much stronger there. The lagoon beaches were selected, with plans drawn up to land reinforcements on the west coast, or bird's head, when the opportunity arose.

The lagoon beaches presented a narrow sliver of white coral sand, fronted by a barrier reef that ran an average of five hundred to twelve hundred yards from the island to deep water and was backed by the seawall. The division staff split the beaches of Betio into five-hundred-yard landing zones, color coded and numbered right to left: Green Beach, Red Beach 1, Red Beach 2, and Red Beach 3 along the lagoon, and Black Beaches 1 and 2 along the oceanside. The lagoon beaches of nearby Bairiki Island, a possible early objective, were code-named Blue Beaches 1 and 2.

A scout-sniper platoon and detachment of assault engineers of the 2d Marines were to lead the invasion by landing at H hour minus 15 minutes (H - 15) at the end of the pier and clearing it of Japanese positions. The capture of this feature was vital to the operation, to eliminate the enemy's ability to deliver a devastating cross fire across the reef and into the assault waves. It had to be taken quickly, if casualties were to be kept to a minimum and the assault troops were to be free of fire into their flanks and exposed rears.

The 3d Battalion, 2d Marines, under Maj. John F. Schoettel, of Lima, Ohio, would form the right wing. It would drive into the reentrant angle of Red Beach 1, cross the bird's head to the northern coast, envelop

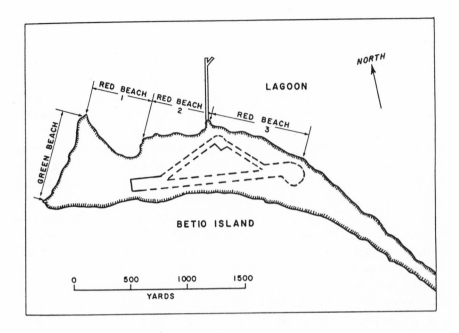

and clear Green Beach from behind, and then turn left to drive down the oceanside of the island.

The 2d Battalion, 2d Marines, under Lt. Col. Herbert R. Amey, Jr., of Ambler, Pennsylvania, would come in to the right of the long Burns-Philp pier on Red Beach 2, secure it for the unloading of supplies and equipment, seize the airfield, and then wheel to drive down the center of the island.

Meanwhile, the 2d Battalion, 8th Marines, under Maj. Henry P. "Jim" Crowe, of Boston, Kentucky, was to land on Red Beach 3 on the left flank of the invasion front. This formation would drive inland on the left of the pier, and hold on its left shoulder to impose itself as a blocking force against any Japanese elements that would try to move up from the tail of the island. With the broader part of the island secured and all gains consolidated, artillery and another rifle battalion would land and sweep down the tail of the island.

At Makin, known to the soldiers by its code name Horse Island, the reinforced 165th Regimental Combat Team (RCT) of the 27th Infantry Division would attack according to a plan devised by its commander,

Maj. Gen. Ralph Smith, and approved somewhat reluctantly by the V Amphibious Corps commander. Two battalions—the 1st and 3d—would land on the western coast of Butaritari Island, followed by tanks and artillery. Two hours later, another battalion—the 2d, reinforced by elements of the 1st Battalion, 105th Infantry—would land four thousand yards east of the main assault on the northern, or lagoon, side of the island.

The object was to envelop the main Japanese defenses in a pincers movement, the first time such a daring tactic had been tried in an amphibious assault. After the two elements had linked up and secured a beachhead, the 165th RCT would make a powerful drive to the west and down the long "handle" of the island, all the while supported by a heavy concentration of field artillery. According to the official army history of the operation, "The plan for getting these troops ashore on Butaritari was elaborate in the extreme and unlike any adopted before or after in the Pacific war."

As the marines had done with Tarawa, the 27th Division staff split the beaches of Butaritari into individual landing zones. They color coded and numbered them—Red Beach 1 and Red Beach 2 along the western, or hammerhead, end of the island where the H-hour landings would be made, and Yellow and Blue Beaches 1, 2, and 3 inside the lagoon. Auxiliary beaches along the oceanside, where no movement of troops was planned, were coded Purple; along the lagoon side on the western end of the island was an area designated Black Beach.

One particularly serious difference of opinion, among many, arose during the tactical planning for the Gilberts. At a joint planning conference in October in Hawaii, Maj. Gen. Julian Smith, who would be in command of the ground forces at Tarawa, asked the navy for more LVTs (landing vehicles, tracked), also known as "amtracs" or "alligators." The vehicles, twenty-five feet long and capable of carrying two dozen men, mounted one or two machine guns, and had been first used at Guadalcanal and in the North African landings in 1942. Since then they had gone through several modifications. They were valued by the marines because they could, as navy historian RAdm. Samuel E. Morison would later write, "do everything but fly." They could make four knots in the water, rumble over shoals or reefs, smash through wire and other light infantry obstacles, and reach fifteen miles per hour on land.

The 2d Division had a motley collection of one hundred LVTs of

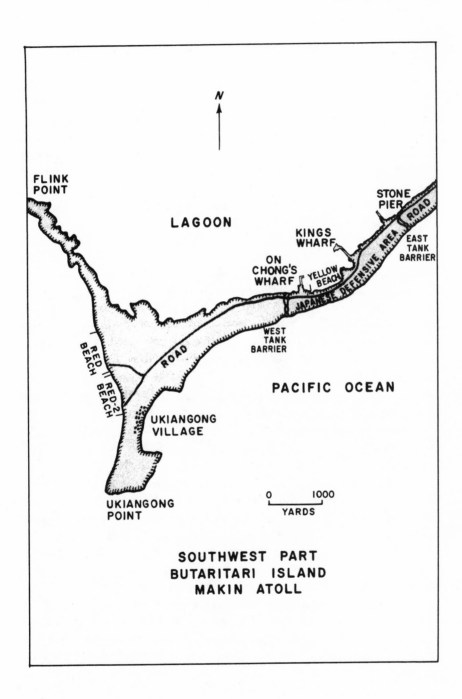

SOUTHWEST PART
BUTARITARI ISLAND
MAKIN ATOLL

its own in New Zealand, but many were either ungunned and unarmored versions of antiquated older models, or had long since passed the operational lifetime of their engines and tracks, or were broken down mechanical wrecks. Seventy-five of these were in fair condition and judged combat capable. These were to be taken along to Tarawa. To ensure success, however, the marines estimated that they needed a minimum of one hundred more. They suggested that the lack of intelligence concerning tidal conditions in the Gilberts alone was reason enough to employ more tracked landing craft. Any possibility that the tides might be low on D day could mean disaster for the assault troops who would have to wade ashore under fire.

"How soon can we have the vehicles, Kelly?" asked "Howlin' Mad" Smith.

Rear Admiral Turner shook his head. They would not be needed, he said. He was convinced that there would be favorable tidal conditions for the marines to make their landings. Furthermore, there were no LVTs available in the Pacific, or ships to transport them. The marines would have to get along with the flat-bottomed LCVPs (landing craft, vehicles and personnel)—commonly called "Higgins boats"—and LCMs (landing craft, medium) manned by navy crews. In Turner's opinion, more LVTs were simply unnecessary. "Besides," he added, "I don't have time to collect more amtracs."

Turner was mistaken in his belief that the equipment already at the division's disposal was adequate for the job at hand, but in truth the navy was wrestling with the effects of a critical worldwide bottleneck in the Allied shipping pool. In the South Pacific alone, hundreds of ships were sometimes idle for weeks for lack of equipment and facilities to unload them. Some transports and LSTs that had been used in the invasions of Sicily and Italy had been detached from the Mediterranean theater but would not arrive in time for Galvanic.

Thus navy opposition to providing more LVTs had less to do with insensitivity to the plight of the marines than with the shipping shortage. At this late date in planning the operation, it was unthinkable in Turner's view to change the vast global shipping schedules merely to accommodate "a few more amtracs for Tarawa." The navy was hard-pressed to meet all the supply and transport needs of Galvanic even without the extra LVTs.

"Howlin' Mad" Smith was not impressed by the navy problems. "By God, Kelly, I want amtracs and I'll have them," he thundered, emphasizing the demand by pounding the table. "On Oahu, I obtained irrefutable proof of the amtrac's efficiency," he wrote later. "They walked clear through seven lines of barbed wire in tests. We knew that a double-apron barbed-wire fence practically encircled Betio and a series of concrete tetrahedrons had been nearly completed. If the reef proved impassable for boats—and it did—the only way to get the men ashore was in amtracs."

But Turner was immovable on the subject. He tried to mollify the marine general. "There's no need to blow up, General," he said. "You won't need amtracs."

Smith minced no words. The fate of the marines assaulting the beaches had been prominent in his mind since he had arrived at Pearl Harbor five weeks before. He was haunted by the spectre of the reef becoming the battlefield. He feared what might happen if the assault troops were caught in the open without armored protection amidst the fury of merciless machine-gun fire. In his crusty and belligerent estimation, the navy rejection was nothing short of callous disregard for the safety of the men who would be required to overcome the obstacles to assault. Anything less than the minimum necessary support requested by Julian Smith would be considered hazardous at best—a needless sacrifice of lives at worst. He pointed out that it was essential to have more LVTs made available, if for nothing else than carrying supplies.

Facing Turner, "Howlin' Mad" Smith said, "Admiral, don't tell me what I need. You handle your ships, and I'll take care of my men."

"You won't need amtracs," insisted Turner.

But the 2d Division commander and Holland Smith were old friends. The former had been chief of staff to "Howlin' Mad" during the large navy and marine amphibious training exercises in the Caribbean in 1940. If Julian Smith said he needed more LVTs, Holland Smith was inclined to believe him. Have them he would. He was appalled that the navy would stonewall him on this point. He already had been forced to accept the untested 27th Infantry Division for the assault on Makin, he reasoned. His suspicion that CINCPAC was not taking the Gilberts invasion seriously seemed well founded. The navy appeared unable to overcome its belief that Galvanic was a mere training operation prior to the invasion of the Marshalls, which in their view was the grand strategic prize.

By now the general's fiery temper was directed in all its fury at Turner, who continued trying to calm him down. "Howlin' Mad" only hardened. Army, navy, and marine staff officers feared what was about to happen. The disagreement had reached an unbroachable impasse. When rejected one last time, the marine general astonished everyone present. He leaned over the table toward Turner. "Julian asked for amtracs and he'll get them," he said. "I'm telling you straight out, Admiral, either produce a hundred amtracs or the deal's off."

Turner remained equally adamant in his opposition.

Then the V Amphibious Corps commander laid down a declaration that in any other forum would have been viewed as an ultimatum. "Kelly, it's like this. I've got to have those amtracs. We'll take a helluva licking without them. No amtracs," he stated, "no operation. You know me, Kelly, I mean it."

Turner threw up his arms in exasperation and sighed wearily. "Yes, General, I know you. I'll rustle up a hundred amtracs for you and find room for them on the ships. Now let's get back to business—there's been enough bullshit."

A shipment of the latest 1943 models was located in San Diego. It sailed from the West Coast to American Samoa, where as it turned out only fifty of the LVTs were diverted for use by the 2d Division. They were rushed aboard LSTs to join the Southern Attack Force in the Ellice Islands en route to Tarawa. Scratch crews were raised, and these also joined the vehicles en route. "It galls me to remember this instance of Navy stubbornness," growled Smith in his memoirs. "I was appalled to find Kelly Turner shortsightedly opposing the use of amtracs." In his final report to Admiral Nimitz, Smith would flatly say, "Without the amtracs, it is believed the landing at Tarawa would have failed." And he was right.

A further flash point of disagreement, as far as the V Amphibious Corps staff was concerned, was Spruance's naval gunfire support plan. Makin, the far weaker of the objectives in the Gilberts, was assigned four battleships and four cruisers. In contrast, Tarawa, which looked to present an infinitely greater threat to the operation, would have only three battleships and four cruisers. Although the attack at Tarawa would be supported by three more destroyers than the assault on Makin, the distribution of naval gunfire worried the marines.

This objection was overruled by Rear Admiral Spruance. He said it could not be helped. He believed that another battleship could not be spared for the bombardment of Tarawa because the amphibious attacks should occur simultaneously. If in the unlikely event Admiral Koga sortied the still dangerous Kido Butai during the assault phase of Galvanic, the Northern Attack Force would most certainly be the first American element to feel its wrath.

In fairness to the navy planners, they had envisaged a greater commitment of naval gunfire support for Tarawa. However, the surprisingly violent Japanese reaction to Vice Admiral Halsey's invasion of Bougainville had knocked a heavy cruiser out of action and rendered it unavailable for the Gilberts operation. The ripple effect of this unexpected loss distressed Spruance exceedingly. But he was firm in his observation that the Japanese naval threat was still sufficient to require a greater concentration of American naval forces in the northern Gilberts than against Tarawa.

The straw that broke the camel's back was "Howlin' Mad" Smith's discovery that he was not going to be present for the invasion. Rear Admiral Charles H. McMorris, who had succeeded Spruance as CINCPAC chief of staff, had directed that Smith and his staff be left behind in Hawaii. McMorris decided that Turner, as overall commander of the 5th Amphibious Force (and therefore the V Amphibious Corps as well), would not need the assistance of Smith and his headquarters staff during the operational phase of Galvanic.

"Apparently," Smith recalled, "the Navy intended to employ the V Amphibious Corps and leave me, the Corps Commander, twiddling my thumbs at Pearl Harbor." Spruance, who was unaware of the directive, restored the marine general to command. Room for Smith and his staff was found aboard Turner's flagship *Pennsylvania,* which would be off Makin. Smith preferred to be available at Tarawa but he did not press the issue, since he was lucky to be going at all. "Looking back on this period from the vantage of years and distance," General Smith wrote, "I sometimes wonder if we didn't have two enemies—the Japanese and certain brass hats in the Army and Navy."

Besides getting the army and marine assault forces into action, there were endless logistical problems caused by the maintenance and sea movement of numerous support and garrison forces. Several Seabee (naval construction battalion) detachments specializing in the development of airfields were to go with the 5th Amphibious Force to the Gilberts. The army 102d and 105th Combat Engineer Battalions were assigned to Makin. In addition, the army air corps cousins of the Seabees, air service support squadrons (ASSRONs) of the Seventh Air Force— the 1st at Baker, the 3d divided among Nukufetau, Funafuti, and Nanomea—were also assigned to Galvanic. The 2d ASSRON was readied in Hawaii for immediate movement into the Gilberts once the objectives were secured. These service groups would supply the bulk of the labor for unloading supplies and clearing away debris and undergrowth from occupied areas.

Two hospital ships, *Relief* and *Solace,* were assigned to the operation. The army forces at Makin would have their own medical service, the 102d Medical Battalion. Marine divisions did not have their own surgery teams. Rather they used the services of "Pelicans," the doctors and aid men of the U.S. Navy Medical Corps. At Tarawa these services were provided by the 2d Medical Battalion, made up of one-third marines and the rest navy medical specialists. Casualty collecting teams and first-aid groups were drawn from the special service troops of the division.

Everything for the assault forces had to be provided via shipping. Besides troops, the transports, cargo ships, LSDs, and LSTs bound for Makin, for example, were crammed with ten days' worth of rations for each soldier, five gallons of water for every man on board, fuel for armored fighting vehicles and motor transports, medical supplies, diesel oil, and all types of ammunition, including that for infantry weapons, artillery, and tanks. All this was in addition to chemical warfare supplies, and signals and communications equipment. The navy was supported by a fleet of tenders, tugs, minesweepers, concrete fuel barges, ammunition ships, and thirteen oilers carrying fuel and aviation gasoline.

Ships began loading in mid-October. The assault forces for Makin boarded their transports at Pearl Harbor on October 29 and 30. Between Halloween and November 3, final rehearsals were held by the Northern Attack Force at Maalaea Bay, Maui, with simulated naval gunfire and air support. Poor weather conditions and rough beaches made the training unsatisfactory. An aura of undesirable artificiality affected the maneuvers. Some units did not participate, or their equipment was already stowed away. The army also feared that the equipment might be damaged, so the exercises were carried out with little zeal. Meanwhile, in New Zealand, the 2d Marine Division was loaded and departed Wellington on November 1. It held final rehearsals with supporting naval forces between November 7 and 12 at Mele Bay in the New Hebrides. These exercises proved only slightly more satisfactory than the army maneuvers in Hawaii.

Nevertheless, by the eve of battle in the Gilberts, more than two hundred vessels ranging in size from battleships and carriers to tugs and coastal auxiliaries would be assembled in their assigned areas off Makin and Tarawa, and off the Marshalls and Nauru. In his berth aboard a transport bound for Tarawa, soaked in sweat, a marine carefully went over the index card he held in his hand. He wanted to be sure that his beloved knew where he was, so he had arranged an elaborate code that would secretly reveal the information. His greeting would indicate his whereabouts:

My Darling—Australia
Darling—New Zealand
My dearest—East Indies
My dearest Violet—Rabaul
Violet—Burma
Honey—Hawaii
Sweetheart—Solomons
My darling Violet—Truk
Violet darling—New Britain
Violet dearest—New Guinea
My dearest Darling—Salamaura
Precious—Aboard Ship
Princess—New Caledonia

Like most people, he probably had never heard of Tarawa. A chaplain later found the card on his dead body.

Chapter Nine

The first planes of the U.S. Seventh Air Force, the army land-based strategic air arm in the Central Pacific, took off from Funafuti on November 13 to attack Tarawa, the heart of Japanese resistance in the Gilberts. For every airman, from commanding officer Maj. Gen. Willis Hale down to the youngest machinist, it was a special event. The Seventh Air Force was marking the official beginning of Operation Galvanic by flying the longest continuous combat missions yet attempted in any theater of the war.

In this first flight were eighteen B-24s of the 11th Heavy Bombardment Group, commanded by marine Brig. Gen. Harold Campbell. Nearly every one of the planes had been recently moved up from Pearl Harbor, and all had been specially modified with extra machine guns for increased defensive firepower. Crisscrossing Tarawa at night from heights of eighty-five hundred and fifteen thousand feet, they dropped fifteen tons of bombs, composed of 126 twenty-pound fragmentation clusters and 55 five-hundred-pound HE general-purpose (GP) warheads. All but one of the bombers returned to Funafuti. Excited crews reported that they could see Tarawa burning from as far away as sixty miles in the darkness.

Meanwhile, the vanguard of the new U.S. Fifth Fleet, the most powerful naval force yet to put to sea in the war, had steamed out of Pearl Harbor on November 10 and from Espiritu Santo in the New Hebrides on November 15. In these advance elements bound for preinvasion air assaults of the Gilberts and Marshalls were four new Essex-class fleet carriers, two light carriers, the veterans *Enterprise* and *Saratoga,* six new fast battleships, six heavy and light cruisers, and twenty-one destroyers.

Rear Admiral "Baldy" Pownall, the technically minded seaman who had commanded the hit-and-run raids against Marcus and the Gilberts, was in overall command aboard the new *Yorktown.* The carriers destined for the northern Gilberts and eastern Marshalls included *Lexington, Cowpens, Enterprise, Belleau Wood,* and *Monterey.* The main task force passed southwest of Hawaii, heading toward the waters between the Marshalls and Gilberts. It refueled at sea on November 15 northeast of Howland and Baker islands and met the supporting battleships before splitting up for attacks against the eastern Marshalls and Makin.

The land-based air forces for Galvanic included seven squadrons of Bomber Command and three squadrons of Fighter Command of the Seventh Air Force. Navy and marine aircraft rounded out these land-based air forces, which were under the overall command of RAdm. John H. Hoover. In all, the land-based air forces included one hundred B-24s, twenty-four Catalinas, and twenty-four Venturas, based chiefly at Funafuti and Canton. All through the week preceding the amphibious landings, the B-24s concentrated on enemy islands from which Japanese aircraft could interfere with Galvanic.

On November 14 the big bombers were back in action. This time they attacked not only Tarawa but also the major enemy airfield at Mili in the eastern Marshalls less than 250 miles from Makin. Mili supported twenty-four medium bombers, two thousand defenders, and five hundred airmen. Ten B-24s struck, inflicting twenty casualties and burning to the ground two barracks and a warehouse in which aerial bomb fuses were stored. The raid on Tarawa was even stronger than the first had been. Twenty-four B-24s dropped thirty tons of bombs, starting numerous fires and causing many casualties.

As D day approached, then, the real intent of the vast American air and sea movement in the Central Pacific began to reveal itself. The B-24s also flew missions against Wotje, Jaluit, Maloelap, and Kwajalein in the Marshalls; they concentrated, however, on the main prize of the Gilberts, flying twice as many missions over Tarawa and Makin as all the other targets. They were over Tarawa every night, dropping a total of seventy-five tons of bombs. But the results were somewhat disappointing. "These attacks," concluded COMAIRPAC, "did little damage of any military importance, and there is no indication that any enemy airfields were closed for more than the duration of the attacks."

Although the heavy bomber raids caused little real damage to fortifications, they did inflict losses on the enemy. Time for rest and work was disrupted, and the poundings exacted a tremendous psychological toll on the garrisons. The Japanese proved unable to put up a stiff resistance to the raids. The American aircrews were annoyed more by poor weather conditions and the long eleven-hundred- to fifteen-hundred-mile round-trip flights than by the enemy. Still they did encounter opposition on every mission. Flak of varying intensity and effectiveness was experienced over all the targets. Enemy fighters battled the bombers over Kwajalein, Jaluit, and Maloelap. In fact, the Japanese had detected the American buildup and actually succeeded in striking first. A dozen bombers from Mili attacked Nanomea on November 11; on November 13 and 17 they hit Funafuti. These attacks destroyed four B-24s and damaged another two dozen.

Despite such handicaps, and although the results were not as great as had been hoped by Major General Hale, the Seventh Air Force still managed to contribute to Galvanic. Sixty-seven B-24s launched 13 raids on the Marshalls and Gilberts, totaling 141 sorties by the time the assault elements of the V Amphibious Corps went ashore at Tarawa and Makin. They dropped 175 tons of five-hundred-pound and one-hundred-pound GP bombs and twenty-pound fragmentation cluster bombs. Five Japanese planes were shot down or destroyed on the ground and as many as seven damaged. In addition to the B-24s destroyed or damaged in Japanese counterstrikes, American losses were two bombers lost in combat, another pair to operational causes, and one lost at sea. Crew losses amounted to seventeen airmen killed or missing in action and nineteen wounded.

On November 18 the fast carrier forces struck. The top target for TF 50 was, of course, Tarawa. By now the B-24s had attacked it four times—with uncertain results. Carrier planes from *Essex, Bunker Hill,* and *Independence* swept over the atoll and pounded it even harder than the far-ranging Seventh Air Force had. The naval aircrews unloaded 115 tons of bombs on Tarawa this day. Similarly, whistles and sirens shrilled out the warning for Mili as American aircraft also revisited that island in the eastern Marshalls, far to the north of Tarawa.

The raid took Mili's defenders by surprise. Shortly after sunrise the first planes appeared. The crack of AA guns, along with the baleful wailing of the air raid sirens, was deafening. American raids had become almost predictable, but the defenders realized quickly that this attack

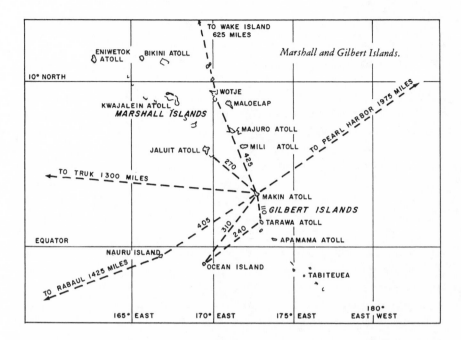

Marshall and Gilbert Islands.

was different. The planes were not the heavy high-level bombers, which invariably attacked at night. Instead this raid came in the morning, and from the east.

Roaring in at seven thousand feet, scores of American carrier aircraft banked and dived for the island through puffs of ugly black flak and streaks of yellow and white tracer. Time and again the planes dived through the furious AA, which came up in a shotgun scatter of fire and smoke that obscured not only the airfield but AA gun positions too. The planes emptied their armaments into all targets of opportunity. Men ran in all directions. They dived for trenches, scrambled for bunker entrances, or headed for dugouts as wave after wave of planes hit the island. Coral erupted, sending shards ripping through the air. Tons of bombs smashed down into hardened shelters, and towering columns of smoke swirled up from a dozen places, covering the island in a soot gray cloud of ruin. As quickly as the American squadrons released their armaments, they sped off to the east, to be followed by others soaring into the assault. Casualties were heavy.

Captain Masanari Shiga, the island commander at Mili, was stunned. Up to this point, since November 15, Mili had been attacked by a score or more of heavy bombers. Yet his command had survived largely unhurt. During the raids Shiga had been able to scramble the Bettys from the airfield. A few had tried to intercept the enemy planes but were unsuccessful. Only one plane had been caught on the ground in all the attacks, and it had been only damaged. But this morning's carrier air raid caused great devastation. A half-dozen planes on the airfield were destroyed or damaged, and numerous AA gun positions were knocked out. This was something very different.

The first supporting raid on Nauru was made the same day by Rear Admiral Sherman's carrier group of *Saratoga* and *Princeton,* which had struck Rabaul on November 5 and 11. At 0300 eighteen fighters were launched for a dawn strike. Three hours later, twenty more fighters followed. Throughout the rest of the day, dive-bombers, torpedo bombers, and yet more fighters swept over the island. Before they were finished, ninety tons of bombs had been dropped and nearly all of Nauru's installations had been severely damaged. One ship had been left burning and four Bettys had been destroyed on the ground. Five enemy fighters had sought to intercept the raids, but all were shot down and crashed into the sea.

The next day the naval air forces launched missions against numerous islands throughout the area. At Tarawa they complemented the effort of nineteen B-24s, which dropped twenty-one tons of bombs and damaged the airfield and started fires all over the island. Then the carrier planes roared in and unloaded sixty-nine tons on the same targets. More damage was achieved than in all the previous B-24 attacks. Between November 13 and 19, 35 Japanese had been killed at Tarawa and 169 wounded in the American air attacks. Returning aircrews reported that "by the end of the day, AA fire had practically ceased."

At the same time on November 19 similar attacks were occurring nearby. At Makin, a dozen B-24s from Nanomea dropped twenty-three tons of bombs; navy planes of the carriers *Enterprise, Belleau Wood,* and *Monterey* dropped an astounding ninety-five tons—more than the Seventh Air Force had been able to unload in a week of raids on a single target. Four Japanese planes—one off Makin, three near Tarawa—were encountered by American fighters and shot down.

Pownall's carrier battle group meanwhile moved into position northwest of Makin, halfway between the Marshalls and that northernmost objective in the Gilberts. His planes struck Jaluit once and Mili three times, further pounding this Marshalls' air base nearest to the Gilberts with 130 tons of bombs. The navy aircrews destroyed the power stations on both islands, burned out hangars, and scored hits on other buildings. The airfield at Mili was rendered unserviceable, and three ships in the lagoon were damaged. In all, seven Japanese aircraft were destroyed on the ground. Lieutenant Frederick W. Gwynne, who flew an Avenger torpedo bomber based aboard the "Lady Lex," scored four five-hundred-pound bomb hits on the Mili airfield "although it already looked like a piece of cheese." He concluded: "It was a picnic. Mili is a beautiful atoll, but it is a Jap cemetery tonight."

The carrier raid of D day minus two on Nauru was followed up the next day with a strike by the B-24s, accompanied by naval photoreconnaissance aircraft. They bombed both of the airfields on the phosphate island, causing much damage to the light industrial areas and to all above-ground installations. As a result of this and the previous carrier raid, Nauru was effectively removed from the list of potential threats to the invasion of the Gilberts. Of all the American preinvasion air attacks, the suppression of Nauru's offensive air capabilities proved the most successful.

Shortly before noon on this day before the army and marine landings, the navy also briefly unleashed some of its big guns. Rear Admiral Ernest G. Small led Cruiser Division 5 in a two-hour bombardment of Tarawa. The 8-inch guns of *Chester, Pensacola,* and *Salt Lake City* flung in 1,941 high-capacity shells. The destroyers *Erben* and *Hale* added 82 rounds of 5-inch fire. The Japanese garrison challenged the bold American action by firing off 46 shells from the massive 8-inch guns without effect and 104 rounds of equally misdirected 5-inch fire. Three pillboxes were destroyed by the American warships before they called it quits for the day. Only about four hundred more pillboxes remained.

The carrier captains were pleased with themselves. The raids by the navy flattops of D day minus two and D day minus one on Nauru, Tarawa, Makin, Jaluit, and Mili had equaled or surpassed the combined results of the heavy bomber raids. Nine Japanese planes had been shot down, eleven destroyed on the ground, and perhaps another ten damaged; and one enemy ship had been set afire, three coastal vessels damaged, and extensive destruction inflicted upon every enemy airfield within range of the Gilberts. Navy losses were five pilots, six crewmen, and five aircraft.

In all, in a week of combined attacks by navy and Seventh Air Force planes, fourteen Japanese aircraft had been shot down or destroyed on the ground and as many as eighteen damaged. Overall American losses were ten aircraft lost and twenty-two airmen killed and about thirty wounded. For this price nearly six hundred tons of HE bombs had been dropped on Japanese air bases in the Marshalls and Gilberts. In far-off Tokyo, a military analyst for Domei, the Japanese news agency, wrote, "The United States is obviously planning to thrust into waters fundamental to our Pacific strategy. The Gilbert Islands have now become a theater of decisive war between Japan and the United States."

The Attack

PART TWO

Chapter Ten

By the middle of November, on the eve of battle in the Gilberts, Tarawa could not have been much stronger. Yet Ens. Kiyoshi Ota of the amphibious transport section continued to spend all his time moving about the adjoining islands, assisting in the unending construction effort. Following the American carrier air raids on the Gilberts in September and Wake in October, the work of building hardened shelters had continued under the supervision of a civilian engineer. The thirty-six men and six landing barges with drop-down ramps under Ensign Ota's command could carry and land eighty troops on an enemy beach, but there was little use for that now. Instead hundreds of men were busier than ever sawing and cutting down coconut trees, which Ota and his unit transported for use in reinforcing bunkers and redoubts.

The construction work had become dangerous, because of the ominously increasing American air raids, but the felled trees were crucial to strengthening fortifications. Sinkings by submarines in the Marshalls and around Truk, as well as the increased tempo of the war in the South Pacific around Rabaul, had long ago slowed to a trickle the flow of steel, cement, and other supplies into Tarawa. The last *maru* to make a port call had been a small coastal freighter, which sped down from Jaluit in late September after the first air raid on Tarawa. It delivered one last shipment of concrete mix.

Soon after, Imperial General Headquarters issued a warning that action was imminent in the Gilberts. This forecast was soon changed to indicate that it would be the Marshalls the Americans would attack. Then the forecast was upgraded to include both island groups. Finally, the beam narrowed until nearly everyone in the Japanese chain of command believed intuitively that the blow would fall on Tarawa and the Gilberts.

All this meant little to the Japanese garrisons. They were now thoroughly alert that something unusual was developing. The frequent flyovers by American long-range reconnaissance aircraft, the end of sea movement between the Marshalls and Gilberts, the incessant air attacks, and the evacuation of the 755th Naval Air Detachment from Tarawa were proof enough for them. At Truk, Admiral Koga, with what was left of the Kido Butai, mourned the loss of his air forces at Rabaul on what appeared to be the eve of the decisive engagement he had sought.

Captain Shigeru Sugano, an engineer with the 6th Yokosuka SNLF, had been building fortifications at Tarawa since February. He was not surprised when Rear Admiral Shibasaki reacted strongly to the American carrier air raid in September. The island commander immediately issued a special directive, his eighteenth since arriving on the island in August, ordering the construction of a bombproof shelter for a massive communications and headquarters command center. "Work was started immediately," wrote a 6th SNLF artilleryman in his diary, "and is scheduled to be completed during October. After the work is completed, one transmitter and three receivers will be installed in the station. No matter what happens, we hope to be able to maintain radio communications."

The walls and roof of the command center were made of formed concrete several feet thick, reinforced with steel beams and coconut logs. The building was carefully constructed, with huge steel doors and ventilation ports on the roof. Artillery and machine-gun positions were laid out around the man-made massif. Nearly a battalion equivalent of infantry were dug in nearby in bunkers and pillboxes of cement and coral. When the command center was finished it had three levels and could accommodate up to three hundred men. It was virtually impregnable to frontal assault.

As summer turned into autumn—not that any significant difference can be discerned in the Central Pacific—the Americans also had been busy in the Gilberts, though the Japanese did not know it. On September 25 and for eighteen days thereafter, the U.S. submarine *Nautilus* operated at periscope depth, alternating time off the coasts of Makin, Tarawa, and Abemama. The boat's crew took soundings and photographs of all the invasion beaches—information vital to the landings—and raced back to Pearl Harbor with the data.

The huge fleet submarine *Nautilus,* one of the two largest in the U.S. arsenal, was no stranger to the Gilberts. In August 1942, with its sister ship *Argonaut,* it had transported Carlson's Raiders, the famed 2d Marine Raider Battalion under Lt. Col. Evans Carlson, to Makin for its spectacular commando raid in support of the Guadalcanal invasion. By November 18 *Nautilus* was back on station in the area to act as lifeguard for the preinvasion air bombardment by the fast carrier forces. The submarine also carried the assault element of the V Amphibious Corps Reconnaissance Company, commanded by Capt. James L. Jones, which would land by rubber boat at Abemama.

Chief Petty Officer Tadeo Oonuki had arrived at Tarawa in July aboard a cruiser with a shipment of volunteers who had answered the call for "hazardous duty in the south." Oonuki was a navy truck driver who had been assigned to Yokosuka Naval Base in spring 1943. He had never been in combat and had no idea what to expect. But he had been in the service for several years and had performed well on shore duty in China and Indochina. Because of his experience driving a truck, he was given a Type 97 light tank. He was proud that he and his crew had been chosen to protect Rear Admiral Shibasaki's headquarters, performing as a mobile armored guard with their 37mm gun and two 7.7mm machine guns.

Torpedo Officer Yoshio Tanikaze commanded one of Ensign Ota's landing barges. He and CPO Oonuki had become close friends. They spent many evenings together, drinking sake, playing cards, entertaining each other with stories, and listening to Radio Tokyo. But when the American carrier planes appeared out of the east on the morning of November 18, Torpedo Officer Tanikaze and CPO Oonuki were not together. The unlucky small-boat commander and his crew had been on routine patrol in the lagoon and were caught in the open during the surprise air raid. They never had a chance.

The sight that greeted the pilot of the Hellcat fighter did not surprise him. He had been thoroughly briefed, and had studied the three-dimensional scale models of Betio that had been built at Pearl Harbor. Everything was exactly where it should be. He also had memorized the charts produced by naval intelligence analysts, showing nearly all the Japanese installations, the many field guns, the AA guns, and the coastal artillery. The information had been updated after each Seventh

Air Force bombing raid and confirmed that the enemy aircraft that earlier had been based at Tarawa were no longer there. Any aircraft would have been the primary targets. With the airfield no longer supporting air operations, however, big guns, above-ground installations, and patrol craft would be top-priority targets.

The Hellcat pilot completed his survey and looked down at a landing barge heading for the tiny island of Eita southeast of Betio; the barge was in the lagoon seeking the safety of the island's broad beach. The pilot passed over the vessel, firing his .50-caliber machine guns, lacing the water with a stretch of furious splashes but missing. He pulled back on his stick and climbed, then swung quickly around for another run.

Torpedo Officer Tanikaze focused on Eita, which lay dead ahead, as the enemy fighter came back. Bullets ripped into the landing craft and it quickly began taking on water. Tanikaze ordered everyone overboard, then dived into the lagoon himself. They began swimming for shore as the boat sank. The plane made another strafing pass, machine guns blazing. Tanikaze and the others disappeared beneath the surface of the lagoon in a spreading pool of pinkish sea.

The American naval bombardment on D day minus one had become so terrible that Ensign Ota, at his command post on the beach, took refuge with six others in a pillbox. The hardened shelter had been wracked several times by nearby bomb hits during the morning air attacks, even before the deadly naval gunfire began falling around it. Everywhere now, Tarawa's defenders were being forced to take shelter. So great was the damage to the communication system that runners had to be used instead. Few who ventured forth ever returned.

The sailing of the American convoys from Hawaii and in the South Pacific was known almost immediately to the Japanese, although no one at Truk or Tokyo knew for sure where they were headed. Nevertheless, Admiral Koga instinctively activated the first phase of the Yogaki plan. On November 15 the extensive movement of Japanese aircraft in the Marshall and Gilbert islands area began. Admiral Nimitz was advised of this sudden development by his naval intelligence staff and passed the ominous news to the Fifth Fleet commanders.

Japanese air patrols over the seas east and southeast of the Gilberts and Marshalls were increased on November 16. A dive-bomber flying patrol out of Mili late in the afternoon of November 18 picked up several heavily laden cargo ships about 150 miles east of Abemama and 200 miles southeast of Tarawa, apparently headed for Makin. In closing to within three miles of the surface contacts for a better look, the Japanese crew braved a spurious barrage of 5- and 3-inch, as well as .50-caliber machine-gun, AA fire. Upon identifying three LSTs escorted by a single destroyer, the crew turned their plane away and took the bad news home. Meanwhile, another Japanese aircraft spotted an American reconnaissance plane about 120 miles east of Abemama. All troops along the Central Pacific perimeter were put on battle alert.

The next day, November 19, a Japanese search plane failed to return from a patrol east of Abemama; American fighters had pounced and shot down the plane so fast that the crew had not had time to radio its predicament. Then, three hours after midnight, in the leading plane of three bombers returning home from a six-hundred-mile search, Lt. Kioki Yoshoyo confirmed the worst. "Enemy contact report!" he excitedly radioed his base. "Fleet sighted. Several carriers and other types too numerous to mention." The plot of the report revealed that the course of the American armada would bring it to Tarawa within twenty-four hours.

In the afternoon eight Japanese fighters and scout bombers found the northern group of carriers heading for Makin, and they engaged the American CAP in a freewheeling dogfight. One of the scout bombers was shot down. The others did not fly close enough to the ship formation to be fired at, content merely to follow and report on the American course during the daylight hours. The Makin-bound LSTs, carrying all the invaluable LVTs for the amphibious assault of Butaritari, now were only forty-five miles from their objective.

As the sun was setting, however, another pair of scout bombers arrived on the scene and dropped float lights to indicate the presence of enemy vessels. Well after nightfall starboard gun crews of LST 31 sighted the exhaust flames of two planes coming in low and fast, following the range of the lighted buoys. When the gun crews detected aircraft engine noise they opened fire immediately at a range of fifteen hundred yards. Soldiers manning the machine guns of their deck-stowed LVTs lent their firepower to the effort to shoot down the intruders.

The first burst of 20mm AA fire set one of the attacking planes aflame. The Japanese pilot tried to make a suicide dive on LST 31, but his plane crashed into the sea after passing over the ship's bow. For ten minutes the other Japanese raider strafed the vessels. He made two passes over the ships before heavy AA fire drove him off into the darkness. As he thought of the LVTs his ships were transporting, the LST group commander, Comdr. Adrian M. Hurst, observed: "Had the attack been successful, it might have seriously jeopardized the mission of the Makin attack force on the following morning."

Commander Goro Matsuura, a veteran of seventeen years in the navy, now directing the operations of the 24th Air Flotilla at Kwajalein, alerted Truk. Admiral Koga alerted Tokyo. Rear Admiral Shibasaki, clearly recognizing the severity of the threat, also radioed Tokyo. The Japanese defenders at Makin and Tarawa had wasted an alarming amount of their precious ammunition against the unending air attacks. In particular, Shibasaki noted, "We must quickly replenish ammo for the 13mm machine guns on both Tarawa and Makin." Finally, it had been confirmed. The first American objective in the Central Pacific would be the Gilberts, Shibasaki assured Truk.

That night the Imperial Rescript to Soldiers and Sailors was recited by the garrison at Tarawa. All units assembled in their assigned areas and pledged to die for His Majesty, the Emperor, if necessary. They vowed to prefer death—if not in battle then by ritual suicide (hari-kari)—to surrender. They promised to overcome all obstacles and hardships, and not to rest until vengeance had been exacted upon the enemy, whose ships even now were coming within sight of the Gilbert Islands.

Chapter Eleven

The ships sailed in massive convoys from all over the Pacific, on elaborate schedules. They were screened by the fast carrier forces. Rear Admiral Harry Hill's Southern Attack Force for Tarawa included minesweepers and the fire support group—three battleships, four cruisers, nine destroyers, and five escort carriers.

The first ships to see action in the operation—other than the LSTs bound for Makin—were the submarines. Primarily because of the need to keep a watch on Truk in case the Kido Butai sailed, but also to waylay any last-minute Japanese reinforcements destined for the Marshalls and Gilberts, many submarines had been on station long before the amphibious assault forces reached enemy waters.

Nautilus, the big transport submarine that had reconnoitered Tarawa and Makin in late September and early October, led the way on November 8. Off Tarawa on November 18–19 she was shelled by the Japanese 8- and 5-inch coastal batteries but escaped unscathed. *Paddle* was off Nauru as early as November 15 acting as a weather station. *Thresher,* covering a quadrant near Truk, sank a forty-six-hundred-ton transport on November 13, but she was forced to return to Pearl Harbor prematurely because of an engine problem.

Corvina, patrolling on the surface at night southwest of Truk on November 16, was spotted by the Japanese submarine I-176. Before the American crew even knew they were in danger, their submarine was sunk by two torpedo hits. She was the only U.S. submarine destroyed by a Japanese counterpart during the war. Her entire crew of eighty-two men was lost. As tragic as the loss of *Corvina* was, she was not the only American submarine lost in Operation Galvanic.

Sculpin, the command boat of a three-submarine wolf pack, had left

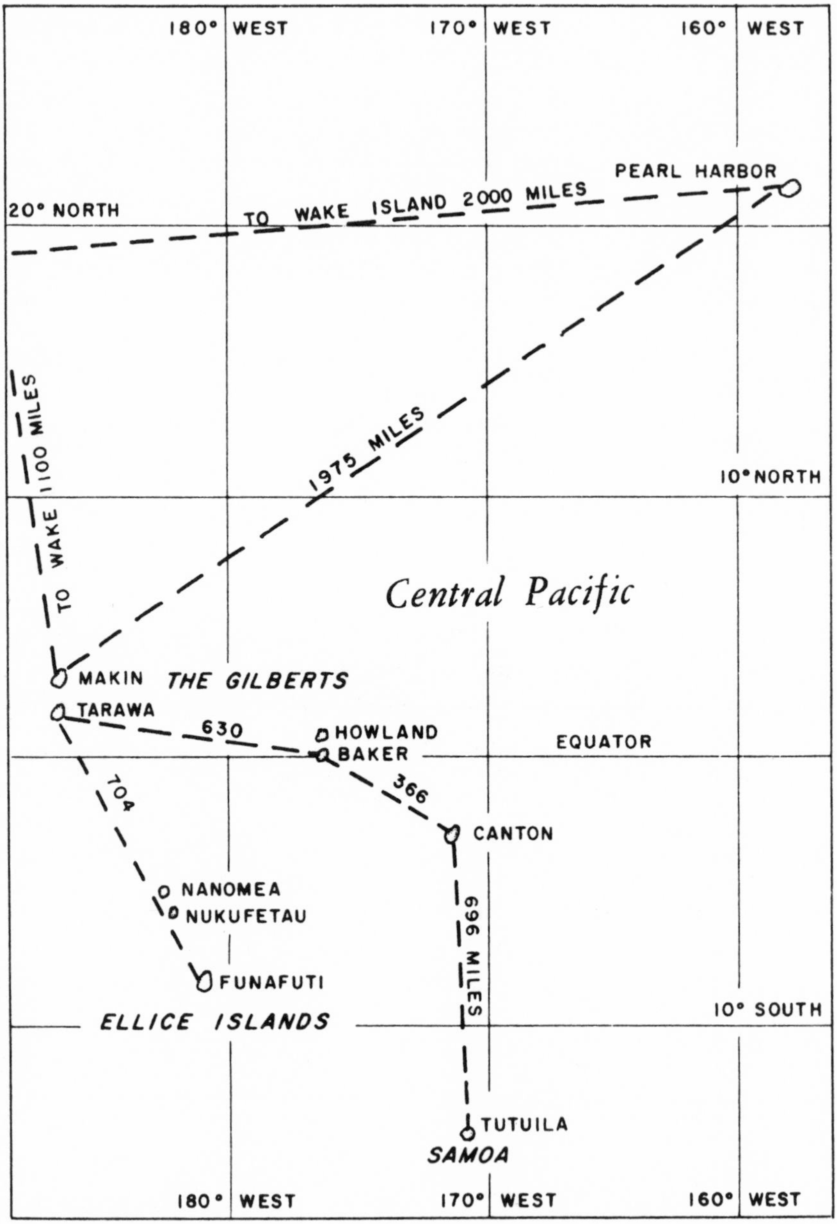
180° WEST
170° WEST
160° WEST
PEARL HARBOR
20° NORTH
TO WAKE ISLAND 2000 MILES
TO WAKE 1100 MILES
1975 MILES
10° NORTH
Central Pacific
MAKIN
THE GILBERTS
TARAWA
630
HOWLAND
BAKER
EQUATOR
366
704
CANTON
NANOMEA
NUKUFETAU
FUNAFUTI
699 MILES
10° SOUTH
ELLICE ISLANDS
TUTUILA
SAMOA
180° WEST
170° WEST
160° WEST

Pearl Harbor on November 5 and refueled from a tanker at Johnston Island on November 7. She arrived on station one hundred miles north of Truk on November 16, and had patrolled for two days without luck when her search radar established a target before dawn on November 19.

"Radar contact bearing two-two-five!" shouted the executive officer up through the hatch from below. Captain John Cromwell, the wolfpack commander, and Lt. Comdr. Fred Connaway, commanding *Sculpin,* were on the bridge. They swung their binoculars in the direction of the report.

"Range one-one-seven-five-oh." The OOD spotted the shadowy silhouette of the enemy convoy at a point fifteen degrees off the starboard bow.

"Contact bearing two-two-seven. Range one-two-oh-double-oh."

Connaway fought the temptation to sound "battle stations." He decided to wait until there was enough light to use the periscope for a submerged attack. At this stage in the war, radar attacks were still unreliable.

"Target bearing zero-zero-nine. Range one-two-five-oh. Speed one-four."

"Come right to zero-zero-nine," ordered Connaway. "Answer bells on four engines. Speed one-eight."

Sculpin surged forward under increased speed. Connaway hoped to put her ten miles ahead of the target in a position for a submerged attack. The reports from the radar plot continued. The executive officer reported seven targets. Judging by their disposition, it appeared that six ships were in screening formation around the seventh.

Connaway went below to examine the charts on which the radar contacts were being plotted. Two parallel tracks revealed that *Sculpin* was drawing ahead of the convoy. The enemy formation appeared headed for Minami-Tori-Shima, or Marcus Island, which Rear Admiral Pownall's fast carrier forces had worked over in August. Connaway climbed back to the bridge. An hour and a half passed. As the rising sun began to illuminate the eastern horizon, he gave the word.

"Battle stations—torpedo!" he said. "Clear the bridge." The alarm claxon echoed throughout the interior of the ship. The lookouts scrambled from their perch and slid down the hatch. Connaway took one last look at the sky. The darkness was receding. The sun was barely visible, the sea black and ominously calm. He was the last man down the hatch.

He slid down the ladder, pulled it shut behind him, and dropped into the control room. A quartermaster slammed the lower hatch and spun the locking wheel as far as it would go.

"Take us down," ordered Connaway, moving to the periscope. The executive officer hit the diving alarm, and the hull reverberated with a racket. *Sculpin* was filled with the noise of rushing air as vents were opened and water entered the tanks.

"Up scope." Connaway adjusted the lens and swung the periscope toward the last reported target bearing. The view revealed a single *maru* with five destroyers and a cruiser escorting her. He stepped away from the instrument. "Down scope."

"Sound reports many propeller noises. Bearing two-four-zero, growing louder."

"Up scope," Connaway said. He remained at the eyepiece for only a moment before he jumped back. "Down scope! Emergency dive! Two hundred feet."

Sculpin's diving planes slanted steeply downward, the whine of the electric motors rising to a high pitch. The convoy had suddenly veered directly toward the submarine, too quickly for Connaway to set up a head-on shot. The enemy ships could be heard passing directly overhead, then the sound of their propellers diminished.

"Bring her up to sixty feet. Up scope."

Connaway walked the periscope in a complete circle, and nodded. The formation was disappearing. The sound room reported that the propeller noises were further diminishing.

"Surface."

The chief quartermaster opened the hatch. Connaway climbed the ladder to the bridge, followed by lookouts. The men had been topside only a few seconds when they all tumbled back down the hatch.

"Dive! Dive!" Connaway shouted. "Emergency—two hundred feet."

"High-speed propeller noise," reported the soundman, "bearing two-four-zero and approaching."

"Battle stations—submerged."

Connaway had surfaced *Sculpin* in a heavy fog and had been greeted by a destroyer charging out of the haze just six thousand yards away. The submarine now plunged for deep water again. Any doubt that she had been seen wallowing briefly on the surface was nullified by the telltale sound of a sonar pinging in a wide sustained search.

"Rig for silent running," ordered Connaway.

The destroyer passed overhead and faded. The first depth charge was wide, but *Sculpin* shuddered violently in the explosion of the one that followed. The destroyer was attacking along a line established by the bearing of its sonar. A fourth depth charge wracked the hatches, fractured air lines, and short-circuited the lighting system. Damage reports revealed that the after engine room was taking on water. The explosions ceased as the enemy came around for another attack.

"On the first run he dropped sixteen six-hundred-pound depth charges, which jarred holy hell out of us," recalled Fireman J. N. Baker. "After the second run we were leaking, our lighting system was gone, and every man was knocked all over the deck. We couldn't get a trim on the boat. All this time the air was getting worse and the heat was terrific. Still they didn't let up on us. At one time we could hear his screws going right over our heads, and all we could do was just sweat it out."

"Sound reports a rainsquall bearing zero-four-five."

"Come right to zero-four-five. All ahead full," ordered Connaway. He was hopeful that the noise of the rain beating the sea would mask the submarine. Perhaps then a chance to surface and escape at full speed would arise.

The submarine, tilting upward because of the flooding, remained beneath the squall while bucket brigades worked to move the surge of water forward from the stern. The chief engineer was having difficulty with the pumps. Meanwhile, the destroyer continued searching.

Connaway ordered the ship up seventy feet to the hundred-foot level in order to reduce the pressure on the hull leaks. Suddenly *Sculpin* began rolling violently. The malfunctioning depth gauge spun crazily, coming to a stop at zero. They had broached the surface. The explosions had damaged the depth gauge and the submarine now was horribly exposed.

"All ahead full," shouted Connaway. "Take her deep!"

Sculpin emergency-dived past four hundred feet—far below the ship's operational safety depth. Depth charges followed her down. Damage reports flooded the control room. The forward torpedo room was deep in water. Sound heads had been blown in. The after torpedo room reported cracks in the hull. The main lighting circuitry had failed. Water continued to rise throughout the ship. Finally, the steering controls jammed.

Yet another depth charge—worse than any they had previously survived—shattered the sea around *Sculpin*.

"Battle stations!" ordered Connaway grimly. "Gun action."

With the submarine settling by the stern, battery power nearly depleted, and every system now operating on emergency drive, Connaway
resolved to surface and attempt to fight clear. The ship rose slowly
as pressurized air leaking through fractured lines pushed water from
the tanks.

Connaway was first up the hatch, followed by the gunners, who raced
to the bridge to man the weapons. "Up we went," remembered Baker.
"The hatches opened and we dashed quickly out on the deck to man
the 3-inch gun and our two 20mm. Once and for all we were going to
fight it out. The day was a pretty one, with whitecaps coming up over
the decks. At first we couldn't find the enemy ship and then we spotted him about three thousand yards off.

"We got the first shot in, which went over [the Japanese ship]," recalled
Baker. "The second fell short. We got in about eight shots, but our
men were being killed as they came out of the hatches."

The destroyer bore down on the stricken submarine, then veered away
to avoid the light American armament. What followed was the single
most methodical destruction of an American submarine in World War
II. The enemy turned broadside out of range of *Sculpin*'s guns and
unleashed a furious barrage of 5-inch AP fire. *Sculpin* was hit by two
full salvos. The first obliterated the forward deck gun and its crew.
The second shredded the conning tower, disintegrating the bridge and
all personnel on it, including Connaway.

"All hands abandon ship!" ordered Lt. George E. Brown, the engineering officer, who succeeded to command upon the death of Connaway
and the executive officer. Men streamed through the control room, heading
topside. Soon only two officers remained, and Brown ordered them
up and out. One, an ensign, expressed preference for death in the depths
to Japanese capture. He was last seen in the wardroom laying out a
hand of solitaire. The other, Captain Cromwell, also refused to go topside.

"I can't go with you," he said. "I know too much."

"Your decision, sir," answered Lieutenant Brown. He and another
man flooded the ballast tanks and rushed topside.

The Japanese destroyer continued shelling long after the submarine
had disappeared beneath the surface. Besides Captain Cromwell and
the ensign, ten other men—some dead, some wounded, some trapped
in flooded compartments, some unwilling to leave—rode the boat down.

"After strafing us in the water and killing several men, the Nips pulled us aboard the destroyer," reported seaman Paul Todd. "One sailor was wounded in the arm and above the eye. He could have been saved, but the Japs threw him overboard." Another man, who was vomiting violently, was about to be thrown overboard as well, "but he kicked free just in time."

In all, the Japanese took forty-two men prisoner. For decades after the war, it was still suggested that Captain Cromwell, who was post-humously awarded the Medal of Honor for his self-sacrifice, had chosen to die in order to protect the secrets of Operation Galvanic—which was scheduled to commence the next morning. In truth, however, Cromwell had often stood top watch at COMSUBPAC headquarters and handled top-secret Allied intelligence. He sacrificed himself in order to protect one of the most incredible strategic advantages in the history of war in the modern world—the secret that the Japanese naval communication codes had been broken.

Chapter Twelve

As *Sculpin* slid beneath the sea in her last dive and the survivors of her crew were taken to Truk for interrogation, Operation Galvanic approached its apex.

Converging on the Gilberts from points all across the Pacific were more than two dozen transports carrying the 2d Marine Division and elements of the 27th Infantry Division, LCSs (landing craft, support) specially modified to fire rockets, and hundreds of amphibious assault craft. Since November 14 the marines had known their objective by its real name, Betio. They had studied every feature of the island on relief maps made of plaster and plywood.

In his final words to the 5th Amphibious Force, Rear Admiral Turner revealed no doubts about the coming battle. As night fell on the day before the invasion, "Terrible Turner" told all hands:

> Units attached to this force are honored in having been selected to strike another hard blow against the enemy by capturing the Gilbert Islands. The close cooperation between all arms and services, the spirit of loyalty to each other and the determination to succeed displayed by veteran and untried personnel alike, gives me complete confidence that we will never stop until we have achieved success. I lift my spirit with this unified team of Army, Navy and Marines whether attached to ships, aircraft or ground units, and I say to you that I know God will bless you and give you strength to win a glorious victory.

On the day before the battle, Maj. Gen. Julian Smith told the men of his 2d Marine Division:

A great offensive to destroy the enemy in the Central Pacific has begun, American air, sea and land forces, of which this division is a part, initiate this offensive by seizing Japanese-held atolls in the Gilbert Islands which will be used as bases for future operations. The task assigned to us is to capture the atolls of Tarawa and Abemama. Army units of our own Fifth Amphibious Corps are simultaneously attacking Makin, 105 miles north of Tarawa.

For the past three days, Army, Navy and Marine Corps aircraft have been carrying out bombardment attacks on our objectives. They are neutralizing and will continue to neutralize other Japanese air bases adjacent to the Gilbert Islands. Early this morning combatant ships of our Navy bombarded Tarawa. Our Navy screens our operations and will support our attack tomorrow with the greatest concentration of aerial bombardment and naval gunfire in the history of warfare. It will remain with us until our objective is secured and our defenses established. Garrison troops are already en route to relieve us as soon as we have completed the job of clearing our objective of Japanese forces.

This division was especially chosen by the high command for the assault on Tarawa because of its battle experience and its combat efficiency. Their confidence in us will not be betrayed. We are the first American troops to attack a defended atoll. What we do here will set a standard for all future operations in the Central Pacific area. Observers from other Marine divisions and from other branches of our armed services, as well as those of our Allies, have been detailed to witness our operations. Representatives of the press are present. Our people back home are eagerly awaiting news of our victories.

I know that you are well-trained and fit for the tasks assigned to you. You will quickly overrun the Japanese forces; you will decisively defeat and destroy the treacherous enemies of our country. Your success will add new laurels to the glorious traditions of our beloved Corps.

He ended solemnly with, "Good luck and God bless you all."

Commanders up and down the chain of command also had final words en route to Tarawa. Lieutenant Colonel Herbert Amey, commander of the 2d Battalion, 2d Marines, briefed his staff in the wardroom of a transport. The main landing, he said, "will consist of three assault battalions, plus detachments of artillery and engineers. Ours is the center battalion, as you know. The entire operation depends on our combat team, and we are the center of it. The whole thing hinges on our three battalions. We've got to get that island and the airfield on it."

Amey recited to his officers the exact schedule of the preinvasion naval and air bombardment, as well as the neutralization of Japanese bases in the Marshalls and at Nauru prior to the actual landings. "On Tarawa itself," said Amey, "the navy will put about 3,000 tons of high explosives on that little square mile in that time. There's never been anything like it. As we hit the beach the planes will be strafing very close in front of you to keep the Nips down until you can get in there and knock off what's left of them. I think we ought to have every Jap off the island—the live ones—by the night of D-Day."

Finally, Amey noted: "We are very fortunate. This is the first time a landing has been made by American troops against a well-defended beach, the first time over a coral reef, the first time against any force to speak of. And the first time the Japs have had the hell kicked out of them in a hurry. Maybe we'll walk ashore. I don't know. It depends on the effect of gunfire and air bombardment."

Several days later Amey was dead.

His intelligence officer, Lt. Adolph W. Norvik (inevitably nicknamed "Swede"), briefed the staff on the defenses at Tarawa and nearby islands, and instructed them how to deal with the native residents of the Gilberts. He summed up the task at hand. The Japanese "will be punch-drunk from the shellfire, so hit 'em before they can pull themselves together."

Several days later Norvik lay wounded.

Colonel Shoup, who would command the assault troops at Tarawa, told a group of officers two days before the battle: "I don't give a damn if there is not one Jap on the island. Our objective is the airfield, and if we get that without losing a Marine, I'll be happy. Killing every Jap on Tarawa is not worth losing one Marine's life."

The rugged assault commander carefully explained the situation to *Time-Life* correspondent Robert Sherrod:

> What worries me more than anything is that our boats may not be able to get over that coral shelf that sticks out about five hundred

yards. We may have to wade in. The first waves, of course, will get in all right on the "alligators" [LVTs], but if the Higgins boats draw too much water to get in fairly close, we'll either have to wade in with machine guns shooting at us, or the amtracs will have to run a shuttle service between the beach and the end of the shelf. We have got to calculate high tide pretty good for the Higgins boats to make it.

Several days later Shoup sat wounded, his back against the outer wall of a Japanese pillbox just off the beach.

Each day as the convoys moved on the Gilberts, the heat grew more oppressive. The equatorial nights were clear, but even they were stifling hot. Long lines of ships, two hundred in all, steaming from Pearl Harbor, Efate in the New Hebrides, Samoa, Funafuti, San Diego, and San Francisco, their massive engines driving them onward, ploughed great troughs of phosphorescent wakes, which fanned out behind them. A transport surgeon noted caustically, "There won't be a damned Jap on Tarawa, and I'll bet we haven't got an alternate target. Why in the hell don't we just take this force and keep going to Tokyo and get the goddamn war over with?" Correspondent Sherrod watched Protestant chaplains hold services on deck and Catholic priests hold confession in a corner of a wardroom.

More than two dozen combat correspondents were dispersed throughout the Fifth Fleet—sixteen were assigned to the 2d Division for the Tarawa landings—and press access to the various commanders was unusually open. The navy had not always been so easy with the press. But the war situation had improved immeasurably since the dark days of Guadalcanal. For much of that grim campaign, "Terrible Turner" had imposed an almost total news blackout—a policy that, besides leaving the public uninformed, had other unexpected side effects.

The lack of information available about much of the Guadalcanal operation had led to wild editorializing in magazines and newspapers, and on the radio. Indignation swept over the troops—whose morale on the island had been a problem from the start—when they heard the speculative news accounts of their efforts. It seemed as though they had been abandoned and forgotten. The speculation arising from the lack of hard news about the operation created the impression that the battle for Guadalcanal was futile. The troops heard more about their plight from the propaganda of Radio Tokyo than from American sources. This infuriated them.

By the time of Operation Galvanic, however, the navy had wised up and a flock of war correspondents was taken along. The navy hoped to provide fresh and accurate news to the public and avoid some of the problems experienced at Guadalcanal. It was generally thought among the correspondents that of the two main objectives, Tarawa would be the tougher target. Jockeying for choice assignments occurred before departure. There seemed to be no end of good stories.

At a November 16 press conference aboard his flagship, Turner told correspondents, "The Japs are probably out there in the Gilberts waiting for us. But we are going to get them. They're wise to the ways of taking advantage of the terrain and they are probably dug in. We will dig them out." Of Tarawa, RAdm. Harry Hill said on November 14: "Just six days from today at 0830 we're going to hit Tarawa Atoll in the Gilbert Islands. We're going to land on this island at the end of the atoll. The natives call it Betio. Before we land on the place, we're going to pound it with naval gunfire and dive-bombers. We're going to steamroller that place until hell wouldn't have it."

Indeed, the navy was bullish on the effects they believed the naval bombardment would have on the Japanese defenders. At a press conference shortly before the invasion, RAdm. Howard F. Kingman, whose duties included commanding the fire support group and devising the bombardment plan for Tarawa, sounded a similarly optimistic note. "Gentlemen," he said, "it is not our intention to wreck the island. We do not intend to destroy it. Gentlemen," he emphasized dramatically, "we will obliterate it."

Julian Smith listened impatiently to these and other boastful predictions. His demeanor was grim when a navy captain talked about taking his destroyer to just a thousand yards offshore in order to saturate the beaches with 5-inch naval gunfire. The destroyer's armor, the naval officer said, would make him almost indestructible to fire from shore. Yet another naval officer declared that his ship's armor was lighter and stronger; it would allow him to move in even closer to shore. Eventually, the marine general had listened to enough. He stood up and looked around the crowded room. "Gentlemen," he said, "when the marines meet the enemy at bayonet point, the only armor a marine will have is his khaki shirt."

Also attached to the invasion force for Tarawa was a special marine photographic section, commanded by thirty-three-year-old Capt. Louis Hayward, the Hollywood movie actor who had starred in several films, including *Count of Monte Cristo* and *Man in the Iron Mask.* But for the past sixteen months he had been a marine. The job of the unit was to capture as much as possible of the battle on film, for use in publicity, planning, and training. Hayward told his men: "I know all of us are fed up with hearing about the 'marvelous' photography coming out of the European war. This time let's really give 'em something to talk about—from the Marines in the Pacific." Of his fifteen men, Hayward said, "As photographers, they honored their profession. No one could ask for more valiant, more capable workmen than those it was my privilege to command at Tarawa."

Ahead of the massive fleet, the struggle for the Gilberts had already started. The B-24s of the Seventh Air Force had begun hitting Tarawa on D day minus four. Then precisely at sunrise on November 18, the same hour at which Rear Admiral Sherman was launching planes against Nauru, Rear Admiral Montgomery's southern carrier battle group appeared southeast of Tarawa and started launching planes. In the afternoon the Japanese bombers from Mili located the LST group headed for Makin and that day and the next attacked without success. Four of the enemy bandits were shot down by American fighters and AA fire. All the while other enemy reconnaissance planes located various American naval formations.

Rear Admiral Shibasaki was waiting for them at Tarawa. He shot off an urgent *gungokuhi* (very secret) report to Truk. In his message, Shibasaki informed Admirals Kobayashi and Koga that the entire American navy was approaching the Gilberts. There never again would be a better time for the Kido Butai to sortie and fight the decisive battle. Since it was known that the Americans would attack the Gilberts, now was the time to send reinforcements. It was the time, Shibasaki admonished finally, to make good on the "hornet's nest" that Koga had said the Americans would find when they hit Tarawa.

The reply was quick in coming. Koga reminded Shibasaki and the men of his command of their duty to die for His Majesty, the Emperor, and to pin down the American invasion forces in support of the ground campaign. What was most important was time—time to organize a relief force and strengthen the naval air forces in the Marshalls.

As the battle drew near, and reports of still more sightings of American ships streamed into Tarawa, a Japanese airman wrote in his diary: "What terrible news. It seems the enemy has more ships than is possible. And his planes are everywhere."

Koga, by now inundated with a welter of new and more ominous reports, reached a similar conclusion. To everyone the impending Gilberts assault looked like "the real thing" and not another hit-and-run raid. But perhaps recalling the tough, prolonged resistance that the Japanese garrisons in the Solomons had put up against enemy attacks at Guadalcanal and elsewhere, Koga did not react fast enough and certainly not strongly enough.

He already had transferred the headquarters of the Fourth Fleet under Vice Admiral Kobayashi to Kwajalein. Now he ordered two light cruisers—the *Isuzu* and *Naka,* both lying at anchor at Truk—and two destroyers to Ponape, and directed their commanders to load twelve hundred troops there and rush to the Marshalls. Another light cruiser, *Nagara,* was also loaded with troops at Truk and dispatched to Mili. Although it was Koga's plan to reinforce Tarawa with these troops, the whole affair was managed with much improvisation. The combined cruiser-destroyer force did not succeed in departing Truk until November 21. By then the battle already was at its height. Everything the Japanese could do to defend the Gilberts had been done. All that remained was the waiting.

On the night of November 19, the first naval action in the Gilberts occurred in the Tarawa-Maiana gap, which, with the area slightly northwest of the primary objective, was the main naval marshaling area for the battle for Tarawa.

The sky appeared unending, with more stars than a man could ever count in a lifetime, a naval officer noted. The red planet, Mars, was visible. The sea was relatively calm but marked by a westerly current of 1.5 to 2 knots when the starboard lookout aboard the destroyer *Ringgold,* which was on forward picket duty, shouted the news that all hands had been waiting to hear. Captain Thomas F. Conley flashed the word over the TBS. The message was received by Rear Admiral Hill aboard the flagship *Maryland* and he notified the fleet, "We now have Tarawa Atoll in sight."

The report barely had been acknowledged before Conley suddenly broke in on the naval radio net again at 2130, alerting the task force to something else. "Skunk bearing two-seven-eight degrees true. Distance seven miles."

Hill detached the cruiser *Santa Fe* and the destroyer *Gansevoort* from the fire support group. They plunged ahead to investigate. He instructed Conley aboard *Ringgold* to "maintain contact but do not fire torpedoes."

Hill's options were slim. He knew that the organization and approach plans for the task force had taken into account the possible presence of friendly submarines in the area, but he had not expected to encounter any friendlies in the vicinity of Tarawa. *Nautilus* was believed to have left the area in the afternoon to rescue a downed carrier pilot, and it was assumed that her skipper would submerge if friendly forces were encountered. The odds that the enemy had secretly moved in light naval forces or perhaps resurrected one of the torpedo boats destroyed in the September carrier raids could not be discounted. Even one diminutive, high-speed enemy vessel, if it were bent on destruction at any cost, could cause ghastly damage in a night attack. The threat to the transports was particularly great.

Rear Admiral Hill relented: "Torpedo him if you have a favorable opportunity but avoid gunfire. Some of our small boys may be in the vicinity."

Conley and the commanders of *Sante Fe* and *Gansevoort* collectively pinpointed the unidentified target and tracked it at long range for more than twenty minutes. They assured Hill that it was a surface vessel and estimated its speed at an alarming twenty knots—headed south, directly for the Southern Attack Force. A few seconds later, Hill gave the word to attack: "All restrictions on the use of your offensive weapons are removed. Open fire!"

Conley pushed *Ringgold* to flank speed, maneuvering into an approach for a torpedo attack. He fired two torpedoes. One "fish" ran true and detonated at approximately the correct time to have reached the target. The other went wild. It circled crazily and came around. The lookouts saw it coming. Conley ordered the engines to full speed ahead in an effort to swing the destroyer so that the torpedo would pass behind the ship. He shouted, "Hard aport! Full ahead starboard!"

The torpedo sliced through the destroyer's wake. Conley slowed to twenty knots. The radical maneuvering swung *Ringgold* around to a course that brought her main battery of 5-inch guns to bear on the target. Conley opened radar-directed fire. *Santa Fe* joined in, and the whole area of sea soon erupted in a roaring storm of fire. The thunder of naval guns sounded back and forth as the warships slammed away at the fast-moving target. The night was illuminated with the flash of their guns. In a matter of just nine minutes, the target disappeared from the radar.

Hill congratulated *Ringgold*: "Job well done."

Five miles away the submarine *Nautilus,* with seventy-eight marine reconnaissance troops aboard, had been proceeding to Abemama after being released from lifeguard duty around Tarawa. Her radar picked up a strange, unreal picture on the sea directly ahead. On the bridge, Capt. Bill Irvin found that he was almost face to face with a stunning array of warships, what seemed to be the entire American fleet—he hoped. Towering ahead were battleships, cruisers, and destroyers.

"We were in a bad way," Irvin said. "We believed the ships were friendly but they were acting very belligerent. Our batteries were low and we were without air supply. We were about two miles off a reef toward which the current was setting at about two knots. If we submerged, we would be in for a nasty time. If we didn't we weren't sure we could properly identify ourselves in time."

As Irvin watched, three of the surface targets increased speed to twenty-five knots and headed directly for the submarine. That heightened his suspicion. He fired a green recognition flare—and got the shock of his life. Shells—very large ones indeed—almost instantly began to fall around his vulnerable ship. With *Nautilus* in grave danger of being sunk, the startled submarine commander acted without a moment's hesitation—the reef be damned.

"Emergency dive—two hundred feet!"

The first salvo missed. Lieutenant Commander Richard B. "Ozzie" Lynch, the executive officer, was just clearing the bridge when another shell exploded nearby. As *Nautilus* slid beneath the surface a shell struck the conning tower, ripped into the superstructure, and delivered the submarine a fearsome, near-fatal blow. Miraculously, the shell failed to detonate. It was a dud. This fluke—estimated at one chance in a thousand—saved the submarine.

Yet *Nautilus* shuddered under the blow and sparks spurted from the conning tower bilges. Although there was no resulting fire or blast, the concussion caused damage. More salvos were heard lashing the sea all around as the submarine dived deep and out of control—fifty fathoms down. Another explosion ruptured a water line to the port main motor cooling system and triggered leaks in the bilges. The gyro was knocked out of commission. In addition, in the haste to vacate the bridge under fire, the crew had failed to close the valve of the outer voice tube. Through this opening and a ruptured seal around the conning tower hatch—not to mention flooding of the main induction—torrents of water streamed down. *Nautilus,* now filling with water, plummeted to a depth of 310 feet before Irvin regained control.

"We had decided they were Japs," he reported. "We felt time was running out fast; we had an important date at Abemama which we were going to keep, even if we had to surface and fight our way through. The seventy-eight Marines were stoic, but unanimous that they would much prefer a rubber boat on a very hostile beach to their predicament." The stunned submarine commander decided to lay low for some time.

After the naval forces had passed, Irvin surfaced. He reported the encounter to CINCPAC at Pearl Harbor, which was greatly alarmed by the report. Before long, however, through analysis of Fifth Fleet dispatches, COMSUBPAC determined that the American submarine had been attacked not by Japanese forces but by elements of the Southern Attack Force's forward screen. Hill had reported *Ringgold*'s sinking of an enemy patrol boat, and *Santa Fe* claimed credit for assisting in the action with seventy-six 6-inch shells.

In all respects, it had been a close call. *Nautilus* had been badly damaged—in fact, nearly lost altogether—but Irvin and the crew worked her cautiously southward, taking advantage of the favorable current. They proceeded on their way to Abemama, shaken by their dramatic encounter but still alive and determined to fulfill their mission.

Chapter Thirteen

There had never been a night such as this in the Pacific. Up and down the Gilberts chain, dozens of ships appeared. In front were destroyers and cruisers, the vanguard of the mightiest fleet yet assembled in the Pacific war. They moved relentlessly forward, in some cases so close to islands that their crews could clearly see Japanese installations. Needless to say, these ships did not go unnoticed.

Behind them, churning through choppy black seas and bearing down on the outer edge of Japan's empire, were legions of ships—the strength and awesome power of the United States Navy, newly constructed and now unleashed at last. They came, steaming in line—a dozen convoys, miles wide, two hundred ships of every description, and behind them nearly a hundred more in support at Hawaii, Samoa, and Efate in the New Hebrides. There were fast new attack transports and slower, battle-scarred veterans of the South Pacific, chartered civilian freighters and tramp steamers of the merchant marine, hospital ships, shining new oil tankers, towed concrete ammunition and fuel barges, and mine-sweepers. There were convoys of shallow-draft landing ships—cav-ernous, wallowing, seagoing container vessels, as long as a football field, their holds filled to capacity with equipment and supplies. Many of these and the plodding transports carried smaller landing craft lashed to their gunwales and decks—more than five hundred LVTs, LCMs, LCVPs, LCTs, LCSs—for the actual assault landings.

Ahead of the convoys and on their flanks were the powerful men-of-war—battleships, cruisers, and destroyers. On the decks of heav-ing carriers, squadrons of fighters and bombers were spotted for Dawn Launch. This supremely majestic naval and amphibious assault force was packed with planes, men, guns, tanks, motor vehicles, and supplies. Including smaller naval and coastal landing vessels carried on board larger ships, a fantastic array of seven hundred vessels of all shapes and sizes and 108,000 men now was organizing in the Gilberts.

The old battleship *Pennsylvania*, Rear Admiral Turner's flagship, which the Japanese had written off at Pearl Harbor, led the three major groupings of ships. Just seven months before, the "Keystone" battlewagon had carried the flag of RAdm. Francis P. Rockwell, commander of the north Pacific amphibious assault forces, to Attu, a snow-swept, barren island of the Aleutians, for the first of the ship's many encounters with the enemy in the Pacific. Yet again she was a floating command post, bristling with radar and radio antennae, serving as the nerve center of the landing operations. Nearby, steaming fearsomely, with all their battle flags flying, were the battleships *Idaho, New Mexico,* and *Mississippi*.

Leading the five carrier and assault convoys bound for Tarawa and Abemama was the cruiser *Indianapolis*, the flagship of Rear Admiral Spruance, the man who had pounded the pride of the Imperial Combined Fleet—the carriers *Kaga, Akagi, Soryu,* and *Hiryu*—in the battle for Midway in June 1942. Close by was the battleship *Maryland*, the flagship of Rear Admiral Hill, commander of the Southern Attack Force. He would actually direct the Tarawa invasion.

Elements of this great armada moved deliberately on the targets. They followed an elaborate schedule of a kind never before undertaken. Transports steamed out of line and, moving in assigned lanes, converged on the assembly areas off Tarawa and Makin. There they organized themselves. Aboard *Zeilin*, second in a line of transports at Tarawa, a calm voice announced their progress as they closed on the assembly area around 0215:

"Target at one-one-two true, 26,800 yards ahead."

"Blackfish"—the code name for the transport leading the way to Tarawa with a faint red signal light on her fantail—"870 yards."

"Blackfish 1,000 yards."

"Blackfish 900 yards."

Each transport took a predetermined position aligned in echelon for the particular beach and assault waves to which its forces were assigned. Out of the assembly areas, the men-of-war—the battleships, cruisers, and destroyers—headed for their bombardment stations. There were ships everywhere. To the men aboard them, this historic armada appeared the most powerful imaginable. "You felt the muscle, the pent-up power, ready to be hurled against that spit of land which was our target," recalled Lt. Comdr. Kenneth McCardle, "and you felt that nothing on earth could resist the momentum of this vast seagoing war machine."

For the troops who would go ashore—soldiers, marines, sailors, and coast guardsmen—despite the uncertainties that lay ahead, the affair was marked by contrasting features of an adventurous lark and a great crusade. Aboard the transports, men wrote last-minute letters, played high-stake games of acey-deucey, adjusted their gear and weapons, joined in crowded bull sessions, or attended religious services. In the sweltering heat of the wardroom aboard *Zeilin,* correspondent Robert Sherrod, a veteran of the invasions of Kiska and Attu in the Aleutians and the combat in New Guinea, recalled, "Some five hundred men knelt in the dripping room or in passageways leading to the room" as they were led in prayer by a chaplain.

More than two-thirds of the tens of thousands of army and marine troops were going into battle for the first time. Many were replacements new to the Pacific. Some had spent as many as two years on garrison duty in the Hawaiian or Fiji islands. "The younger guys, especially those ones of us who were on their first cruise, practically all of us not even twenty-one yet, were excited," recalled GySgt. L. L. Lucas, of Orange County, California. "None of us had any idea about what we were in for."

On the crowded deck of his transport, Lucas, a veteran of Guadalcanal, and a coast guardsman whose name Lucas did not catch were watching the teaming mass of ships assemble. The coast guardsman "was detailed to a shore party and was worried about how to protect an illegal clutch of hootch he had aboard after he went ashore," said Lucas. "He was more worried about his booze than his rear end. He survived the battle and I later ran into him again at Okinawa. I asked him about the liquor. He told me that before his section boarded their Peter boat he had given it to a corpsman to share with the wounded. I'm sure it was put to good use." Associated Press correspondent William Hipple approached a green marine, obviously a new replacement. "Are you scared?" asked Hipple. "Hell, no, mister," said the young man defiantly. "I'm a marine."

A private attached to an army support unit was on the deck of an old transport watching Makin loom on the horizon. He found little comfort in the long, sleek lines of the ships all about him; his thoughts were on the job ahead. Turning around, he heard a sergeant talking to a group of infantry who would land at H hour: "This kid with a Bronx, New York, accent made the remark that he didn't see how in hell they could come out of it alive. The sergeant—he looked old enough to have charged up San Juan Hill with Teddy Roosevelt—grunted and said, 'When your time's up, your time's up.' The kid thought about it for a minute and nodded. Hearing this actually seemed to please him."

There was morbid joking too. Aboard *Zeilin,* Sherrod listened as one marine said to another, "Hey, Bill, I just remembered I still owe you a pack of cigarettes. I want to pay you back before we get killed. Say, you want to buy a good watch?" Said Bill, "We'll get that watch off you on the way back." As the marines "jested with one another," observed Sherrod, "only a few even whistled to keep up their courage." He heard another man shout at a marine wearing eyeglasses, "How many of them you going to kill, Bunky?" "All I can get," said the man without smiling as he cleaned his rifle barrel. Said another, "I should have joined the Boy Scouts. I knew it."

Nineteen-year-old Pvt. Jack R. Stambaugh, of Bowie, Texas, a green replacement who had joined the 2d Division after Guadalcanal, was confident. He had contemplated how he would perform in his first fight. During the long passage to Tarawa he had confided in a boyhood friend, Pvt. Leon C. Randall, also of Bowie: "I don't know how I'll feel when I get into battle, but I don't think I'll be yellow. Maybe I'm just blowing off now, but I think I will be a fighting fool." Aboard another transport, a marine lieutenant remarked that D day was his seventh wedding anniversary and he couldn't decide when he had been more frightened. Rhetorical regrets that Tarawa looked as if it would amount to a "coral Kiska" were expressed. An abundance of jokes about native girls in grass skirts and sarongs circulated through the fleet.

It was not uncommon to see whole platoons of hot, sweating, seasick men hanging over a rail vomiting up what, in some cases, amounted to the finest food they had seen since coming to the Pacific. Although the traditional "last meal" varied from ship to ship, for the most part special efforts were made to give all hands the best fare possible. Aboard *Zeilin,* the marines were fed steak, scrambled eggs, fried potatoes, and two cups of coffee. On other ships the meal consisted of mountainous sandwiches of roast beef, chicken, and ham.

The mess crews had begun serving meals at 2000 on November 19. It was a little after 0330 when they finished. Throughout the task forces, the men who would take the first great amphibious step in the Pacific tried to get what rest they could before battle. As Gunnery Sergeant Lucas climbed into a vacant bunk aboard his transport, he rolled over and saw an enlisted marine lying on his back, a Bible resting on his chest. He thought that the marine had fallen asleep reading. But then the man opened his eyes, stared at the bottom of the bunk above him, and said, "Amen."

Meanwhile, Iva Toguri, better known by her pseudonym "Tokyo Rose," announced to the world over Radio Manila that an American fleet with the 2d Marine Division, "the butchers of Guadalcanal," was concentrating in the Gilberts. From this, she said, it was obvious that an enemy landing and large-scale attack at Tarawa was imminent and that one of the bloodiest battles in American history was about to begin. This time—unfortunately—her propaganda was horribly accurate.

Down the atoll, squatting ominously on the sea, were huge, hulking shadows of ships. Rota Onorio, a fourteen-year-old boy, ran to the beach of the tiny islet where his family had been relocated by the Japanese. In the week before, he had become accustomed to the sound of large aircraft in the distance and overhead, the muffled booms of exploding bombs and the sharp staccato crack of quick-firing flak batteries. But this was something different. As full comprehension came to him, the young boy realized he was looking at an invasion fleet.

On the island everything was peaceful. The moonlight was bright, and the groves of palm trees and pandanus were still and quiet, casting long shadows. Onorio climbed into his dugout and plunged the hollowed-out coconut-log craft into the sea to investigate. In the midst of the staggering array of huge warships, his dugout seemed like a child's toy. Everywhere he looked there were battleships, cruisers, and destroyers towering over him. Marine sentries aboard a ship spotted him and brought him aboard. He was taken immediately to a naval intelligence officer.

The Americans were greatly interested in the disposition of Japanese forces in the island group. Onorio and other natives who had come out in their boats told them in crisp British English that there were but two dozen Japanese based on Bairiki, the island nearest Betio, and perhaps a few hundred others scattered up the northern leg of the atoll. All the rest, as many as five thousand, were on Betio. The American naval officers asked too about the Allied prisoners of war and civilians who had been left in the islands when the Japanese came. Their fate, the natives said, was unknown, but it was generally believed that they were all dead with the exception of the French priests and nuns on Taborio.

Finally, American interest turned to a critical factor, the tides. What would the conditions be over the reef the next day? they inquired anxiously. Could small assault boats, drawing between three and four feet of water, navigate their way ashore? "No," answered the natives. "Tomorrow the reef will be impassable." The Americans were at first disbelieving, but the natives insisted. "It will be impassable—even at high tide," they said. When, the officers asked, would the tides be capable of floating small boats? Perhaps in two days was the answer. The autumn tides in the Gilberts were unpredictable.

This information was relayed to The Flag, but there was nothing that could be done. It was too late. It was nearly dawn—the sunrise that eighteen thousand marines had been preparing for since August. In a few hours the gun crews of the fire support group would begin the preinvasion bombardment of the island. Then men who were already lowering themselves into landing craft off Tarawa would be on their way to secure a beachhead for the bulk of the invasion forces that would follow. Now everyone awaited the sunrise. H hour was scheduled at 0830. The event that had been planned over the past six months, and that had thrown Allied shipping schedules in the Pacific and around the world into chaos and confusion, was at hand.

Now there could be no turning back—not for Rear Admiral Spruance in the cruiser *Indianapolis,* not for the seasick marine private in an LCVP rapidly filling with water in the three- to four-foot seas.

Ensign Ota in his bunker overlooking the invasion beaches at Tarawa had heard nothing from his superiors since the afternoon of the previous day. He was hungry, tired, and frightened. He felt isolated. He could not understand why there had been no advance warning. And now, what was he to think about the scores of ships surrounding Tarawa, the massed formations of transports? And worst of all, the leviathan mass of a battleship that had appeared as if out of nowhere. His uneasiness gnawed at him and threatened to consume him.

One hundred miles to the north, a chief petty officer named Sasaki had much the same dreadful experience as the scene was repeated off Makin. Already he and his men had been bombed and strafed relentlessly for two days by carrier planes and land-based bombers. Butaritari, especially its lagoon beaches and the main fortified area that the Americans had dubbed "The Citadel," was pockmarked with huge craters. But at 0245 Sasaki swung his artillery glasses over the edge of his dugout and a feeling of hopelessness swept over him. He picked up the dark mass of first one battleship and then another.

Greatly alarmed, Sasaki swept the horizon. He caught a glimpse of another warship, then another, until it seemed that he had fixed on ships of every size and description—almost the entire enemy fleet, he thought in a moment of wild speculation. Huge battle flags snapped in the South Seas trade winds. He began counting ships. He did not stop until in the shimmering moonlight offshore he had discerned three battleships, two cruisers, three destroyers, and numerous other ships he could not identify. This, then, was it. The light of dawn would surely bring all this awesome force of enemy naval and military might down upon them. This the Japanese defenders of Makin and Tarawa knew.

Chapter Fourteen

It was Sunday, November 20. All along the beaches of Betio, in the silent darkness before dawn, the Japanese waited beneath the camouflage of palm fronds. They manned weapons that were zeroed in on the approaches to the island. For some time now Rear Admiral Shibasaki had known of the presence of the American ships off Tarawa. Observation posts and sentries had spotted the navigation lights of ships at 0300 and had immediately contacted the command bunker. All lights on the island had been quickly put out.

In these last few hours before dawn, Shibasaki conferred with his staff. He reached a decision a little after 0400—not that it had taken any great deliberation. His plans were well-rehearsed. All troops knew their assignments by heart. Messengers came and went. Officers took reports of sightings and noted the pleas of gun crew chiefs to open fire. But Shibasaki refused to let them fire on the ships in the dark, so worried was he by the poor aim they had exhibited the day before against the enemy cruisers and the submarine that had been seen lurking about offshore. By withholding fire until sunrise, he reasoned, the waste of his precious ammunition stocks would be minimized.

A powerful AA searchlight suddenly stabbed the darkness, probing tentatively from the northwest corner of the island. With white hot intensity, it focused on the task force, silhouetting a transport in its brilliant glare. It lingered for only a moment, then just as suddenly went out. Shibasaki ordered that flares be fired to assure that all defenses were ready.

A brilliant red star shell cluster suddenly soared into the night sky from the south shore just outside the command bunker at 0441. It hung for several minutes, suffusing the island and the surrounding sea in a strange, eerie incandescence. The reflection shimmered on the lagoon. Only seconds had ticked away before all over the island, smaller meteor-like flares streaked through the sky, creating orange and white parabolas. Total darkness fell again on the island. Shibasaki had his confirmation. The flares told him that the defenders were ready.

Runners were sent out with the message for which the gun crews had been pining. Shibasaki told them, "When you have a good target, fire at your own discretion." He wished them good shooting and ordered them to make every shell count.

Offshore the transport rendezvous area was a teeming mass of ships, stirring with noise and intense activity. Helmsmen fought to keep ships on station in the strong current as milling assault craft circled in the choppy seas, waiting their turn to come aside for their loads. Davits, winches, and pulleys rattled as cargo booms hoisted landing craft over the high steel sides of the transports, and the assault troops began climbing down the scramble nets into them. On the ships men crowded the rails, shuffling their way toward debarkation stations. Most of the LVTs and LCVPs were in the water by 0430, and were now being organized into assault formations by control boats.

Chaplains threaded their way among the assault troops: "In a few minutes you will be over there. . . . This will be a great page in the history of the Marine Corps. . . . Wherever you men are, stop and give a prayer. . . . God bless you all." One chaplain distributed a page of selections from the Scriptures entitled "Spiritual Ration for D-Day." Another closed his service with, "God bless you—and go out there and bring glory to our Corps." Father Francis E. Kelley, of Philadelphia, a veteran of Guadalcanal, ended his service similarly. "God bless you," he said, "and God have mercy on the Japanese."

Over intercom systems and through loud-hailing bullhorns, among officers and veteran NCOs, all manner of words were heard: "Remember Pearl Harbor!" "This is it. The real thing." "Now hear this. Marines report to debarkation stations." "Adjust your sights." "Do you wanna live forever?" "Our Father who art in heaven." "Two-eight, away. Let's go." Then there were the words common to all the amphibious operations of the war—words that everyone from The Flag to the lowliest private and seaman heard: "Away all boats," and "Land the landing force."

All over the crowded decks men moved about as they could, looking for friends who were going in aboard other boats in later waves. It had been impossible for marines, sailors, and coast guardsmen not to come to know one another during the long voyage. Now they shook hands and exchanged good wishes. Hundreds took time to kneel where they were to be led in prayer by the roaming chaplains. Gunnery Sergeant Lucas looked out over the score or more of ships and the thousands of men scrambling down their sides into landing craft. He wondered about his brother, who was also a marine but on another ship. "Of course, I could never have picked him out," said Lucas. "We hadn't seen each other since we joined up." The two brothers would not meet again until eighteen months later at Okinawa when they would stumble into each other near Shuri Castle while on forward reconnaissance missions for different divisions.

While topside aboard *Heywood,* Princeton graduate Lt. Alexander "Sandy" Bonnyman, of Santa Fe, New Mexico, whose 18th Marines assault engineer platoon would assist Major Crowe's battalion landing team on Red 3, encountered his company commander, Capt. Joseph Clerou. Bonnyman was married, had three children, and owned several copper mines, an essential wartime industry. He was at Tarawa by choice, since on nearly all counts he need not have been in uniform. The company commander insisted that his young platoon leader accept payment for a ten dollar debt incurred drinking in New Zealand, but Bonnyman refused. Finally they agreed jokingly that if Clerou were killed, Bonnyman could have his brand-new combat boots.

Dr. Edwin J. Welte, a young, crop-haired Minnesotan who was the surgeon of the 2d Battalion, 2d Marines, was in the junior staff officers' bunkroom aboard *Zeilin* with several others when Capt. Benjamin T. Owens entered. "Doc, I'm going to get shot in the tail today," said the young battalion operations officer from Oklahoma. Remarked Doc Welte, "Oh, you want a Purple Heart, huh?" The waiting men laughed when Owens thundered, "Hell, no, I want a stateside ticket."

Elsewhere officers finished up their debarkation talks as best they could, sometimes with unusual twists. A warrant officer from Cincinnati walked among the waiting men aboard his transport. He overheard a marine NCO tell his men that Tarawa was nothing more than a flyspeck of sand and coral in the middle of nowhere and that the penalty for fooling around with the Gilbertese women was death. From somewhere among the knot of stoic young marines, a hardened voice remarked, "Then why the hell do we want it? We should let the little bastards keep it."

Many marines were going into battle for the first time. Veterans told them what to expect. Shortly before the troops climbed into the landing craft, Lt. Stacy C. Davis, whose 8th Marines platoon would land in the first wave on Red 3, gathered his men aboard *Heywood*. "For those of you who were not with the 8th on Guadalcanal," he said, "I don't want you to feel cheated when this one is over. What we're really doing is just a little police work. We'll all be coming back right after we secure the place. We probably won't see a single Jap."

"But don't worry," Davis continued, "there's plenty of islands left and you'll get your share of combat. This place is only a little over two miles long and about half a mile deep at its widest point. We've already shelled it enough to sink the place. The few troops the enemy have here are Japanese marines and I sure hate to see us kill marines." The men laughed as he summed up, "But, after all, they are Japs, so I guess it's all right."

Debarkation, a complicated and dangerous process under any conditions, was by now fully underway on the sixteen transports off Tarawa. More and more churning, troop-filled assault craft were lowered and joined those already endlessly circling the mother ships. Soaked to the bone and seasick, the marines were soon miserable in their bobbing landing craft. The difficulties in just getting the marine, navy, and coast guard troops topside in orderly fashion aboard the jammed ships proved immense.

Some men carried as much as ninety pounds of equipment. The typical marine was burdened by his combat load, which included his M-1 Garand rifle, bayonet, rations and water for three days, bedding roll, grenades, 125 rounds of ammunition, inflatable rubber life preserver around his midsection, gas mask, toilet articles, three pairs of socks and underwear, entrenching tool, first aid kit, and (if he smoked) fifteen packs of cigarettes in individual waterproof bags. The special weapons sections and combat engineers, especially the flamethrower teams, were so burdened that they were hardly able to get to their feet without help.

As in probably every major amphibious assault of World War II, the first casualties were taken during the debarkation phase, long before the assault troops were even fired on. Landing boats, jostled and bounced about by the rise and fall of swells, smashed into the hulls of ships or were swamped. In loading the first three waves, three of the precious LVTs, older models and already in precarious condition, were rendered useless after being battered against LCVPs while transferring men. In such condition, the vehicles were at the mercy of the current and drifted around aimlessly, unable to reach their formations for the run to the line of departure or the nearest ship. Six sank in this manner before they reached the lagoon.

In addition, the swift current and choppy seas surrounding the reefs further added to the confusion. Boats and LVTs were considerably scrambled and separated from their formations. One boat scheduled to land at Red 3 in the fourth wave became lost and did not reach the reef until late in the afternoon. When it did, the marines in it found themselves heading into the wrong beach. There were hundreds of other similar stories of landing craft mixed up, but there were far more serious mishaps too.

As troops began hitting the deck aboard *Heywood,* a marine rose hurriedly and the spoon of one of his grenades became entangled in the wire mesh of his bunk. The grenade exploded in the ship's compartment. Eight marines were seriously wounded, knocked out of the battle before they had even made it topside to climb into their landing craft. Sergeant Lucas watched marines balancing themselves as they went over the side of a transport near his. One man, heavily burdened with an 81mm mortar plate, appeared to be having trouble. Lucas looked just as the marine fell headlong from the scramble net and disappeared into the sea.

Meanwhile, aboard the flagship *Maryland* lying off the west end of the island, Rear Admiral Hill stared at the silent, dark shadow ahead. Ever since the star shell had illuminated the island and the ships around it, then fizzled out, there had been no signs of life from the Japanese garrison. The battleships and cruisers were lined up in the arc of a half circle for maximum effectiveness of direct and enfilading fields of fire. The ground forces, the men of the 2d Marine Division, were queuing up for their rendezvous at the line of departure. The massive naval bombardment, which the navy was certain would destroy Betio and make the job for the marines all but symbolic, was scheduled to begin at 0615. The naval bombardment would be preceded by a carrier air strike at 0545.

It was now 0500.

A signal light ashore blinked out a recognition challenge to a cruiser, but it received no answer. Captain Carl H. Jones, skipper of the flagship, gave the order to put the battleship's floatplane aloft. Its pilot— Lt. Comdr. Robert A. MacPherson—would be the eyes of Maj. Gen. Julian Smith and Admiral Hill during the landings. He would track the landings and spot for the bombardment. At 0505 the catapult launcher aboard *Maryland* screeched and MacPherson's little Kingfisher plane was flung airborne. The grinding of the catapult created a brilliant red flash of sparks as the floatplane was thrust out over the sea in its quest for altitude.

The sight of the red flash silhouetted the battleship only momentarily. But the tension and strain caused by waiting, holding their fire, startled the Japanese into action. For the Japanese spotters groping in the darkness for suitable targets, the sparks from the catapult seemed like a signal to begin the battle. With orders to fire at their own discretion when a target revealed itself, the chief of one of the big 8-inch naval guns on the west end of the island ordered his crew into action. The power lift of the gun was activated and the massive barrel was elevated to bear on the battleship. The crew chief gave the word: "Fire!"

In an instant, there was an omnipotent crack of thunder. The long, rifled naval barrel became a deafening torch as the first glowing high-velocity AP shell left its powerful muzzle, headed for *Maryland* eleven thousand yards away. The deadly enemy missile rumbled in over the superstructure of the American flagship and splashed into the sea a few hundred yards behind the big battlewagon, throwing up a phosphorescent geyser more than a hundred feet high.

As the transports unloaded, the fire support group had been lining up according to the size of their main armaments—destroyers in front, the cruisers and battleships behind them, with their 14- and 16-inch guns elevated for counterbattery fire as needed. With the destroyers darting about up front, the larger warships swung round, turning into line for broadside firing. Even before the echoes of the enemy 8-inch coastal artillery piece had receded, Capt. William Granat, commanding the battleship *Colorado,* ordered his fire control sections to respond. His ship let go with a salvo from its forward guns, which rumbled in over the island and landed in the lagoon. *Time-Life's* Robert Sherrod noted, "The curtain was up in the theatre of death."

Hill and the others had seen the gun flash on the island. They positioned themselves on the bridge and adjusted their powerful binoculars. Other staff officers crowded the bridge or watched anxiously from elsewhere for the fire support group to open up en masse against the island. Nearly every eye in the task force was focused on the battle line in anticipation of the massive retaliation they knew was forthcoming. Marines and seamen rushed topside aboard every noncombatant ship in the task force. The men-of-war wasted no time.

All eyes on *Maryland*'s bridge were on Rear Admiral Hill when the staff gunnery officer asked expectantly, "Shall we go ahead, sir?"

Hill answered simply: "Yes."

The gunnery officer turned to the TBS. "Commence firing," he told the ships. "The war is on."

From the speaker system of *Maryland* came the static squawk: "Stand by for main battery."

An ominous warning buzz followed, then, at 0507, the four 16-inch guns aft of the bridge fired, bathing the ship in a burning light as the huge tubes spat flame.

Lieutenant Commander Kenneth McCardle remembered the moment vividly: "The big ship flinched as though a giant had struck her with a hammer. Old trouper that she was, she quivered in every corner, dust filtered down from the overhead fixtures in flag plot. Several lighters were jarred out in that first blast, and I thought several of my teeth had been jarred out. Then the forward two turrets let go in unison, and then they alternated, forward four and after four, WHAM! WHAM!"

Every warship in the battle line opened up almost at once. They continued their massed fire on the island as sailors and marines cheered deliriously. As the battle line closed the range, the crescendo mounted steadily until the noise became unimaginable. Tremendous concussions were created from the concentrated fire. Veterans of the naval battles of the Solomons braced themselves for the strange sensations caused by the shock waves rolling across the water. Others were less cautious. Several men, carelessly exposed on deck, were knocked overboard by the bracketing aftershocks of the big guns.

Amid the stupefying bombardment, the Japanese gunners fired back, though only sporadically, since the explosions around them had forced them to abandon any pretense of spotting for accuracy. Instead the crews sought refuge in their blockhouses and fired only randomly in the general direction of the ships. The hurricane of naval gunfire swirling down upon Betio was so intense that coral boulders and the splintered trunks of entire palm trees were blasted hundreds of feet into the air. Where a courageous enemy crew would attempt to man its weapon, a ton or more of shells would pound into the vicinity of the winking fire flashes.

The American counterbattery fire ceased abruptly at 0542—thirty-five minutes after it had started—in expectation of the arrival of the fighters and bombers of Rear Admiral Montgomery's carriers. The pandemonium had been unearthly, but now an impenetrable silence hung over the area. "We weren't used to the quiet, and still shouted at the top of our voices as though everyone was stone deaf," a gunner aboard *Maryland* said. "It took a little time to realize we could speak in a normal manner."

Aboard the flagship, the communications shack was flooded with reports of direct hits by the score on gun emplacements and the apparent destruction of several magazines and fuel dumps. Officers began evaluating the reports. This had not been possible during the bombardment because the flagship's radio had inexplicably malfunctioned with each salvo fired from the ship's guns. Hill's comments during the affair had been terse. Now, like everyone else, he watched the sky.

Sailors and marines looked up, searching for the air cover that would knock out any surviving enemy guns with bombs and pin to the ground any Japanese manning beach defenses. The planes would provide the coup de grace, they hoped. They would pave the way for the marines to stage a cakewalk over Betio. Then the vast stores of ice cream in the holds of the transports could be brought ashore. But as the minutes ticked by, 0545 came and went and the planes did not appear.

Anxiety reached a new threshold. By now the first three assault waves had been loaded and the fourth and fifth waves were going over the sides of their transports. Having been meticulously briefed on the components of the attack, men began grumbling and venting their frustrations at "flyboys" and the navy in general. There were references to the days on Guadalcanal when not an American plane could be seen in the sky, whereas scores of enemy aircraft roamed at will.

Suddenly attention was riveted toward the island. Men were jerked back to the reality of facing a more serious problem at hand. Another red star shell cluster blossomed above the shadowy island, now becoming visible in the dawn light. Then the big guns on Betio, the guns everyone assumed had been neutralized once and for all during the bombardment, opened up again and began blazing away. The display was a stunning confirmation of the strength of the enemy fortifications, and throughout the task force men looked to their officers for reassurance.

The Japanese commenced their second sustained burst of firing at 0548—less than ten minutes after dawn, just six minutes after the American bombardment had lifted for the missing air strike. Almost immediately shells began dropping into the center of the assembly area, evidence that the enemy fire control sections were back in action. The shells fell among transports and cargo ships, which at the time were consumed in the delicate business of unloading men and material into landing craft. All along the smoke-shrouded coastline, pinpoints of bright light winked as the Japanese guns fired, their crews having reoriented themselves during the lapse in American firing and put their weapons back into action. Aided by the first light of day, they had easily discovered the helpless transports and quickly brought the heavy weapons to bear at ranges of ten thousand to twelve thousand yards—point-blank range for guns of such large caliber.

First Lieutenant Earl J. Wilson, a twenty-six-year-old marine public relations officer, formerly a reporter for the *Washington Post,* watched at the rail of his ship. "Suddenly about 100 yards off from where I was standing, I saw a huge geyser of water, and I was very surprised. At first it occurred to me that one of our ships had misjudged and her shot had fallen short. Then, I realized that the Japs were using their coastal guns and were shooting back at us."

When the cannonading began, Robert Sherrod, like thousands of others, had rushed topside. "My God, what wide shooting," he said, turning to Maj. Howard J. Rice, of Detroit, executive officer of the 2d Battalion, 2d Marines. "They need some practice." The battalion staff officer looked at him quizzically. "You don't think that's our own guns doing *that* shooting, do you?" For the first time, Sherrod realized that there were some Japanese on Betio. "Like a man who had swallowed a piece of steak without chewing it, I said, 'Oh.'"

In fact, many men thought that the shells were the result of American destroyers overshooting the island. But the size of the splashes—great geysers of foam and water erupting all around—was an indication that the fire was unfriendly. Many 8- and 5-inch shells, following one another in quick succession, scored near misses. "They splattered steel against the sides and decks of the ships," said one transport commander.

For the marines preparing to assault the island, this was the first realization that there would be Japanese defenders waiting for them. And, worst of all, they must be unbelievably well dug in to have survived such a terrific naval bombardment. Utterly bewildered at the rude shock, all hands began scrambling for cover on the decks.

Technical Sergeant James G. Lucas, a twenty-nine-year-old combat correspondent from Tulsa, had been around. He had been in action with four Raider battalions, jumped with marine paratroopers, made a patrol in a submarine, and hitched a ride in a bomber on a night raid over Bougainville. But even he was taken by surprise when the enemy retaliated. "Without warning," he wrote, "an eight-inch shell hit and exploded 10 yards off our side. We dived behind a hatch, laughing at each other as we came out. A second shell hit five yards off, killing a sailor and spraying our deck with shrapnel."

The crew of LST-34, which had carried one-third of the valuable LVTs from Samoa, found themselves almost in the exact center of the transport area. Geysers were rising everywhere, drenching the ship in water and splaying shell fragments across her deck. Clearly what was a miss for the other ships was a serious affair to LST-34, stationed in the focal point of the Japanese line of sight.

One of the first shells splashed into the sea a mere thirty feet from the vulnerable LST. Another impacted not more than fifty yards from *Zeilin*. In the next quarter of an hour, the transports *J. Franklin Bell, William P. Biddle, Harris, LaSalle, Virgo,* and *Monrovia* were also straddled by numerous salvos. What made matters worse for the transport group was that they could not respond to the enemy shelling for fear the assault forces then boated and in the water might be struck by inaccurate fire. The transport crews chafed at not being permitted to use their light 40mm guns.

"Behind, our boats strung out in a long chain and I thought what would happen if one of those shells should hit in the middle of them," recalled Lieutenant Wilson. "Another whine and whispering note, and again we hit the deck. We were learning fast. The shell passed through our rigging and landed a hundred yards off our port side. We all began to ask, Where are our planes? For Christ's sake, why don't they get here? Why don't they get in there and knock out those big guns?"

On the flagship bridge, Rear Admiral Hill also was deeply concerned with the plight of the transports and LSTs. It had been thought that the ships were marshaled well beyond the range of enemy guns. But the charts of the Gilberts that had been used by the planners were nearly a hundred years old and inaccurate. Thus the transport group, because of navigational error, found itself in the midst of a fire zone—in fact, closer to the island than the big warships were.

The admiral had been confident that the bombardment would quickly and decisively dispose of the Japanese gun emplacements. But it was obvious that the planners had grossly overestimated the effect naval gunfire would have on the forts and blockhouses that protected the enemy artillery. Even now those guns were wreaking havoc with the transport group, threatening to halt the debarkation of the assault forces. The actual number of guns firing from the island was unknown, but fire control officers were reporting that at least two 8-inch and six 5-inch pieces were still in use. If their observations were at all accurate, simple addition led Rear Admiral Hill to conclude "that out of four 8-inch guns and eight 5-inch guns on Betio, from 50 percent to 75 percent survived" the B-24 and carrier air raids before D day as well as the cruiser bombardment of D day minus one. All that was in addition to the forty-minute bombardment in the previous hour.

There was ample reason for concern. The situation could easily become critical if any of the crowded transports were hit or, perish the thought, sunk. The loss of life could be horrific. Hill contemplated his options with his staff. Something had to be done—and fast. Even as the men consulted, ships continued to log near misses as they hurried with the procedures of unloading. Japanese fire control would surely improve as the morning became brighter.

That the planes had not arrived as scheduled complicated matters. If the aircraft arrived while the fire support group was engaged in working over the enemy coastal artillery, with *Maryland*'s TBS fading in and out, there could be a disaster. It would be impossible to call off the bombardment, and the planes might fly into a wall of naval gunfire. Hill determined that he had no choice. When it was finally confirmed over the naval air net that the air strike would not arrive until 0610, he decided to resume counterbattery fire until the planes were in sight. He was not a happy man at this point.

At 0605 the battleships and cruisers opened up again, pummeling the troublesome—and, should their crews improve their aim, deadly—enemy guns. Just as before, when the first shells of the task force found their mark, the Japanese quit firing and "went to ground." More precisely, they pulled back into their fortifications and waited for the counterbattery fire to end. Once the naval gunfire commenced, the whole island was again blotted out by a cloud of dust and smoke. It was impossible aboard the ships to determine whether the enemy guns were being destroyed or if the crews were just sitting things out. In any event, Betio now presented an incredible scene of devastation, and The Flag staff were encouraged.

The bombardment was halted at 0612 for the carrier planes, which still had not arrived. The sun climbed fully over the eastern horizon, turning a flaming orange. Again the enemy guns opened up when the bombardment lifted, though at first there appeared a marked difference in their rate and volume of fire. Then the Japanese crews, as if somehow sensing that this was their final opportunity, let go with a supreme effort. So dense was the pall of smoke and dust that they in effect were forced to fire blindly despite the improving light. Once again it was the transports and LSTs in the center of the transport area that received the most attention.

The perplexed crew of LST-34 watched anxiously as the enemy crew of a 5-inch gun on the northeast point of the island began to find the range, tracking their misses by the splashes created. Inside of three minutes, they found it. The first salvo struck seven hundred yards off the port bow. Then another came over, leaving its telltale plume three hundred yards off the port beam. The geyser from the third salvo was plotted one hundred yards off the starboard quarter.

At 0615 the skipper of LST-34, Lt. James J. Davis, watched the fourth shell explode just thirty yards astern. The next one was bound to be dead on target. He promptly got underway in an effort to achieve an evasive course that would take the clumsy ship beyond range of the improving enemy marksmanship. LST-34 shuddered and her engines strained for power as Lieutenant Davis demanded, "Speed forced flank!" Several shells slammed into her wake as she plodded away.

The skippers of LSTs 242 and 243 were watching, and they wasted no time in getting their vessels underway too.

For a seaman watching LST-34 from the bow of a nearby ship, the scene stood out in his memory.

> I recalled pictures of Union gunboats on the Mississippi shelling Vicksburg—but this was the other way around. The LST was smack in the center of all that fury. Those of us watching hardly had time to brace ourselves for the next salvo. The urge to put our hands over our eyes was strong, but we couldn't pull ourselves away. First there was a bright flash from the island, then two fire-balls arced out over the lagoon. They sounded like a freight train. Then they crashed into the sea and straddled her. It was awful to see. I remember thinking, so that's what it's like when your ship is sunk. But she came out of it and got away.

Meanwhile, the transport *LaSalle,* under Comdr. Fred C. Flugel, was also straddled by many near misses, which burst all around with fearsome implications. It was apparent that the ship's luck was running out when a salvo of undetermined size landed only twenty feet from her bow. The ship was rocked by the explosion. The deck was flooded with water and the plating lightly dented. The shelling was serious enough that Capt. Herbert B. Knowles, commander of the transports, ordered his helpless flotilla to retreat northward at 0616. He did so reluctantly, vacating the area, as he said, "only when enemy shells up to probably 8-inch size began getting too dangerously close."

Transports and LSTs maneuvered from the area under fire all the way. Captain John B. McGovern's division of ships was the last to leave. His group remained in the area until 0625, as he saw it, "under desultory enemy fire from the beach." However, as the Japanese gunners began concentrating against his vessels, he was also "obliged to move out of range to a distance of 18,000 yards."

The crews of landing craft in the water, many already loaded, followed the zigzagging transports out of harm's way. The action, reminiscent of similar encounters in the Solomons, made strong impressions on all hands. As Lieutenant Wilson watched, "The ship opposite us, steaming along at full speed with a wide 'bone' of foam at the bow, had a string of landing craft following her. It reminded me of a string of black beads against a wide strip of lace." Lieutenant Commander MacPherson in his Kingfisher spotting plane from *Maryland* also witnessed the forced retreat. "The transports," he noted curiously, "reminded me of fat mother ducks followed by their broods." Another officer observed that it "looked like boat-race day at New London."

By the time the transport area was cleared, the ships had withdrawn ten miles from the island. Before all the maneuvers had been accomplished, however, two men aboard *Harris,* two coast guardsmen aboard *Arthur B. Middleton,* and another aboard *William P. Biddle* had been struck and wounded by shell fragments. In other instances, men had been knocked or blown overboard and fished out of the sea by landing craft. Elsewhere there were bruises and broken bones. The Japanese not only had fired first but—for all anyone aboard the American ships knew for certain—they also had drawn first blood.

Chapter Fifteen

Another sound—a buzzing or massed drone—roared over the task force at Tarawa at 0615 when the navy fighters and bombers at last appeared. In perfect formations, flying almost wing to wing, Hellcats, Avengers, and Dauntlesses headed for the island over which an appalling curtain of smoke hung and fires burned. As the planes screamed in, there appeared here and there sudden bursts of flak. In other places crisscrossing streams of tracer fire from dual-purpose machine guns swept the sky. Men watched the planes with admiration. They reasoned that everything was going to work out after all, and they took heart in the ferocity of the air attack.

Disregarding the smoke and AA fire, the carrier planes—not just a few but more than a hundred from *Essex* and *Bunker Hill*—began to blast Betio. Again and again they bored in. One preinvasion attack was conducted by eighty planes, but Rear Admiral Hill was not relieved in the least. The late arrival of the planes threatened to disrupt the assault plan and tax the flexibility of the whole operational timetable. Apart from that, Japanese guns were still firing on the fleeing transports and LSTs.

The air attacks appeared as merciless as the naval bombardment had been, with planes pounding preselected targets in deliberate fashion as they made their runs into the fiery conflagration beneath them. Three squadrons of Avenger torpedo bombers struck the enemy's main gun positions with two-thousand-pound blockbusters. Dauntlesses hit the numerous Japanese dual-purpose guns with thousand-pound bombs, while yet another squadron of Avengers dropped sticks of hundred-pound antipersonnel and incendiary explosives. The fighters formed a protective umbrella high above during the bombing phase, then zoomed in, strafing the beaches and inland areas with their multiple .50-caliber machine guns.

The planes originally had been allotted thirty minutes for their attack, but their late arrival had shortened this to just ten minutes before the warships would open fire again at 0625. Fearing a rain of shells from the task force, the aircrews hurried their attacks, so that their contribution was quite uncoordinated. Most of the aircraft were in and out of the area in seven minutes, but a squadron of fighters remained aloft until 0625 to carry out strafing runs. The warships held their fire and the bombardment plan had to be further modified. The fighters had barely cleared the island when the warships began hammering away again at 0627. Every delay in the intricate schedule was making a shambles of the invasion plan.

It had been anything but a milk run for the aircraft—by any stretch of the imagination. Besides operating under the mistaken impression that they were not wanted over the island until sunrise at 0615, the crews had considerable difficulty assembling after takeoff. Darkness and the lack of airspace needed to join formations led to hectic conditions over the carrier group. With so many planes in the air at one time in such a constricted area, just getting started toward Tarawa proved a chore.

When the planes arrived, according to a fighter squadron commander from *Independence,* "it was still dark enough for tracers to blind the pilots." To make matters worse, flak had been quite heavy, especially for the Avengers, which were given the task of demolishing the enemy coastal guns. Japanese flak batteries, range finders, and directors were sited opposite the intervals between the big guns. This created effective AA cross-fire zones into which the planes had to fly. Deck crews were stunned when twenty planes returned to the carriers with various degrees of damage, some trailing smoke and fuel, some riddled with steel splinters, others with ailerons shot up.

At least one plane did not return at all. Aboard *Maryland,* Lt. Comdr. Ken McCardle had watched as the plane dived on a Japanese position. Coming under fire, presumably from a 120mm AA gun, the plane was shot down in a matter of seconds. "One moment there was a plane— the next moment a stick of fire blazed down toward the ground." McCardle could not help but suspect that the crew had been killed, "for there was no parachute." In any case, it would not have mattered. There would be no sanctuary for downed American airmen at Tarawa this day.

The Southern Attack Force had been in action off Tarawa for more than an hour when one hundred miles away the bombardment of Makin began at 0640 and Butaritari erupted with a roaring storm of fire. A deadly symphony reverberated over the island as the big ships slammed steadily away at their targets. The gray dawn brightened with the flash of their guns, but along the assault beaches and inland areas there were no great clouds of smoke as at Tarawa. Makin was in places swampy and marshy, and a rainsquall had recently passed over the area. This moisture reduced the likelihood of a firestorm similar to that which the marines would encounter at Tarawa. But there was devastation all the same.

The battleships *Idaho, Pennsylvania, New Mexico,* and *Mississippi* fired tons of steel from their 14- and 16-inch guns at Japanese gun batteries protecting the main fortified area. Meanwhile, cruisers and destroyers leveled streams of shells into pillboxes, bunkers, and dugouts. Of the supporting air bombardment, the naval historian RAdm. Samuel Morison, then a lieutenant commander aboard the cruiser *Baltimore,* recalled: "One could see coconut palms shooting up into the air, the trunks being separated from the foliage and the tops coming down like shuttlecocks."

With steady fire control, the accurate *Pennsylvania* knocked out a trench complex from six miles offshore. It was later determined that the salvo had killed sixty-two Japanese. Rear Admiral Turner noted that the superb shooting "considerably scrambled the trench, Japs, and trees for some distance." In addition, buildings were flattened, and a battery of 80mm AA guns and two light tanks were severely damaged. Mounting a total of 12 14-inch and 16 5-inch guns, *Pennsylvania* alone pumped 403 14-inch and 246 5-inch shells into Makin in an all-out effort to soften up the island for the soldiers who would land on the beaches.

Concentrated in the mile-square main assault zone in the center of the island, dubbed by army intelligence officers as The Citadel, were a dozen concrete and coconut-log bunkers and bomb shelters; seven pillboxes; six 5-inch naval guns; seven pieces of field artillery of 70mm and 80mm caliber; six 37mm AT guns; a mile or more of fire trenches, antitank ditches, and barricades; and no less than thirty machine-gun nests, including heavy 13mm dual-mounted weapons. There were also numerous spider traps, mortar pits, and observation posts. The inexperienced army troops heading for the island would need all the help the big warships could give them.

At Truk Admiral Koga and the impotent Combined Fleet waited for news of landings. Koga had done all he could. He had alerted his garrisons throughout the Central Pacific and called up the air reserves in the home islands. No one yet knew the true strength of the impending enemy action. No one had calculated—or could even estimate—the total size of the American naval forces. If the reports made by search planes from Mili, Makin, and Nauru in previous days were any indication, then the enemy strength appeared staggering—larger even than the immense Japanese fleet that had sailed against Midway in 1942. And although the main attack appeared concentrated against Tarawa and the Gilberts, no one was really sure if there would not be others—perhaps in the Marshalls and at isolated Nauru too.

Everything now depended on the Japanese naval infantry holding the islands. With the Kido Butai crippled and the carrier air forces lost in the disastrous battles that had raged around Rabaul, the outer islands had suddenly become all that lay in the way of American mastery of the Central Pacific. These islands were now very important. From the island fortifications these men of Nippon looked out to sea, and contemplated how long they could hold out against such overwhelming enemy firepower.

Chief Petty Officer Sasaki, manning his 70mm artillery piece at Makin, was worried. The garrison's floatplanes were long gone. All but one had departed for Jaluit the day before. The crew of the one plane left behind, an Emily shot up in the carrier air attacks and stranded near King's wharf, had spread themselves out on the wings and fuselage and committed suicide on D day minus one. Sasaki wondered why there were still no orders forthcoming from the command post. To be sure, communications throughout the island were out, but runners could have been sent out at night before the shelling had begun. That he had received no messages from runners must mean that everyone was at his battle station.

But what of the enemy battle line offshore, now shelling the island with impunity, and the massed formations of planes? Sasaki did not know what to think. All he knew was—as he managed to write in the diary he had been keeping since the American carrier air attacks had begun the previous day—"We were being horribly shelled." Indeed, salvos landed all around, showering the area with dirt, coral, and steel splinters. The explosions became so furious that Sasaki abandoned all hope of manning his weapon. For a moment the bombardment shifted to somewhere far behind his position. He surveyed the carnage. Casualties among the gun crews were light, and he was shocked to find that his artillery—howitzers of various calibers—was still intact. Apparently the enemy was mistaking dummy gun positions along the coast for the real thing, but he could not see how his weapons, protected by coconut-log stanchions, could escape destruction much longer. The devastation around his own piece seemed to prove that. He decided that it was futile to remain in the open any longer.

Sasaki took advantage of the lull to seek safety. He assembled his crew and led them to an observation post for refuge—some distance away. Nobody in the dugout appeared injured, but again and again shells smashed into the vicinity, making it clear that there was little safety to be found here either. "Then, gathering up the personnel of the observation post," he wrote, "we all ran for the air raid shelter."

They remained in the bunker as enemy planes came over, bombing and strafing. He moved to an aperture and watched. His frightened men beat their fists against the walls of the shelter in frustration at their helplessness. But there was nothing Sasaki or anyone else could do. There were more planes in the sky than ever before. Shocked, even mortified by the force assailing them, Sasaki wrote, "From both sides, inside and outside the lagoon, the enemy is pouring concentrated shelling and bombing into the area of our headquarters. Bombs are dropping by the score." Soon, it seemed, the island would break apart and sink under the weight of the enemy naval and air bombardment.

Sasaki would not have been comforted to know that landing craft carrying the 27th Infantry Division troops to their assault zones on the hammerhead end of Butaritari Island were just a mile away. Behind the scrub brush and swamps bordering Beaches Red 1 and 2, all but a handful of Japanese defenders had pulled back into their redoubt, into The Citadel in the center of the island, leaving no one to resist the Americans when they landed.

Things were much different at Tarawa.

Chapter Sixteen

With the sun rising higher in the sky, Tarawa was still there, squatting menacingly on the sea against the brightening horizon. All who gazed upon the island thought it seemed strange to find it intact, after all the fury that had been directed against it in the previous two hours.

To Rear Admiral Spruance, it was a symbolic first step toward Tokyo, the focus of much planning and preparation over the previous six months.

To Rear Admiral Hill, on the bridge of *Maryland,* Tarawa was a task he hoped to be done with quickly. Though he was alarmed by the ferocity of the Japanese reaction, he remained confident. The night before he had passed a message to Spruance via a destroyer.

> We had a fine training period in Efate, and I think the boys are all prepared to do their job in good fashion provided we get a break in the weather and tidal conditions on the beach. I have had a little trouble convincing some of my fire support boys that when I say I want close fire support I mean *close*. The 2nd Division has done a fine job in their loading and are streamlined down to a point where I fully hope we may get the transports completely out of the area in approximately twenty-four hours. They have been a wonderful crowd to work with and I think they will put on a good show.

To several marine riflemen, veterans of the jungle campaign at Guadalcanal whom correspondent Robert Sherrod cornered on their transport, Tarawa looked "tougher than anyone has said."

By 0635 the transports and LSTs were in their proper position and

128

the naval bombardment began anew. It was incredible to behold. The earlier firing had been purely reactionary—counterbattery fire intended to silence the enemy guns, which had opened up first. Phase II was different.

The heaviest prelanding bombardment in history, it was painstakingly planned to methodically and deliberately reduce the island fortifications to rubble. The patterns would leave not a foot of the island unscathed, from the bird's head to its tail end. In all, three battleships, four cruisers, including Spruance's flagship *Indianapolis,* and nine destroyers would fire three thousand tons of shells into the island in two hours. More clouds of smoke and dust began to rise again from Betio, obscuring it from the warships.

The minesweeper *Pursuit,* slow and armed with only a 3-inch deck gun and accompanied by two smoke-laying LCVPs, started through the narrow main channel into the lagoon at 0646. At the same time the first three assault waves were leaving the boat rendezvous area. Another minesweeper, *Requisite,* followed *Pursuit* in at 0700. The LCVPs and a whaleboat from *Pursuit* laid smudge pots, while the little wooden-hulled minesweepers (YMSs) went to within three thousand yards of the beaches, searching for mines, shallows, sandbars—anything that might obstruct the progress of the assault craft.

The appearance of ships so close to shore startled the Japanese gunners. Despite the smoke screen and dust, long-range machine guns and light artillery fired on the ships as they did their work, but they escaped any damage. No mines were discovered, but the current was running fast. *Pursuit* charted the bottom and marked assault lanes for the landing craft by laying flagged buoys. *Requisite* turned to lead the "inshore close fire support" group through the swept channel.

The destroyers *Dashiell* and *Ringgold,* battle pennants snapping from the mastheads and guided by a Royal New Zealand Navy officer who had lived at Tarawa before the war, followed *Requisite* into the lagoon to put point-blank fire into the beaches and protect the minesweepers. The water in the narrow channel was shallow, which made it impossible for the ship to dash through to the lagoon until it was clear of the knife-edged reef. Almost as soon as Lt. Comdr. Thomas Conley began maneuvering *Ringgold* through the channel, Japanese guns began dropping shells all around the ship. One gun in particular—its fire flashes revealed it on the northwest corner of the island—

fired exclusively on the channel until it seemed that the valiant destroyer was running a gauntlet. Suddenly *Ringgold* ran aground halfway through the entrance. In backing off the shoal, her sonar gear was torn from the hull.

The sight of the troubled warship a mile and a half out seemed too good to be true for the Japanese gunners. There would certainly be no better chance than this. It seemed that *Ringgold* was the only ship the enemy gunners could see. In an instant numerous AP shells ranging in size from 3- to 5-inch caliber rained down around the destroyer—and close. One of the first landed just fifty yards away. Then a full salvo of 5-inch fire straddled the ship.

Conley got the engines going again, but not soon enough. He was easing *Ringgold* off the reef just as a Japanese gun crew found the range. A shell struck the ship below the waterline. Although it did not explode, the dud knocked out power aft of the bridge and made a ragged hole through which an arc of black water rushed into the ship. Immortalizing himself in the annals of the U.S. Navy, the chief engineer, Lt. Wayne A. Parker, controlled the flooding by shoving his backside against the hole until a mattress could be found. For his action, he was awarded the Navy Cross.

Several rounds exploded in the air over *Ringgold*'s fantail. One passed through the rigging, knocking out the radar. Others dropped nearby, blasting great chunks of coral from the reef. There was no respite from the Japanese fire. In the next few minutes, dead in the water and drifting, *Ringgold* was hit again—this time amidships. The shell passed clean through, ricocheting through a 40mm magazine, the sickbay, and the emergency radio room, and into the midst of a 20mm battery. The hapless gun crew was bowled over in all directions before the live shell exited the ship.

On the command ships, operations staff crowded the radio shacks, listening for any information. Through it all, over the TBS came a steady flow of frantic messages. All who heard the radio traffic listened with mounting anxiety. Rear Admiral Hill's staff was stunned that the Japanese were still resisting. Within minutes, it seemed that all four of the ships in the lagoon were in danger. *Ringgold*'s messages told the story: "VISIBILITY IS POOR. WE ARE BEING SHELLED BY HEAVY AND LIGHT GUNS FROM SHORE." "WE ARE HIT. TAKING ON WATER." "OUR PORT ENGINE IS OUT." "WE ARE TAKING

HEAVY FIRE FROM NORTHWEST CORNER OF HELEN." "WE ARE HIT SECOND TIME." "OUR FIVE INCHERS ARE ENGAGING ENEMY GUNS."

Ringgold was in a bad way but still battleworthy. She had been hit three times, although not all the hits and near misses exploded. The port engine was knocked out, power to the after third of the ship was down, her radar was inoperable, her sonar array was gone, and minor fires had started in several places. The destroyer drifted toward the reef, threatening to block the way of any vessel larger than an LCVP, before Conley got her underway again. All the while, *Ringgold*'s guns fired back at the enemy. Nearby, *Dashiell* saw the danger and also began firing on the northwest corner of Betio. Meanwhile, with *Ringgold* bracketed in the midst of the enemy shells, Conley coaxed the destroyer into deeper water. Once clear of the channel, he ordered, "Full speed ahead!" *Ringgold* surged forward into the lagoon, the crew fighting the fires and making temporary repairs to the hole in the waterline while under heavy shelling. Shells slammed into the ship's wake, creating great geysers of water and blasted coral.

Miraculously, although a dozen men had been shaken up, no one had been killed or seriously injured. In the midst of the action, *Ringgold*'s gunnery officer, Lt. Lyttleton B. Ensey, had kept the ship's guns firing, eventually silencing the 5-inch coastal gun that had been the most accurate. A lucky salvo detonated its ammunition dump, which went up in spectacular fashion. The gun was knocked out of action.

The LSD *Ashland,* a specialized landing ship with dock facilities, which had loaded the 2d Division's tanks at Noumea and joined the Tarawa convoys at Fila, was next through the narrow passage. The destroyers and minesweepers, still under fire, formed a line offshore, and enemy guns fell silent all along the coast under their heavy fire. The high-bosomed *Ashland* came on slowly, followed by the first three assault waves loaded in the invaluable LVTs—nearly a hundred of them in long columns. Lieutenant Commander Roman F. Good turned on *Pursuit*'s searchlight at 0746 to guide the LVTs through the smoke and dust that blanketed the lagoon. They passed through the channel en route to the line of departure, an imaginary line six thousand to sixty-six hundred yards from the beaches.

The battleships and cruisers continued their shelling. With each salvo, enormous tongues of orange flame licked their dual superfir-

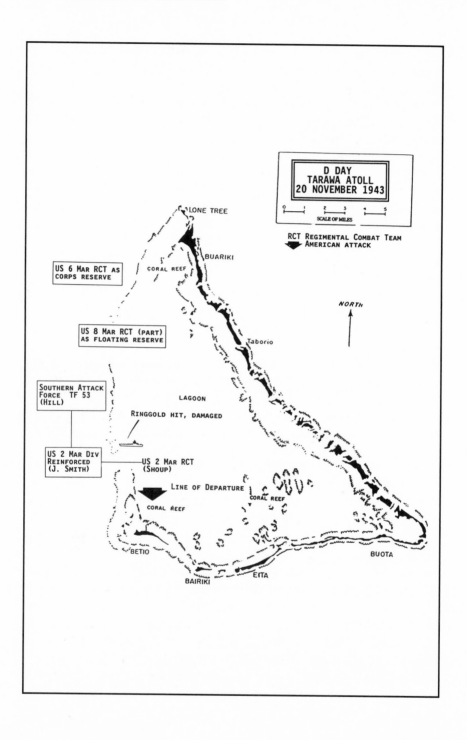

D DAY
TARAWA ATOLL
20 NOVEMBER 1943

0 1 2 3 4 5
SCALE OF MILES

RCT REGIMENTAL COMBAT TEAM
▼ AMERICAN ATTACK

LONE TREE

BUARIKI

CORAL REEF

US 6 MAR RCT AS
CORPS RESERVE

NORTH

US 8 MAR RCT (PART)
AS FLOATING RESERVE

Taborio

SOUTHERN ATTACK
FORCE TF 53
(HILL)

LAGOON

RINGGOLD HIT, DAMAGED

US 2 MAR DIV
REINFORCED
(J. SMITH)

US 2 MAR RCT
(SHOUP)

LINE OF DEPARTURE

CORAL REEF

CORAL REEF

BETIO

BUOTA

BAIRIKI   EITA

ing turrets. Concussions displaced the sea beneath the guns, and the massive force unleashed when the guns fired bounced the mammoth ships backward. The roar of the 14- and 16-inch guns, the lightning crack of 5- and 8-inchers from destroyers and cruisers, and even the 3-inch fire of the minesweepers delivered the mightiest preassault bombardment the marines had ever seen. A hundred shells a minute smashed into the island.

The main assault forces had been boated and waiting to land since at least 0400. Now the lagoon was crowded with vessels stretching nearly seven miles from the boat rendezvous area. Lieutenant Commander Good, tracking their progress with *Pursuit*'s radar, calculated that the line of departure would not be established on time. The LVTs had been expected to reach the line by 0745, but it proved impossible. The distance from the transport area was greater than planned, and a strong current and choppy seas slowed the LVTs. In addition, *Pursuit* had mismarked the line of departure.

Pursuit notified Hill that the assault waves were twenty-four minutes behind schedule. Lieutenant Commander MacPherson in his spotter plane also reported their slow progress. Nothing could be done but postpone H hour. Hill pushed the landings back fifteen minutes to 0845, but he was unable to call off the final preassault air strike, which was already airborne and on its way to Tarawa. The fire support group was ordered to resume its bombardment until 0835. Milling about in the lagoon, the marines scanned the skies for the army B-24s, whose two-thousand-pound blockbusters would flatten the island.

Seven hundred miles to the south, at Funafuti in the Ellice Islands, RAdm. John Hoover, directing all land-based air forces for Galvanic, and Maj. Gen. Willis Hale, commanding officer of the Seventh Air Force, were both stunned. In the hours before daylight a full squadron of army Liberators had been readied and their pilots and crews briefed for this last big mission against the Gilberts. The strike against Tarawa was to be carried out from high altitude in support of the carrier-based strike. But in the darkness, something had gone awry. It could not have happened at a worse time.

The bombers had been spotted on the runways for takeoff. All had been set. The first plane, piloted by the squadron leader, failed to achieve proper altitude and crashed into the Pacific after running out of airfield. The next four planes managed to make it aloft, though with great difficulty, and proceeded to assemble into formation for the long flight. Beneath them, however, yet another heavily laden bomber also crashed on takeoff.

With two of six aircraft already lost, some of the crews aboard the remaining eighteen B-24s refused to take off with the oversized and unwieldy payloads on the short runways, and the mission was scrubbed. Though shocked at the dismal performance of the crews, no one blamed them for refusing to fly the mission with such loads—slightly more than four thousand pounds each. The payloads would have constituted the largest heavy bomber strike yet tried in the Central Pacific, with forty-eight tons of bombs.

The four Liberators that had managed to get airborne carried on with their assignment. But they were not even sure that the island they hit was Tarawa. It was not. It is believed that one or two at most found Makin, and the rest bombed nearby Maiana or an uninhabited island of the Marshalls group.

This was to have been a great prestige mission for the army. Major General Hale was aware that Holland Smith and the marines were hopeful about the Seventh Air Force contribution to the main thrust against Tarawa. He was also aware that the navy was doubtfully watching to see what the big bombers could do in a tactical role. But the proposal to send the B-24s against Tarawa on D day had been flawed from the start. The distance of the mission alone made any tactical use of the bombers impractical, and the ambitious bomb loads proved too great for the short coral runways in the Ellices. Yet another crimp in the Tarawa assault plan had appeared.

Pursuit and *Requisite,* performing as control vessels, marked the line of departure, and along the line red and yellow flags fluttering from buoys indicated the assault lanes. *Ashland* opened her huge bow doors and launched LCMs carrying fourteen Sherman tanks of C Company, 2d Tank Battalion. Each of the medium tanks mounted a 75mm gun and two machine guns. They would land in the sixth wave and provide the marines with instant heavy firepower ashore.

At exactly 0824 the first wave of assault troops crossed the line of departure and the battle for Tarawa was on. Forty-eight LVTs carrying 1,464 marines headed in, with 5-inch, 40mm, and 20mm fire from

Dashiell and *Ringgold* roaring overhead. Two LCSs, which would each smother the beaches with one hundred 4.5-inch rockets, marked either end of the line that lay parallel to the beaches. The second wave, 600 marines in twenty-four LVTs, then crossed. Up to eight more waves strung out behind them, and prepared to land at five-minute intervals. In just a half hour it was hoped that there would be 3,000 combat troops ashore, by noon as many as 6,000 more.

Just as the LVTs crossed the line of departure, the naval bombardment lifted to allow the last air assault to come in. This was the original H hour minus five minutes mission, which the assault troops assumed would pin down the Japanese until the minute they landed. The planes roared over the beaches, strafing and bombing, and were up and away again in less than five minutes. However, the LVTs still had thirty-five hundred yards to go. Rear Admiral Hill again postponed H hour—this time to 0900. As bad as things seemed, very few men realized that matters were to become much worse before the day, much less the battle, had ended.

Chapter Seventeen

The marines of the first wave could not yet see anything of Tarawa. They were still too far away. All that could be distinguished ahead of them was a boiling mass of smoke and dust. Otherwise, visibility was limited to about a thousand yards. The destroyers were still dueling with Japanese coastal batteries. The noise was fearsome. The deafening roar overhead reminded many men of thunderstorms of mythical proportions. Bone-rattling shock waves created from the massive concentration of naval gunfire rolled out from the island. Decades later men would vividly recall the violent thunder of the bombardment.

Misery had plenty of company in the landing craft, where the men, chilled by a strong headwind, were drenched by the gallons of foul milky green and brown water of the lagoon that spilled into the craft with the butting of each wave. Though confident, from what they could see, of the effect of the naval gunfire and air attacks, most of the marines had been boated for four hours or more. Their disgust with their discomfort was reaching its apex. One marine in an LCVP of the fifth wave, loaded with about thirty-six men and all their equipment, saw a young corporal overwhelmed by a deluge. They were riding so low in the water, a long white wake fanning out behind them, that the swell swept over the side and into and out of the boat again. The unfortunate marine sat in the corner coughing, gasping for breath, and covered with foam, which gave him the lurid appearance of "a rabid dog."

Such misery was commonplace throughout the little flotilla. From the moment the landing craft, especially the LCVPs, had left the transport assembly area, they had been filling with water. Correspondent Robert Sherrod had climbed down the nets and into a Higgins boat at 0635. "Within five minutes after we pushed off," he noted, "a half barrel of water was splashing over the high bow of the Higgins boat every minute. Everyone of the thirty-odd men was soaked before we had chugged a half mile." Men heading for Red 1 were shocked to see the dorsal fins of sharks swimming among their wallowing landing craft, which seemed ready to sink at any second. The scavengers had been stirred up by the activity and vibrations in the water. Danger lurked everywhere, it seemed.

The naval gunfire continued overhead as the assault waves bored in. With each rolling aftershock, landing craft would shudder as if struck by some mighty unseen fist. One correspondent, boated in a later wave, noted curiously that whereas the roaring canopy of shells traveling overhead "numbed a man's senses," the "explosions jarred you to the marrow." Upon catching a glimpse of the roaring flames and boiling cauldron that was Betio, a private was amazed at the sheer power of naval gunfire. Watching, he croaked in an incredulous voice to no one in particular, "It's a wonder the whole goddamn island doesn't fall apart and sink."

In other craft, men who were not incapacitated by seasickness ignored their unlucky companions and the water filling their craft, and stood and cheered the onslaught. For the marines who had not experienced the ferocious Japanese shelling of Guadalcanal, the whole affair was awesome and unbelievable. They shouted as though the Japanese were already defeated. Aboard the warships there were similar thoughts.

A sailor aboard *Tennessee* observed the bombardment with detachment. "I couldn't see anything but black smoke and flames from one end of Betio to the other, and figured that's what hell must be like." Rear Admiral Howard Kingman, who commanded the fire support group, was aboard the same ship. From the bridge, he stared out at the tiny island in disbelief, thinking "it seemed almost impossible for any human being to be left alive on the island." On some ships naive bets were made that Betio would no longer be there when the bombardment ended.

In the lagoon, a crewman aboard *Ringgold* noted, "The whole island was ablaze. You couldn't see anything but fire and smoke. Every once in a while a great pillar of flame shot skyward as though a volcano had erupted. A sailor standing near me gave a sickly grin. 'Mate, they need firemen in there—not marines,' he said. And I thought, it's going to be a cinch for our guys . . . they'll find nothing but splintered palm trees and dead Japs." Another observer with an astute flair for symbolism described the maelstrom as the voice of doom for the Japanese, not only on Tarawa but throughout the Pacific.

One hundred miles away at Makin the naval gunfire in support of the landings by the 27th Division was also astounding. In a bombardment exceeded in tonnage until then only by that of Tarawa, destruction was massive all along the assault beaches and inland. Whole tracts of mangrove and native villages disappeared. Coral, dirt, parts of entire coconut trees, and dummy gun positions spewed into the sky, and scrub brush began to burn. In all, the ships expended nearly two thousand rounds of 14-inch and 1,645 rounds of 8-inch shells against the island.

The first wave of LVTs was coming in against virtually no opposition. A few rifles flashed behind the beach, a machine gun or two raked along the reef, but there was nothing of the intense fire feared by the untested New York infantry of the 165th RCT of Maj. Gen. Ralph Smith's 27th Division. To many soldiers the amphibious assault had all the appearances of a rehearsal. In fact, the dry runs at Maalaea Bay and Kahoolawe in the Hawaiian Islands had been more difficult.

Major Edward T. Brandt, in a leading LVT of his 3d Battalion, 105th Infantry, assault team, watched as the tracked landing craft fired off their batches of rockets. Expecting to see the missiles blanket the beach ahead, he was disappointed when most misfired or flew off wildly, their firing mechanisms ruined by the saltwater. Others fell short, but some succeeded in hitting the beaches. The sixteen LVTs taking in the soldiers—the primary reason the assault proved such a welcome anticlimax—lumbered out of the sea in the first wave, sporadic enemy fire rattling against their fronts.

Before long, however, the enemy firing stopped. The .50-caliber machine guns of the LVTs and supporting 5-inch fire from the destroyers *Phelps* and *MacDonough* appeared to have driven off the few Japanese manning positions behind the beach. Yet, although there was not the heavy resistance at the water's edge the troops had been briefed to expect, the landing was not entirely bloodless. Almost as soon as the LVTs reached the reef, one seaman was killed and another wounded by the enemy fire.

The LVTs hit the coral reef about forty yards offshore and, encountering no wire, mines, or other beach obstacles, roared up the low embank-

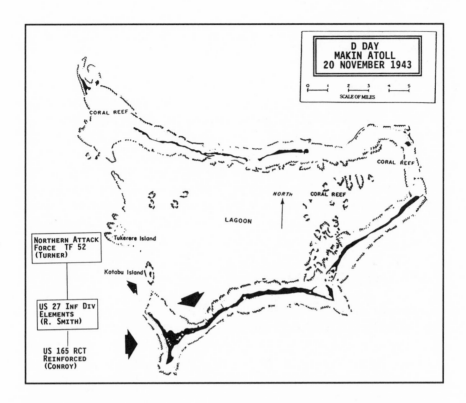

ment. "One could see them," recalled the historian Morison, "crawling up on the beach like prehistoric monsters foraging for game, while the second and third waves of landing craft pressed in, throwing spray." The LVTs slewed to a stop amidst the scrub brush behind the beach, and infantry scrambled over their sides and sought cover.

Once aground, nobody seemed to know exactly what to do, or where the Japanese were. There certainly was no enemy on the beach to put up a fight. Many men simply stood still, serenely waiting for enemy fire before hitting the ground, but not a shot was fired at the little band of soldiers. To Brandt, seeking the comparative safety of the back side of his LVT, the important thing was to organize his troops and get them inland. "I jumped down from my [LVT] and stood straight up for two or three minutes, waiting for somebody to shoot me," he said. "Nobody shot! I saw many other soldiers doing the same thing."

As the second and third waves, loaded in LCVPs, hit the reef, they bottomed out. A dozen ramps went down, and 165th RCT assault troops of Lt. Col. Gerard W. Kelley's 1st Battalion and Lt. Col. Joe Hart's 3d Battalion, the infantry commanders leading the way, surged forward into the sharp coral rock formations, the swells often breaking over their heads. Reaching the beach, they moved off north and south to secure the flanks of the beachhead, supported by Stuart M3 light tanks. At five-minute intervals from then on, successive waves of three hundred landing craft with men and material were supposed to land— chief among them twenty-two hundred men with tanks, jeeps, AT guns, and field artillery. Everything depended on moving as fast as possible before the Japanese recovered from the shock of the preassault bombardment. The landing had been successful and casualties light, it seemed. Kelley regrouped his main body of troops directly forward of the beachhead. "Move out," he told them. The men of the 27th Infantry Division struck off inland.

Aboard the Fifth Fleet flagship *Indianapolis,* rounding the southwest corner of Tarawa after completing an independent fire mission, Rear Admiral Spruance trained his binoculars on the squat, unwieldy LVTs making their top speed of four knots toward the beaches. As the flagship drew nearer Betio, she joined in the bombardment again, and the island shuddered under the impact of more HE shells. The troops, the men of the 2d Marine Division, were moving steadily in and "Sprew" wanted to watch. Up to a few hours before, he had hoped that the naval and air bombardment would make the massive operation almost superfluous. His chief of staff, Capt. Charles J. "Carl" Moore, shared his confidence. "Fires were burning everywhere," he said. "The coconut trees were blasted and burned, and it seemed that no living soul could be on the island . . . the troops approached the beach, and it looked like the whole affair would be a walkover."

But now, although the clouds of smoke seemed to confirm that the warships were finding targets, few men on the bridge were as certain as they had been. They had heard over the TBS the shocking news from natives who had paddled out to the task force that the tides at Tarawa would be low and erratic. No one was prepared to alter the plans, even if it were possible, and only a few were prepared to accept the information as the truth. Supremely confident of the men he had chosen to plan and command the operation, Spruance declined to intervene or inquire about the intelligence. The information, if it was at all accurate, had simply arrived too late for it to make any difference. The orders remained the same—"The 2nd Division will attack and seize Tarawa Atoll."

Thus, even more emphatically, it became everyone's prayer that the naval gunfire and air attacks would provide the margin of victory— that the Japanese defenders would be shell-shocked and incapacitated, their coastal batteries and field artillery destroyed, and the island cratered with massive shell holes. But, with gunnery observers unable to see clearly through the smoke and dust surrounding the island, and frightened that the big warships would shell friendly forces, the bombardment was lifted at 0855. The assault waves were still an astonishing twenty minutes from shore.

The last air attack by Dauntlesses and Hellcats was similarly affected. Diving from high altitude, the bombers loosed their loads indiscriminately wherever they suspected a target. The unnatural darkness ruled out any possibility of aimed bombing. After making strafing runs, one after the other, the fighters zoomed back out to sea. The well-meaning aircrews unloaded their bomb loads and .50-caliber cartridge belts as best they could but not where they were needed most—on the deadly guns and fortifications behind the lagoon seawall.

That the timing of the operation had been thrown completely out of sync was unknown to most of the marines. Neither was it suspected that before the first LVTs would hit the beach, the Japanese would be afforded ample time to make the appropriate dispositions to meet the landings in force. But Spruance was not greatly alarmed. Unaware of the delays in the air attacks, and with nothing to rely on except what infrequent radio reports his staff aboard *Indianapolis* could intercept and piece together, he had no reason to suspect that anything was drastically wrong. The men of the 2d and 8th Marines were heading for Betio, similarly unaware that the jagged, rock-hard coral reef might be exposed, forcing them to wade in under murderous fire.

By now the island was in sight, and troops still entertained thoughts about an easy landing. But when the long lines of assault craft began to draw AA airburst artillery fire while still three thousand yards from shore, it was clear that the enemy guns would no longer remain silent.

The battle had suddenly become very real and life threatening. As the naval bombardment dissipated and the planes left the area, H hour was not far away for the men in the first three waves.

The airbursts exploded overhead like giant firecrackers, and peppered the assault craft with shell fragments and buckshot. Marine drivers controlling the LVTs of the 2d Amphibious Tractor Battalion became the first casualties in the drive for the island. They stood erect and exposed in the open control cabs as they went about their jobs of getting the vehicles and loads ashore. In contrast, the marines crouched low in the craft suffered few serious injuries from the airbursts. The rounds were too scattered and highly charged to be effective against targets so low in the water. Yet the marines and landing craft crews would never forget the concussions and the hot grains of steel that stung their faces.

At two thousand yards, through all the deafening noise from the enemy AA artillery and gunfire from *Ringgold* and *Dashiell,* which alone among the warships had continued firing, another more ominous racket could be heard. It was infinitely more frightening and possibly more deadly than anything else. Japanese long-range heavy machine guns had opened up, and their bullets were ricocheting off the sloped, lightly armored fronts of the LVTs. In a matter of minutes a few vehicles fell out of formation, their mechanization and drives gone haywire from lucky hits, or driven off course, zigzagging crazily as their drivers struggled to regain control.

An infectious anxiety spread among the men in the assault waves. The awful sound of the naval cannonade combined with the Japanese fire seemed to be right on top of them. It appeared impossible that men could have survived the holocaust of steel and fire that had flayed the island over the past three hours, so how could there still be Japanese firing at them, they wondered. Here and there squad leaders raised their heads above the sides of landing craft to check the distance yet to be covered, and, disconcerted, ducked down again.

Up ahead close combat already had commenced at the end of the six-hundred-yard Burns-Philp pier. With naval gunfire still roaring, a scout-sniper platoon led by twenty-nine-year-old Lt. William D. Hawkins, of El Paso, Texas, assisted by assault engineers, was going in to silence enemy positions along the pier. "Hawk," as everybody knew him, had been commissioned in the field for "conspicuous courage and strong leadership" in the furious first month's fighting at Tulagi and Guadalcanal. Later, still at Guadalcanal, for days at a time behind enemy lines, he had led long-range reconnaissance patrols of the 2d Marines forward intelligence section. Since then he had trained his men until he believed, "The thirty-four men in my platoon can lick any two hundred-man company in the world."

Long-range patrols would not be necessary on Betio, but there were plenty of other things to deal with. Machine-gun nests were slung beneath the pier on platforms and protected by sandbags, rifle positions were located among the shacks near the seaplane ramp at the end of the pier, and mines or booby traps probably had been laid. Intelligence believed that the enemy positions could endanger the assault forces with enfilading fire on either side. One rumor had it that the Japanese had rigged explosives to the drums of gasoline stacked on the pier head, intending to blow up the pier to deny its use to the Americans, who needed it intact to supply the beachhead.

Hawkins and his men were supposed to land at the base of the pier fifteen minutes ahead of the first assault wave at 0845. Under the cover of the naval bombardment, they would knock out the enemy positions, clear the pier head, and drive down the finger to the shore. Yet their three LCVPs were nowhere near the pier when they should have been. The adjustments to the timetable had led to chaos, and the current had slowed the LCVPs. By the time Hawkins got the landing craft on track, much time had been lost. The delay cost the commando force their naval gunfire cover, which lifted at 0855. Not a shot was fired at them directly until they were near the objective. Then it was a different story. Small-arms and machine-gun fire flayed the high plywood sides and slanted steel bow ramps of the boats.

Second Lieutenant Alan G. Leslie, of Milwaukee, Oregon, commanding a five-man team of combat engineers of the 18th Marines, approached from the west flank in the lead boat. The crew nudged the LCVP close enough for Leslie and his men to climb onto the pier, then backed off and began circling. Some of the marine and naval officers doubted that Leslie could accomplish his mission. A former enlisted man, he had only recently been made an officer. Warrant Officer John F. Leopold recalled, "On the ship they were giving odds of ten to one against that he would come out alive."

It was now 0857. The boat with Hawkins and his section approached from head-on. They would storm the pier itself after Leslie and the engineers had cleared the seaplane ramp. Hawkins leapt onto the pier. The commandos were twelve minutes late, but it was clear that the first assault waves also would not land on time. For now the forlorn entourage was alone.

The fighting was wild and frantic. Again and again Leslie's flame-thrower roared, spewing long streams of flaming liquid. An equipment shed and another small building shielding enemy riflemen were engulfed in fire. Mortar shell after mortar shell rained down from shore, and 13mm machine guns raked the pier head. Out in the lagoon, the assault waves "were still about fifteen hundred yards offshore," Warrant Officer Leopold remembered, "when there was a tremendous explosion at the end of the Japanese main pier. 'Thank God,' someone yelled. 'Leslie made it.'" A fuel dump near the seaplane ramp had blown up. Marines in the landing craft cheered and slapped each other on the back.

Off the pier head, the commandos waited, circling. Japanese popped up from their hiding places in protective niches under the pier, or in light landing barges moored along its side, and lobbed grenades and fired their *arisakas*. Hawkins and Leslie led the engineers across the broad planked esplanade, moving from cover to cover. They were peppered by splinters of wood from the pier flying all around them. Blasting the Japanese, the marines hurled demolition charges, threw grenades, and fired their carbines. Hawkins used his "grease" gun with tremendous ferocity.

The skirmish was as frenzied as it was brief. Some of the men in the LCVPs didn't wait for Hawkins to give them the word to land. One boat maneuvered closer in, and Cpl. Leonce "Frenchy" Olivier, of Eunice, Louisiana, led three marines onto the pier to cover the assault with their rifles. No sooner had they taken cover and let go a few rounds than the Japanese pinned them down. The Rigosentai fought fanatically, despite the fury directed their way by the small group of Americans.

As his messmates watched, horrified, Hawkins hurled himself down the pier, with all the grim, heroic determination that had earned him a commission in the Marine Corps and would make him a legend before his fighting was finished. Some suspected that he was fighting not only the Japanese but hateful memories—of growing up with the severe scars of a childhood burn accident, and of losing work, of being rejected as a volunteer by the army and then the navy because of his cosmetic disfigurement. Within him seethed a defiance, a determination to settle a score of his own for all the difficulties he had had to overcome. A marine sergeant recalled: "You see, 'Hawk' loved trouble. If there was a tough job to do, he'd ask for it." Somehow he kept on going down the pier, twenty to thirty yards toward shore before he turned back.

When the fighting died down the scene was incredible. The pier head itself was afire. The plank decking was burned and blasted. In all, Hawkins, Leslie, and four engineers and four scout-snipers had knocked out at least six machine guns, and now there was not a live Japanese to be seen. The dead—perhaps twenty-five men—were lying all around. The furious fight to clear the end of the pier had lasted all of six minutes. The marine commandos were the first Americans to invade a Japanese-held possession in the Central Pacific. But in the great scheme of things, their preassault action provided merely a footnote to Operation Galvanic. Hardly had Hawkins led his men back to their boats than the Japanese reoccupied the pier.

Three hundred yards farther out, the landing craft moved relentlessly forward. The LVT drivers and their accompanying naval guides saw it first. So did the officers and NCOs peering over the sides. The reef. They could see the *reef*. In between the swells of the outer lagoon, the jagged, razor-edged barrier of coral was visible. A mere three feet of water covered it, and even that appeared to be fast receding. It would be close for the assault waves boated in untracked landing craft.

The marines in the LVTs were cautioned to brace themselves as the amphibious vehicles went aground with sickening crunches—some of them a thousand yards from shore. They were jarred violently, and the men within them were jostled about helplessly. The craft, so ungainly in appearance, shuddered as their crews shifted gears into overland drive and slammed engines to full speed ahead. Treads began grinding and biting into coral.

Admiral Spruance saw the LVTs hit the reef. Some of them stopped dead, their crews unsure what to do; others continued on, climbing up the outer edge of the barrier. They alternately crawled and ploughed their way toward the island. As he watched, their lines became ragged and disorganized. Some vehicles lagged behind, and others appeared to be in trouble. For the first time, Spruance was alarmed. A marine observer aboard a ship off the lagoon said that the Civil War carnage of Pickett's charge at Gettysburg came to mind.

Aboard *Maryland,* Rear Admiral Hill and Maj. Gen. Julian Smith were also watching. Although the delays had been troublesome, it was not thought that matters were serious enough to cause undue worry. But when the LVTs approached the reef, things changed quickly— for the worse. The demeanor of the men on the bridge became one of horror, and there were gasps from the staff officers as LVTs came to a stop. They watched as some of the marines leapt over the sides into the water and began wading, their weapons held high. Other LVTs managed to go on, though poorly organized and incredibly slow. It did not take long for the officers to determine that the worst possible scenario had become a reality: Many men were going to die as they struggled just to get ashore.

Chapter Eighteen

In the large operations room of his massive three-story command post (CP), Rear Admiral Shibasaki listened to the sketchy reports and information about the American tactics received by his staff. Around him, hundreds of men, some of them horribly wounded and screaming in pain, sweated out the bombardment. The way the Americans were going about their attack, by advancing on the island from the lagoon, surprised Shibasaki, but the sheer ferocity of the naval gunfire was his chief concern. That the fortifications would stand up against such unbelievable shelling was something he dared not doubt.

Yet the wasteland around the CP provided no encouragement. Everywhere the island was a devastated no-man's-land of wreckage and blackened sands, uprooted trees, and cavernous craters. Here and there smoke from some unseen fire spiraled upward in billowing columns. There was no sign of life anywhere except in the lagoon, where strange craft—"little boats with wheels," as the Japanese called the American LVTs—were churning steadily for shore. Nearly all above-ground structures—barracks, storehouses, kitchens, garages—were gone. Only ash outlines remained as proof that they once existed. Around the airfield, the hangars, revetments, repair shops, control tower, and observation posts were gone or wrecked. The skeletons of several burned-out aircraft smoldered around the runways. Everything else—ammunition and fuel dumps, vehicles and heavy equipment, including concrete mixers and the narrow-gauge railroad—had been either incinerated or damaged.

Shibasaki could not know, but nearly all the big coastal guns were twisted and broken wrecks. The AA searchlights were shattered. Camouflage screens and netting, which had hidden dugouts and bombproof shelters with great skill and cunning, were stripped away in the storm of fire. The communications network, most of which had been laid above ground, was for all intents and purposes obliterated and the system of signal communications paralyzed. Betio appeared incapable of resisting the enemy about to land on its beaches.

But the island's appearance belied its hidden strengths. As Shibasaki suspected, most of the garrison survived and the men were even now emerging from their hardened shelters. They had lived through the four hours of unprecedented naval and air bombardment protected by bunkers and pillboxes, covered by four- to six-foot layers of concrete, crushed coral, and sand. Each structure had been strong enough to withstand all but direct hits by 16-inch naval gunfire and two-thousand-pound bombs dropped from aircraft. By official counts, no more than three hundred of the defenders were believed to have succumbed to the bombardment. The survivors had quivered and trembled throughout the pounding and earsplitting blasts. The majority of those who died did so not from the destruction of their shelters, but from the concussions and unearthly pressures created by the massed explosions in so small an area. They were found in bunkers after the battle, crushed by the sheer pressure of the air around them.

Though many men had cracked mentally and some committed suicide, most were able to sweat it out. Ensign Ota steeled his frightened men by reminding them of their sworn duty. "The earth shook," he said, and "the sky was a fiery ball. . . . I stayed with my men at our machine guns in a bunker which covered a field of fire on the western lagoon side beach. . . . I thought of my family as shells slammed around us . . . we were flung about like rag dolls by the explosions. . . . I thought of honor and courage and the Mikado. . . . We had taken an oath to give our lives for the Son of Heaven . . . and this was the acid test. I told my men we must not fail or we would dishonor the Emperor, our country and our ancestors . . . and so we endured."

When the bombardment suddenly ceased and the planes flew off to the east, the tense break afforded the Japanese an opportunity to regain their sanity. They emerged to crew their infantry weapons, most of which they found virtually undamaged. Others raced to occupy rifle pits. The defenders positioned on the ocean side of the island rushed for the fortifications facing the lagoon, following trench systems where possible. Small signal flags emblazoned with the symbol of the Ris-

ing Sun appeared from rifle pits and through the firing slits of pillboxes and bunkers. Along the lagoon beaches and the positions emplaced
around the CP, the tiny pennants indicated that defenders lived. It also
meant that the attackers would encounter the deadly fire and bitter
resistance of a determined foe who had survived the most heavily
concentrated bombardment in history.

But Shibasaki had no way of knowing how many had survived. When
the shelling finally ended, he and his staff needed to make contact with
far-flung units, but communications were out. The only radio that had
survived the enemy's bombing attacks of the previous day was a powerful
shortwave transmitter that could communicate only with the Naval General
Staff headquarters in Tokyo. Thus Shibasaki had direct control only
over the three hundred handpicked men of his tough SNLF guard who
were veterans of the fighting in the Solomons and now protected the
area around the command center.

The dazed defenders, shaking uncontrollably from shock, some with
blood running from their ears, noses, and eyes, were amazed that they
were still alive. Some still wore the *hachimaki,* the white headband
that demonstrated contempt and defiance in the face of an enemy and
unqualified willingness to die in battle. Samurai had worn them for
centuries. Other defenders, scratched and cut, their clothes ripped and
shredded, wore *sennimbari,* or "the belt of a thousand stitches," made
by women in the home islands and sent to the men on the various fronts
in the Pacific and Asia. In ancient times, the cotton article had warded
off enemy arrows. In World War II, it was worn around the midriff
as a charm against bullets. Although communications were knocked
out, each man knew his job and the ultimate task of the 3d Konkyochitai—
to engage the enemy at the water's edge and destroy them while they
were still in the water. Wasting no time, the Rigosentai began to do
just that.

The Japanese fire began to grow in volume as the thin line of LVTs
closed in on the focus of all the destruction. Only the destroyers lying offshore in the lagoon continued their shelling, and hundreds of
shells from their fast-firing guns whooshed over the heads of the marines.
Another fearsome sound joined the terrible racket when multibarreled
rocket launchers aboard the LCSs at either end of the assault force
flashed off their racks in packages that careened through the sky, trailing

wisps of white smoke behind them. Fired much too far from shore, none of them reached the island. Instead the projectiles impacted short of the assault beaches. The reef ahead seemed to disappear momentarily behind a wall of bursting rockets and coral.

In the bounding LVTs the drivers and machine gunners could now see the deadly phalanxes of steel and concrete dragon's teeth and barbed wire in front of them. There seemed to be far more obstacles than anyone had briefed them about. In back of the seawall the Japanese still could not be seen. Nothing was exposed. If not for the scattered gun flashes that stabbed the haze and the pinpoints of winking light ahead, the island itself would have appeared deserted.

Nearer and nearer the LVTs moved. Eight hundred yards. Seven hundred yards. Enemy fire was growing heavier, but it was still irregular. In water that was three to four feet deep the LVTs pressed onward as machine gunners began firing. The first wave was about six hundred yards from shore when the Japanese heavy weapons—the ones that the navy presumed would not survive the historic naval and air bombardment—opened up en masse, the likes of which had never been seen in an amphibious assault.

Dual-purpose antiboat guns cracked. Mortars thumped. Artillery thundered and machine guns chattered. From all along the fifteen hundred yards of invasion beaches Japanese guns poured forth a storm of fire into the assault waves, seeking a terrible and swift vengeance for the massive shelling to which they had been mercilessly subjected.

When it became obvious that landings would occur on the lagoon side of the island, the majority of the defenders shifted, so that now in the center of the invasion front more than eight hundred Rigosentai—the equivalent of a reinforced battalion—were dug in and waiting. All along the beaches the Japanese had the advantage. Shibasaki counted on this to be decisive. He did not expect to stop the Americans from reaching shore. But in many places the reef actually jutted out of the water. It would negate any attempt at quick reinforcement of any beachhead that might be established. For the most part the enemy would have to cross the reef on foot, and throughout the journey they would be under the sights of machine guns and small arms. Shibasaki anticipated that the first waves would be pinned down on the beach, while his gunners decimated the reserves.

The farther the Americans had to wade, the better. The guns had long been zeroed in on the reef, with exact coordinates predetermined and notched on the shields of the weapons. There, on that cruel and ugly barrier, was the sole chance to stop the attack. Shibasaki knew that the Americans would want to reach the island and engage the Japanese as far inland as possible.

Behind the seawall there were more than forty artillery pieces and dozens of machine guns. Ammunition was sufficient for only about three days of battle; much of the machine-gun ammunition had been shot off in the past few days during the relentless air attacks. Half of the tanks had been entrenched so that only their turrets showed. The armor stationed around the CP was ordered to move out. Trundling from their harbors, shaking loose sand and debris from themselves in the effort, five tanks left to find suitable firing positions behind the beaches.

It now remained for Shibasaki's troops to hold off the Americans, destroy them if feasible, and await help from the Imperial Combined Fleet in the air and at sea.

PART THREE

The Horror

Chapter Nineteen

The Americans crested the reef at Tarawa in the lightly armored LVTs that Holland Smith had insisted be provided for his marines. The men hunched lower in their landing craft as the sudden impact of the Japanese fury became evident.

In the assault waves were men who had survived the horrors of the fighting in the Solomons. Leading on the right and in the center were the 2d Marines, who had bled during the darkest months of the savage fighting on Guadalcanal. They had earned battle stars at obscure, strange-sounding places such as Halavo, Gavutu, Tulagi, Tanambogo, Gurabusu, and Koilotumaria. Many had actually landed at Guadalcanal with the 1st Marine Division and fought there throughout the entire campaign. On the left, the assault was spearheaded by the 8th Marines, whose jungle tactics had so harassed the Japanese in the final drive on Guadalcanal. Although every unit in the South Pacific had suffered from malaria, the 8th Marines had experienced an additional agony—elephantiasis, a disfiguring enlargement of tissue caused by parasitic worms. Many of its men had been stricken with the monstrous affliction in Samoa.

Among the 2d Marine Division also were units—and a few veteran NCOs and officers—that had fought at Chateau Thierrey and the Meuse Argonne in World War I. Many others had been in action during the Long Armistice in the "banana wars" in Latin America. Now here was another battle ahead of them. This one, before it would end four days later, would go down in military history as "the Tarawa killing ground." After the battle, *Time* magazine would trumpet, Tarawa "gave the nation a name to stand beside those of Concord Bridge, the *Bonhomme Richard,* the Alamo, Little Big Horn and Belleau Wood."

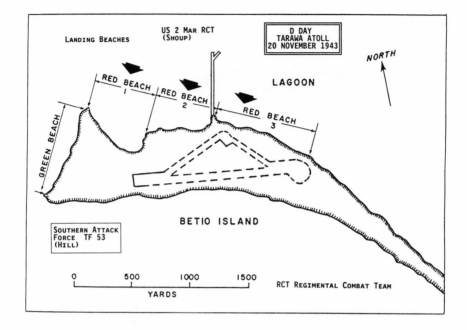

LANDING BEACHES

US 2 MAR RCT
(SHOUP)

D DAY
TARAWA ATOLL
20 NOVEMBER 1943

NORTH

RED BEACH 1

RED BEACH 2

LAGOON

RED BEACH 3

GREEN BEACH

BETIO ISLAND

SOUTHERN ATTACK
FORCE   TF 53
(HILL)

0   500   1000   1500

YARDS

RCT REGIMENTAL COMBAT TEAM

The most intense fire was coming from a large complex of pillboxes and bunkers in the center of the 2d Marines front—in the 3d Battalion's zone to the west and 2d Battalion's zone to the east. Here at the junction of Red 1 and Red 2, the Japanese had their heaviest concentration of machine guns and artillery positioned to create precision-sighted cross-fire zones across a thousand-yard front. Some marines would remember the area as "Hell's Kitchen," but it would later be better known as "The Pocket." Fully two-thirds of the approaching LVTs were subjected to unavoidable enfilading fire from these positions.

To make matters worse, Red 1 was the only irregular-shaped assault zone, indented with a deep cove. The boundary with Red 2 occurred where the shore straightened out again in a smooth sweeping pattern to the tail end of the island about two miles away. Within that crescent-shaped cauldron the marines met fire so heavy that hopeless chaos was immediate. Aboard the battleship *Colorado,* QM Walker M. Gunter could see all too well what it was like for the men going in: "I had a panoramic view of the invasion. As the waves of craft approached Betio, a shore battery opened up. You could see its flash as it fired. Sometimes the big shells splashed in the water; at other times you could see the black smoke of a direct hit."

On all three invasion beaches men met heavy fire as their LVTs moved in, but the assault troops headed for Red 1 never had a chance. Japanese gunners behind the seawall were almost eye level with the LVTs that crawled and swam into this beach. To the defenders, the ungainly, terrapin-like vehicles hardly seemed to be moving. Even over the most favorable terrain, the LVTs would have been no match for the battery of 70mm dual-purpose guns emplaced on the western end of the cove, or for the batteries of 37mm rapid-firing field guns and 70mm howitzers farther east. A half-dozen heavy twin-mounted 13mm machine guns were also in action. Their interlocking fields of fire were devastating.

The main assault troops for Red 1 came in aboard thirty-one LVTs and were very hard hit. Five of the tracked vehicles were struck by shells and burned or were sunk outright. Drivers at the controls, trying heroically to coax the craft ashore, were fully exposed to the storm of steel and fire. These men were swiftly hit. Some LVTs had been slowed by the outer reef, then were unable to climb the shelf in the face of the enemy fire. The ones that made it as far as halfway to the cove were, for the most part, driven off course and channeled by obstacles and gunfire toward the extreme northwest corner of the island—the "bird's beak."

Some drivers, finding that they were unable to thread their way through the offshore jungle of concrete tetrahedrons and barbed-wire obstacles, instinctively veered right or left, seeking less heavily defended stretches of beach. Trying doggedly to reach the shore, they where shelled fiercely. Here and there an LVT would be hit, begin burning furiously, then stop dead. If the men in the doomed vehicles were alive and able to do so, they plunged over the sides into the water, where they were mauled by machine-gun fire as they started wading.

"An anti-boat gun stopped our craft about thirty yards from shore," recalled Pfc. Richard M. Larsen, riding in a first-wave LVT. "We were in the midst of all kinds of fire. We jumped out into the shallow water and ran around to the back of the craft. A bullet hit me in the left side of the back of my neck. There were four of us behind the tractor, and we were trapped there. They threw mortar shells, machine gun bullets, and rifle bullets at us."

The driver of Pfc. Newman M. Baird's LVT, loaded with twenty-five men of Company I, was killed by machine-gun fire one hundred yards from shore. A lieutenant leapt forward, pulled the dead man from the controls, and drove the landing craft until he too was hit. Then a shell struck the LVT and it stopped thirty yards from shore. The men were bowled over by the concussion and sent sprawling all over the LVT. Stunned and under machine-gun fire, Baird, an Oneida Indian from New York, looked around and found his assistant, who had been feeding the LVT's machine gun as Baird had fired. "He was crumpled up beside me," said Baird, "with his head forward, and in the back of it was a hole I could put my fist through. I started to shake him and he fell right on over."

Baird noticed that some of the men's helmets and gear had been lost. Several men were dead or seriously wounded; others had simply disappeared. Just five feet away one of his buddies lay on the deck of the LVT. "He was on his back and his head was all bloody and he was holding his hand over his face and mumbling something." Baird took charge of the stunned group, shouting, "Let's get the hell outa here!" He grabbed his rifle and an ammunition box and went over the side. For Baird and the remnants of the platoon—about a dozen men—the horror had just begun. It would seem like forever before they got to the beach and found shelter behind the seawall. There, another marine would pull an inch-long sliver of steel from Baird's back. Only Baird and three others from the LVT made it to the cover of the coconut-log barricade.

Though the fire was intense and the noise of the battle deafening, here and there men were coming through. The storm into which Company K ploughed was typical. Commanded by Capt. James W. Crain, a Guadalcanal veteran, the unit was supposed to land on the left side of Red 1. However, it was so hard hit that when its first elements touched shore at 0910—the earliest of all the Tarawa landings—casualties already were serious enough that it seemed doubtful they could even establish a foothold. In effect, the company no longer existed. It had been decimated. Survivors who had endured a nightmare to reach the beach now were subjected to constant enfilading fire from The Pocket.

First Lieutenant Joseph O. Schulte moved to the front of his LVT with the riflemen who had been manning the vehicle's .30- and .50-caliber machine guns. He commanded the 1st Platoon. To his right was 1st Lt. Wilbur E. Hofmann heading into the center of the cove with the 2d Platoon, followed by 2d Lt. James Fawcett with the 3d Platoon. As Schulte came within two hundred yards of shore, he ordered his machine guns into action. No sooner had he begun to direct their fire than enemy machine guns began responding from all directions. As he stood erect pointing out targets, a hail of fire fell upon the LVT, and bullets struck his shoulder and wrist. In the same instant, the LVT driver was killed and his assistant rushed to the controls. Both machine gunners were wounded but refused to abandon their weapons until the vehicle reached the seawall. Schulte succeeded in getting his men out of the craft before he fell unconscious on the beach. When he regained his senses, he found himself in the sand beside the body of his dead radioman.

Fawcett came in some distance away from Schulte, whose LVT had been driven off course by heavy fire. Fawcett, a fourth-year marine, had commanded a tank at Guadalcanal; now the twenty-four-year-old Washingtonian was an infantry officer. He watched intently as Lieutenant Hofmann's platoon went in. Several machine guns converged on the 2d Platoon vehicle as men began leaping over the sides. Fawcett watched for Hofmann to get out but did not see him. He knew why when one of the LVT machine guns opened up. Hofmann had stayed behind to cover his men as they dashed to the seawall. Just as Fawcett landed, Hofmann's LVT took a direct hit and exploded, disappearing in a suffocating cloud of smoke. Hofmann and several wounded were killed in the blast.

Company I, which had been farthest away from The Pocket, suffered less, but only by a matter of degrees. Its veteran company commander, Capt. William E. Tatom, disregarding the heavy enemy fire, raised himself over the bulkhead of his third-wave LVT. He was trying to pick out his lead platoons, or possibly one of the shore batteries or machine guns firing on the assault waves. Although it may have been a natural act on Tatom's part, it proved an unfortunate one. "He had been standing for only a moment when he just fell backward onto the troop deck," said a man who had been watching. "He just sort of grunted when he was hit. He'd taken a bullet directly in his forehead. He was dead before he hit the deck."

A coconut-log barricade on the western half of the beach offered some protection from the merciless fire, but not nearly enough. About twenty yards from shore Company I riflemen, some with their clothing on fire, jumped from their LVTs and quickly sought whatever cover could be found. Within a few minutes some survivors had gone over the log barricade and infiltrated inland about the same distance as Company K on their left—to a depth of fifty yards. Here they were pinned down, unable to either defend themselves or pull back to the beach. Along the way they silenced a brace of dual-purpose guns firing from the bird's beak.

As the fourth wave grounded on the reef off Red 1, the men could see through the smoke and dust a graveyard of burning, twisted hulks and tiny knots of men seeking shelter behind the seawall. The lagoon was under heavy fire, evident by the splashes of large-caliber shells and the tracers of machine guns. It was into this inferno that Company L arrived. Their young and tough commander, Maj. Michael P. Ryan, of Osage City, Kansas, scanned the shore. It was clear that there had been a disaster. Red 1 was a shambles. More than half of the beach was still in Japanese hands. Very few LVTs were visible; to Major Ryan it appeared that "most if not all" had been knocked out. Only a few marines could be seen on the eastern half, where by now there should have been hundreds. Little could be seen of the western half, where heavy smoke indicated that frantic close combat was taking place. Ryan grimly ordered his men into the water. They would have to wade to shore.

The Sherman tanks that were scheduled to support the assault troops were held up at the reef. The plan was for a platoon of six tanks under the command of twenty-three-year-old Lt. Edward Bale, of Dallas, Texas, to land in the fourth wave as near the beach as possible, then crawl over the reef to shore. When the LCMs carrying them reached the reef, their coxswains turned the barges away in search of a gap in the reef. Overcome by the destruction before them, the LCM crews were milling about when the command boat carrying the battalion commander, Maj. John Schoettel, appeared at the reef. He directed Bale to land the tanks where they were and take them in. The ramps were dropped and the Shermans were launched in four-foot swells—eight hundred yards from shore. Bale, in his command tank "China Gal," led them toward the island.

Tragedy was swift in finding the special armored reconnaissance troops who jumped into the water to guide the tanks. No sooner had they gone ahead to place flags marking craters and other obstacles than they were met by fierce enemy fire. Nearly all were killed or wounded. Bale led the tanks into the eastern half of Red 1, which was under the heaviest fire. The beach was littered with destroyed LVTs and the inert bodies of dead, dying, and wounded marines who could not be moved because of the intense fire.

Rather than run his tanks over the pitiful forms, Bale decided to land on the northwest corner of the island. As the tanks maneuvered in the water, buttoned up under the enormous fire, four fell into shell holes. One after another, they foundered and sank or their engines were drowned out. Men came scrambling up out of the hatches and plunged into the water. Many succeeded in reaching the seawall, but some were cut down before they could find cover. Only two tanks, including "China Gal," battered repeatedly by 40mm and machine-gun fire, were still heading for shore. The loss of these tanks would cost the 3d Battalion dearly.

Schoettel surveyed the hell of Red 1. Company L was wading in, and it was apparent that the volume of fire its men were taking was terrible. But that was the extent of Schoettel's knowledge. He and his command group began to disembark, but they encountered equally severe fire. Schoettel decided to remain at the reef and direct the operation from his boat. Before the first LVTs had returned from the beach, an unidentified voice, believed to have been a Company K marine, broadcast in the clear: "Have landed. Unusually heavy opposition. Casualties 70 percent. We've had it. Can't hold. We're licked."

As the fourth- and fifth-wave boats beached and the men began to wade ashore, the Japanese machine-gun and 70mm artillery fire seemed to increase, and many shells burst among the incoming troops. Dozens of men went down and did not get back up. A bullet struck Sgt. James A. Bayer a stunning blow on the crown of his head, just above the hairline. Blood gushed over his face as he fell helmetless into the water. The shock did not last long. Perhaps the water revived him. Realizing that to stay in the water meant certain death, he was soon up and moving the only way he could—on all fours. He reached the seawall and scrambled around a pillbox until he found cover.

Coast guardsman Carl Jonas and a shore party entered the water at the reef and immediately encountered groups of men returning to the boats. "Suddenly," he said, "we realized with a shock that they were some of the wounded." The shore party helped the injured marines as best they could. The carnage was terrible; the dying men, fighting to keep their heads above water, "were reaching up, like the men in the Italian primitive paintings of the damned in hell."

The boat in which WO John Leopold was approaching the island tried four times to cross the reef with its load of 37mm antitank (AT) guns. On each occasion the coxswain turned back because of the heavy opposition. In one instance a 5-inch shell exploded ten feet from the bow. "It was just too damn bad," recalled Leopold. "The tracers and bullets cracked through the air like pistol shots, coming so fast it was like popcorn. The tracers crisscrossed, and the whole area was a pattern of thin red lines of flame. Every now and then an amtrac would go up in flames, and I saw two Higgins boats go the same way."

Hundreds of wounded, weaponless, leaderless men streamed back toward the boats and reef—away from the wholesale slaughter off Red 1. Companies K and I suffered the highest casualties—50 percent each in sixty minutes—and Company L suffered nearly as badly. Every hundred yards they waded, their ranks were thinned as men were killed or wounded, disappeared in explosions, took refuge behind burned-out wrecks, or simply turned back. By the time Major Ryan reached the beach—he had hitched a ride on an LVT until it was destroyed and the driver killed—the company had lost 70 marines. Only 110 were left, and these were scattered and disorganized. By noon the company's effective fighting strength would be reduced even further.

It seemed that the 3d Battalion had been all but eliminated. Of the assault troops who had answered roll call aboard the transports before dawn, half were now killed, wounded, or missing. The remainder were dispersed or held up at the edge of the reef. Of the three hundred men ashore, only the remnants of Company I were operating effectively, and they were out of contact with everyone. The assault waves had been reduced to forlorn little groups of men fighting merely to stay alive against heavy rifle and machine-gun fire sweeping the narrow shelf of sand and forbidding movement.

"We swore everybody on the beach was dead," said Warrant Officer Leopold. "We thought no one was alive because we didn't see how any got in. I had asked the night before how many men were going in before me. They told me several hundred in each wave. That would be more than a thousand men. I don't believe more than three hundred came through unscratched. The beach should have been called Annihilation Beach," he said. "It was red with blood."

Schoettel contacted Col. David Shoup, the overall assault commander, and explained his situation: "Receiving heavy fire all along beach. Unable to land. *Issue in doubt.*" Shoup himself was at the time under heavy fire off Red 2. He was unable to acquire a clear picture of what was happening immediately in front of him, much less on Red 1. He told Schoettel to land on Red 2 with the survivors of his shredded battalion and attack The Pocket from the rear. All who heard Schoettel's distraught reply were shocked. "We have nothing left to land," he radioed.

Chapter Twenty

The heroic marine commando force, led by Lt. William Hawkins and his scout-snipers, had continued with the dangerous duty of securing the pier between Red 2 and Red 3. Not only were they still under murderous fire but they were unable to navigate the length of the pier in their LCVPs because of the reef. They went to work knocking out enemy strongpoints among the pilings. In the brief time the commandos had before the assault waves bore down on Betio, they cleared half the length of the pier.

Working under conditions of furious desperation, the assault engineers under Lt. Alan Leslie were similarly frustrated in their attempts to get ashore. Their boat became fouled on the reef and they had to back off as Japanese riflemen sniped at them. The engineers watched helplessly as the first assault waves came in aboard LVTs, rumbled over the reef, and waddled past them toward the island. When Leslie saw an empty LVT returning from the beach, he waved it down and ordered its wild-eyed driver to take the engineers into the battle.

The difficulties that Leslie encountered in finding a ride were no worse than those that held up Hawkins and his men. The LCVP carrying the scout-snipers in ahead of the assault waves had been machine-gunned. The fire indicated that the gun was located beneath the pier. Hawkins made several passes but found nothing. He set about finding a way to get to the beach. When the boat grounded, he commandeered an outbound LVT. The Japanese, seeing the LVT working its way down the pier, singled it out for special attention. Gears grinding and treads clanking, the LVT was immediately taken under fire by an antiboat gun, which straddled it with several near misses.

Small-arms and machine-gun fire raked its sides. Again and again mortar rounds rained down, spraying the vehicle with shell and coral fragments. The LVT machine gunner poured a steady stream of lead into the pier at point-blank range as the driver tried to maneuver close to shore.

The scene was savage. The LVT gunner kept up his intensive fire until he fell over dead, his chest blasted open by a machine-gun burst. Hawkins leapt forward and took over the weapon. In a matter of minutes the LVT crashed through a spur in the seawall and up onto the base of the pier. Some of the scout-snipers did not wait for the craft to clear the narrow beach before vaulting over the sides. Said a lieutenant of Hawkins, he was "a madman. He cleaned out six machine-gun nests, with two to six Japs in each nest. I'll never forget the picture of him standing on that [LVT], riding around with a million bullets a minute whistling by his ears, just shooting Japs. I never saw such a man in my life."

The commandos plunged into the smoke of the explosions and fire sweeping the base of the pier. They rushed into a no-man's-land of trenches, rifle pits, and buildings. Mortar rounds fell in their midst, and small-arms and *nambu* fire poured out to oppose them. Out front the commandos dived for cover, pulled themselves up, and advanced again and again. Bullets whined. Sergeant Francis P. Morgan, of Salem, Oregon, went down mortally wounded, "shot in the throat," said a corporal. "He was bleeding like hell, and saying in a low voice, 'Help me, help me.' I had to turn my head."

By the end of the day casualties among the commandos would be almost a third. Hawkins himself would be one. But nightfall would find him still fighting despite a shoulder wound from the shrapnel of a shattering mortar blast. He would not be alone. Although only one of their number had been killed, several of the scout-snipers had been wounded to one degree or another. And all of them were fighting on.

The dozen first-wave LVTs leading the 2d Battalion into Red 2, which extended from the eastern curve of the cove to the central pier, were also hit by all types of gunfire. Some were disabled and came to a stop, starkly silhouetted in the sights of enemy guns that zeroed in on them. Others went wildly off course, drivers dead, controls mangled, occupants helpless to do anything but wait for the craft to stop. Eventually they would crash into the seawall, become tangled in dense barbed-wire jungles, smash into some other form of barricade, or end up on the wrong beach—if they were not knocked out first.

LVTs spilled shocked, wounded, and dead men indiscriminately. In the center of the attack there was nowhere to maneuver forward to avoid the flanking fire from The Pocket. The whole area ahead was swept by machine guns placed in pillboxes all along the seawall on Red 2—no more than thirty yards from the water's edge. These positions kept the narrow strip of sand and the reef under saturating fire. Before the first LVTs beached at 0917, many drivers and gunners had been either killed or wounded. As the amphibious craft were hit, crews and assault troops went over the sides. Once in the water their chances of survival lessened dramatically again.

Staff Sergeant William J. Bordelon's LVT carrying Capt. Warren "Lefty" Morris, the twenty-five-year-old Company F commander from Arkansas, and a flamethrower and demolitions platoon of the 1st Battalion, 18th Marines, was blown out of the water twenty yards from shore. Hit successively by several shells, it was finally rent apart in a tremendous blast. It seemed impossible that anyone could have survived. Bordelon, an assault engineer from San Antonio, had enlisted right after Pearl Harbor. Now he led four others, including Morris, in salvaging what they could. They climbed out of the twisted wreck and started wading. By the time Bordelon, Sgt. Elden H. Beers, of Deer Park, Washington, and Pfc. Jack G. Ashworth, of Los Angeles, reached the island, they and the company commander had become separated. The other survivor had been killed.

The second-wave LVT carrying Maj. Henry C. Drewes, from Jersey City, New Jersey, commanding the 2d LVT Battalion, made three tries to get ashore, only to be driven back on each occasion by hostile fire. As shells exploded all about his vehicle, Drewes, standing beside the machine gun in the cupola, made light of each burst and the fierce Japanese opposition with a smile or humorous gesture. The former insurance salesman was killed by a bullet through his head, and was dead before he could have possibly known what hit him. "He died," the men with him said, "with a grin on his big, ruddy face."

Drewes's executive officer, Capt. Henry G. Lawrence, of Albany, Georgia, succeeded him. He was convinced that quickly few defenders had been killed or were shell-shocked. He watched dumbstruck as his vehicles were hit by shell fire. Small-arms rounds came through the sides of his vehicle. As the craft bored in on the beach, he was amazed to see enemy troops standing on the beach and seawall, throwing grenades. His driver was killed and the LVT disabled. His crew chief had his hand blown off while throwing an enemy grenade out of the vehicle. Lawrence put a tourniquet—a piece of hemp line—on the man's arm. He took control of the damaged LVT and ran it over barbed-wire entanglements just off the beach. Marines ahead crouched behind the seawall. Some were up and over it, engaging the enemy in hand-to-hand combat. Japanese and American dead lay on the beach and in the water.

Japanese also lobbed grenades into another first-wave LVT, coined "The Old Lady" by her crew, as it lumbered up to the seawall. Corporal John J. Spillane, a semipro baseball pitcher before the war, scooped up the first one and threw it at the seawall, then grabbed others and flung them back. One he caught in midair. He snared a third, fourth, and fifth, and threw them at the Japanese. Screams were heard behind the seawall. A machine gun ceased firing. A sixth grenade tumbled into "The Old Lady" and he snatched it up, but his luck had run out. It detonated, tearing his pitching hand to shreds. The men tended his wound as best they could, then clambered over the sides of the LVT and into the fight. For Spillane the war was over. A surgeon later amputated his ruined right hand.

Five hundred yards from shore twenty-three-year-old Cpl. Byron D. Beckwith, of Greenwood, Mississippi, a machine gunner aboard a first-wave LVT, directed .50-caliber fire left and right, trying to keep the enemy pinned down. Beckwith fired until his gun thwarted him. When it jammed four hundred yards out, he moved the rear-mounted .30 caliber to the forward gun mount. Enemy fire poured in from the front and flanks and penetrated the sides of the LVT, killing and wounding men in the troop compartment and disabling the light machine gun. Beckwith remained fully exposed behind the useless weapon as encouragement to the marines about to leap into the fight. He remained there until he was shot from his perch. A bullet struck him in the thigh, "like someone driving a hot spike all the way through."

Corporal Obie E. Newcomb, a thirty-four-year-old combat photographer from Westchester, New York, was going into action for the first time. He was amazed that the twenty-six assault troops in his first-wave LVT were wisecracking on the way in. With mortal danger ahead of them, shells dropping around them, and bullets ricocheting off the LVT's frontal armor, these veterans of Guadalcanal harassed Newcomb about getting their pictures in *Life* or *Look* magazines. "Anybody want to buy a good watch?" asked one. Another young marine quipped: "I forgot my rubbers—hope I don't get my feet wet." Five men were killed before the LVT reached the beach; another died just as the vehicle landed and took a direct hit.

All along the front the chaos and confusion among the American ranks seemed to whip the Japanese into an increased frenzy of firing. The marines had but one aim—to get through the water, cross hundreds of yards of the obstacle-strewn reef, rush the narrow sand shelf, and then take shelter behind the dubious cover of the seawall. Unable to run in the knee-deep water, burdened by their gear, hundreds were caught in crisscrossing machine-gun and small-arms fire.

Company F, landing on the left half of Red 2, was severely disorganized. Shaken and under heavy fire, its survivors could do little more than dig in where they landed near the base of the pier. Some marines reached the seawall and took cover behind it. A few crawled over it and moved inland. At no point did they gain more than seventy-five yards. From hidden dugouts, from pillboxes just behind the seawall, and from the tops of trees, Japanese fired relentlessly into the men lying exposed in the coral sand.

Company E was able to establish a toehold, but at tremendous cost. In scenes reminiscent of Verdun and the Somme in World War I, men had fallen in uniform rows as they tried to cross the seawall. Small pockets of others huddled here and there behind it.

Meanwhile, Company G landed in the center of the sector and was immediately pinned down. Unable to move, the men had no opportunity to organize, so in pairs and threes, sometimes just one rifleman, they dug in. Only a handful were able to climb over the seawall. First Lieutenant Phillip J. Doyle leapt from his LVT near a pillbox. The Company G platoon leader from Neola, Iowa, scrambled to the top of the seawall and single-handedly charged. He threw a grenade into the pillbox, then jumped in with the enemy. He killed four of them, one after another, with his carbine before they could shoot him.

Everywhere marines were learning that they had landed in assault zones other than the ones to which they had been assigned. The collapse of the assault plan was reflected in the experience of Captain Morris, the Company F commander. Taking a head count, he found that he had under his control six men from his own company, sixteen from Company E, ten from Company C, and fifteen from Company H. Some had landed five hundred yards from their assigned sectors. Numerous platoons scheduled to land on Red 2 and fight westward toward The Pocket discovered themselves east of the strongpoint—in a wholly isolated strip of fire-swept sand in the center of the beach that was the hell of Red 1. Similarly, an H Company medium machine-gun platoon was driven off course by heavy fire and ended up on Red 3. To complicate the confusion, every small group, no matter where it landed along the three-hundred-yard front on Red 2, found itself pinned down by enemy fire and without communications.

One of the first platoons to reach the beach was that of 2d Lt. Tiove H. Ivary. His LVT was caught in a beam of machine-gun fire that the Japanese kept up all the way in. Suddenly, slugs began penetrating the unarmored sides of the vehicle. Horrified, Ivary shouted to his men to get out. As the LVT hit the beach, those who were not dead or injured went over the sides. Ivary was hit in one arm by a bullet, and no sooner had he dropped to the sand than a grenade exploded and shattered his right leg. His men propped him up against the seawall. In shock, weak from loss of blood, he somehow remained in command.

Others were not so fortunate. Men were killed by the score throughout the area marked by the reef, central pier, and northwest corner of the island. Among the dead off Red 2 was twenty-nine-year-old Lt. Col. Herbert Amey, the confident 2d Battalion commander from Pennsylvania. He had commandeered an LVT that took him and half his command group to within several hundred yards of shore before it was stopped by barbed wire and hit by a shell. "Come on! Let's go!" he thundered while leading the eighteen men into the water and splashing forward, gesturing memorably toward shore with his .45-caliber Colt automatic. "Those bastards can't stop us!" Hardly had he taken another breath than he was hit by machine-gun fire, which ripped open his chest and stomach. The courageous battalion commander was killed instantly.

Shortly before he died, Amey had turned to Associated Press correspondent William P. Hipple and said, "I suppose you got a story. Guess the Japs want a scrap." Hipple and the rest of the group now found themselves "in a crossfire from the right and left—machine guns, rifles and occasionally heavy caliber automatic weapons. The bullets hissed in the water alongside all of us," he said. "As the water was now shallower, most of us got down on our hands and knees. We made spurts upright. My head was knocked back slightly. I felt the top of my steel helmet and it was red hot where a bullet had creased it. I dived completely under water, as I did many times afterward, and tried to swim submerged as far as possible." Amey had been in the lead when he went down. Only nine men—half of the group—reached shore.

"It was like being completely suspended, like being under a strong anesthetic, not asleep, not even in a nightmare, but just having everything stop, except pain, and fear and death," said Lt. Comdr. Patrick Grogan, who observed the macabre scene from his fourth-wave boat. "I was afraid. Everybody was afraid. And no one was too proud to admit it."

Those who were hit and were still able to move dragged themselves to the water's edge and lay there. Lieutenant Colonel Alexander B. Swenceski, commanding the 2d Tank Battalion, was blown out of his vehicle into three feet of water. Severely wounded and deep in shock, he was alone and in danger of drowning. He could not reach the water's edge. All about him small islands of dead bodies dotted the reef. Swenceski did the only thing he could think of: With great effort he crawled on top of one of the ghastly cairns of American dead and lay there. He closed his eyes. He would be found there thirty-six hours later, raving but somehow still alive.

Not only were most of the LVTs knocked out, wrecked, or disabled, but soon the twisted wrecks of other types of vehicles contributed to the fearsome seascape. Landing boats piled up on the reef and were blown apart by gunfire. Before long they were joined by tanks, bulldozers, and half-tracks, most of which had had their engines drowned out or had been sunk in deep water. All along the pier and in some places up to the base of the seawall, thousands of dead fish floated.

Gilbert Bundy, of New York, a civilian artist for King Features Syndicate on his first combat assignment, transferred to an LVT at the line of departure. He got to within two hundred yards of the shore when the craft was hit successively by 3-inch naval shells. Miraculously it did not sink. However, twenty-one of the twenty-three men aboard were killed instantly—only two, Bundy and a badly wounded private, survived. "I was standing in the starboard rear behind three

Marines, all of whom were killed outright and blown over me," recalled Bundy. The weight of their lifeless bodies pinned him in the horrific human wreckage on the deck.

Freeing an arm, Bundy opened his first-aid kit and sprinkled sulfa powder into the other survivor's wounds. After struggling for two hours, he eventually freed himself from the pile of dead and pulled the wounded marine inside the LVT's battered cupola. Here the two men sat throughout the rest of the day, as the smoldering craft drifted out of control and Japanese machine guns periodically raked its sides. The men were later rescued, but not before Bundy was mistaken for a Japanese and nearly shot by an LVT salvage crew.

Robert Sherrod and fifteen other men flagged down an LVT, which took them in part of the way. They went over the side into neck-deep water. No sooner had their feet hit the coral than as many as six machine guns were firing at the group of men. Numbed by fear, Sherrod watched as bullets hit all around him, "six inches to the left or six inches to the right." Wading on, he "was scared, as I had never been scared before," but finally Sherrod pulled himself into the shelter of the stanchions under the pier four hundred yards from shore. Bullets splashed around him "like raindrops in a water barrel."

Within thirty minutes the 2d Battalion had been badly beaten. Twenty-nine LVTs had started in. Three were lost in fiery blasts that killed every man in them; three others were sunk in chest-deep water and two were disabled and crashed. One entire company had been put out of action—it actually ceased to exist—and two others were in grievous condition. In all, less than half of the battalion had completed the journey from the edge of the reef to the beach. Casualties in the three assault companies were 30 percent. Many of their officers had been killed or wounded, or were missing. In Company E alone, five of six officers were killed and the other wounded. The men, often without weapons and in shock, huddled at the base of the seawall all morning.

Major Harold K. Throneson, a former Raider who had been at Midway and Guadalcanal and in the Russells, was part of Amey's command group. He returned to the reef to bring in 81mm mortars, which were desperately needed. This meant that Captain Morris was not merely the only company commander ashore on Red 2, he was also the highest ranking remaining officer of the entire 2d Battalion. He was with his understrength composite company behind the seawall. Thus Lt. Col.

Walter I. Jordan, an observer from the 4th Marine Division, assumed command of the battalion.

Jordan, who would later distinguish himself in command of the 24th Marines at Iwo Jima, was stunned to find himself suddenly the senior officer on Red 2. At 1000 he set up his CP in a shell hole in the center of the sector and tried to establish communications. Behind him chaos and confusion reigned. The fourth and fifth waves had arrived in their boats. All along the reef the lowering of their ramps attracted furious Japanese fire as marines jumped into water four to eight feet deep.

Jordan sent out the word: "Situation bad. We need help."

The Tarawa Atoll island of Betio in the central Gilbert Islands. Air reconnaissance photo shows Betio's critical airfield and coral barrier reef, as well as Bairiki and other lesser islands of the atoll stretching to the northeast.

On the deck of a transport en route to the Gilbert Islands a marine intelligence officer uses a terrain model to brief junior officers on Betio Island's formidable strength: heavily gunned steel and reinforced concrete fortifications as well as a labyrinth of anti-invasion and antitank obstacles.

Aboard the battleship USS *Maryland,* bespectacled Maj. Gen. Julian Smith, commander of the U.S. 2d Marine Division, watches D-day naval bombardment and landing craft heading into Tarawa invasion beaches. In center background, arm resting on the splinter shield, is RAdm. Harry Hill, Galvanic Southern Attack Force commander.

Minutes before H hour at Tarawa waves of amphibious tractors race for shore carrying spray-drenched marines. The special landing craft, dubbed "amtracs" by the marines and "little boats with wheels" by the Japanese, proved crucial to the success of the operation.

Struggling inland of the seawall on Betio Island, marines take cover behind blasted palm trees, debris, and sand-covered Japanese bunkers while under heavy enemy fire. Beach sector is unknown, but it is probably Red Beach Three.

One of the most dramatic and human of all Galvanic photos. Two navy corpsmen brave severe fire to help a heavily-laden and wounded marine back to shelter behind the seawall at Betio. Twenty-nine Navy Medical Corps personnel were killed and fifty-two wounded in action at Tarawa.

A burned-out American Sherman medium tank lies amidst the ruins at Tarawa. The Japanese concentrated heavy-weapons fire against supporting American armor whenever an opportunity arose. Such kills, coupled with operational losses, to obstacles and mishaps, cost the 2d Marine Tank Battalion a score or more Stuart light tanks and all but two of fourteen Shermans.

Floating in the surf and sprawled inland of the seawall and around knocked-out amphibious tractors, corpses of marines killed by point-blank fire from hidden machine-gun nests testify graphically to the ferocity of the Japanese defense of "Fortress Tarawa."

Sitting atop a half-sunken Sherman tank (*center background*), a pair of marines survey the gruesome vista of bloated American dead, cut down coming ashore on bloody Red Beach One.

Soldiers of Maj. Gen. Ralph Smith's U.S. 27th Infantry Division prepare to move inland in order to secure the H-hour assault sector on Makin Atoll's Butaritari Island. Although Japanese resistance was light, tough terrain conditions on narrow Red Beach One prevented an orderly landing.

Columns of black smoke from Japanese fuel dumps destroyed by naval gunfire tower behind Makin's Yellow Beach Two as soldiers of the 165th RCT wade ashore against sporadic enemy fire. The third wave was called off until the most dangerous Japanese positions were silenced.

Looking past a dead Japanese, an American soldier considers what is ahead at Makin. In contrast to the marines at Tarawa who fought for control of a sand-swept island, the soldiers on Butaritari contended with jungle and swamps where each tree was a potential hiding place for Japanese snipers.

Chapter Twenty-one

Meanwhile, the third component of the assault from the lagoon was falling into place on the eastern side of the Burns-Philp pier. Major "Jim" Crowe's 2d Battalion of the 8th Marines was coming in on Red 3. In comparison to the raging battles to the west, enemy fire was light on Red 3. But comparison mattered little to the keyed-up men in the assault waves. Shells hit the reef, and machine-gun and rifle fire swept three feet above the surface of the water. Although not the overwhelming enemy opposition that was concentrated against the men landing on the beaches a mile to the west, the enemy fire on the center of the landing beaches at Red 3 was nevertheless plenty heavy.

Thirty-one LVTs began hitting Red 3 at 0922. Two found exits through the seawall near the base of the pier and continued on to the ground beyond. Not many of the Red 3 defenders had been killed by the naval bombardment, but many of those manning the beach fortifications were too dazed to react quickly. The Japanese had been astonished and demoralized to see *Ringgold* and *Dashiell,* the "in close fire support" group, lay to a mere two thousand yards offshore and keep the assault zone under furious 5-inch fire until the marines landed. In some places defenders were found convulsive, lying face down in dugouts and pillboxes, so incapacitated by the destroyer fire as to be helpless. These were bayoneted or dispatched with bullets to the head.

The main reason for the success at Red 3 was blind luck. The landing, for the most part, was heavily concentrated and occurred largely on one half of the beach. Smoke and dust had obscured the landmarks, and heavy wire and concrete obstacles had channeled most of the LVTs to the left half of the sector, to a place where the beach was less heavily defended.

To the men of Lt. Stacy Davis's 1st Platoon of Company F, the landing was a hot one. Private First Class Richard Spooner was aghast at the ferocity "of fire we were pouring at the Nips" as his LVT headed for the island. "Then it appeared as if our craft had been hit, which surprised me. I looked over toward Lieutenant Davis and almost went into shock. Half of his face looked as if it was shot off. 'No, no,' I pleaded, 'this can't be.' It didn't look as if he could possibly survive." Minutes later the LVT took a direct hit and was blown up. Spooner found himself "in water up to my chest, still trying to keep myself in one piece." Davis survived and within minutes of reaching shore led an attack against the Burns-Philp wharf east of the pier where he was wounded again before pulling back to the beachhead.

One LVT after another caught Japanese attention. As the craft carrying Pvt. Donald M. Libby, of Donora, Pennsylvania, came in on the extreme right of the second wave, bullets came through the unarmored sides and he was wounded in both legs. An instant later a mortar shell rocked the vehicle, and Libby was hurled bodily into the lagoon. When he came to, he looked himself over. His body was peppered with bullets and shrapnel, the larger fragments of which he pulled out himself. He clung to the wreckage of the LVT, which now lay on its side.

For hours he waited for help. Finally, about noon, a marine approached. "What state are you from?" the man yelled. Libby, by this time suffering from the onset of shock, realized that something was not right. The man's helmet appeared too large for his head, his rifle was slung across his back, and he carried a bayonet—with a blade shanked at the hilt. Libby rose weakly just as the Japanese, disguised in marine fatigues, attacked. He slashed out with the bayonet, piercing Libby's left hand. The wounded American wrenched the weapon away with his right hand, and clubbed the enemy to the reef. He held the man's head under the water until he drowned. Unwilling to risk further unwanted adventure, Libby began swimming back out into the lagoon. Many hours later, his uniform ripped and torn, his body scratched and bloody, he was fished out of the water by a passing LVT crew.

The assault troops who hit the beach intact were elated, none more so than Major Crowe. The forty-four-year-old redhead was already a Marine Corps legend. He had been an old-time enlisted man as late as 1940. The mustachioed officer—the only battalion commander to successfully land with the assault troops at Tarawa—had cajoled and connived to get this H-hour assignment for his battalion. His first attempt had been turned down, but Crowe had not given up. He argued his case on the grounds that his battalion had earned the right during the training in New Zealand. Colonel Shoup agreed and assigned the 2d Battalion what everyone believed at the time was the toughest objective.

Shoup's gamble paid off. Now behind the assault waves a dozen LCVPs lowered their ramps on the reef, and reinforcements jumped into the water. Ahead lay one thousand yards of gently shelved reef surmounted by the seawall and a belt of pillboxes and bunkers. Crowe's journey to the island had been maddening. As his charging command boat drew abreast of the reef, Crowe viewed the enemy fire pouring out at his men with a fearless intensity. It was known throughout the 8th Marines that he could hardly wait for the fighting to begin.

As the fourth-wave landing boats headed into Red 3, they not only ran afoul of enemy machine guns, they also came under mortar fire. Men dived for cover behind ramps and gunwales. Not Crowe, their commander. He remained standing on the foredeck. A marine remembered, "The boys all hunched low on the troop deck—all except 'Big Jim.' He remained upright, staring angrily at the positions of the Jap guns behind the beach." The man concluded then and there that Crowe was "likely the finest soldiering marine I ever knew."

Crowe's LCVP ground to a halt five hundred yards from shore and its navy coxswain hesitated. Nearby another landing boat bottomed out and the men watched it disintegrate under the impact of a direct hit by a large mortar round. Amid the roar of the diesel engines and the thunder on the reef, Crowe shouted to the coxswain: "Now! For Christ's sake—drop the ramp!" Afraid of sinking, the sailor refused and prepared to turn his boat back toward the lagoon. Nothing the infuriated Crowe said or did could persuade the coxswain to drop the ramp. Crowe yelled over the crump of exploding mortar shells, cursing the sailor roundly, and ordered his group over the sides.

As he plunged into water up to his shoulders, Crowe could see bullets splashing in the water all around. He struck off abreast of his group for the shoreline. Smoke was building up behind the beach. When another man in the party, 1st Lt. Kenneth J. Fagan, saw the fantastic storm into which they were wading, he yelled out to his battalion leader, suggesting that they could all return to the transport for a coffee break if things did not work out. Crowe burst out laughing and continued toward shore.

As Crowe and his men splashed through the surf, other men streamed past them—going the opposite way. Waist deep in the water, oblivious to the gunfire, Crowe halted and, with a strange, maniacal look on his face, moved among their wavering ranks. He turned them around with the sheer force of his personality—and a menacing 12-gauge pump shotgun he waved in their faces—and ploughed on. He had been machine-gunned before—except that in the Solomons he had been in the jungle. As a captain at Guadalcanal, he had howled, "Goddamnit, you'll never get the Purple Heart lying in a foxhole. Let's go get 'em!" He charged a Japanese trench and single-handedly knocked out a machine-gun emplacement. For this conspicuous action he had won a Silver Star and had been promoted on the spot to major. Said a marine combat correspondent of Crowe, "His men spoke about him reverently, in subdued whispers, as one worthy of the highest respect of man and God."

Fifty yards from shore, men going down around him, Crowe came across a crippled LVT. Its motor was running irregularly and the driver was coaxing it shoreward in about three feet of water. Crowe and several others veered toward the LVT and, with machine-gun bullets whining all around, took cover behind it the rest of the way in. As the LVT drove up onto the beach, Crowe suddenly pitched back into the water; the vehicle had run over a mine and exploded with terrific force. The men were knocked on their backs, cut and bruised but otherwise unhurt. The LVT was destroyed. Crowe was angry that it had taken him so long to reach shore but was happy to have made it.

Private First Class William Clear also found himself going in against heavy resistance. "The fire was heavy as hell as we went in. I was scared to death. An eighteen-year-old marine over on my right was not at all concerned. 'Christ, Bill,' he said, 'ain't we giving those Japs hell!' I didn't have the heart to tell him most of that stuff was going the other way." Crowe landed at 0940 and radioed that his battalion was ashore but encountering "heavy opposition." There were casualties, but fewer than he had expected to see after his own experience getting ashore. Totaling his losses after the battle, Crowe would report just twenty-five killed and wounded in landing.

A swift move inland pushed the beachhead to the airfield in several places, widening the area forward of the water's edge to give the assault troops some breathing room. In forty minutes the marines had established a hundred-yard front between the lagoon and the Japanese defenses back of the seawall. One by one, enemy strongpoints over-looking the lagoon fell, but overall little of Red 3 was in American hands. Although no firm contact would be established between the lead assault companies until late afternoon, and enemy small-arms fire was still serious within the beachhead, the 2d Battalion's assault landing was a triumphant success by the standards of Tarawa.

Crowe was personally committed to getting the attack moving. Ignoring the enemy gunfire, he paraded defiantly up and down the beach. Most men, such as Private First Class Spooner, were taken aback at the sight of this burly, straight-backed major with the booming voice who moved fearlessly among them, exhorting them to "move out" and to "get off your asses and over that goddamn wall!" While he was stomping about, five men around him were killed by snipers.

Few dared to defy Crowe's words or risk his wrath; men could see that he clutched his swagger stick in one hand and his shotgun in the other. The effect was all the heroic battalion commander could have hoped for. "I wasn't about to try and swim away," recalled Private First Class Spooner. "I figured if I tried to, that old tiger would beat me to death with that cane of his." Even as Crowe was moving among the frightened survivors of his battalion, reinforcements, guns, tanks, and supplies were piling up at the reef.

Chief Petty Officer Tadeo Oonuki, the former country boy from Kasumigaura, watched the assault landing operation through the ob-servation slit of his navy gray and green camouflaged Type 97 light tank. He could see as far as the reef line through the smoke. He had studied the various approaches to the island for many months. He knew them well. There were sectors where the island was flat behind the beach, with the seawall running for hundreds of yards in either direc-tion east and west. In other sectors, such as the one behind Red 2 where he was, the beach was backed by a low, shallow crest behind the seawall halfway between the airfield revetments and the crescent-shaped cove that was Red 1. The tank was largely hull down, screened from the lagoon by scrub foliage and the cover of coconut trees along the edge of the airfield.

Oonuki had personally chosen this sector, partly because of its suitability for allowing a wide firing arc for his 37mm main gun and twin 7.7mm machine guns, but primarily because it was a point from which he could withdraw quickly if necessary. A strong mobile position was the most important single factor in such a defensive mission. The trails and paths among the pillboxes and bunkers would allow him to range along the perimeter of any beachhead the enemy might succeed in establishing.

Oonuki oriented himself, checking his line of sight. The long pier lay several hundred yards to his right, broken and burning furiously near its end where terrible fighting had raged. The northeastern point of the island, the bird's beak, was far to his left. A terrific wall of smoke blotted out the lagoon. The enemy assault troops had appeared from out of the unnatural haze and come in all the way to the beach aboard the dual-drive "little boats with wheels." Now, however, the direct fire of dozens of pieces of heavy and medium artillery blocked the reef approaches to the enemy reinforcements who disembarked from untracked boats.

The enemy reserves appeared as tiny toys sloshing forward through the water with their heavy packs and equipment, and Oonuki was mesmerized by the spectacle. A ragged wave of tractors returned to the reef and commenced shuttling additional troops, with their heavy radios, machine guns, and mortars, to the far shore. The battle was very different from what Oonuki had imagined it would be during the anti-invasion exercises. There was an uncommon orderliness in the overall direction of the enemy movement, in the desperation of men hurrying to accomplish their crossing of the reef, with sudden violent death hounding them. The noise level, even now that the naval bombardment had lifted, was nothing short of apocalyptic.

There appeared to have been little success to the landing in this sector. The beaches here were shallow—little more than sand strips—and blocked by the seawall. There were no easy points of exit for vehicles or men, and the Japanese artillery shot methodically at the boats on the reef. Despite the ferocity of the enemy bombardment and the devastation it had wrought, numerous guns had survived and now their shells found their mark, shredding the green-clad figures, hurling them about in eruptions of white coral and brown water, and setting their ungainly vehicles ablaze in shattering fountains of flame. Oonuki was astonished by the courage of the Americans.

The blasts and smoke made it difficult to see, but Oonuki soon made out a line of infantry crossing the reef on foot, and he opened fire with his machine guns. He poured short bursts of bullets into the advancing American ranks. Enemy troops fell everywhere, but it was impossible to determine whether the hits belonged to Oonuki or some other Japanese gunner hidden in a bunker or entrenchment nearby. Beyond the pier he saw enemy armor crawling ashore. To his left another pair of tanks was making for the bird's beak. What, wondered Oonuki, would happen if he engaged the tanks in a gun duel?

As he contemplated the alternatives, he was relieved of the necessity to decide. Several hammering blows on the hull of the tank compelled him to look through the lower vision slit. Banging on the tank with his rifle was an exhausted Rigosentai. Oonuki, the man said urgently, was to immediately move his tank back to the command post. With the unpleasant decision of whether to attack the American armor made for him, Oonuki turned his own tank around and wasted no time in driving inland. Behind him the American tanks came ashore. They took up positions and quickly began cracking open Japanese pillboxes with their 75mm guns.

Chapter Twenty-two

A firm grip on what was happening along the invasion front had so far eluded the 2d Marines commanding officer, Colonel Shoup. He had been trying to track the operation's progress from an LCM circling off the reef. The command post of Lieutenant Colonel Amey's battalion was supposed to be in the center of Red 2, about fifty yards from the water's edge. Shoup was unaware that the indomitable Amey had been killed, since contact had been lost with the assault battalions.

The area beneath the pier among the pilings was crowded with marines heading in two directions. Some men were cautiously picking their way forward; others—wounded, fearful of the Japanese resistance—were moving toward the reef, away from the island. The LVTs returning from the beach seemed in equally bad shape. Shoup's radioman broadcast hailings again and again but to no avail. As the command boat circled, it was clear that conditions ashore must be terrible. Shoup was uneasy and worried.

Shoup decided to commit his reserve. The situation seemed the worst on Red 1, so at 0958 he ordered Maj. Wood B. Kyle's 1st Battalion, 2d Marines, to land on Red 2 and work to the west, reduce The Pocket from the flank, and link up with Major Schoettel's isolated and pinned-down remnants on Red 1. Shoup wanted desperately to know what he would find when he finally reached shore.

Determined to get there, he and the 2d Marines command staff boarded an outbound LVT that was transferring its wounded to their boat. Shoup decided to take a roundabout way which would bring him first to the sector of Red 3, lying east of the central pier, before he struck out for the 2d Battalion command post somewhere near the center of Red 2.

180

Though the detour would add almost three hundred yards to his journey, Shoup had good reason for the diversion: Red 3 was apparently under less enemy fire than Red 2.

But as his LVT navigated the boat passage along the eastern side of the pier, things changed. They met a terrific storm of fire, and one of the men in the craft was wounded. A few yards farther, the LVT was delayed. A marine beneath the pier indicated that the enemy still controlled the base of the pier nearest Red 3, and that if Shoup landed there he would be unable to reach Red 2. Shoup could see for himself that troops were retreating under the lee of the pier and he was shocked. The situation was much worse than he had feared. It appeared that the entire assault was endangered. He could not believe that the Japanese defenders had recovered so quickly, or that so much of the front remained in enemy hands. It was also hard to accept that he had to turn back, as his staff was urging him to do.

Shoup ordered the LVT driver to double back and again try the Red 2 side of the pier. They had rounded the pier head and gone about two hundred yards down the western boat passage when a shell struck nearby and the LVT's engine stopped. The driver dived overboard. In the midst of airburst artillery fire, Shoup looked around and saw that further progress was hopeless. Several enlisted men in the craft were wounded.

"Let's get out of here!" shouted Shoup. "Everybody out!" He led the staff over the side but hit the reef and badly wrenched his knee. Nevertheless they worked their way toward the shelter of the pier, which they reached at 1030. Here Shoup commandeered an LCVP he spotted navigating a narrow channel on the west side of the pier. He boarded the craft and ordered it toward shore. They were turned back by heavy fire. He commandeered another outbound LVT filled with casualties. Shoup jumped aboard and discovered that most of the casualties were dead. He ordered the crew to help him throw the bodies overboard, and demanded of his staff: "All right, who's coming with me?"

Only one man rose—Lieutenant Colonel Carlson, the former commander of the raid on Makin. Carlson, an observer of the 4th Marine Division, already had personally led two groups of marines to shore and returned. Shoup shamed the rest of his staff into his waiting LVT. On the way to shore he spotted groups of marines huddling beneath the pier and behind wrecked landing craft. "Which of you yellow sons of bitches are coming with me?" he shouted. Some men reluctantly got up and started for shore.

Shoup headed for the base of the pier, where it appeared that some of the 2d Battalion had landed. It would be noon before he touched sand. Just as he hit the beach a large shell landed with telling effect. Two riflemen behind the group were killed in the blast, and in the concussion Shoup fell to his knees. His horrified staff rushed to his aid, but he pushed them back. "Keep away!" he shouted angrily, battling back nausea and struggling to his feet without their help. Limping, he led them inland. About fifteen yards from the water's edge, the command group found shelter behind a bunker in which three Japanese had been killed. The structure was forty feet long, eight feet wide, and ten feet high. Here, in a hole in back of this fortification, Shoup established his headquarters.

Shoup crawled into the hole, recalled correspondent William Hipple, and said, "OK, let's get going. If we don't secure a piece of this island by nightfall, we're in a spot." His staff tried not to show unnecessary alarm at the sight of his torn and bloodied trousers. The stocky regimental commander had not only badly wrenched a knee but in the explosion on the way in he had taken a painful shotgun blast of shrapnel in the back of his legs.

The determined colonel began to learn the truth about the invasion. Its center ran along the beach and its indentations for a distance of about 250 yards—roughly from the pier now at his back to a point 200 yards east of The Pocket. From Major Rice, the 2d Battalion's executive officer, who had mislanded in the center of Red 1 with a radio, it was confirmed that the western flank was a mess. On the bird's beak and elsewhere around the crescent-shaped cove of Red 1 were the leaderless and embattled survivors of Major Schoettel's shattered battalion. On the west were the companies of the 2d Battalion, 8th Marines. Shoup could piece together very little information about the strength of any of these assault forces.

In his own area, between the two other beachheads, the 2d Battalion, 2d Marines, was holding on precariously but had been badly mauled. Other than the troops holding out around him, Shoup had little but the scant remains of ghost companies. Other groups, officers told him, were not concentrated, and there were units that still could not be accounted for. The bulk of his artillery was immobilized at the reef, sitting on the decks of landing craft near the pier head, which was still burning. A group of Sherman tanks and half-track–mounted 75mm guns were supposed to have landed by now. But one of the tanks had sunk in deep water and the rest had diverted to Red 3. The half-tracks had not even reached the reef. Thus on Red 2 at this moment Shoup had at best only about six hundred men.

Although reserves and any stragglers and splinter groups yet to land would presumably strengthen the forces in the center of the front, at the moment Shoup had nowhere near the reinforced battalion he had expected. Neither he nor Carlson were overly optimistic of the outcome of the battle. But both men refused to give in to defeatism. They saw what many younger, green marine officers did not—that what the 2d Division lacked in veteran troops and experienced officers it might still make up for with the grim dedication and fierce tradition that the Marine Corps imbued in its combat forces. But either way it would be a close thing.

The carnage among the assault troops at Tarawa had been awful. Two battalion commanders—those of the 2d Battalion, 2d Marines, and the 2d LVT Battalion—had been killed outright. A third, the CO of the 2d Tank Battalion, lay critically wounded offshore atop a pile of dead marines, his whereabouts unknown to anyone. A fourth battalion commander was stranded offshore and out of contact with his troops. The assault commander, Colonel Shoup, had been wounded but was still in action. Owing to heavy casualties among leaders and tremendous disorganization, no company had landed with its officer and NCO cadre at full strength.

Not more than twelve hundred marines, the remnants of a reinforced marine amphibious assault regimental combat team, had landed by the time it had been planned there would be three thousand men over the seawall and fighting inland. The only positive thing that could be said was that elements of the 2d Marine Division were ashore.

Aboard the flagship at midmorning, the navy and marine high command gathered in grim knots on the bridge. Over the unreliable radio net they had been able to monitor only brief fragmentary reports of the battle. Excerpts from communications journals give an almost hour-by-hour account of the crisis at Tarawa up to the time troops began to dig in for the night.

0910. "CO Red 3 reports heavy opposition."

0912. "Troops landing Red 2 meeting heavy resistance."

0917. "Boats held up on reef right flank of Red 1. Troops receiving heavy fire in the water."

1105. "Third Battalion is landing to rear of troops on Red 3 and catching hell."

1203. "Large-caliber guns on west coast firing on boat waves. Request immediate air attack."

1345. "Red 3 reserve team unable to land. Heavy enemy fire. Is there another beach where we can land?"

1350. "Antiboat guns holding up reserves. Troops on Red 2 are 400 yards away from Jap guns on the right."

When word reached The Flag that Shoup finally had arrived on the beach, Maj. Gen. Julian Smith crossed the bridge of *Maryland* and rushed over to Col. "Red Mike" Edson, the hero of Guadalcanal.

"They've done it!" exclaimed Smith, extending his hand to his icy-calm chief of staff.

Edson demurred. "I'd rather wait, sir," he said.

The incredible view from the cockpit filled navy Lt. Comdr. Robert MacPherson with a sense of personal grief. The sight through the Plexiglas window of his Kingfisher spotting plane brought the veteran air observer deep sorrow. Below him were wave upon wave of amphibious vehicles, landing craft, and support units creeping forward. Behind them dozens of artillery pieces and armored vehicles were hung up in barges on the reef, and still more waves were circling or forming up in the lagoon.

MacPherson flew along the reef line, flying low, revealing the big white star on the underside of the wings of the diminutive naval aircraft. Quite simply the navy commander, whose job it was to report the progress of the assault waves and call in naval gunfire from *Maryland,* was humbled and awed by the enormity of the horror occurring below him. He watched as the marines and their machines flowed toward the island like a ragged parade, each of them part of a process far greater than the nightmare that surrounded each individual.

In all respects, it was alarming. Some assault waves were at a standstill. The hulks of navy landing craft were burning where the enemy's artillery had stopped them. Here and there the protection afforded by these wrecked or burning vehicles and the pier sheltered small knots of men. So confused and frightened were they that one could in places hear their curses and prayers above the din of battle. Fantastically horrid vistas spread before the ranging spotter's plane.

MacPherson had swept low and scanned the exposed coral reef since before H hour, and it now appeared to him that the battle had become a monumental mess on the verge of collapse. In the planning, the navy staff had anticipated little trouble in getting ashore. Yet from the sky, from his bird's-eye view, it was obvious to MacPherson that only the first three assault waves had moved well. Of the hundred LVTs that had loaded in the transport area, perhaps three-quarters actually crossed the reef as planned. Despite the intense enemy fire, the bravery of the LVT crews had carried the spearhead of the 2d Division ashore. But for every six or seven LVTs that had rushed toward land along orderly parallel routes in the right general direction, three or four sooner or later had gone off diagonally toward wrong sectors, or had been sunk at sea or knocked out.

MacPherson could see that the battalion on Red 3 had already pushed its lead elements across the seawall and inland in the west, even as desperate fighting just to cross the reef had been occurring in the other two battalion landing zones. The Japanese capacity to strike back at the tide of assault troops moving toward shore had proved remarkably heavy. MacPherson could only guess about the fearful casualties that already must have been suffered.

Long after H hour, by which time it should have been knocked out, enormous fire continued to pour forth from the huge concrete bombproof shelter blocking the way of Major Crowe's assault troops on Red 3. Over the naval air observation net MacPherson pleaded for naval gunfire to take out the deadly position. "Can't something be done about that enemy blockhouse?" he radioed frantically. A dispassionate voice responded affirmatively, but no naval gunfire fell near the strongpoint. "The water seemed never clear of tiny men, their rifles held over their heads, slowly wading beachward," noted MacPherson. "I wanted to cry."

Chapter Twenty-three

These were hours of anguish. Marines scrambled to the shelter of the coconut-log seawall and lay there, exhausted and scared out of their wits. The battle was only a few hours old, yet already events were like nothing anyone had dreamed in their worst nightmares. "It was," a marine later said, "like fighting in the middle of a pool table without any pockets." Men crawled forward over the seawall in ones and twos, and began to work in among the pillboxes and bunkers, assaulting some and avoiding others. Overhead the equatorial sun was getting hotter, and all along the Tarawa invasion beaches Japanese artillery shells and machine-gun and small-arms fire were registering horribly well.

By 1030 Major Kyle, a Guadalcanal veteran, had commandeered enough LVTs to begin landing two companies of his 1st Battalion, 2d Marines. He had been flagging down the precious vehicles since 1000 as they returned from the H-hour landing waves to the edge of the reef. As his fresh formation arrived at the reef, they had been shocked to learn that the water was too shallow to float their LCVPs. When they had been ordered to leave the line of departure, no one had told them about the condition of the reef. Soon the confusion began. Boats began piling up in a terrible, confused traffic jam. During the process of moving men from their bobbing boats to LVTs, Japanese fire had continued heavily throughout the lagoon. Three of the ramp boats were sunk by direct hits during the transfer phase.

During it all the marines revealed a courageous if curious eagerness to get into the fight. The LVTs turned and started back to Red 2 with these reinforcements as quickly as they could be loaded, without waiting to form into organized waves. The first vehicle reached the beach without trouble; the Japanese were still concentrating for the most part against the marines already ashore. The second LVT, coming in several minutes later, did not fare so well. At least two machine guns and possibly three shifted their fire from the marines pinned down on the beach to the LVT just as it ground to a halt behind the seawall to debark troops. Marines scrambled out of the craft from all sides under converging streams of machine-gun fire. Two squads, about twenty men, were wiped out, every man falling dead or wounded.

The rest of the two companies encountered the same intense fire that had riddled the assault troops earlier. Before 1100 most of the LVTs were knocked out by hits from large-caliber shells and raked with machine-gun fire. The vehicles on the right were forced off course and driven toward Red 1, where a total of 115 men would misland and attach themselves to understrength units of the 2d and 3d Battalions. Marines forced to wade in were cut down in sweeping rows along the reef. In all, not more than 400 men of Kyle's group reached shore as planned. The LVTs ranging in number from one to eight would continue to attempt the journey throughout the day, with heavy loss of life. Colonel Shoup's first attempt at rapid reinforcement of the beachhead had failed ignominiously, battered to pieces by overwhelming Japanese opposition.

Meanwhile, the 3d Battalion, 8th Marines, under Maj. Robert H. Ruud, arrived off the reef for the reinforcement of Red 3. They had been ordered forward at 1018 and crossed the line of departure at 1100. Like those units before it, this battalion also was unable to cross the reef in LCVPs. As the boat waves approached they came under rapid 20mm and 40mm fire. They were still closing the reef when—WHAM!—a thunderous crack near the tail end of the island was heard. Marines ashore, stunned, moved instinctively closer to the protection of the seawall. Almost immediately the roar of the battle faded momentarily. Behind them a strange sound—like the noise of "a steel girder hitting concrete," said United Press correspondent Richard Johnston—reverberated across the lagoon.

The noise, recalled Johnston, "pierced the ears, above the howling fury of the battle, and echoed for seconds. Out in the blue water, the westernmost Higgins boat disappeared. Quite literally. It had been there and suddenly it was not. In its place, for a split second, there was a blur in the air, and then there was nothing." What had happened was all too clear. The crew of a Japanese 5-inch coastal artillery piece had spotted the six waves of reinforcements and opened fire. Within the span of a minute, two landing craft disappeared in blinding flashes before rapid counterbattery fire from *Ringgold* silenced the powerful enemy gun. The Japanese shelling, said Johnston, "was a terrifying and heartbreaking sight."

The coxswains of the other craft immediately stopped. Shouted one terrified sailor: "This is as far as I go!" The ramp was dropped and twenty marines jumped off into water ten to fifteen feet deep; all but one or two drowned. In another LCVP, a marine platoon leader panicked and ordered the ramp lowered against the counsel of the crew; one of the first men off, a private, weighed down by two heavy ammunition chests strapped to his shoulders, disappeared the instant he hit the water.

Other boats—their crews killed, wounded, or missing—drifted out of control. Some men were picked up by rescue boats; others would float around for hours before being picked up. But a startling number of men, with messmates trying to close their minds to the screams, were pulled under by their battle burdens and drowned. They died just yards, often feet, from the coral reef—killed even before they were in the fight.

Lieutenant Paul S. Hospodar, of Lorain, Ohio, was in the midst of the fury. The story of his 1st Machine Gun Platoon, Company I, is typical of what occurred in the first attempt to reinforce Red 3. The platoon was loaded into two LCVPs and two LCMs in the fourth wave. "We circled about, awaiting further orders," he noted, "and finally proceeded to make a four-abreast landing on the northeast side of the pier under intense enemy fire." Scattered mortar shells fell around them during their approach to the reef. At a thousand yards, they began to receive artillery and heavy machine-gun fire.

Boat number four, an LCVP, was hit dead on and began to sink. Sergeant Kenneth W. Seymor, of Fredericksburg, Virginia, and sixteen others abandoned the doomed craft. They worked their way to the burning pier and during the journey to shore killed several enemy snipers hidden among the pilings. Along the way five men were killed or wounded. The survivors were the lucky ones. The other three boats ploughed to within eight hundred yards of the shore, where a mortar shell exploded on the deck of boat number three, another LCVP. Exactly what happened to the men and material in this landing craft was never determined. No one was able to say for certain, but it was believed that about a half-dozen men were lost in the shattering mortar blast. Others drowned, claimed by the sea after scrambling into the deep water to escape the sinking LCVP. That left about ten men who struck out for shore. Perhaps five made it but were soon killed.

The other two boats, both LCMs, grounded unscathed in the same area and dropped their ramps. From boat number one, all hands jumped into water over their heads. At least one man drowned, doomed by the heavy weight of equipment he carried. The same thing happened to the marines in boat number two. Twenty-five men jumped out before they realized that the water was too deep. Five were dragged back aboard before the ramp was raised, and the boat backed off under heavy fire. The remainder of the men were left clinging to debris or to the wrecks of other destroyed landing craft in pathetic attempts to stay afloat. Some succeeded in reaching the end of the pier; at least one drowned.

Before any of the platoon reached shore, three-quarters of the men were lost to enemy fire, drowning, or inability to disembark; the unit had practically ceased to exist before it even fired a shot. It was all over by 1145. Mortars, machine guns, and antiboat fire had inflicted heavy casualties and completely disorganized the battalion. Hospodar's boats were so badly butchered that Ruud withdrew the rest of the beleaguered landing waves. It would be late afternoon before what remained of the battalion could take an effective part in the battle. Survivors would continue to show up after nightfall.

In everything that has been written about Tarawa, less attention has been paid to the travails of such "reserve" battalions as 1/2 and 3/8 than to units that landed at H hour. Not by any stretch of the imagination, however, was the worst hostile fire limited to the H-hour waves. In fact, even before the first wave had jumped into the chest-deep water, Ruud's battalion had suffered severe casualties. Of the first wave only 30 percent reached shore; of the second, 20 percent. The third wave was, according to Ruud, completely "wiped out." In fact, "They were pulverized before they got ashore," said Pfc. Rick Spooner, who had been watching from the beach. "Those poor guys were dropping in bunches." Only one out of three of these men made it ashore. The survivors moved off toward the central pier to make their way to the beach under its cover.

*   *   *

By midafternoon of D day, five reinforced battalions of marines had been committed at Tarawa. All but one had suffered crippling casualties and were in bad shape. On Red 1 the disorganized elements of three battalions were practically fighting an independent action. On Red 2 elements of two battalions struggled to hold on where they had landed. Little headway was made in the attempts to clear out the positions from which fire was being directed against the narrow, two-hundred-yard front. On Red 3 elements of two battalions held a front of 250 yards and a beachhead about 100 yards deep. Their major effort was under Maj. William C. Chamberlin, of Seattle. He had been a professor of economics at Northwestern University when the war began. Though wounded, he directed the attack toward the heavily defended area of Burns-Philp wharf.

Within six hours, the matter of greatest concern had become not how quickly the Japanese could be crushed but rather the fate of the five battalions on the narrow beaches of the island. With their backs to the lagoon, the marines were manning essentially two disjointed beachheads in the area of the bird's head and along the outline of its belly. These were small toeholds really, and the marines had little armor support and no artillery except for the two destroyers in the lagoon. If the five battalions were attacked in strength at any point along the coast, the situation could become perilous.

Optimism was a rare commodity at this time. The American high command had thrown all the naval and military might at its disposal against this "vitally strategic objective," yet the walls of "Fortress Tarawa" barely had been scratched. Now the question had become, could the marines hold on? Julian Smith radioed Maj. Gen. Holland Smith, the crusty, pugnacious commander of the V Amphibious Corps, aboard the 5th Amphibious Force flagship *Pennsylvania* off Makin, to brief him on the situation as it was then known and request release of the corps reserve, the 6th Marines, to 2d Division control. "The issue," reported Julian Smith in all seriousness, "is in doubt."

Aboard *Indianapolis*, the commander in chief, Central Pacific, Rear Admiral Spruance, conferred with the chief of Fifth Fleet operations, Capt. Emmet P. "Savvy" Forrestal, about the shocking "issue in doubt" message sent to V Amphibious Corps headquarters at Makin. The highly regarded former destroyer man had hurried to the bridge with the message to see firsthand what Spruance thought of it.

Looking across the lagoon, Forrestal was flabbergasted at the sight of the vast disaster developing. Boats circled offshore in the lagoon in milling confusion. It was impossible to determine if the marines were winning. All morning Forrestal had monitored reports of marines moving along the exposed reef and Burns-Philp pier and being cut to pieces. He feared that reinforcements and supplies would never reach shore, and that it was only a matter of time before the small assault force would be overpowered. If the 2d Division was to continue fighting as an effective combat unit, Forrestal insisted, the plight of the understrength assault forces had to be eased. Forrestal urged the Fifth Fleet commander to inform CINCPAC of the deteriorating situation.

The chief of operations and others of the Fifth Fleet staff strongly believed that their big picture view of the battle was sharper and broader than those of the men actually directing the desperate fighting. This, given the awful chaos and confusion, led to a heightened sense of serious crisis. They urged Spruance to send messages to Rear Admiral Hill and Maj. Gen. Julian Smith to affirm the urgent requests for men, armor, vehicles, air support, and guns that must be satisfied. Finally, COMCENPAC himself should intervene, Forrestal told his boss.

Spruance, however, refused. "I pick men who I believe are competent to do the job," the soft-spoken victor of Midway said, "and I'm going to let them do it." He stood wordlessly, watching through binoculars when there was something to see, calmly waiting when there was not.

At Makin, Maj. Gen. Holland Smith, commander of the V Amphibious Corps, was pacing near the radio shack aboard *Pennsylvania*, observing in his opinion "the dilatory Makin operation," when the alarming message from his friend Julian Smith came in. He rushed to the admiral's quarters, where the irascible "Terrible Turner" was catching his first rest in nearly forty-eight hours. Smith personally woke him, and the two ill-tempered commanders conferred privately for thirty minutes.

The fight for Makin, though infuriatingly slow and one that "Howlin' Mad" Smith believed marines would have finished in a few hours, was going well, and it appeared to be only a matter of time before the army overran the island. Turner told Smith to do what he thought was best under the circumstances, and went back to sleep. The marine general approved the request to commit the 6th Marines to action at Tarawa, but he was sorely worried. The battle was only a few hours old. "Howlin' Mad" counseled himself and the naval and marine staff on the bridge to the effect that, "Julian Smith would not have asked me to commit our last reserve unless conditions demanded this desperate action."

Chief Petty Officer Oonuki had never encountered a more frustrating time. As the commander of perhaps one of only two surviving Japanese tanks, a staff officer explained, it now was Oonuki's job to conduct combat reconnaissance. He was to determine the locale of friendly forces, probe the enemy front and locate, if possible, any gaps or weaknesses, and then report back to the command post. Oonuki was to be "the admiral's eyes," he was told. Yet he ran into problems from the beginning.

In the chaos at the command post he lost his crew. He had no idea where they had gone or what had happened to them. They should have been waiting for him at the entrance to the bunker. Oonuki was in a fix. Obviously his comrades had become separated from him in the confusion surrounding the huge headquarters complex, which now was under infantry and naval gunfire from the enemy's forward assault elements and was crowded by the hundreds of wounded who sought shelter behind its thick walls. Oonuki had no tank-operating capability without a crew.

A scratch team was put together. Among them was the wounded commander of another tank whose vehicle had been lost during the prelanding naval bombardment. The fire flash of a near miss had burned out the tank and scorched the crew, who were friends of Oonuki's. An untrained seaman also bravely volunteered. Oonuki assigned him to the main gun. The CPO got into the driver's compartment and, after a jerking start, edged the tank slowly toward the airfield. Together in the belly of the 7.5-ton tank they moved out down the main runway.

Under the best of conditions the Type 97 light tank proved a tough, if under-armored and sometimes unreliable, little combat package. It was certainly the Japanese tank most frequently encountered by the Allies during the war. But here, attempting to work around shell craters, its engine malfunctioning in the heat and dust, its ammunition nearly depleted, and without the covering fire of accompanying infantry, it was nearly helpless. Oonuki could only hope for the best.

Time weighed more heavily on his mind than it ever had before. The crew feared that they would be caught by an enemy plane or AT gun while moving so conspicuously down the runway. The volunteer gunner reported American infantry rushing across the airfield farther ahead, and rapidly opened fire with a series of 37mm shells. The other crewman, the former tank commander, manned the machine guns, firing short bursts at the enemy column. Oonuki realized that he could carry out his essential mission only as long as he kept the tank running and under control.

They lost sight of the American troops.

Oonuki was spuring the tank on, pushing it as far as it could go, when it broke down. Eminently conscious of their vulnerable situation, the crew continued firing as Oonuki tried to nurse the engine back to life. He was about to order the tank abandoned when oddly the engine sputtered back into action. Although the clutch was burned out and the tank was stuck in low gear, Oonuki was able to turn the tank around and return to the command post. There he waited into the afternoon as important papers were burned, wounded were moved, and dispositions for relocating the command post to the southern shore were made among the three hundred men crowding the huge shelter. Oonuki received new orders. He would help create a diversion for Rear Admiral Shibasaki's movement and interfere with American countermoves once the dash toward the ocean began.

Sometime before Oonuki struck out, a navy captain demanded the attention of all who were crowded in the shelter. By some miracle Shibasaki had succeeded in maintaining contact with Tokyo. The navy captain held aloft a communications blank and announced that Shibasaki had received a message from His Majesty, Emperor Hirohito. The Americans were getting very close now. However, the vast facility grew quiet, and men stood rigidly out of respect for their figurehead monarch. "You have all fought gallantly," the officer read loudly so that everyone in the bunker could hear. "May you continue to fight to the death. Banzai!"

For the second time Oonuki was compelled to recruit yet another scratch crew. In the chaos the other men had vanished. Oonuki had last seen the former tank commander who had gone out with him on the brief reconnaissance when the latter returned to the shelter after a daring personal foray into the battle. "I've just killed a dozen Americans!" the man shouted, wielding a bloody samurai sword. "I'm going back out to kill more. Who will come with me?" Several defenders followed the wild man back outside. Oonuki never saw any of them again.

Now he improvised once more, enlisting two others who climbed into the unreliable tank with him and departed the headquarters. They had fired off the last of their ammunition when the engine broke down again—this time for good. Again they were clearly visible, in the open. The recruits escaped and took off. Oonuki rigged the tank to burn, then dismounted; but before he could toss in a grenade to ignite the fuel, he was in the midst of heavy shelling. The body of a man—whether Japanese or American, he did not know—landed nearby with a sickening thud, as if it had been dropped from a great height.

Oonuki, now alone, ran for cover. Tumbling into a crater, he found it filled to capacity with dead men. He stumbled on into a second shelter, a first aid post, and into a new nightmare. The bunker was small and crowded with dead and dying men. The dismounted tanker counted six occupants—among them two dead men—jammed so close together that it was difficult to move about. He recognized two defenders. Ironically, they were friends, the badly burned crewmen from the tank whose commander had gone scouting with Oonuki and was last seen brandishing a bloody sword.

For a while there was a lull, but Oonuki soon suspected that it was only a matter of time before they were all killed. The shelter was hit from all sides by machine-gun, mortar, and rifle fire, and was surrounded. It was hot and dark in the cramped quarters, and the men were hungry and thirsty. They clawed at the ground with their fingers until a puddle of brackish water formed and they were able to drink from it. Oonuki passed around a vitamin Syrette, and each of them squeezed a drop through dry, cracked lips and onto their tongues.

As the Americans assaulted the area around the shelter, the desperate, wounded tank crewmen sat and listened. The firing outside swept over them. Suddenly one of the men recognized a new danger and yelled, "Grenades!" In a small ventilation shaft in the roof over their heads they heard a scraping noise followed by a metallic "clunk." They stuffed a blanket into the air shaft, which muffled the explosion. Now the only thing they could do was wait. The only means of escape from the bunker was through the narrow entrance beyond which the Americans continued to blaze away with machine guns and rifles and, infinitely more harrowing, their awful flamethrowers.

Everyone was beginning to succumb to the heat and stench of the indescribably foul air in the shelter. They began to collapse from exhaustion. Oonuki leaned back against a sandbag wall; his knees buckled and he slid down in a partly upright position. His strength and his capacity to resist were utterly spent. Suddenly the sanctuary of the bunker was no more. A frightful commotion occurred as the terrifying WHOOSH of a flamethrower swept the interior of the shelter. The brilliant orange fire filled the constricted space, and Oonuki lost consciousness amidst a roaring hell of flame and shrieking screams.

Chapter Twenty-four

The issue was indeed in doubt for the American navy and marine commanders aboard the ships of the Southern Attack Force off Tarawa. With the spearhead of the 2d Division now severely blunted, the problem of how to hold on and what could be done was causing increased tension and anxiety. Junior officers and NCOs in each sector, as soon as they had taken stock of their much-depleted ranks of assault troops, were frantically calling for more reinforcements in order to maintain their shallow footholds. Logistics and gunnery officers aboard the transports and cargo ships and warships were beset by an incomprehensible babble of conflicting requests for supplies and equipment and naval gunfire and air support. "A disaster is developing," repeated "Savvy" Forrestal, the Fifth Fleet operations staff officer, to Admiral Spruance aboard *Indianapolis.*

Up to this point Spruance, although aware that everything was not going according to plan, failed to see any reason or practical opportunity to intervene. The absence of water over the reef and the chaos and confusion that gripped the command structure left him uncertain whether he even had any positive contribution to make at this time. He had not been intimately focused on the attack on Tarawa since he had proposed it as the first American objective in the Central Pacific campaign. Rather he had concentrated on the possibility of a general naval engagement northeast or west of the Gilberts, not to take place until the Combined Fleet had revealed itself. After further anxious consultation aboard the flagship, and against the advice of his staff, Spruance reaffirmed his decision not to interfere. He instructed his advisers to "let Hill and his people work it out."

*　　　*　　　*

Meanwhile, at Makin the last major phase of the epic Galvanic assault was underway. The sentinel island of Kotabu had been seized without difficulty by a combined force of army and marine scouts, and now along the lagoon beaches of Butaritari the rest of Maj. Gen. Ralph Smith's 27th Infantry Division assault troops were going ashore.

There was unusual levity among the soldiers of the 2d Battalion, 165th Infantry, commanded by Lt. Col. John F. McDonough. As the first wave drew abreast of the destroyers *Phelps* and *MacDonough* and headed for Yellow Beach 1 and Yellow Beach 2, some men were actually singing. Watching them pass, a warrant officer aboard *Phelps* wondered "what kind of hell it was into which they were hurrying."

Captain J. M. Baker recalled: "Some of the men read magazines. Although there was singing all along the line of landing craft, a few men fell asleep. Others were eating cold lunches and horsing around, all the way in." Ahead of them Baker observed that "the smoke from exploding fuel dumps a mile or so apart was rolling over the tree tops thousands of feet west of each fire. The low swells that backed up into the lagoon from the ocean to the west were spilled into choppy little waves by the breeze that knocked the top off a few of them."

As they encountered the reef, they were met by machine-gun and rifle fire about five hundred yards from the beach. "The bullets were dropping all around them and the boats of the succeeding waves," said Colonel McDonough. "With naval gunfire exploding ammunition and fuel dumps on the shore, planes strafing and bombing the beach, the [LVTs] firing their rockets and machine guns and the [LCMs] conveying the medium tanks (right on the tails of the [LVTs]) firing their machine guns, it was almost impossible for anyone to certify just where the enemy fire was coming from."

The soldiers crouched low in their LVTs during the last three hundred yards to shore. The first landing was at 1041. Of the sixteen LVTs carrying the assault troops into the Yellow beaches, two were destroyed, two were wrecked, and four were damaged but reached the beach. On the right, one went out of control and careened across the island toward the ocean through the enemy's main fortified zone. It finally plunged into a crater. Before everyone could find cover, two of its occupants were killed by machine-gun fire. Two other LVTs were hit by enemy shells; among the men who were caught dismounting, five were killed and a dozen wounded.

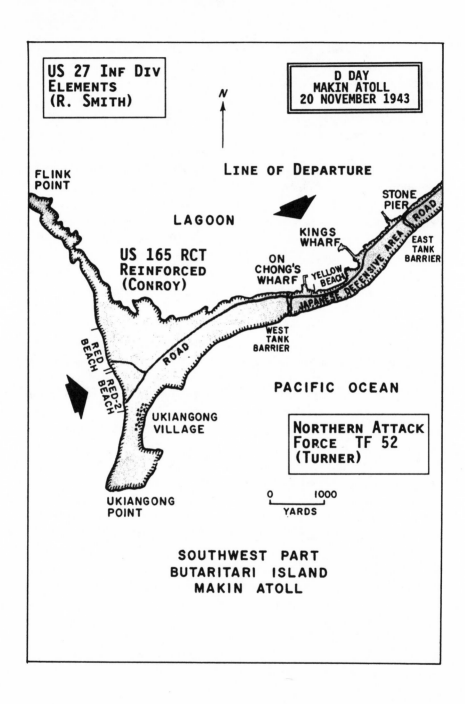

To the left, one of the tracked landing craft ran up the seaplane ramp on King's wharf, machine guns blazing. The soldiers leapt out and seized the pier by crawling along the slope of the causeway, which shielded them from enemy fire. Unable to return the fire, the Japanese fled. All of the other LVTs landed as planned and moved inland, swerving to the left or right before disembarking assault troops.

As the assault troops touched down on Yellow 1 and Yellow 2, M3 Lee medium tanks of Company A, 193d Tank Battalion—fifteen of them commanded by Capt. Robert S. Brown—plunged off their landing craft into the water 150 to 200 yards offshore. All along the Yellow assault sectors, for almost 2,000 yards from the village of Butaritari near the stone pier to the west tank trap, the Lees clanked toward shore. Captain Brown could see smoke sweeping across the beach ahead and the action around King's and On Chong's wharfs flanking either end of Yellow 1. As the tanks floundered toward the island, two were lost in shell holes. Captain Brown was in one of them.

The sergeant commanding the other foundered tank recalled, "We went forward about 25 yards and hit a shell hole. We got out of that and went about 15 yards more and hit another. The water was about seven feet deep and our tank drowned out and immediately filled with smoke. My driver said the tank was on fire. The crew dismounted right there with great speed through the sponson door. I remained inside. As soon as the crew got out they were machine gunned from the shore and with more speed they came back inside. Something like an hour and a half later we were picked up."

For most men of the 2d Battalion landing behind the tanks, wading in over the reef in water two to six feet deep proved to be the toughest part of the battle for Makin. Once they were dumped into the water and surged forward, the hesitant troops found only spotty enemy opposition along the lagoon beaches. Nevertheless, they did not all charge off the boats. A few had to be coaxed to go ashore; and when they were in the water, they had to be told what to do. In some craft, grounding on the reef north of Butaritari, no one moved when the bow ramps were dropped.

Officers yelled at them to get off, warning that while they remained in the boats they were sitting ducks for Japanese artillery. "Get out!" they shouted in effect. "Do you want to be killed here? Move to the beach and get inland." As squad leaders leapt into the water, a soldier would follow, and then another. Finally, all would follow, in a bunch. "Get inland! Keep moving!" officers shouted above the din of battle. Struggling over the reef in undisciplined knots, a few soldiers were caught by snipers or a machine gun that fired from Butaritari village.

The officers and NCOs weaved back and forth among the ranks, separating groups of men, getting them to disperse. The soldiers moved in knots as many marines did at Tarawa, seeking the deceptive safety they instinctively believed could be found in numbers. No enemy shells fell, but several men went down here and there from small-arms fire. None drowned but two were killed by gunfire. The worst was still to come and it would decide the fate of this component of Galvanic.

Some of the enemy fire came from a pair of battered derelict hulks partially sunk off the end of On Chong's wharf. Ensign Andrew P. McConnell mounted three machine guns to starboard on his LCVP and maneuvered into position so that all the guns could fire at once at the hulks. The Japanese fired back—and hard. From shore men watched in admiration and amazement as the sailors, bullets flying all about the boat, directed a rain of lead against the enemy wreckage at close range. The firing continued until one of the guns jammed and the cross fire from shore compelled the crew to withdraw. One seaman aboard the LCVP was seriously wounded in the action and later died. For the next two hours all scheduled activity ashore and in the lagoon ceased while carrier planes bombed and strafed the hulks. At the same time the destroyer *Dewey* slammed 5-inch shells at the wrecks.

Other strong pockets of resistance were encountered. From one dugout a Japanese officer emerged and approached Lt. John Campbell of M Company as if to surrender. However, at the last second the Japanese struck out with his sword and before he was shot down Campbell was severely wounded. Once across Yellow 2, men of the 105th Infantry fought through several pillboxes and trenches and fortified redoubts before breaking through and driving inland. Behind them were fifty-five enemy dead and captured. In one elevated trench, which a platoon had overrun and now sought cover in, two large enemy groups emerged from connecting tunnels and fell upon the unsuspecting and outnumbered Americans in a vicious hand-to-hand melee. Before the Japanese were driven off and the position mopped up with the help of an artillery barrage, eight soldiers lay dead or wounded. More than thirty enemy bluejackets were killed.

Despite such incidents of furious opposition, all resistance within the beachhead area was mopped up within four hours. Often it was accomplished with help. The eleven Lees that reached the ocean shore of the island split up and moved east and west against the tank barriers, overrunning numerous enemy positions. One tank crushed a shelter as infantry stood by and gunned down a dozen Japanese who rushed out. Another wiped out a machine-gun nest en route to the east. One tank drove directly into the village of Butaritari and without much difficulty destroyed several machine-gun nests and pillboxes, using its 37mm turret gun and hull-mounted 75mm howitzer.

Meanwhile, on the hammerhead end of the island two miles to the right of The Citadel, things were curiously quiet. The assault troops on Yellow 1 had moved off the beach, avoided enemy contact, slanted southwest, and set out to link up with the assault force from the Red sectors. They expected to meet by noon. But this was not to be. Unlike the 2d Battalion, which had landed and advanced quickly, the 1st Battalion had been held up by the few Japanese defenders entrenched on the western half of the island. After advancing slowly against desultory opposition, the 1st Battalion momentum had stopped cold when it came up against the islandwide obstacle of the western tank barrier.

The terrain also delayed the advance. Tangled undergrowth and swamps on either side of the only road led to confusion and extreme caution among the troops. Worse, the naval and air bombardment had badly cratered the road. The huge, mud-filled shell holes were more effective than any enemy barricade in holding up vehicles, and the soldiers were reluctant to go forward without their tanks. When they were able to advance, the Stuart light tanks of this force clattered forward nose to tail along the lagoon beach, on the narrow coastal road to the west.

After encountering little resistance for more than a mile, just 150 yards short of the tank trap the battalion of the 165th Infantry came under heavy fire. Several men were hit, and the march petered out, the soldiers going to ground for cover. The delays, coupled with the poor condition of the Red beaches, already were so critical that Rear Admiral Turner diverted follow-up forces to the lagoon beaches. The confusion became even worse. But even now at least one man in the chaos of Makin was acting.

Along the lagoon beach, a confident Col. Gardiner J. Conroy, the 165th Infantry's defiant commanding officer, a prominent Manhattan lawyer in peacetime, walked up to the crews of the tanks and the assault troops, yelling at them to get a move on and silence the enemy strongpoints ahead. Along the beach, behind felled coconut trees and in the coarse undergrowth, exhausted and drained soldiers lay shoulder to shoulder, all along the line of advance, unprepared to move against the enemy fire. The intrepid Conroy rallied the troops and, showing the way, led the tankers up the road, oblivious to the rifle and machine-gun fire that raked the area.

Here and there, others were roused and came to life. Word came to bypass the Japanese strongpoint rather than launch a direct assault on it. Second Lieutenant Daniel T. Nunnery, a platoon leader, and his company commander went up through the undergrowth to a large coconut tree to reconnoiter a way around, and spotted the machine-gun nest. As Nunnery considered the tactical problem, one of the Japanese riflemen saw him and cut loose. Nunnery was killed instantly, shot through the head. Nearby, a chaplain rushed to aid a wounded point man, and was himself wounded. Another soldier who gallantly dashed from cover to help them was killed.

Colonel Conroy came upon the scene, leading four light tanks. He was walking upright. "Get down!" shouted a battalion commander. Conroy hesitated, and was struck dead by a hail of bullets. From the moment he had landed on Red 1, Conroy had been setting an example, practically booting men forward. For all the daring and dash with which Conroy had urged his beloved but inexperienced 165th Infantry into action, its forward movement had been pushed home without determination or conviction. What momentum the heroic colonel had sparked simply evaporated upon his death. In fact, until 0800 the next day, with the enemy long gone as the battle moved far ahead of this area, Conroy's lifeless form lay by the road. This was the pattern at Makin, where command now fell to Lieutenant Colonel Kelley.

When the advance stopped for the night, the 27th Division assault troops were inland of their beachheads but woefully short of their objectives. The linkup had been achieved, but the forces were partially separated by an enemy pocket blocking the western approach to The Citadel. D day losses were about a hundred casualties, perhaps one-quarter of whom were killed. Rough fighting lay ahead in the next days, but for now the 27th Division commanders were pleased to be ashore. By evening, possibly five thousand troops and a hundred vehicles and guns had landed.

The last significant action at Tarawa on D day was the drive by the combat group composed chiefly of survivors of the 3d Battalion, 2d Marines, commanded by the aggressive Maj. Michael Ryan. Had Colonel Shoup but known, the difficulties on Jordan and Crowe's beaches were somewhat offset by the success on the western end of the island— the personal triumph of Ryan, who played the important role in the accomplishment. This decisive, intensely determined marine again demonstrated the outstanding qualities that would earn him a Navy Cross and a British Distinguished Service Order for his part in the battle. Even as Ryan and the marines began their advance out of Red 1, the two surviving Shermans of Lieutenant Bale's tank platoon began driving right up to enemy bunkers, ramming their way through obstacles. The tanks, leading the advance, came so close to enemy positions that they ran the risk of being isolated, but, at point-blank range, they knocked out Japanese strongpoints all along the rear of Green Beach.

Behind the armored support and under covering rifle fire, assault engineers began the demolition job of blowing up bunkers and pillboxes with fused TNT charges. This force drove ruthlessly toward the south shore of Betio across open ground, driving headlong into the flank of the main Japanese fortifications. The troops did not stop until they had come to within three hundred yards of the sea. Reports of their dramatic gains, however, failed to reach either the flagship *Maryland* or Colonel Shoup. For this reason the improving situation on Red 1 was not realized beyond Ryan's makeshift command group.

While fighting was raging behind Green Beach, the rest of Ryan's group was struggling to hold on farther east. On the left half of Red 1, a mixed team of assault troops from three battalions fought a desperate action against The Pocket and the fortifications inland dominating the junction with Red 2. Wherever the Americans advanced, Japanese defenders fought with all their customary ferocity to resist withdrawal. A single Type 97 light tank cut through a marine platoon, and a fierce counterattack was forestalled only after naval gunfire was called in and aircraft were vectored to the scene. In some instances, marines came across bunkers whose occupants had committed suicide rather than fight. But overall there was little sign of demoralization among the enemy at this time. Ryan's command post was charged by several sword-swinging Japanese who were cut down by rifle fire in their mad rush.

Lieutenant Bale in "China Gal" was out front with another Sherman—clearly visible, in the open, crawling forward at walking speed to allow the marines to keep up with them—when a storm of Japanese artillery and mortar shells fell around the clearing. There was a pause, and Bale was shocked to find no sign of the marine infantry who had been covering the tanks. He suddenly knew why, as a solitary Japanese tank raced headlong toward him, its gun already beginning to traverse to meet the Sherman. The heat in "China Gal" was oppressive. Bale rushed to turn and set up a shot, but the enemy was upon him too quickly. The American fired first—and missed.

The Japanese tank commander did not hesitate; he fired, and hit. The enemy 37mm shell struck the Sherman's turret and disabled its traverse mechanism. Unable to fire again, Bale charged "China Gal" forward and rammed the enemy tank. He then roared hastily backward, leaving the fight to the other Sherman—and leaving behind his precious 75mm gun, lost in the collision. To the marines' amazement, the Japanese commander promptly set the other Sherman ablaze with a rapid succession of direct hits. Said an observer: "She lit up like a Christmas tree." The crew abandoned the burning tank and ran for cover.

When at last the marines encountered heavily dug-in defenders near the western battery of 8-inch coastal guns, the consequences of further advance looked too great. A dozen men were cut down. Without armor or sufficient demolition equipment, this was too much for the marines. The 3d Battalion was a mere shadow of its former self. No longer at even half strength, it simply lacked the ability to hold what it had taken. Ryan determined that their gains made them vulnerable to Japanese infiltration or counterattack. He withdrew the troops back into the Red 1 beachhead. By late afternoon, they were dug in compactly on the bird's beak with the support of a few machine guns and "China Gal," whose 75mm gun was gone. Their lines were separated from the nearest marines on Red 2 by six hundred yards of enemy-held ground.

Two thousand miles away in the Hawaiian Islands, Makalapa lay quiet and peaceful in the late afternoon. The day was comfortably breezy and cool, and the clouds scudded low over the surrounding mountains. At Admiral Nimitz's secret mountain headquarters, however, this was not just another routine morning. Rear Admiral Charles "Soc" McMorris, CINCPAC's intelligent chief of staff, had been up since before dawn. Nimitz had directed the principal commanders of Operation Galvanic to send him information copies of all important communications, and now, in the operations room, they were considering the most recent report.

The news from the Gilberts was bad. Makin had not fallen in one fell swoop as had been hoped. Rather, although Turner had reported that the 27th Infantry Division forces landed on schedule and advanced against no opposition at first, Maj. Gen. Ralph Smith's troops were finding it tough to gain ground. The Japanese had disengaged their few combat forces and successfully withdrawn to new positions in the east.

However, at the moment the big concern was Tarawa. The news from there was worse—far worse. McMorris had been carefully following the developments. He had monitored Maj. Gen. Julian Smith's message to "Howlin' Mad" Smith at Makin, which concluded with the ominous words "issue in doubt," requesting release of the V Amphibious Corps reserves, and had taken it immediately to Admiral Nimitz.

"The 2nd Division has asked for the Force Reserve," McMorris reported bluntly. The report came as a shock. A staff officer reminded Nimitz and the others that "issue in doubt" had been the phrase used by Major Devereux and the marines at Wake just before that American island had fallen to the enemy in 1941. As an officer recalled, there was a long silence as Nimitz pondered the situation. He sat quietly, revealing no emotion. He had directed that the amphibious assault forces "get the hell in and get the hell out," and it was apparent to his staff that he was troubled by the predicament of the marines at Tarawa.

Finally, he said to the naval officers who were expectantly gathered around him: "I've sent in there everything we had, and it's plenty. I don't know why we shouldn't succeed." Along the base of the embattled beachhead at Betio, any marine private who was not yet dead or wounded could have provided many good reasons.

Chapter Twenty-five

The situation at Tarawa improved only slightly as D day dragged on. On Red 3 Major Crowe's battalion directed its efforts toward knocking out a strong, steel-reinforced bunker complex on its left flank. In vicious fighting the Japanese doggedly resisted every effort to eliminate the enormous stronghold. Buildings near it were burned or demolished by assault engineers with dynamite and flamethrowers led by 1st Lt. Sandy Bonnyman. Tanks were used. A section of 37mm AT guns was wrestled over the seawall by hand in order to take the position under point-blank fire. But it was all to no avail.

The complex was repeatedly hit and partly wrecked but refused to crumble; fire still came from it. A platoon of Company F was entirely wiped out by heavy fire from a steel pillbox protecting the larger emplacement. Another platoon was pinned down until nightfall by the endless shower of grenades and machine-gun fire that poured forth from its apertures and produced heavy casualties. These losses forced Crowe to hold what he had until he could get more men into action.

On the right, mixed elements of Major Crowe and Major Ruud's battalions penetrated as far as the airfield and consolidated control in that area—for what it was worth. The area proved to be a killing zone that was nearly untenable. It was swept by machine-gun fire from bypassed enemy troops who used every conceivable means of hiding from which to harass and hold up the American advance. They lay in wait in bunkers built flush to the ground or in spider holes, emerging just long enough to fire into the rear of advancing marines and duck down before they were spotted.

Meanwhile, a Japanese counterattack was beaten off—fortunately before it really got started. Even as the depressingly slow and bloody fighting on the beach was going on, the first large-scale Japanese move-ment was taking place. A forward observer reached the Red 3 command post almost immediately, bringing this information to Crowe. For the first time since landing, the marines had seen live Japanese. Perhaps two hundred of them were moving forward through the sparse undergrowth that fringed the south shore of the island. Crowe's beachhead was already under ferocious pressure when they received news of the Japanese move.

The enemy troops had filtered up from the tail end of the island and were preceded by two navigating tanks for armored support. The Japanese tanks rumbled forward, side by side, out of the great dust cloud raised by the naval and air bombardment in the chaos of dev-astation that was the center of the island. For the marines hugging the ground, the spectacle was fantastic—and frightening. Within minutes of the report, Crowe sent out a call for artillery and men. Soon a group of marines, some of them "walking wounded," rushed toward the axis of the enemy advance. A 37mm AT gun section was manually hoisted over the seawall and also went into action.

The crack of the American light artillery was recognizable to the marines up front and gave them heart. One Japanese tank was destroyed and the other damaged and driven off. When the enemy troops began to move forward, the marine gunners opened up with a fury of canis-ter shot that dispersed the attack and left many enemy dead and wounded strewn beyond the front. The marines had averted the first serious threat to their toehold at Tarawa.

There would be others.

For now the most confused situation was on Red 2, where Colonel Shoup remained unable to organize a determined attack from the shallow beachhead established by the H-hour assault waves. Small groups of men had infiltrated 125 yards inland, but most marines were still pinned down behind the seawall on the narrow sand strip at the water's edge. Units were disorganized and hopelessly scrambled. Large gaps existed in the lines throughout the landing zone. Survivors of 1/2 had strengthened the assault forces somewhat at various places, but nowhere was there an organized line. One company commander reported to Shoup that the situation was "impossible to control" and doubted his ability to hold his sector of the front. No officer knew where all the component elements of his command were, nor did he have the communications to control men he could not see.

Nevertheless, some marines had not waited for things to straighten out on Red 2. They had taken matters into their own hands. Staff Sergeant William Bordelon, the assault engineer who was one of four survivors of a third-wave LVT, had gone into action almost immediately by himself. After reaching shore he and two companions salvaged a satchel of TNT. They wrapped demolition charges, and Bordelon went over the seawall under the covering fire of nearby riflemen. He rushed two pillboxes, one after the other, throwing the TNT charges into them as he passed. Both enemy positions were blown up. When he ran out of TNT, he returned to the beach and wrapped another charge. Although he had been shot in the left arm on his previous excursion, he immediately went back over the seawall after a third pillbox from whose slit machine-gun fire poured. On this second trip, he charged the weapon and was wounded again.

Upon taking cover Bordelon grabbed a rifle from a dead marine and gave covering fire to men who were going over the top. A navy corpsman sought to treat his wounds. Bordelon waved him off. An enemy grenade exploded in his midst, ripping open the stomach of one of his companions. Behind him a wounded marine struggled to reach shore under fire. Bordelon plunged into the water to help the man. Going in he spotted yet another wounded marine. Grasping a wounded man beneath each arm, the sergeant got them to the shelter of the seawall.

Although suffering from loss of blood from his wounds, for which he continued to refuse medical aid, Bordelon ran back to the seawall. He destroyed a fourth pillbox with a rifle grenade. Then with more TNT he wrapped another demolition charge. But as he went over the seawall a third time a Japanese machine gun caught him in its withering fire. The twenty-three-year-old Bordelon was killed instantly. He was posthumously awarded the Medal of Honor, the first of four marines to win the nation's highest award for valor at Tarawa.

In dying, Bordelon (and hundreds of other nameless men) demonstrated what had to be done. The key move of the battle lay in getting men inland. The seawall had to be crossed to stop that horrible enemy fire on the beaches and the reef. Calls for help had gone out not long after the assault waves had hit the shore. The LCMs carrying the Shermans comprising the fifth wave had rushed in but were held up when they encountered the reef. Besides Lieutenant Bale's shattered tank platoon, which had reached Red 1 and gone into action with Major Ryan's combat group, it had been planned to land two platoons of five tanks each on beaches Red 2 and Red 3.

The tanks attached to the 2d Battalion, 2d Marines, sought to land eight hundred yards from shore shortly before 1000. The first of the thirty-two-ton monsters to trundle off its ramp was tragically lost when it sank up to its turret. The other tank crews ordered the sailors to back their LCMs off the reef and try to land on Red 3. There the 3d Tank Platoon could be seen crawling over the reef, apparently with less difficulty. However, only two of the Shermans eventually succeeded in reaching Red 2.

In making their detour, the coxswains of two LCMs tried to navigate the boat passage on the Red 3 side of the pier, but were soon taken under fire. The first LCM and tank were sunk in the narrow channel not one hundred yards from shore by a direct hit, blocking the landing barge behind it, which was also soon hit. The damaged LCM moved back a couple of hundred yards until it sank and bottomed out. The navy crew finally dumped the Sherman on the reef and it began churning toward the beach. While maneuvering to reach Red 2, however, it fell into a shell hole and the entire crew drowned.

Shoup put the two remaining tanks to work against The Pocket, but within twenty minutes of finally getting into action both of these were also eliminated from the fight. One was caught in a cross fire of AT weapons and tried to crawl out of range. As shells smashed all around, the driver ran it blindly into a shell hole from which it could not be extricated. This tank had to be abandoned. Soon afterward a Japanese bluejacket rushed from a hiding place and knocked out the other tank by placing a magnetic mine on its hull. Thus ended the heavy armored support for Red 2.

The Shermans destined for Red 3 fared better, but for only a slightly longer period of time. Led by twenty-five-year-old 1st Lt. Louis E. Largey, of Hollywood, California, the 3d Platoon came in under equally severe conditions. A medium-caliber shell delivered Largey's command tank, code-named "Cannonball," a direct blow on its frontal armor and disabled the radio. All five tanks were hit, but the crews held them on course and reached shore, where they soon attracted an even greater volume of enemy fire. The marines who were dug in behind the seawall were skeptical about the tanks, since they drew such furious fire. Major Crowe immediately ordered them off the beach and inland.

"Go in there and blast anything and everything," said Crowe to Largey, who had dismounted upon hitting the sand. "Clear the way for our men." An engineer widened a gap in the seawall with a demolition charge and Largey, in his damaged command tank, led the others, code-named "Charlie," "Condor," "Colorado," and "Commando," inland. One after the other, the tanks ground up the slight embankment and into the center of the island, and began blasting away with their 75mm guns. The fighting was brutal. Within ninety minutes the armored fist that Crowe hoped would lead his breakout across the island had been reduced to one operational but badly battered and burned tank.

"Condor" and "Charlie" were knocked out almost simultaneously. The first of the hapless pair was mistakenly dive-bombed by a navy pilot who had been vectored to the scene in order to work over the Japanese tanks that earlier had been seen rumbling toward Red 3. In the explosion of the thousand-pound bomb, the American tank was wrecked and the crew bailed out. "Charlie" engaged a heavy AT gun and lost. Largey, in "Cannonball," was also indirectly stopped by the same gun or one nearby. In seeking to evade the enemy fire, the driver slewed the tank into an excavation that he hoped would afford some cover from the deadly fire. Unfortunately he unknowingly drove into an underground Japanese fuel dump, which another strafing plane promptly set afire. Largey and the crew escaped, literally under fire, but were stuck behind enemy lines for most of the rest of the day.

"Colorado" was hit by a heavy shell and also caught fire, but the driver fled back to the beach and into the water, extinguishing the flames. After quick makeshift repairs, the crew returned the tank to the seawall and by nightfall they were anchoring the left flank of Crowe's beachhead. "Commando," the final 3d Platoon tank, advanced the farthest from Red 3—nearly to the southern, or ocean-side, shore. En route she was hit no less than eighteen times by light artillery fire, but her gunner, plucky Pfc. William E. Duplessie, of Charlevoix, Michigan, destroyed two AT guns and knocked out five pillboxes before a 40mm shell clipped the fuel line and set "Commando" aflame. In bailing out, Duplessie was wounded. It would be two days before the crew, trapped deep within enemy lines, encountered fellow marines.

Half-tracks mounting 75mm howitzers, which Shoup called into Red 2, were similarly eliminated before they were able to make a difference. The LCM carrying one of the upgunned half-tracks took a direct hit by a 3-inch coastal piece and was sunk as it approached the reef. Another half-track succeeded in reaching the beach but bogged down in some deep sand. By nightfall its crew, working furiously under unending enemy fire, still had not succeeded in digging it out. As confusion mounted among the scores of milling landing craft in the lagoon, the rest of the half-track platoon failed even to reach the reef.

Two LCMs, each with a 3d Battalion, 18th Marines (Seabees), bulldozer and metal beach mat, were supposed to land on Red 2 with the fourth wave, but were unable to land their cargo for forty-eight hours. In fact, it would take three days for many landing craft with supplies and equipment to get rid of their loads. At the end of the day only the Shermans "China Gal" and "Colorado," both damaged, and one half-track were operational. "I never had much use for tanks," said one marine, but "'China Gal' and 'Colorado' sold me."

The navy steamed for deep water at sunset, doubtfully leaving Tarawa to the embattled marines ashore and a few destroyers to guard the lagoon entrance and provide naval gunfire support.

The other destroyers departed the area first, blasting with their sonars at the shallow coastal water for Japanese submarines known to be converging on the area. The cruisers and battleships followed, forming slowly into two columns. Zigzagging as it steamed through the Tarawa-Maiana gap and back into the Pacific, the bombardment fleet left the battle behind for the night.

Thirty miles west of Tarawa, a squadron of sixteen Kate torpedo bombers advanced in a V formation, their crews scanning the sea ahead with their eyes and probing the airwaves for American radio transmissions with their equipment. They flew from air bases in the Marshalls— half from Roi and half from Maloelap. Presently the pilot of the lead Kate found himself looking down on a collection of a dozen ships in line astern formation, traveling due north at twenty knots. This was the American southern carrier group that Japanese submarine intelligence reports had told them about, the flight crews decided. They must have noted with satisfaction that the enemy was out in the open, right where they could get at him with their backs to the setting sun.

Almost instantly, long-range, high-proximity fused AA shells began to explode around the dodging, twisting aircraft, even as American fighters bored in. Without a moment's hesitation, the confident

Japanese naval aircrews deployed expertly into an oblique line. Nine broke through the American air defense screen, divided into equal groups of three torpedo-armed bombers, and attacked. Minutes later, in the only enemy air offensive of D day, numerous powerful Japanese torpedoes knifed through the water in the very midst of the American carrier battle group.

On the bridge of the light carrier *Independence,* Capt. Robert L. Johnson saw them coming. So did officers on the bridges of the other carriers. The enemy aircraft had come in so low that they were seen by the fliers on CAP before they were picked up by radar. *Independence,* which had been caught in the vulnerable process of recovering planes returned from ASW patrol and had just secured from a submarine alert, promptly slammed her engines to full speed astern and commenced zigzagging. The AA gunners aboard the ships opened up with everything they had, but three torpedoes sliced between *Essex* and *Bunker Hill* before the Japanese planes that had launched the deadly missiles could be shot down.

The rest of the enemy planes had concentrated against *Independence,* which was isolated and could not fight off the attackers by herself. Johnson fought to swing the carrier back and forth to evade the torpedoes. But in the aim of so many torpedo tracks—at least five at once— the radical maneuvering could not keep the carrier unharmed. A torpedo crashed into the stern on the starboard side.

As *Independence* was slammed sideways, it shuddered and slowed. She began to list immediately. A fighter plane and AA gun and crew were lost overboard. Fires sprang up here and there, and steering from the bridge was knocked out. There were sixty casualties. These included seventeen dead, some of whom were killed when the after engine room, fireroom, and magazine compartments below deck were flooded to right the list. Half the Japanese planes were knocked down—five by *Independence* gunners. The rest escaped back to the Marshalls. Rear Admiral Montgomery detached a cruiser and destroyer to escort the severely damaged carrier to Funafuti in the Ellice Islands for quick repairs— and from there back to Pearl Harbor for extensive drydock time.

Under any other circumstances, this chance confrontation west of Tarawa between the Japanese torpedo bombers and the southern group of American carriers would have been merely a historical footnote. But in the balance sheet of Galvanic, when the operation was in such jeopardy and every means of defeating the Japanese quickly was needed if a combined arms effort to seize the Gilberts was to succeed, the loss of even one light carrier with its thirty-eight planes and the warships escorting it was a hard blow. This was particularly so, since the fate of the Fifth Fleet and the V Amphibious Corps had taken yet another turn. Throughout the Marshalls area, despite the hard work of Rear Admiral Pownall's fast carrier forces in the north, the air reinforcements promised Rear Admiral Shibasaki were beginning to arrive from all over the Pacific in a determined, if erratic, flow.

Chapter Twenty-six

Along 1,500 yards of beach, marines controlled not more than 750 yards of disconnected front at Tarawa. The foothold on Red 1 was at most 150 yards in width; the beachhead of Red 2 and Red 3 combined stretched perhaps 600 yards. Here and there men lay over their weapons peering out into the darkness lit up by flares and tracers. Some slept the sleep of unconscious exhaustion in shell holes and blasted bunkers, but most remained tensely awake. Some units, such as the commandos under Lieutenant Hawkins, were still probing warily through bunkers within their own lines.

The triumph of getting ashore was eclipsed by the numerous disappointments and setbacks of D day. Japanese guns had had the reef ranged for months. It was impossible to locate the enemy. Often his weapons could not be seen even when they fired. Throughout the day a live Japanese was rarely encountered. And although naval gunfire and air attacks rained down all over the mile and a half of island, enemy fire had continued to roar from the front and the flanks—from pillboxes, bunkers, trenches, the tops of trees, and spider traps. The carnage was terrible.

Time-Life's Robert Sherrod was one of thousands of awed survivors of the amphibious assault who had been compelled to wade to the island under fire. Now Sherrod and another correspondent were seeking a place to rest their heads for the night. Just a few feet beyond the position they selected below the seawall on Red 2 lay the mangled, rapidly decomposing bodies of four Japanese. The two men peered over the seawall into the darkness. "I was quite certain that this was my last night on earth," recalled Sherrod. "We had twenty feet along perhaps one sixteenth of one-half of one side of the island,

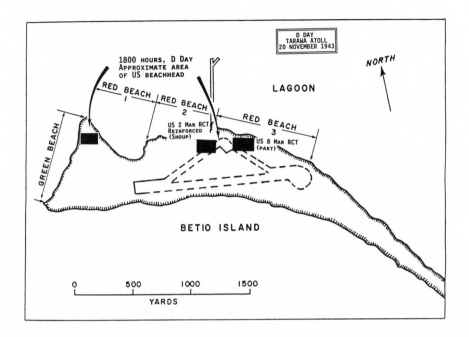

plus a few men in shellholes on either side of the airstrip. The Japs
had nearly all the rest." With grim fatalism, he noted, "If the Japs coun-
terattacked, what could we do except shoot at them from behind our
seawall until they finally overwhelmed us?"

"Pelicans"—navy doctors and corpsmen—had landed with the assault troops and were engulfed in a flood of blood as automatic weapons
fire and artillery raked the beaches and reef, and grenades exploded
among marines and shore parties. Inland, from the southern shore, from
the center of the airfield and the revetments around it, from the tail
end of the island, enemy reinforcements appeared steadily throughout the day, as if they had been untouched by the most awesome
preinvasion naval and air bombardment in history.

Lieutenant Herman R. Brukardt and three corpsmen, landing with
3/8 in the fifth wave, set up a hospital less than ten yards inland in a
Japanese pillbox recently cleared of enemy machine gunners in the
initial assault. Brukardt, a twenty-nine-year-old battalion surgeon from
Menominee, Michigan, worked without rest for thirty-six straight hours,
using flashlights to illuminate the pillbox. As the battle raged about

him and casualties were brought in, he treated a total of 125 seriously injured men, of whom only 4 died. In the midst of operating on one badly wounded man, two live Japanese were discovered in the bunker and killed.

In one LVT off Red 1, an entire medical section had been wiped out when their landing craft took a direct hit. When the twisted wreckage bobbed alongside the transport *William P. Biddle,* a coast guardsman moved to get a closer look as the boom lifted it aboard. "She came along about 1300 and had been floating for three hours or more," he said. "There was a pool of blood an inch deep on the deck; the stuff was thick but sort of sloshed everywhere. One of the mangled bodies was a navy doctor. We buried them right there at sea."

The doctor was Lt. Ward R. Vincent, a 4th Marine Division surgeon and observer. There were two other men in the landing craft, perhaps corpsmen. They were also dead. Ten wounded had been taken off by another transport before the smashed LVT had floated away. Also among the dead on that first awful day of combat in the Gilbert Islands was Lt. Edwin J. "Doc" Welte, the popular battalion surgeon from Minnesota, killed coming ashore on Red 2 with the 2d Battalion, 2d Marines. During the battle, about a hundred navy medical corpsmen were wounded and twenty or more killed.

Chief Pharmacist's Mate Roy J. Barnhill, thirty-three years old, of Salt Lake City, assisted by members of the division band, went into the enemy lines numerous times that first night and returned with wounded marines. They hobbled in with them all night long, dragging injured men in ponchos or litters. Japanese twice hurled grenades in Barnhill's direction, but fortunately the explosives failed to go off on both occasions. Another surgeon, Capt. French Moore, treated casualties at the end of the pier where he arrived about 1730. Under his charge the wounded were given first aid and evacuated in boats as supplies were unloaded on the pier. Here and there, wherever the seawall, pier, or wrecked LVTs afforded some cover, corpsmen rigged plasma bottles—if they had them. Medical supplies were in such short supply that volunteers were recruited to wade back into the lagoon to grimly retrieve first aid kits from the bodies of marines killed trying to walk ashore.

The invasion front that night at Tarawa had to be seen to be believed. The vast area from the beaches to the reef line was a gruesome graveyard of smashed landing craft, bodies floating in and out with the surf, wrecked or abandoned burning vehicles, and crates of supplies. An appalling number of men were casualties. Five hundred sailors and marines were dead; one thousand others were wounded. Most still lay in improvised first aid stations or positions from which they could not be evacuated.

It is impossible to calculate how many men died while waiting to be evacuated. The senior officers of the division already feared that their casualties were the heaviest in Marine Corps history. They were right. Although they could not know it then, only one other battle in the Pacific war would produce more first-day casualties than D day at Tarawa. At Iwo Jima, February 19, 1945, two divisions, the 4th and 5th Marine Divisions, suffered twenty-three hundred killed and wounded. In contrast, at Soissons, July 19, 1918, in World War I, two marine brigades had thirteen hundred casualties. In both instances, however, the casualties at Tarawa were proportionally far greater. Here the advance elements of one division did all the suffering.

The terrible attrition was caused chiefly by the inability of the assault forces to get heavy weapons support ashore. Not only had tanks and half-tracks been unable to land effectively, nearly all the artillery had remained boated in the lagoon throughout the day. There was simply no earthly way to get the guns in. The commander of the 1st Battalion, 10th Marines, blue-eyed, mustachioed Lt. Col. Presley M. Rixey, of Virginia Beach, Virginia, was the first artilleryman ashore. He came in with Colonel Shoup at noon and was promptly pinned down—without any of his twelve powerful 75mm pack howitzers.

According to the plan, his artillery battalion was to have landed on Red 1, the only area from which the guns could give the assault troops full support. However, the heavy enemy guns in The Pocket remained unsilenced, as were many on the tail end of the island. Much small-arms and machine-gun fire had been reduced in the bird's beak, which was now the beachhead on Red 1, but throughout the sector enemy fire was still heavy. Yet the marine artillery was vital, and by 1400 it became apparent to Rixey that if he were to get his weapons ashore at all on D day, he would have to bring them in over Red 2. A short time later he sent an officer out to the reef with the order to land the guns, and the 1st Battalion started to move its heavy weaponry ashore piece by piece.

The artillery spotters, called forward observers for lack of any better description of their dangerous jobs, had gone in at Red 1 ahead of their guns and were with Major Ryan. Since landing boats still could not cross the reef, LVTs were procured. Carrying two sections of the 75s and their six-man crews, the tracked landing craft waddled ashore. A partially dismantled section from Battery A was the first across the reef and into Red 2, followed by another from Battery B. At 1800 one gun let go, firing its fourteen-pound HE shells toward the southwest.

Not enough of the invaluable LVTs remained afloat to bring in the entire artillery battalion. Therefore, the guns of a third battery unloaded at the end of Burns-Philp pier. These nine-hundred-pound guns also were dismantled and miraculously carried in pieces by their crews through waist-deep water into the beachhead. It was dark by then, but five sections of the 10th Marines (Artillery) were landed and dug in. The guns were ranged and in position to "fire for effect" at dawn.

It was late afternoon when Brig. Gen. Leo "Dutch" Hermle, the assistant division commander, arrived at the end of the pier under sniping fire. Hermle was determined to see for himself what was happening. As he attempted to raise the command post ashore, the pier was still burning where Lieutenant Leslie and the assault engineers had set it afire in the morning. Debris and wreckage littered the lagoon—the effect of the day's fighting. Dead marines and smoldering landing craft were evidence, as Hermle would later say, of "an untried doctrine that was tested in the crucible of actual combat." Yet for now he had no clear picture of what was happening. Unable to establish reliable radio contact with either Julian Smith or Colonel Shoup, he sent a messenger out to one of the ships in the lagoon to apprise the division commander of the situation via the TBS.

Meanwhile, aboard the flagship *Maryland,* southwest of the island, Julian Smith was too remote to comprehend the confusing situation. By now the division commander, impatiently awaiting word from Hermle, with Edson at his side grim and tense, had received the first few fragmentary reports of the battle from Shoup. Smith was astounded by the heavy casualties suffered by the assault troops. The messages coming in carried a note of anxiety, attesting all the more to the shock and gravity of the situation. Although he had not yet received full news of the disaster that had befallen his command, Smith now began to realize that it was no longer a question of merely overrunning the enemy but possibly of saving his division from being destroyed.

It was not practical to break off the fight—had it even been considered—so Smith resolved to renew the battle the next day with the V Amphibious Corps reserve, the 6th Marines, in an effort to deliver the Japanese a decisive blow. He sent orders to Hermle to relieve Shoup and take command ashore, fearing that the situation was beyond the experience of Shoup, whom he suspected was too junior for the job at hand. At 1900, as darkness was descending, Smith sent orders to Shoup to "hold what you have. Develop contact between your battalions. Clear isolated machine guns still holding out on the beach. Make provisions to meet organized counterattack." It was not necessary for him to add that the success of the operation depended upon the marines holding firm through the night.

From what he could see, it was acutely clear to Hermle even from his offshore vantage point that the exhausted troops would be hard-pressed to hold on to their slim gains through the night. They could hardly be fit to defend themselves much less engage in night combat should the Japanese counterattack. Supplies were not getting ashore; the marines had used up their water rations; much of their ammunition, armored vehicles, and landing craft lay everywhere wrecked; and the end of the pier was crowded with casualties. All the battalion commanders were calling for help, and little equipment had gotten to shore by then. A staff officer accompanying Hermle scouted ahead and confirmed the "horrible" supply conditions. The marines could not be expected to bear it much longer. It was essential to organize a makeshift supply service.

Since he had not yet received Smith's instructions that he take command ashore, Hermle concentrated on what he could accomplish. The pier to a point thirty yards toward shore was stacked high with crates containing much-needed water, plasma, and ammunition. Hundreds of landing craft that had been unable to unload milled about in the lagoon. Also huddling about the area were remnants of Major Ruud's 3d Battalion, 8th Marines—the reinforcements that had been cut to pieces wading into Red 3 in the early afternoon. Through Maj. Stanley E. Larsen, the battalion's executive officer, Hermle organized them into carrying parties. "You men get the hell up that pier," he directed, "and get these supplies moving." It took some time, but soon a hundred or more marines, all that was left of three of Ruud's shattered companies, reluctantly started ashore in ragged columns through a fifty-yard, fire-swept lane.

Hermle sent two other officers—Maj. Rathvon M. Tompkins, of La Jolla, California, assistant division operations officer, and Capt. Thomas C. Dutton, of East Cleveland, Ohio—to find Shoup and determine when and where the 6th Marines reserve should be landed. The two men did not return until nearly dawn. When they did Hermle moved back out to the lagoon to the destroyer *Ringgold* to inform the flagship of Shoup's preferences. Again he was foiled by the breakdown in communications, but word came through from Smith angrily ordering Hermle to return to the flagship aboard *Ringgold* when the destroyer came alongside to replenish ammunition. Hermle left a staff officer to coordinate the movement of supplies. He had been on the pier a mere eight hours, long enough to confirm for himself and the 2d Division CG that the battle was in grave danger of being lost.

Meanwhile, Capt. Herbert B. Knowles, commander of the Tarawa transport group with his headquarters on *Monrovia,* in fact had been sending in thousands of tons of supplies and equipment throughout the day—with no report of its receipt. Because Hermle had been unsuccessful in communicating the situation via radio, and messages from the island continued to bear Shoup's authority, it was assumed that Hermle was incommunicado or, even worse, killed or wounded. Knowles sent Maj. Benjamin K. Weatherwax to locate either Hermle or the 2d Marines command post and determine the supply situation. Weatherwax left the transport at 2100.

Weatherwax and Hermle passed within feet of each other at the end of the pier, but in the darkness they failed to meet. Better luck was had with Shoup. Said the 2d Marines assault force commander when Weatherwax crawled into his foxhole: "This is the damndest crap game I ever got into." Weatherwax made numerous attempts to transmit the coordinates of Shoup's preference for landing the reserves but was unsuccessful; in the end, he was not able to report back to Knowles in person with the information until shortly before dawn.

Only through the combined personal reconnaissance efforts of Brigadier General Hermle and several marine staff officers did The Flag and 2d Division CG, Maj. Gen. Julian Smith, learn the terrible truth about the landings. It was impossible to estimate the surviving strength of the Japanese defense forces, but everyone, from "Howlin' Mad" Smith at Makin on down, suspected that it must be considerable. They were convinced that the hours before dawn would be critical. It would be necessary not only to plug gaps all along the front but to get supplies flowing to Shoup's troops at the same time.

Worried about Shoup's ability to direct a divisional battle of this size, harassed by the "outstanding communications deficiency" connecting him to that tired junior officer and by the absence of any communication at all with the battalion on the left, Julian Smith was far less than sanguine about the situation. Just as the confusion caused by conflicting requests began to overwhelm the division staff, Hermle reappeared. Smith was infuriated. His specific order to Hermle to move ashore and take command had not been carried out. Hermle explained helplessly that he had not received the message. The combat command of the 2d Division was to remain for another day the responsibility of Colonel Shoup, destined by a quirk of fate to be both architect and executor of the Tarawa plan.

Chapter Twenty-seven

Offshore several destroyers put in a night-long barrage inland of the marine positions at Tarawa. In return Japanese mortars and artillery thumped irregularly. Supplies and equipment were stacked on the pier, shore parties were working on the beaches and beneath the pier, and casualties lay everywhere. Navy coxswains and medical parties had evacuated more than seven hundred men during the day, but hundreds more still lay ashore. The dead had begun to decompose, and a sickly, sweet smell was noticeable.

In the close-quarters action it was impossible to see the enemy or locate his weapons. In this respect the first night was not much different from the first day. Since H hour, twelve hours before, a live Japanese had rarely been encountered. Only a few Korean laborers had been taken prisoner, and only a few hundred Japanese dead counted. Volunteers and medical corpsmen climbed in and out of destroyed landing craft in search of supplies and equipment, ranging from dry cell batteries for radios to machine guns and ammunition lifted from sunken LVTs or wrecked tanks. Others carried wounded men back out to the reef for evacuation. There they would be placed on boats and taken to hospital ships or transports.

By midnight enemy fire along the Burns-Philp pier was so heavy that the slightest movement was fraught with serious risk. The pier was on occasion ordered off-limits. Although at the end of the pier men worked under fire, only one or two vessels were able to unload at the same time. There were scores of craft floating without purpose, waiting for someone to lead them in. Few navy or coast guard crews tried to come in through the arcing tracer fire and scattered shelling.

Inside the beachhead, runners slid in and out of shell holes and captured bunkers—carrying reports, relaying orders, evading enemy fire. Throughout the night, stretcher bearers brought in the wounded. Men in all three assault sectors were looking for their units or buddies. So many marines had been separated from their units in the chaos that no exact count of the D-day casualties could be attempted. However, everyone knew that they were plenty heavy. Nearly as many marines had fallen in the first day at Tarawa as had been killed in the whole six-month Guadalcanal campaign.

The battalions lying between the airfield and the lagoon tried to make the best of the confusing situation. Colonel Shoup maintained his regimental forward command post where he had established it—in back of the knocked-out enemy bunker—in order to permit runners to easily relocate him and to prepare for the morning assault out of the beachhead. Leaning against the outer wall, his wounded legs stretched out before him, Shoup studied maps and issued orders for the next day. Radiomen nearby worked carefully to bring order to the fouled-up combat communications network.

Many Japanese were moving about. Here and there small groups wandered into the marine lines. Some enemy detachments even managed to swim out into the lagoon and man machine guns on old hulks west of the pier or in burned-out LVTs. About 0200 it was determined that some of the enemy fire was coming from the wrecked hull of the *Saida Maru,* the Japanese tramp steamer on the reef off Red 2. The Japanese fired these weapons into the rear of the American beachhead or along the pier where stragglers and shore parties moved. There were several attempts at infiltration. One enemy unit came in at dusk to try to recapture the Burns-Philp wharf. Riflemen of 2/8 hit back hard as the enemy attacked, driving off the raid. The Japanese left behind eight dead.

Huddled in foxholes and shell holes, and behind the seawall, men stood watch, looking for enemy movement. Most by now had not slept in twenty-four hours. They took turns straining their tired eyes, struggling to remain awake—waiting, anticipating the dreaded banzai attack. Everyone believed that a counterattack was inevitable. Even out in the fleet and on the vessels in the lagoon a restlessness dominated the mood of the Americans at Tarawa. Now and then, rifle and machine-gun fire broke out when a Japanese patrol revealed itself or when the shadows of trees and wreckage appeared to move in the eerie light of flickering fires burning all over the island. Still the big push did not occur, and overall the night on land passed quietly compared to the day.

Nevertheless, attrition among the marines was steady. Second Lieutenant Ernest A. "Matty" Matthews, combat intelligence and assistant public relations officer, of Dallas, had come in aboard an LCVP that was able to reach the end of the pier shortly after midnight. He had spent fifteen hours boated, including at least ten hours at the line of departure. After a failed attempt to land during the day, the former *Dallas Morning News* reporter had determined that his chances of surviving were not good, and he instructed his buddy, TSgt. James Lucas, to let his mother "know how it happened."

The son of a career army officer, Matthews was no stranger to war. He had fought for the loyalists in the Spanish Civil War and had made the assault landing at Guadalcanal. He was not enthusiastic about landing at Tarawa, but he nevertheless was the first one out of his boat and onto the pier. He gave Lucas a hand up. Together they had not moved ten feet down the pier when a shell exploded, knocking them flat. Before they were able to rise and move on, another shell landed directly beneath the planking on which they lay. The blast rocked the pier in every direction. Matthews was mortally wounded; he moaned briefly and died. Lucas prayed for the fallen marine, then staggered toward shore, stunned by the loss of his close friend.

Major Lawrence C. Hays's 1st Battalion, the last of the 8th Marines, had been boated since early morning, bobbing around offshore while waiting for word to move to the line of departure. At 1625 the combat unit was ordered to land, but the message was never received. The last formation of the 8th Marines remained boated, awaiting orders that did not come. Overhead in a navy Kingfisher spotter plane, Lt. Col. Jesse S. Cook, Jr., of Earlander, Kentucky, 2d Division staff supply officer, observed the 10th Marines artillery going ashore on Red 2, and mistakenly reported the movement as that of Hays's battalion, which was only then assembling in the lagoon. Thus, well into the first night, Julian Smith wrongfully believed that 1/8 was ashore. The confusion might have been cleared up had Cook himself not run into trouble.

The water seemed covered with vessels as Cook and his pilot, Ens.

G. K. French, flew over the lagoon just after sundown during their return to the fleet, which had put to sea for the night. The plane commenced a shallow glide at three hundred feet in order to land near a cruiser. At that moment up ahead bright yellow flashes peculiar to AA shells burst in the night sky like so many sparks against black velvet. Hundreds of streams of tracers reached toward the clouds, throwing up an erratic, sweeping lattice of AA fire.

It was impossible at that distance and in the dark for anyone aboard the warships to tell whether the plane was friendly or belonged to the enemy. Because of the plane's sudden unexpected appearance, its low-level approach on the flagship, and its failure to identify itself, jittery gun crews had not had time to think twice. They opened up en masse on Rear Admiral Hill's personal orders, the second time in less than twenty-four hours that navy guns had taken American seamen and marines under direct friendly fire.

The incident led men ashore and afloat to conclude that the Japanese were striking back at the fleet with planes from the Marshalls. Some men, among them war correspondent Robert Sherrod, mistakenly believed that a naval battle was taking place, and feared the worst. For the men in the landing craft, particularly the 1st Battalion, 8th Marines, the situation was horribly frightening. As they watched the enormous volume of tracers coming from the fleet, they expected to be strafed at any moment. Many inflated their life vests and prepared to leap into the water, despite the presence of sharks that had been seen scavenging bodies in the lagoon.

However, the AA barrage broke up when the blip disappeared from the radar screens. Ensign French had landed the Kingfisher immediately. Although Cook was able to identify himself and his plane, he and the pilot were forced to spend the night afloat—twenty-five miles west of Tarawa—since they could not safely approach the fleet in the darkness.

Eventually—through the reports of Lieutenant Colonel Cook; the former Raider Colonel Carlson, whom Colonel Shoup had sent back out to the fleet around noon; Brigadier General Hermle; and messages from the commanders ashore—it became apparent that 1/8 was still afloat. Julian Smith ordered Hays to take his battalion into Red 2 at dawn. The eyes of the Southern Attack Force would be on this formation.

At 2100 "Washing Machine Charlie," in this case the first of several Japanese medium bombers operating singly, appeared overhead. Flying lazy circles, the first plane dropped a stick of bombs, half on the Japanese side of the island and half on the Americans; a dozen marines were killed or wounded. Another nuisance raider appeared about an hour before dawn and dropped its bomb load scattershot, here and there. Among the damage it inflicted was the random near miss of an outbound LVT loaded with casualties. The vessel, although not directly hit, was swamped and sank. Perhaps as many as fifteen wounded men drowned.

Thus the first night ended, and, although there had been no dreaded banzai attack, men had continued to die through the hours of darkness. It was the Japanese plan that many more would be slaughtered before this first American amphibious assault in the Central Pacific was finished.

At dawn of the second day, American soldiers, sailors, and marines were on their major objectives of Tarawa and Makin, still fighting grimly. Through long hours of savage combat with an unexpectedly strong and tenacious enemy, they had gained only the barest of beachheads on islands that planners had hoped they would seize swiftly and with little difficulty. At Tarawa the gallant troops of Colonel Shoup's reinforced 2d Marines clung to their miniscule gains on Betio, and at Makin the inexperienced soldiers of the late Col. Gardiner Conroy's 165th Infantry RCT struggled to move forward on Butaritari. Everyone was uncertain about what new horrors the second day would bring. Heavy casualties, confusion up and down the cumbersome chain of command, and unanticipated communication setbacks had taken their toll. All in all, from Rear Admiral Spruance down to the army and marine privates who doubted they would see another sunrise, it had been a miserable Sunday outing.

Meanwhile, three thousand yards off the southern point of Abemama—the third of the main objectives in the vast invasion plan—the transport submarine *Nautilus* slowly came to the surface. It was midnight when a crewman opened the hatch. The skipper, Lt. Comdr. Bill Irvin, climbed up into the conning tower. Behind him came marine Capt. James L. Jones and an Australian army scout, Lt. George Hard, a former Gilbert Islands resident.

Below, the seventy-eight marines of the V Amphibious Corps Reconnaissance Company, which Jones commanded, looked glumly at one another. Still rattled by their narrow escape from the guns of the Southern Attack Force on November 19, they were stoic. Nobody was looking forward to spending another full day underwater sweating and breathing stale air. They were anxious to leave the submarine. Shouldered into their combat gear and gathered in the minelaying hold, they hadn't long to wait. There they huddled, tense, in the compact space, as their officers briefed them for a final time.

Irvin, who had directed the critical periscope level coverage of the Gilberts in *Nautilus* in September and October, gave the word to his executive officer. "Now hear this," Lt. "Ozzie" Lynch said thickly over the ship intercom. "Now hear this. Marine personnel fall in on the after deck." The marine scouts moved with drilled efficiency to the hatches and climbed laboriously topside. Rough seas hindered the submarine crew as they launched the six large rubber landing boats with outboard motors. Guide lines were held taut as the scouts prepared to disembark for Abemama.

The marines were only a small force. No one expected much trouble, although the Japanese radio listening station was still in operation. The lack of enemy activity, as reported by navy and Seventh Air Force reconnaissance planes in the past three months, indicated that there were few Japanese here. To be certain, however, the marines had been ordered to scout the atoll and determine whether the Japanese had slipped in any sizable force at the eleventh hour. If any large enemy force was encountered, Jones was to avoid an engagement and withdraw. A contingency plan had been drawn up to land a battalion of the corps reserve, the 6th Marines, and a marine defense battalion of the garrison force, if necessary, after Tarawa and Makin had fallen.

As the rubber boats neared the shore, *Nautilus* vanished behind them, absorbed in a rainsquall. When some of the motors on their boats stalled, the marines rowed with vigor. Yet a strong current, coupled with the rainsqualls and the darkness, swept them leeward of their intended beach. They neared a point where the waves began to break on the barrier reef. Here the surf was treacherous, and the reef threatened to rip their craft to shreds if they did not maneuver around it. Only after four hours of the most strenuous effort did they succeed in reaching shore. That their uniforms and gear were soaked by the sea and rain only added to their discomfort.

Marines jumped into knee-deep water and wrestled their heavy boats, laden with equipment and fifteen days' supplies, into shore. They scanned the beach and scouted inland. Everything was quiet; nothing could be seen in the darkness. Abemama seemed asleep. If there were Japanese on the atoll, none were nearby. The marines had landed successfully, but not where they expected. They found themselves on Kenna, which they knew by its code name Joe—the last islet, their last chance to land before crashing onto the reef, which would have scrubbed their mission.

Jones established a perimeter and sent out patrols.

Chapter Twenty-eight

A towering black smudge in the eastern sky was visible as Lt. Col. Jesse Cook stirred. The 2d Division staff officer found himself in the observer's seat of his navy Kingfisher spotting plane. He had spent the night in this flimsy floatplane bobbing at sea twenty-five miles west of Tarawa after being forced down by friendly AA fire the previous evening. Early morning mists rising from the Pacific swirled around the plane. Seated in front of him in the cockpit was his pilot, Ensign French.

It was a half hour before dawn, and both men, neither of whom had slept much, were wide awake. As the sun began to rise over the eastern horizon on this Monday, November 21, the two men saw lights approaching from the west in the brightening sky. It looked like the lights of aircraft, and they waited anxiously to identify them as friend or foe. They were unable to determine this immediately, but before the planes were overhead it was evident that they were Japanese. They flew in tight V formations of many planes each. Ensign French counted sixteen in number.

The enemy aircraft had barely appeared overhead when it became apparent that the Kingfisher plane had been spotted on the surface of the sea. One of the bombers in the van veered from formation and glided down to have a closer look. The two Americans threw back the canopy of their wallowing floatplane and prepared to plunge into the sea if the enemy raiders opened fire. However, the Japanese plane circled only once, the pilot and crew gawking curiously, and continued on toward the east with the rest of the formation. Cook and French broke in on the navy air net, identified themselves, and contacted The Flag with an urgent warning: "Numerous enemy planes inbound Tarawa."

Rear Admiral Hill already knew of the impending dawn air raid. Radar aboard the destroyer screen shielding the fleet had picked up the "bandits" at a distance of thirty miles out. The radar grids turning atop the mastheads of the picket ships centered on the bearing of the enemy planes. The warning by Cook merely verified the radar report that the Japanese planes were indeed heading for Tarawa. Rear Admiral Hill ordered the picket ships to fire randomly and attempt to decoy the raiders away from the fleet and Tarawa.

Gunners on the destroyers and cruisers opened up first on the fast approaching Betty bombers with a vociferous AA barrage. Soon the battleships joined the fray. One observer mused that it looked like the Fourth of July over the sea around Tarawa. The brightening sky erupted with fiery shell bursts and brilliant streams of heavy AA machine-gun tracer. The swarm of Japanese planes ignored the heavy flak, however, remaining in formation and heading for the island, which they could easily locate by the fires that still burned in places. One after the other, the bombers flew straight over Tarawa and dropped their loads. The enemy defenders fired flares and tracer fire pinpointing the American positions, but most of the "sticks" impacted in Japanese-held territory. These rekindled the smoldering fires that had nearly burned themselves out. Some bombs landed randomly near ships and landing craft in the lagoon and on the reef. The enemy planes then swerved hard and headed back toward the Marshalls—their formation intact.

As dawn broke, Colonel Shoup's men, from their positions along the lagoon beaches, could begin to see the sprawl of the island with its blasted and burned buildings and splintered coconut trees. Nearby, the airfield, with its fifteen-hundred-foot fire-swept runway, dominated the battleground. The American lines had been strengthened during the night, and all the 2d Division's assault units and reinforcements faced grimly south or east—except the 1st Battalion, 8th Marines. Major Lawrence Hays's men stared over the gunwales of the landing boats in which they now had been waiting uncomfortably in the lagoon for twenty hours.

Under the cover of darkness, considerable quantities of ammunition, more artillery, light tanks, water, and other supplies had been brought in. Yet few of the marines, looking warily out from shell holes and foxholes and over the edge of the seawall, thought that this day would be less frightening than the previous one. Japanese reinforcements also had moved into the lines during the night and now lay carefully concealed in the wasteland of broken concrete and rubble. They, like the weary marines, waited for the light of day.

Enemy artillery and machine-gun fire on the pier had raged all night. Twice during the hours of darkness Japanese troops had tried to rush the pier. Counterattacking locally, the enemy had crept through the blackened sands to throw hand grenades into the marine positions. Infiltrating the pillboxes, the Japanese fought deadly, fierce hand-to-hand battles. They partially succeeded in gaining footholds, only to be beaten back with heavy losses. Gunnery Sergeant Jared J. Hooper, of Milford, New Jersey, second in command of the scout-sniper platoon, led the final charge and oversaw the critical reclamation of the pier.

Across the reef, behind the Red 1 and Red 2 sectors, Capt. Henry Lawrence, who although wounded on D day had assumed command of the LVT battalion, had made a night foray against the wrecked landing craft that enemy snipers had occupied. In some instances he was met with fire from American machine guns now manned by Japanese. With a flamethrower, his small group assaulted the occupied vehicles. Japanese clad only in shorts or in fatigues they had taken from dead marines were burned alive and gunned down. During this vicious nighttime action, Lawrence managed to clear out several LVTs and salvage a few others that had sustained only moderate damage or had been abandoned. In others he found stranded and wounded Americans whom his men helped evacuate.

But elsewhere on the island during the night, it had seemed as though both sides were drawing a deep breath. The nerve-racking lull was brief, however. When the fighting broke out again at sunrise, it seemed worse than on D day. The main attack began at 0600 in support of Major Hays's battalion, which had waited so long off the reef for orders to land, victims of communication foul-ups. "We were so seasick and disgusted," recalled a C Company officer, "that we'd have thanked the Nips for shooting us."

At first light, the carrier planes came in, strafing and bombing near the end of the airfield and the tail of the island, where most of the enemy reinforcements were coming from. The destroyer *Dashiell* joined in the bombardment. The other destroyer of the "close-in fire support" group, *Ringgold,* was unable to assist. She had shot off her entire supply of 5-inch shells the previous day. Instead, despite being slowed by a twenty-six-degree list caused by her pre–H-hour wounds and other types of battle damage, her crew made themselves useful taking on wounded. Her deck was awash in blood. Her role in providing naval gunfire support was taken over by the destroyer *Johnston,* which had been detached from the fleet.

Shortly before Hays's "fresh" battalion started in, the marines learned that they would be landing in the rear of the American beachhead opposite the eastern end of Red 1. Their officers instructed them to unload their weapons as a precaution against accidentally hitting friendly forces. Then, while some of the landing boats milled alongside the control boat *Pursuit,* taking on coffee provided by the crew of the minesweeper, Japanese shells began falling among their ranks and they had to be moved. The men frantically loaded their weapons as coxswains tried to keep the boats whole until the vulnerable human loads could be landed.

The enemy fire reached its crescendo at 0615, when the long-awaited landing by the battalion finally commenced. While the navy crews approached the reef, looking for a place to penetrate as close to shore as possible, the enemy guns began to zero in. As the five waves of two dozen or more LCVPs passed the wreck of the tramp freighter *Saida Maru,* at least one enemy machine gun poured a heavy volume of fire into their flanks. There was no place to hide from the Japanese machine guns and mortars that were ranged in on the reef. Before they could drop their ramps, two LCVPs simply blew up and disappeared after taking direct hits from a 70mm howitzer located in the area known ominously as The Pocket.

As the reinforcements jumped into the water, they were almost all felled. Correspondent Sherrod, awed by the calm disdain for death the marines demonstrated, watched with a mixture of fascination and horror: "Within five minutes I see six men killed. But the others keep coming. One rifleman walks slowly ashore, his left arm a bloody mess from the shoulder down. The casualties become heavier. Within a few minutes more, I can count at least a hundred Marines lying on the flats." Stranded at the end of the pier, the former Raider Colonel Carlson calculated that he saw 100 men hit in the span of just fifteen minutes. In fact, only 90 marines of 199 in the first wave reached shore.

Private First Class James Collins, of Spartanburg, South Carolina, recalled: "The water was red with blood. All around me men were screaming and moaning. I never prayed so hard in all my life. Only three men out of twenty-four in my boat ever got ashore that I know of." Collins made two trips back into the water to help wounded men. On his second attempt, a corpsman's head was blown off while Collins carried him toward shore. Private First Class William Coady, of Minersville, Pennsylvania, helped ten wounded men back into his boat before he finally reached the beach. About halfway in, TSgt. Gene Ward, a marine combat correspondent, dropped to his hands and knees. "I wormed along on my belly," he said. "Recalling that coral cuts badly, I kept looking at my hands and wrists. They were bloody but I couldn't feel anything."

A salvage crew from the transport *Sheridan,* busy rescuing men whose boats had been sunk, came upon fifty marines in deep water. Some were wounded but most were unharmed. All of them had lost their weapons and equipment. Although his LCVP was under heavy machine-gun fire and fighting a strong current, the skipper, Lt. Edward A. Heimberger, better known as the movie star Eddie Albert, and his crew lifted thirteen wounded men from the water. Heimberger also offered to evacuate the rest, about thirty-five men in all. They refused, demanding only that the sailors "bring back something for us to fight with."

The marine reinforcements were numbed by the ferocity of the unanticipated enemy resistance. In the mounting confusion, with intense fire from every angle, it was made painfully clear to Colonel Shoup that the opposition remained heavier than anyone had thought possible. There would be no reinforcements left if enemy fire continued unabated. Shoup had few illusions about this most deadly kind of landing—against strong positions held by an enemy who could not be seen. The fiercely determined assault commander knew that it was only a matter of time before Hays's battalion was annihilated. The Japanese obviously hoped to crush the reinforcements, by sheer weight of fire, with little threat to themselves. Against such powerful and concentrated resistance, the only thing that could save the immensely brave marines who were fighting their way across the reef was action by the troops ashore.

Shoup directed all units ashore on Red 2 to jump off immediately in order to offset the enemy fire that was raking the incoming 8th Marines ranks. The attack, backed by naval gunfire, bombing and strafing, flamethrowers, demolitions men, light artillery, 75mm half-tracks, and 37mm guns, surged here and there, but it was slow, dangerous work.

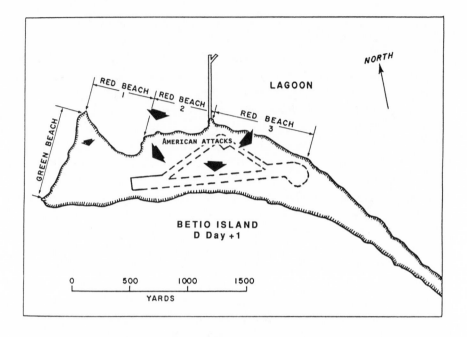

Lieutenant William "Hawk" Hawkins led his scout-snipers in repeated devastating assaults deep into The Pocket. As survivors stumbled ashore, they were fed into the area the commandos had cleared.

In the first of these daring missions against three pillboxes, Hawk and his men fought their way up the beach. At the time the Texan qualified as at least a technical casualty. He had been wounded on D day by mortar fragments and need not have continued fighting. Yet he had accepted only first aid and remained in the battle. "They can't hit me," he had insisted. "They couldn't hit me with a shotgun at point-blank range." Now, fighting among the strongest enemy positions on the island, he jumped to the foredeck of a disabled LVT just as the Japanese opened up. Though he was instantly struck in the shoulder by a bullet, he came up fast, firing directly into the principal enemy position. The Japanese were all killed, and two neighboring pillboxes were demolished with TNT. His men convinced Hawkins, who was now bleeding badly, to have his wounds examined. But when a corpsman insisted that he return to the ships for proper treatment, Hawkins refused. "Forget it" was his answer.

Two hours after clambering from their boats on the reef, having suffered severe casualties while wading in, the first four waves of reinforcements landed. The fifth wave was held back until it could be filtered in piecemeal. By late morning, the movement to shore, although it had been stopped and started several times, was now largely completed. Nearly half of the battalion—four hundred men—could not be accounted for. Three hundred fifty of them had been killed or wounded, and the others were missing. Nevertheless, enough had reached shore to be thrown into the fight.

Shoup ordered Hays to attack westward, through The Pocket, and link up with Major Ryan's isolated beachhead. This was the second battalion to which Shoup had assigned this unenviable mission. While Hays organized his remnants for the drive down the beach, Lieutenant Hawkins received first aid for his shoulder wounds. Gunnery Sergeant Hooper assumed temporary command of the scout-snipers. Though he was a mere twenty-six years old, Hooper had five and a half years in the marines behind him and had fought through the entire Guadalcanal campaign. He led a squad into the plane revetments bordering the airfield. From here enemy snipers were firing on the Red 2 staging area, creating havoc within the marine lines. This assault, in which Pfc. Basil J. Gillis, of Ipswich, Massachusetts, was shot and mortally wounded, allowed the 10th Marines to improve the field of fire of five sections of 75mm pack howitzers in order to support the landing being made by Hays's battalion.

As the 1st Battalion, 8th Marines, was coming in, the 75mm guns of the 10th Marines were firing directly ahead upon the most powerful Japanese emplacements. Using delayed-action fuses in order to penetrate the thick concrete and coconut shelters, artillery smashed a key strongpoint in The Pocket, but machine-gun and rifle fire was still heavy when the shelling was called off. It was redirected against the wrecked freighter *Saida Maru* on the reef. The crews of the guns registered a dozen direct hits—to no effect. Enemy troops still fired into the rear of the marines on the beach and on the men moving ashore. Hays's battalion attacked several positions, but without heavy weapons support his group lacked the strength to breach the fortified area between Red 1 and Red 2.

Before noon the navy planes moved in again and delivered a sudden and savage air bombardment to the *Saida Maru*—again with little effect. Shoup finally resorted to heavy naval gunfire to do the job. With air spotting and assistance from forward observers ashore, the battleships *Maryland* and *Colorado* fired salvo after salvo of 14- and 16-inch shells at the hulk. The naval gunfire fell dangerously close to friendly forces and showered some men with coral fragments, for in this small area perhaps one thousand Americans were working along and under the pier and on the reef. But by the time the two battlewagons finished their shelling, the *Saida Maru* was no more. In her place on the reef sat a mass of hideously twisted, smoking metal. By then, however, much of the steam had been taken out of the drive toward Red 1 by Hays's reinforcements.

Farther up front, the marines suffered casualties from Japanese artillery and mortar fire falling around them. A mortar barrage impacted where the marine tanks had taken shelter for the night. Technical Sergeant Jim Lucas was a mere fifty yards away with another man, eating cold rations and "cheering as we would at a football game." He recalled: "We watched with fascinated interest the chess game that followed. Risking their lives, tank crews went to their mounts and drove them frantically about in zigzag circles. The Japs shifted their range and tried to reach them. Shells exploded in a half a dozen places where the tanks had been, but only one was lost."

As the American armor zigzagged desperately to escape the ambush, a Japanese bluejacket emerged from his hiding place. Rushing forward, he tried to place a grenade on the tread of "Colorado," Lt. Louis Largey's Sherman tank, which had come through D day blackened and dented but still operational. As the courageous enemy saboteur dashed alongside the fast-moving tank, a marine rifleman shot him down.

Chapter Twenty-nine

At Makin the main action of the second day also was underway. The 27th Infantry Division's plan of attack called for the soldiers to jump off at 0700 and complete the drive to the eastern end of Butaritari. The commander of the division, Maj. Gen. Ralph Smith, was hopeful that the battle was nearly won. To knock the Japanese off balance and prevent any kind of cohesive resistance, he had ordered the 2d Battalion on the evening of D day to continue the attack "at any cost" in the morning. However, even before sunrise the Japanese were at work attempting to interpose themselves in the route of the American advance.

The first night on the island had been nightmarish. Enemy stragglers lurked in destroyed shelters behind the army lines, and as soon as night had fallen, these bypassed troops began moving about. They sought to rejoin their own forces, reorganize their dispersed ranks, and harass the green Americans. Whatever their purpose, the Japanese resorted to tricks. One enemy bluejacket moved in close to the perimeter, whispering, "Psst! Hey, Sarge!" Others called out, "Medic, Medic! Send a medic out here!" They dropped firecrackers all night long. At dawn a Japanese ran the length of the Yellow beaches shouting loudly, "Reveille, fellows! Get up! Reveille." Weary American soldiers unleashed a hail of rifle and machine-gun fire, which cut the man down. All along the perimeter Japanese patrols were active throughout the night.

In the confusion of the night's action, orders and counterorders went awry—they were delivered to the wrong units or simply were never sent. The company commander whose outfit had the job of leading the way in the morning mistakenly believed that the jump-off time was 0800. Thus, much of the shock of a devastating morning artillery preparation was wasted. Second, the tanks were not in place by the time the attack was to be renewed. Ten Lees were ready, except for ammunition and fuel, which had not arrived from the beach. While the tank crews waited for gas, navy fighters and bombers were pounding the area ahead. The air attacks occurred uncomfortably close to the front and the soldiers pulled back. Nothing could be done until the air assault ended and the tanks were prepared.

The attack—when it finally began four hours late, at 1110—was supported exclusively by the tanks and gained less than three hundred yards by early afternoon. Without naval gunfire, air support, and artillery, all of which was abundantly available but which the assault leader Col. John McDonough was reluctant to use in a combined arms role because of the unreliable communications, the infantry advanced slowly. By midafternoon McDonough's men had moved down the handle of the island to the base of King's wharf, mopping up Japanese stragglers and driving back the main body of enemy troops. Here the soldiers encountered the stiffest resistance of the day.

Ahead lay the wreckage of the big enemy seaplane smashed on D day and before by air and naval bombardment and now beached on the reef. From the wrecked plane and other positions—underground bunkers, pillboxes, trenches, rifle pits, trees, and behind barbed-wire emplacements—Japanese heavy AA machine-gun, rifle, and 3-inch coastal artillery fire swept across the island on a five-hundred-yard front. Four of the tanks pumped shells into the plane, and later the soldiers retrieved eighteen dead Japanese who had been concealed in its body and wings. For four hours the close combat raged in this fortified zone until one after another the enemy positions were finally overwhelmed.

In the afternoon the tanks moved on. The attack progressed. But by nightfall, the 165th Infantry RCT was only a thousand yards beyond where they had been in the morning. Charged with the quick capture of Makin, Ralph Smith's problems were acute. The movement of his assault forces from the Red beaches to as far as the Stone pier had proceeded at a snail's pace. Troops, equipment, and tanks were easily disorganized by enemy opposition and the press of combat. The single road leading from the beachheads to the front had become a quagmire. Because of constant sniping by enemy riflemen, nearly all work and forward movement was interrupted time and again.

On the positive side, there were fewer American casualties—eighteen killed, fifteen wounded—than had been suffered on D day, and all enemy resistance behind the American lines had been eliminated except for a few isolated snipers.

When the squad under Gunnery Sergeant Hooper returned from their interim mission near the airfield at Tarawa, the indefatigable Lieutenant Hawkins led the commandos on yet another foray into The Pocket. This time they struck a complex of five bunkers and pillboxes lying beyond the three they had knocked out earlier. This action, however, proved far more costly. Despite the bursting grenades and machine-gun fire that engulfed the commandos in their attack, they did not waver. Hawkins led them forward.

In total disregard for his own safety, Hawk crawled from a shell hole toward the first pillbox, in which two heavy machine guns were emplaced. "Don't worry about me," he told his men. "I'll take care of this one myself." He did. His men watched in horror when, only yards from the aperture of the pillbox, the officer took a slug dead center in his chest. He rolled a hand grenade through the aperture and killed all the Japanese inside the pillbox. Although his men pleaded, Hawkins again refused aid for his injuries despite the pain. "I came here to kill Japs, not to be evacuated," he argued, fighting off the accumulated shock of his three serious wounds.

But this marked the onset of tragedy. Private First Class Marcel J. Krzys, of Cleveland, was navigating past a bunker when he was shot through the head and killed. Earlier, in the drive up the beach, a mortar round had killed three other commandos. Although three more of the pillboxes soon fell, enemy fire was still intense, and the noise and carnage of grenades and machine guns all around was enormous. Now, as they came in sight of the fifth pillbox at the base of a sandy knoll, Hawkins told his men to hang back. Almost instantly they knew why. Seemingly unaware for the moment of any pain from his wounds, Hawk insisted on eliminating the last pillbox himself.

Hawkins's plan was to clear the way for his assault by throwing grenades at the pillbox, rushing forward, and then throwing a grenade through the firing aperture. Time after time he had done it, with exceptional daring. This time, however, just as he had lobbed a half-dozen grenades and stood up to charge, one of the Japanese 13mm heavy machine guns opened up. His men watched helplessly as the courageous lieutenant was "practically torn apart." Sergeant Morris

C. Owens, twenty-six years old, of Madison, Wisconsin, was nearby. A bullet struck Hawkins's uninjured shoulder, which shattered in the explosion, and severed an artery. As Owens watched, "The blood just gushed out of him."

Several scout-snipers rushed forward, grabbed Hawk, and propped him up against the back of the seawall. Others, in a rage, swept over the barricade and knocked out the enemy position. There was no question for whom they had done it. Hooper and three of the men got Hawk back to the beach. Miraculously, the Texan hung on. They carried him to the former enemy bunker where Doc Brukardt had set up his hospital. By one count Hawkins was given twenty-five pints of blood in all. He told his men not to worry. "Boys," he said weakly, "I hate leaving you like this." Everyone was humbled by the man's amazing strength and will to live. But fight as he might, his wounds were too grievous. Hawkins died during the night of severe shock and blood loss before he could be evacuated.

William D. Hawkins was posthumously awarded the Medal of Honor. In citing Hawkins for his self-sacrifice, Julian Smith observed, "His relentless fighting spirit in the face of formidable opposition and his exceptionally daring tactics served as an inspiration to his comrades during the most crucial phase of the battle." The airfield for which the marines fought was later officially named Hawkins Field, the first time this had been done for a marine rifleman. Hooper took over command of the scout-snipers again, this time for good.

At Hawaii, Admiral Nimitz anxiously greeted his staff. Following his regular morning conference, the commander in chief, Pacific, had at the request of VAdm. John Towers called a meeting to review the torpedoing of the light carrier *Independence* the previous evening off Tarawa. According to Towers, the chief of naval air forces in the Pacific, the event had been a tragic setback that need not have happened.

More than anything else, Towers argued, the lack of mobility imposed on the fast carrier forces by tying them to support of a contested beachhead had led to the loss of *Independence*. The battle for Tarawa was a gigantic magnet that had attracted the enemy air forces to the carriers. In the original Galvanic plan, Rear Admiral Spruance had based his disposition of the fast carriers on his fear of attack by Japanese carriers. But even now, when the Japanese Combined Fleet showed no signs of coming out to fight for the Gilberts, Spruance's view of the enemy naval situation remained conservative. Towers, backed by several other air enthusiasts, urged Nimitz to give the carrier captains more freedom before further damage was done to their ranks by forcing them to linger unnecessarily around the embattled islands.

When Nimitz asked for suggestions, Towers recommended immediately sending the fast carriers north to knock out enemy airfields that had not yet been hit by the Galvanic air forces. Towers wanted the carriers to go directly to Kwajalein—the center of Japanese air power in the Marshalls and through which all enemy air movement in the area occurred. He also was concerned about Roi-Namur and Maloelap, and wanted these hit hard before any more heavy air attacks could be launched from their fields. Nimitz refused to order Spruance to alter his plans before the Gilberts were captured, but he permitted Towers to draft a dispatch that granted the carrier captains a little more freedom of movement.

In this message Nimitz cited the hazards of continued air attack and possible submarine assault. He advised Spruance: "The use of surface craft by the enemy is unlikely. In the circumstances, operating areas for the carrier groups prescribed in the Galvanic orders are too restrictive. If the carriers continue too long in such narrow confines, they become subjected to progressively greater torpedo hazard. Take corrective action to insure them greater freedom of movement consistent with their mission."

Aboard his flagship *Indianapolis*, Spruance noted the message and notified the carrier captains accordingly. Nevertheless, he instructed them to remain within range of easy interception of any Japanese planes that might yet appear in the area of the objectives of Tarawa and Makin.

At Abemama, the marine scouts learned that there were indeed Japanese among the islets, including combat troops capable of defense. One of the patrols sent out by Capt. James Jones ran into an enemy patrol of three naval infantry shortly after dawn on a neighboring island. A brief but fierce firefight ensued in which one Japanese was killed. The other two withdrew, with confirmation for their commander, a sublieutenant, that they were no longer alone on the atoll.

Jones and the rest of his understrength company manhandled their weapons and supplies, and one of their number who had been injured in reaching shore, to the island where they had planned to land. Here they found a whaleboat, which was quickly put to good use in moving men and material. They had no way of knowing the Japanese strength, but after the difficulties encountered in just getting ashore, and then running into the enemy picket, Jones was cautious. He sent out patrols to find natives who could provide information about the Japanese. They soon found three.

By chance one native knew the Australian scout, Lieutenant Hard. The native told the marines that there were Japanese dug in two miles northward on the end of an island known to the marines as Otto, but not anywhere else on the atoll. He said that their number was about twenty-five. The marines also were surprised to learn that between them and the enemy, on the island of Monaku, was a group of French Catholic priests and nuns whom the Japanese had spared. These civilians were confined to Saint Michael's mission, where their superior, seventy-three-year-old Father Paul Mehl, ran the school at Abemama.

Although the marine reconnaissance party was tasked only with scouting for a follow-up assault force, Jones and his men moved out. They now knew that there were enough enemy troops to give them trouble. If they were caught in the open, they would be sitting ducks for the enemy. Said one: "We had to stay there five days, and there wasn't room for the Japs and us too." Thus, with the Australian army scout, Lieutenant Hard, and their native guides, they advanced up the chain slowly, exploring each island they crossed.

Finally, they reached Otto. The Japanese enclave was a strong one, fronted by a fordable channel but with all approaches well covered by machine guns. After probing the positions, and drawing alarmingly heavy fire that seriously wounded Pfc. Harold J. Marek and another man, Jones considered his options. The heaviest weapons in the tiny marine arsenal were light machine guns. Without mortars, it appeared impossible to dislodge the Japanese. It was late in the day and Jones saw no reason to make a costly rush of the enemy position. He broke off the action and withdrew, setting up a defensive perimeter for the night.

Chapter Thirty

Within hours Maj. Gen. Holland Smith's optimism regarding the resumption of the attack at Makin had faded. The futile efforts to wrap up affairs on this second day seemed to have been the last straw for the irascible V Amphibious Corps commander. He took out his frustration on Maj. Gen. Ralph Smith and the 165th RCT of the 27th Division. He felt that the soldiers simply had not moved fast enough. As he later wrote in his memoirs: "I was very disappointed with the regiment's lack of offensive spirit; it was preposterous that such a small Japanese force could delay the capture of Makin."

By midafternoon the crusty old barnacle of the U.S. Marine Corps could stand it no longer. He went ashore to look over the situation himself. By the time he reached the beachhead command post, he was, by his own account, "furious." He was determined to conclude the battle for Makin quickly so that he could be off to Tarawa, where he badly wanted to be, and the marine general believed that Ralph Smith "was fiddling with an operation that should have been ended long before."

As the corps commander and his aides approached the island, they saw reserves and equipment moving up to the front on the narrow road parallel to the lagoon, but without much haste. Upon reaching the command post, Holland Smith learned for the first time the details of the predicament. Ralph Smith, he surmised, was out of touch with the battle. His "communications with his regiment were extremely poor and he showed little enterprise in improving them. He didn't know where his battalions were, and insisted on sitting by the phone, where he couldn't get any information because the phone didn't work."

More than anything else, "Howlin' Mad" Smith's overriding concern for the beleaguered marines at Tarawa contributed to the anger he directed at the army. In fact, the V Amphibious Corps commander seemed no better informed of affairs at Makin than Ralph Smith. In many ways, things were better than he thought. Even now, messages were finally beginning to pass between the CP and the battalions, and the 27th Division staff's picture of the situation was improving.

Ralph Smith—a brilliant, imaginative, and determined officer—already had been to the front to see for himself how the situation could be alleviated. For the first time since the beginning of the battle he was able to act with confidence. In spite of the many setbacks, the 165th RCT had cleared all the island except the area northeast of the east tank barrier, and he believed that the situation was heartening. Victory, he sensed, was close at hand. By the time the V Amphibious Corps commander came ashore, demanding a quick finish to the battle for Makin, "almost all the day's objectives had been achieved" as provided for in the plan.

Sparing nothing, however, "Howlin' Mad" Smith bluntly restated "the importance of cleaning up the island as soon as possible." He complained that the soldiers, though worn out from heat exhaustion, were lagging. He charged that they were waiting for tanks and naval gunfire to do their jobs for them. Only decisive leadership could turn things around.

The army general calmly acknowledged that the situation was difficult, but he defended his troops, explaining that they were "attacking on a very narrow front and the Japanese were well dug in." He assured the corps commander that he had every hope of finishing off the enemy quickly. The 27th Division headquarters intended to keep the momentum in their favor. Efforts already were afoot to get fresh troops and more armor into action the next morning.

However much he doubted or wanted to rely on the soldier, Holland Smith had little choice. His influence on the situation was affected by the fact that his authority extended only so far—which created a dilemma for him. As corps commander he exercised operational control of the 27th Infantry Division, but since it was an army formation, administrative control lay with Lt. Gen. Robert C. Richardson, Jr., back in Hawaii, who was the commanding general of all army forces in the Central Pacific. There was little the marine could do. "Had Ralph Smith been a marine," he reported to Admiral Nimitz, "I would have relieved him of his command on the spot."

Holland Smith's misplaced fury did not stop there. He was under the mistaken impression that the body of Colonel Conroy, the 165th RCT commander who had been killed on D day, had not been recovered, even though the road where Conroy had died was now far behind the front and clear of the enemy. This struck the marine as an indication of a lack of loyalty of the regiment's troops to their late leader. "There was no danger involved," Smith observed. "Even if there had been, such negligence was inexcusable." In fact, although Conroy's body had remained by the road during the night, it had been retrieved by the time Smith came ashore.

Holland Smith set out on an inspection to confirm his suspicions about the battle. As he came upon the Yellow Beach sectors where troops were unloading supplies, an infantry company came through the area, firing into the trees right and left and forcing hundreds of men to take cover. The general dismounted his jeep and demanded to know what was going on. A lieutenant explained that he was clearing out possible snipers. Smith exploded. "Can't you see there aren't any Japs around here?" the marine general shouted. "Our men are working all over the area and you come shooting at tree tops when any damn fool can see there aren't Japs up there. Why, the enemy is thousands of yards up front." The soldier insisted that he was following orders to continue "shooting at everything so we won't take any chances." Smith revealed his identity and threatened, "If I hear one more shot from your men in this area I'll take your damn weapons and all your ammunition away from you." Soon afterwards, two Japanese snipers were killed "within two hundred yards of the spot."

Finally, despite strenuous efforts to get the 165th RCT moving, the cumbersome attack by the exhausted soldiers came to a halt at 1700—two hours before darkness was to close in on the battlefield. Whatever determination and drive that Holland and Ralph Smith had hoped to instill had come too late. Soldiers established their lines for the second night at Makin only yards forward of the final belt of Japanese defenses. After nightfall infiltrators tried repeatedly to breach the American positions, but they were betrayed by low-hanging trip wires strung thirty yards beyond the front. At least seven Japanese were killed after becoming entangled in the trip wires.

Lieutenant Seizo Ishikawa, the island commander at Makin, had been killed in the prelanding bombardment on D day. His second in command used his initiative, however, and when the infiltrations failed he expertly pulled the remainder of the small garrison from the south to further delay the American advance. The battle at Makin would continue for at least another day. There was not much Holland Smith or anyone else could do.

Inland of Red 1 and Red 2 close to the runway of the airfield at Tarawa, Colonel Shoup's 2d Marines spent the day fighting for their lives. Two Japanese counterattacks toward Green Beach were barely beaten back by Major Ryan's composite battalion. Pack howitzers and some mortar sections pounded the enemy lines as marines sprinted in small groups from shell hole to hummock and across the runway. Closing the gap between Red 1 and Red 2, Shoup's men moved in and out of converging fire lanes, their rifles and grenades blasting out the enemy, their flamethrowers incinerating the Japanese when they revealed themselves in their shelters.

The Japanese fought back hard. "This is worse, far worse than yesterday," observed correspondent Robert Sherrod. From his vantage point near Colonel Shoup's command post some fifteen yards from the lagoon, Sherrod could look out into the wasteland. As the murderous fire continued, he was astounded to see a marine—twenty-year-old Pfc. Adrian C. Strange, of Knox City, Texas, "the dirtiest man I have seen on the island"—emerge from the battle, limping, not bothering to seek the slightest cover. He stopped where the correspondent and others hugged the back of a retaining wall; then he grinned and said, "Somebody give me a cigarette." Strange pointed to a machine-gun crew in a shell hole across the airfield, its weapon clattering. "There's not a cigarette in the crowd." A marine threw him a pack, and he walked casually back across the airfield under fire all the way. "Shoot me down you son-of-a-bitch," he called out to the unseen sniper who was shooting at him. Said a veteran marine officer as he watched Private First Class Strange return to the fighting: "As long as we have boys like him, we're OK."

Shoup radioed to *Maryland*, "We're in a mighty tough spot." He explained that between 0600 and noon he had lost perhaps six hundred men. Only half of the 1st Battalion, 8th Marines, had reached the beach, and they had been quickly swallowed up in the awful maelstrom surrounding the effort to eliminate The Pocket and reach Major Ryan, who remained cut off. Every attempt to reach Red 1 had been mercilessly beaten back. His hands trembling from the enormous strain under which he was working, Shoup alerted the division command, "The situation ashore doesn't look good."

Yet on the western coast of Betio, the embattled elements of two battalions of the 2d Marines—the 1st and 3d, under Major Ryan—were at this time attacking to the south, inland of Green Beach. Aided by the close naval gunfire support of two destroyers, and by the damaged tank "China Gal," commanded by Lt. Edward Bale, and another Sherman that had been salvaged during the night, they drove all the way across the island (the bird's head). By midafternoon the advance, skirting warily past minefields, had carried five hundred yards to the ocean shore. The line in this area of the battlefield was now nearly straight across the eight-hundred-yard stretch of Green Beach, just west of the airfield, and over which the V Amphibious Corps reserves, the 6th Marines, could land safely.

Similarly, in the center of the still dangerously disconnected beachhead, the 2d Battalion managed to establish a line forward of Red 2 and just short of the airfield by late afternoon. Men began to move into the triangular infield formed by the airstrip, where a few forlorn marines had spent the night. Back of these forward positions, assault engineers used demolitions against Japanese stragglers. One by one deadly strongpoints that had wrecked landing operations for thirty-six hours were knocked out and some freedom of movement was at last achieved near the water's edge. At the same time on Red 2 Major Kyle's 1st Battalion concentrated on eliminating enemy positions that blocked the approaches to the airfield, and then drove toward the ocean side of the island.

In fact, although the fighting was hellish and costly, the marines were making progress in every assault zone except on Red 3. Here the primary objective of Maj. Jim Crowe's battalion remained the reduction of the system of enemy strongpoints near Burns-Philp wharf, and no advance was made. Although the 5-inch shells of a destroyer, the direct fire of 75mm and 37mm guns of Sherman medium and Stuart light tanks, and virtually every rifle and AT gun of the battalion were focused on this fortified area, little success was realized in reducing it or silencing the heavy enemy machine-gun and small-arms fire that poured along the beach from it.

The 6th Marines had been surprised when they got orders after noon on D day to boat for landing. "The corps reserve being called in on the first day?" they had wondered. "They won't need us," the men had complained several days before when they learned they would comprise the main reserve for Galvanic. Like tens of thousands of others, they had believed, "It will all be over the first day." Even when they began boating they did so with disbelief that they would see combat. Bandsmen struck up martial music and men dropped into bobbing boats singing lustily, "From the halls of Montezuma . . ." But as their boats proceeded to the lagoon, the 6th Marines were shocked by the terrible wounds and mounds of dead and dying marines they saw among the boats heading to hospital ships and transports. They listened in on their radios and learned just how dreadful the situation had become.

The 1st Battalion of Maj. William K. Jones, whose brother, Capt. James Jones, was leading the marine scouts at Abemama, was ordered to land on Green Beach. They had been milling about the lagoon for twenty-four hours and began landing in the early afternoon on the second day. It was slow going, and it was not until 1640 that the landing was entirely finished.

Some men and material came in aboard LVTs whose crews implemented a makeshift shuttle service reminiscent of the first day. Others came in aboard untracked landing boats, or in rubber assault boats that were towed and paddled ashore, or on foot. But the affair was not a bloodless one. As the LVTs moved into the beach, one was lost in a maze of mines. Hideously destructive "teapot" mines—which exploded upward beneath vehicles with devastating force—had been sowed all across the southern end of Green Beach. Within minutes the vehicle was rent apart in a massive explosion. The LVT "cracked open like an egg" and turned over, killing all hands except one man who was miraculously thrown clear of the wreckage by the blast. Beneath them a fifteen-foot hole had been blown in the coral reef. Behind the marines a platoon of light tanks waddled ashore two hours later. Soon they were sited behind Green Beach, preparing to jump off against the enemy positions the next morning in the first coordinated drive of the battle.

By the end of the second day, only a few hundred Japanese dead had been counted, but everyone believed that there must be many hundreds more buried in the rubble. Scores of suicides were turning up in overrun bunkers and pillboxes. The first large group of prisoners—a dozen Korean laborers, all of them wounded—was taken the second day. Through interrogation they indicated there had been six thousand Japanese on the island.

Bairiki, just three and a half miles to the southeast of Betio, is another of the tiny piles of coral and sand that make up Tarawa Atoll. In the vast and intricate Gilberts invasion plan, the island, code-named Sarah, had gone largely unnoticed except as a possible preinvasion platform for a 10th Marines artillery bombardment of Betio. That was until the second day. Then came reports from air spotters and from the crew of a patrolling destroyer that enemy troops were wading the channel between Bairiki and Betio. Shoup decided that he could not allow the former island to become a means of withdrawal for the Japanese.

To leave Bairiki alone was too risky. No one was prepared to allow even one Japanese to flee across the reef into the far reaches of the atoll and fight a delaying action up the narrow archipelago of islands. Hurriedly on this second day, the 2d Battalion, 6th Marines, began landing on Bairiki two hours before nightfall. As they approached the isle the marines did not expect to encounter opposition—but they did. When the brief prelanding bombardment by cruisers and battleships lifted and Lt. Col. Raymond L. Murray's battalion moved ashore in their landing boats, they were taken under long-range fire by machine guns.

Murray called in navy planes to knock out the guns. The Japanese fire, located by the pilot of a Hellcat fighter, came from a single pillbox practically in the center of the island. In strafing the strongpoint, the plane scored a lucky hit. For some reason, the pillbox in which the defenders had barricaded themselves doubled as a secondary fuel dump. During the first strafing pass, a canister of gasoline exploded when it was struck by a .50-caliber bullet. The whole structure was consumed in a flash of fire, and all of its fifteen occupants were incinerated.

These were the only enemy troops on Bairiki. The men of the 2d Battalion comprised the first American combat formation to land during Galvanic without taking casualties.

Chapter Thirty-one

The violent storm raging over the Gilberts also continued at sea. From naval intelligence alerts issued by CINCPAC, Rear Admiral Spruance knew exactly what the Japanese were up to. Navy code breakers in Hawaii had been listening to enemy radio communications emanating from Truk for days now. On the morning of November 21 they issued a general warning that Japanese submarines were converging on the Gilberts from all points of the compass. That mass attacks might develop, although probably not until November 23 at the earliest, was a threat not to be ignored.

Fifth Fleet destroyers not otherwise engaged in naval gunfire support missions had been put on heightened ASW patrol. Each ship carried a full load of depth charges and the most sensitive sonar gear of the day. Knowing that Japanese submarines might be prowling about was only part of the battle; finding and destroying them was the hard part. It was known that six large enemy submarines that had been operating in the Central and South Pacific had been ordered to the Gilberts by RAdm. Takeo Takagi, commander of the Japanese Sixth Fleet. What wasn't known, in spite of the best efforts of the code breakers, was that at least one of these enemy vessels was already stalking around beneath the surface in search of prey. Even now it was perilously close to the most lucrative and vulnerable American shipping—the transports off Tarawa.

This was confirmed when American planes had unsuccessfully bombed a submarine at dawn near the entrance to Tarawa lagoon. That was too close. An enemy submarine that had penetrated this far could attack the destroyer screen or the transports it guarded. Also, if it were a large enemy fleet-type submarine, it could use its deck guns in a night action—

250

a tactical innovation in which Japanese submariners excelled. Earlier in the war, enemy submarines had shelled oilfields in California and beach fortifications at Hawaii, Guadalcanal, and Wake under the cover of darkness.

Now, at noon on November 21, a few thousand yards from the transport marshaling area, a soundman on the destroyer *Gansevoort* of the fire support group was listening for anything unusual. Suddenly the sensitive sonar apparatus he was operating picked up a contact. He raised the alarm.

"Plot it!" ordered the officer of the watch as he hurried over to check the information. But by the time the destroyer had come round and charged the contact at high speed, the phantom had been lost. *Gansevoort* dropped several depth charges without apparent results. She briefly continued circling on patrol in a sustained wide search pattern without luck, and then returned to her station off Tarawa. Meanwhile, sister ships *Meade,* under Comdr. John Munholland, and *Frazier,* under Lt. Comdr. Elliot M. Brown, were called in to continue the search.

An hour later a full-fledged sea hunt was on when the potential threat was reacquired—and lost again—this time by *Meade.* The deadly game of cat and mouse continued throughout the afternoon as the destroyers patrolled the area, finding and losing the suspicious contact several times. Finally, at 1700 another acquisition was established.

"I've got it!" shouted Soundman George A. Lewis aboard *Frazier.* "Sound contact—bearing three-two-zero true." Ensign Thomas P. Higgins, who was commanding the sonar watch, worked with Lewis to pinpoint the location. Although they knew that a Japanese submarine had escaped a bombing attack at dawn, until this latest contact they could not be certain that they were not chasing a whale. Higgins, however, was definite this time.

"I'm sure it's a Jap sub, Skipper," Higgins advised. The position of each previous point of contact had been plotted on the tactical chart. The bearing of each had been in an erratic pattern, as though the contact were trying to evade the destroyers overhead. That was enough for Brown, who was standing on the bridge.

"Battle stations—depth charge attack!" Brown ordered, and *Frazier* surged angrily toward the contact, located nine miles northwest of Betio. As soon as his own ship made contact, Commander Munholland also led *Meade* into the attack. The quartermaster of the watch aboard

Frazier announced over the speaker system: "Stand by for depth charge attack."

"Range to target one-four-zero-zero, bearing three-two-two," reported Seaman Lewis from his sonar station. The object beneath the surface was no longer a "contact." It was now a "target," a submarine crewed by enemy seamen. Command of the attack lay with Commander Brown, since *Frazier* had been the first to pinpoint the latest bearing and arrive on the scene. Once he had the target's course line, Brown made his approach head on.

All the while Seaman Lewis continued providing updated tactical information. "Target appears to be moving to the right," he said.

"Change course to three-three-two," ordered Brown.

A minute later depth charges started to roll from *Frazier*. Soon *Meade* was also throwing "ashcans" overboard. With each massive explosion, the surface of the sea shattered like broken glass, and a violent mushroom of water erupted.

Amid the tension of a submarine on the run, Seaman Takashi Kawano, a talker in the control room of the Japanese fleet submarine I-35, relayed the dreaded news from the sound operators. "High speed propeller noises approaching."

The heavy pinging grimly dispelled any doubt that the American destroyers had failed to locate I-35 yet again. The crunch of depth charges proved it. The submarine angled sharply down, plunging to the safety of deeper water.

"Two hundred sixty feet," reported the chief engineer.

Although the enemy ships were fully cognizant that he was in the area, Lt. Comdr. Hideo Yamamoto did not want to assist the enemy in pinpointing their location by generating unnecessary noise that would register on the enemy's hydrophones. He rigged the ship for silent running, secured all auxiliaries, and continued working the propulsion unit just enough to allow him to steer. An eerie silence settled over the hunted submarine and its crew of ninety officers and men. Through the hull they could hear the enemy screws converging overhead. With a submerged top speed of eight knots, which her inefficient batteries could not support for long, I-35 could not hope to outrun her attackers. Her only chance of survival lay in the low odds that the depth charge attack might not inflict fatal damage to the hull.

Yamamoto had been lurking east of the enemy destroyer screen at a depth of sixty-five feet just before noon when the lone destroyer suddenly had come charging from the direction of Tarawa. In the brief but violent depth charging that followed, the submarine barely escaped with serious damage. Lighting had been knocked out when bulbs shattered in their sockets from the concussion and the electrical system short-circuited. As Yamamoto dived deep, the explosions followed the submarine down. She began shuddering and sprang leaks in her plating.

And now, with battery power failing and I-35 stopped dead and silent in the depths, there were more explosions. Like the beating of a muffled drum, the depth charges thundered at spaced intervals, battering the hatches and weakened hull. It was not difficult to imagine the American destroyers roaming back and forth on the surface, reversing course and laying strings of depth charges along the line of bearing that their sonar gear had established.

"Take us deeper," demanded Lieutenant Commander Yamamoto. "Three hundred ninety feet."

All hands knew that this was far below the maximum depth for safe operation of their inferior submarines. The hull constricted under the pressure of twenty thousand pounds of water per square foot as the submarine plunged below the depth where the canisters were exploding. Relief was fleeting. They knew that the enemy would tenaciously keep up his attack. And soon the booming of depth charges sounded once again. I-35 lurched and rolled under renewed destruction that followed it down.

Instruments in the conning tower failed, and gauges in the control room malfunctioned. The clocks stopped. Under the enormous pressure, the packing around the diving planes was blown free, and the rivets in the hull began to give way. Suddenly the hull and fuel tanks ruptured, and the submarine began taking on water at an alarming and inexorable speed. With fatalistic expressions all hands turned to their section chiefs for some sense of hope. No such optimism could have convincingly come forth under the circumstances. The terrible burden of decision rested with the commander.

Yamamoto tried one last option. He tried to move out of the locus of the concentrated explosions, but then he learned that the situation was now truly hopeless. The depth charging had ruined the rudder. The boat no longer could be controlled. Another shattering blast, worse than anything before it, caused the submarine to suddenly nose down at a ponderous angle of twenty degrees. They could go no deeper; the water pressure would crush the hull. Yamamoto exercised his final option.

"Surface!" he said. "Prepare for gun action." He blew the tanks, and slowly, as though she did not want to go, the submarine rose toward the surface. Yamamoto's order to surface sent gun crews slogging through the rising water to assemble at their battle stations, ready to open the hatches and rush onto the deck. Desperate planesmen forced the crippled diving planes, in a series of shuddering fits, to yield some uptilt so that the ship would break the surface level and not bow first. But by this time it was a forlorn effort. I-35 was fleeing death from below only to face it squarely on the surface.

"The sea stinks of oil!" shouted Lt. Gilbert H. Scribner, Jr., *Frazier*'s executive officer; Lt. Thomas E. Anderson, her main battery control officer, confirmed his observation.

As if to lend timely credence to the report of the two junior officers, a huge batch of reeking fuel bubbled to the surface nearby. *Frazier* dropped four more depth charges along the leading edge of the spreading oil slick, further polluting the brilliant blue sea. The destroyer steamed at full speed with a wide "bone" of brown scum kicked up by her bow.

"Target is surfacing," advised Seaman Lewis.

"There he is!" yelled a lookout, pointing. "Over there."

"We got the bastard!" hooted an unknown voice on the bridge.

A periscope, then a conning tower, followed by the sleek gray shell of a dreaded Japanese I-boat surfaced between the two destroyers. Two floatplanes from a pair of cruisers nearby circled the wounded enemy vessel like vultures, then swooped down to strafe and bomb. *Frazier* turned round to close the target, her 5-inch and 40mm guns opening fire immediately.

Aboard I-35 a submariner flung open the conning tower hatch, and men began scrambling out. Gunners raced to man the 5.5-inch gun on the main deck and the .50-caliber AA machine guns forward and aft of the bridge. The American destroyer was bearing down on them at full attack speed, obviously eager for the kill. A 5-inch shell struck the tower, and the spotter, the pointer, and the gun chief were all killed in their mad dash to the main gun.

Superior Petty Officer Ichiro Yamashita climbed out of the wrecked, and now red-hot, tower and made it onto the deck. He headed for the main gun. Petty Officer Shigeto Ohata, the chief planesman, was right behind him, headed for a machine gun. Neither made it. Both were hit by bullets from one of the strafing planes and fell to the deck unconscious.

As salvos from the American ships sent monstrous geysers upward and shook the submarine, Petty Officer Kawano also struck out for the main gun. A shattering blast obliterated the forward deck. When the smoke and fire cleared, nothing of the 5.5-inch ammunition locker was to be seen. Kawano decided to try to man the machine gun. No sooner had he armed it than one of the planes zoomed in strafing. Kawano was struck a terrific blow. When he examined his right hand, which was covered with blood, he discovered that two fingers were missing. A few seconds later, he was hit again and fell to the deck, also unconscious.

Below, in the control room, Commander Yamamoto knew that the end of I-35 was at hand. All around him men were streaming into the control room from other compartments. He accepted his final responsibility to his ship and crew: As an officer of His Majesty's Imperial Navy, his obligation was not to permit his crew to die leaderless. He scrambled up the conning tower hatch. Another shell pierced the ship, causing horrific slaughter on the deck. Among those killed was Yamamoto.

"Stand by for collision!"

Unwilling to take any unnecessary risk, Commander Brown heeled over *Frazier* in a deliberate head-on approach, charged in hard, and rammed the submarine just aft of the conning tower. As the destroyer backed off to free her badly bashed bow, I-35 began taking on heavy water and sinking swiftly stern first. More crewmen emerged from the conning tower hatch. As disbelieving American sailors watched, the Japanese rushed to man the deck gun. They were cut down by pistol and rifle fire. No other Japanese got off before the submarine slid below the waves, its bow pointing into the sunset, pursued all the way down by bombs from the now swarming ASW air patrol from the escort carriers. A total of four survivors were left in the water.

The destroyers quickly launched their motor whaleboats, but the rescue was not an easy one. One of the survivors fired on the rescue party and was promptly killed. The other three Japanese were stunned and did not resist. All were picked up. While returning with the prisoners, *Meade*'s whaleboat was mistaken for a submarine's conning tower by one of the planes. It dropped a five-hundred-pound bomb, which landed only a yard away from the whaleboat and exploded under water, lifting the craft into the air. By some miracle the boat was not destroyed. AA gunners aboard *Meade* opened fire. The plane was damaged but managed to return to the escort carrier *Suwanee*.

One Japanese submarine had been destroyed, but others remained in the Gilberts. The fighting at sea was not over.

Chapter Thirty-two

Since the previous night, the man with one of the least glamorous jobs at Tarawa had gone about it with determination. All through the second day navy Capt. John B. McGovern, commander of one of the transport groups, had worked to bring order out of chaos. Told to get control of the ship-to-shore situation, McGovern had moved his headquarters to the minesweeper *Pursuit* during the first night. Only quick action could save the marines, and by early afternoon of D day plus one, eighteen LVTs had been rounded up. Neither McGovern nor his men had managed more than brief catnaps in thirty-six hours. Despite vicious enemy fire and the indescribable confusion of the American supply situation, the motley group of vehicles and marine and navy crewmen under his command had initiated a shuttle service that moved enough supplies to the end of the pier and then to shore to stave off disaster.

But just barely. When Colonel Carlson—whom Colonel Shoup had sent out to the fleet the previous day—arrived back at the beach on the second morning, the situation had improved little. Reinforcements had not arrived as planned; resupply had been short and erratic; and entire rifle companies had disappeared in their attempts to consolidate meager gains. The 2d Division had been pushed close to destruction. Shoup sent the former Raider back out to the flagship with another situation report for Maj. Gen. Julian Smith and Colonel Edson, the division chief of staff.

Only after Carlson's briefing of these officers, coupled with the good news that Major Ryan had secured Green Beach and that the laggard tide had finally come in, did the situation ashore begin to improve. Julian Smith was, for the first time during the battle, able to act with confidence. On the basis of his enhanced understanding of the events of the morning, he was now able to deploy the 6th Marine battalion landing teams. Until then it had been "touch and go," according to Lieutenant Colonel Rixey, the 10th Marines commander, but "then I knew we would win."

Others also began to suspect that perhaps the worst was behind them. The courageous Carlson, who before the battle was over would make four trips into and out of the fire-swept beaches, returned to the command post again at midnight. Although not much had changed for the better, he too instinctively felt that the turning point had passed. Lieutenant Commander Robert MacPherson, in his Kingfisher spotting plane, saw troops along the Black beaches on the ocean side of the island and swooped low to investigate. When they waved to him, he noted optimistically in his log: "There's no mistaking the smile of a grinning marine." In fact, the improved situation at the end of the second day—which, in the words of correspondent Sherrod, was "reflected in everyone's face around headquarters"—had not come too late.

Correspondent Richard Johnston, who had come ashore with Major Crowe on Red 3, looked around him. He also sensed that the worst had passed. He scribbled in his notes: "It has been my privilege to see the Marines from privates to colonels, every man a hero, go up against Japanese fire with complete disregard for their lives. Men have died around me, many lie dead up ahead and more are going in to die. The situation at one time was critical, but the valor of the Marines," he observed, has "won the battle." But, in fact, although the situation had improved, the battle was far from over.

Colonel Shoup's situation report emphasized the turn of events. The marines, he said, were "dishing out hell and catching hell." He noted that Lieutenant Colonel Rixey's pack howitzers were in position and registered to begin firing on the tail end of the island the next day. Finally, he added, "Our casualties are many. The percentage dead is unknown." As for "combat efficiency," he added, "we are winning."

"Red Mike" Edson came ashore and relieved the exhausted Shoup of overall command of the island fighting at 2030. Shoup, whose coolness in desperate straits would later be judged to have saved the day at Tarawa and earn him the Medal of Honor, was now free to concentrate solely on the plight of his own regiment in and around The Pocket. Yet, as positive as events were looking, only now did the veteran

Edson begin to learn the facts of all that had transpired in the previous day and a half. The tally of the 2d and 8th Marines' remaining men told the grim story. All through the afternoon of the second day, battalion leaders and company commanders of the assault teams who were in contact with the command post reported their strength. Speculative and variable as information reported in the heat of battle always is, these reports presented an awful accounting.

Of Shoup's reinforced 2d Marine RCT, only Jim Crowe's attached 8th Marines force of the 2d and 3d battalions on Red 3 was fighting as a coordinated unit. Of this group, no one had any idea how many men were left of Ruud's 3d Battalion, which had been mauled while landing as reinforcements on D day. Few believed that there were more than 350 still uninjured. Crowe's own 2d Battalion had suffered some 300 casualties. In the Red 1 and Red 2 sectors, Shoup's 2d Marine battalions were mere shadows of their former strength. Schoettel's 3d Battalion was at half strength, and still fighting under the inspiring leadership of Major Ryan. The 1st Battalion under Kyle had been splintered to shreds and partially absorbed into any of four different battalions into whose rear they had landed piecemeal. The 2d's strength was down to a few hundred effectives. In Hays's 1/8, also on Red 2, perhaps 400 men were left. In landing on the second day, this battalion suffered losses greater than any unit committed on D day.

The action at Tarawa had not been confined to Betio. In addition to the landing on Bairiki, 2d Division scouts had reconnoitered the islets east of the main battleground. The platoon that scouted Eita located fuel depots and bomb and mine dumps, but no Japanese. Another platoon, which landed on Buota, encountered one hundred enemy troops dug in around a radio station, and withdrew undetected after nightfall. A third platoon, which landed four miles farther up the chain near Tabiteuea village, captured a Japanese laborer.

Although ten thousand men, including seven battalions of marine infantry, had been committed to battle—the figure belied the fact that many attached elements were units such as shore parties, Seabees, special service troops, and others—the attack battalions that had come in on D day had almost ceased to exist as combat formations in and of themselves. The men of these defiant, fiercely proud units were still scattered in small groups, dazed, suffering from battle shock, and too often bereft of officers and noncoms. In addition to the record losses of D day, when fifteen hundred men had fallen, the 2d Division lost another thousand men killed, wounded, and missing on the second day.

The fighting had been so bloody and so terrible that the spirit of even battle-hardened veterans, who made up half of the 2d Division, had been sorely tested. Although small groups of stragglers were common, Shoup and his staff had encountered only sporadic instances of panic. "We were not all heroes," said one officer. "I started inland with about 100 Marines to take out a machine gun that was giving us trouble, but by the time we got there only two or three were with me." But for the most part the marines had fought on against formidable odds.

Now, what remained of the shattered and bloodied assault units was being weakened by exhaustion and, ironically, the collapse of Japanese defenders being squeezed and driven back upon themselves. Too few marines were available in some outfits to move into all the ground that had been taken. All routes of advance seemed to end in the airfield area, with the main body of enemy troops centered around The Pocket and from the southwest corner all down the southern coast. Down that rough corridor to a point inland of Red 3, Edson planned to make what he hoped would be the final drive. By husbanding his strength through the night, he planned to attack relentlessly down this axis the next day with the 6th Marines, supported by Shoup's reduction of The Pocket, and finish the battle.

All through the night of November 21, orders went out for troops to pull back into defensible perimeters, holding as much of their gains as possible. The capture of Green Beach was an important factor in Edson's planning. Admittedly the odds for finishing the battle quickly were still great, even with a clear beach over which supplies and troops could move freely. If The Pocket could be overwhelmed swiftly, and if the men who had been fighting since D day could hold out through the long night ahead—a great many if's, it seemed—there was every hope that the 6th Marines could sweep down the southern coast all the way to the tail end of the island on the third day. Regardless, with the Japanese now split into two groups—the redoubt in The Pocket and the main body still holding on savagely south and east of the airfield—and material getting ashore, the picture had brightened immensely. As night enveloped the opposing American and Japanese troops at Tarawa, Colonel Shoup grabbed his first real sleep in sixty hours.

Elsewhere within the American lines, few men slept easily for fear of counterattack. As the Japanese were driven in upon themselves in narrow fronts, the danger of a banzai attack had become more acute. But again on this second night, no Japanese counterattack occurred. While messengers hand-carried orders of battle to far-flung units, and marines dug foxholes or scrambled into shell craters, everyone waited for the third day.

The End

PART FOUR

Chapter Thirty-three

Neither had there been rest for the soldiers at Makin during the hours of darkness of November 21. Shortly before midnight Japanese, creeping forward from bypassed positions in the area of the western tank barrier, tried to infiltrate the army lines in order to reach their comrades—most of whom had retreated to the east, although the Americans did not yet know it.

Throughout the night alongside the flank of the beachhead inland of Yellow 1, small-arms fire crackled and grenades detonated. The entire western half of Butaritari was stirred by the activity. The company in the thick of it heaved about a hundred grenades during the night, and in the morning found five dead Japanese beyond their perimeter. During a lull, a sentry threw the men in the beachhead into panic, arousing battalion commanders in their foxholes. "There are 200 Japs out there!" the guard shouted, mistaking the approach of navy landing craft carrying supplies as enemy reinforcements.

At the height of the wild spectacle, friendly fire was hurled into the 27th Division command post. "Howlin' Mad" Smith, the corps commander, had been trying to sleep on a cot outside the headquarters tent. He crawled out from under his mosquito net. "Shots whizzed over my head from a 25-yard range," he recalled, "drilled holes in the command post tent and clipped coconuts off the trees." The nervous fire was abated only after officers moved among the troops, talking in loud voices to avoid being shot by their own men. The third day was not likely to be much better than the first or second, Smith feared.

At the front, Col. Joe Hart's 3d Battalion, strengthened by the arrival of a dozen medium and light tanks, went back into action at dawn. Advancing after a ninety-minute heavy artillery barrage, which fired nine hundred rounds of 75mm and 105mm HE shells at the suspected Japanese positions, the soldiers swept forward to the eastern antitank ditch that ran across the island. They gained ground against occasional sniper fire, and were 250 yards east of the barrier as early as 1045.

Meanwhile, an LVT-borne company conducted an amphibious flanking movement to cut off the enemy from further retreat. Landing three miles to the east of the front, they learned from natives that the Japanese already had passed. They were fleeing across the reef to the neighboring island of Kuma, which soldiers had scouted on D day plus one. Another end-around flanking movement was organized, and in midafternoon an infantry company seized Kuma without opposition, trapping the remainder of the Japanese forces on Butaritari.

It seemed that it was only a matter of time until the Japanese were finished. The operation was taking on the telltale characteristics of a rout. Major General Ralph Smith assumed full command for the first time, but even though the battle had become more fluid, overall the going was slow. Holland Smith was anxious to be off to Tarawa, where the danger was still great. He turned on Ralph Smith. "Get your troops going!" he thundered at the army general. "What's holding you up? There's not another goddamned Jap on this island."

Until now Ralph Smith had listened impassively to "Howlin' Mad" Smith's firm reproaches to intensify all attacks and end the whole affair. However, this latest charge that no enemy troops remained on the island was more than he could take. He warned the corps commander: "General, that plain isn't so." Although he had no illusions that the Japanese remained on the island in strength, Ralph Smith was concerned. There was the chance that his own view was too pessimistic, but it seemed that the marine general's optimism was premature. The Citadel had been cleared and the soldiers were advancing beyond it, but fighting was still going on. All day the enemy forces had appeared to be falling back. The possibility of a counterattack could not be ignored.

This view was shared by the army historian S. L. A. Marshall, then a lieutenant colonel attached to the 27th Division staff. "All of the main enemy works in the heavily populated end of the island were in our hands," Marshall observed. "Such enemy soldiers as still lived had faded back into the bush and the sights and sounds of resistance had almost died out. Most of us, however, had the uneasy feeling that the gathering calm was wholly deceptive."

Marshall took a special interest in Holland Smith as he watched the V Amphibious Corps commander confer with Ralph Smith at the division CP. "We three sat there together batting at mosquitoes," Marshall remembered, "while Holland Smith nagged." Too great a force was being tied down in a battle that should have ended by now. "Right then I decided," as Marshall later put it, "Holland Smith was clearly a bully, something of a sadist and, I guessed, tactically a chowderhead."

Nevertheless, by the time the 3d Battalion soldiers dug in for the night, ahead lay five thousand yards of unsecured territory. All that seemed necessary was to mop up a now thoroughly disorganized enemy trapped on the extreme northeastern tip of Butaritari. Rear Admiral Turner judged the island captured, "though with minor resistance remaining." He congratulated Ralph Smith and ordered him to reembark two infantry battalions and all the heavy armor the next day. It was not a foregone conclusion that the marines could finish the job at Tarawa by themselves. There, it was still impossible to say just when the end would come.

On the 2d Marine Division front at Tarawa, the 6th Marines went into action for the first time since landing the previous evening, and they did so with a vengeance. The 1st Battalion was set for an early morning rush, but the axis of their attack appeared to be a difficult one. They faced the narrow hundred-yard-wide corridor of heavily fortified ground between the airfield and the ocean, a strip that was studded with pillboxes and bunkers hiding an untold number of Japanese riflemen. Company C led the way.

They jumped off at 0800. Supported by destroyer fire, three light tanks, and the medium tank "China Gal," commanded by Lt. Edward Bale, they swept forward rapidly, and by 1100 had linked up with the 1st Battalion, 2d Marines. "Those infantrymen were terrific," said Bale. "I never saw such guts. We ranged across the whole end of the island and down the south side and they never flinched but took us straight to the targets." During the afternoon the last battalion of the 6th Marines waded onto Green Beach and moved up in the rear of the assault. Together the two sister battalions, riding the wave of an irresistible momentum, advanced up the southern beaches (the bird's back) as far as the eastern end of the airfield, which they reached in late afternoon.

When the drive ended, behind them lay an estimated fifty pillboxes containing 250 Japanese dead. At least one marine cracked, succumbing to the pressure of two days of combat. Finding his way cut off by an enemy machine gun, he shrieked: "All right, you bastards, I'm coming in!" Disregarding all caution under fire, he threw away his rifle and unslung a grenade from his belt. He crawled on his stomach until he was directly beneath the gun's flashing muzzle, then lobbed the grenade into the emplacement. As the screams of the enemy inside the broiling bunker filled his ears, the marine rolled on the ground, laughing insanely and pounding the sand with his fists. Corpsmen got him to the rear.

Private First Class Felix S. Kranc, of Chicago, found his squad similarly pinned down in the cross fire of three pillboxes. He crawled to within thirty feet of the nearest position, stood up behind a coconut tree, and emptied an entire clip into the embrasure. When this failed to silence the machine gun inside, Kranc grabbed a Browning automatic rifle (BAR) and charged. He stuck the muzzle into the firing slit and emptied the weapon on full automatic fire. Still the enemy gun continued to chatter. Kranc bummed three grenades, which he threw from a distance of only ten feet away. The gun fell silent. On his way back he saw a marine lying wounded in the center of the cross fire. He and another marine rushed into the killing zone, rolled the wounded man onto a poncho, and dragged him to safety.

Elsewhere gains were made, but against heavy resistance and with far less evident results. The 2d and 3d Battalions, 8th Marines, attacked out of the hard-pressed Red 3 beachhead. They slashed east along the lagoon shore, again concentrating against the massive bombproof and steel pillbox complex near the Burns-Philp wharf. Two companies succeeded in knocking out the steel pillbox, together with another supporting position. The bombproof was then assaulted from the front and sides and was nearly surrounded.

At one time elements of Company F of 2/8 were astride the top of the bombproof, but still the Japanese would not give up and the fortress remained in enemy hands. The marines fought with tanks, artillery, mortars, rifles, grenades, machine guns, and multiple charges of

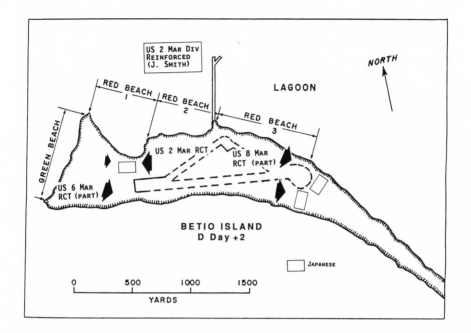

US 2 MAR DIV
REINFORCED
(J. SMITH)

NORTH

LAGOON

RED BEACH
1

RED BEACH
2

RED BEACH
3

GREEN BEACH

US 2 MAR RCT

US 8 MAR
RCT (PART)

US 6 MAR
RCT (PART)

BETIO ISLAND
D Day +2

JAPANESE

0   500   1000   1500

YARDS

TNT. They were supported by destroyers and air attacks. Still the stubborn defenders gave no quarter, even though they must have been near the end of their capacity to resist. These were the men from the 7th Sasebo SNLF, who made up Rear Admiral Shibasaki's elite marine guard. They had fought at Guadalcanal and survived. They would fight to the death at Tarawa.

By midmorning, the marines had made some progress toward reducing enemy fire from the flanks and believed that now was the time to finish the job. At 0930 a 60mm mortar round struck an uncharted ammunition dump. The volatile stockpile blew sky high, taking with it—to the utter shock of the marines—an enemy position that had been a linchpin in the Japanese defense on Red 3 since D day. Several marines were wounded by the ensuing shower of shrapnel or were knocked down and buried by falling debris from the explosion. Lieutenant Louis Largey rumbled forward in "Colorado," his blackened Sherman tank, and flattened the troublesome steel pillbox with successive hits from his 75mm gun at point-blank range. Seabees brought in bulldozers, and the drivers fearlessly pushed sand over the smoking enemy emplacements. Gradually, with supreme effort, the area was brought under control—free from enfilading fire for the first time during the battle.

The mammoth, sand-covered dome, so formidable for these past three days, was now isolated. Perhaps 150 Japanese were still alive inside the mound. The nearby supporting positions all had been knocked out. The trenches were nearly empty of live enemy riflemen; the bunkers were torn from their foundations by naval gunfire; the pillboxes were burned, blasted, cracked open, and buried by sand.

Major Bill Chamberlin gathered a mixed bag of riflemen and assault engineers from a half-dozen units and organized the attack. "Follow me!" he shouted. The tiny force surged over the seawall. Chamberlin and SSgt. Norman K. Hatch, of Washington, D.C., scrambled up the western face. Hatch, a twenty-two-year-old fifth-year marine, was a combat cameraman. Once the two men were through the rubble at the base of the massif, they disregarded the enemy frontal fire and raced to the top. It was strangely quiet when they reached the crest and peered down from a height of seventeen feet above sea level, the highest elevation in the Gilberts. Nearby a Japanese squad suddenly broke into the open and chased the two marines off the mound.

This was the time for Lt. Sandy Bonnyman and his detachment of engineers. The previous day Bonnyman had crawled forty yards in front of the marine line to place demolition charges in the entrance to a bunker. Chamberlin now ordered him to seize the summit and hold it. He also sent a demolition team under Cpl. Harold Niehoff to strike the bomb-proof from the southeast in order to cover the main assault and cut off the access of Japanese reinforcements. Niehoff and his group hurled explosives and used flamethrowers against the position from the south, cleared the summit of an enemy machine-gun nest, and charged uphill.

Bonnyman, executive officer of the 2d Battalion, 8th Marines, shore party and commanding the 2d Platoon, Company C, started out with a dozen men, supported by riflemen to cover the advance. The small force was plainly silhouetted as it moved up the face of the mound. All over the eastern half of the Red 3 beachhead, dirty, tired marines, curious about all the commotion, watched in awe. The smoke of burning palm fronds that had camouflaged the emplacement covered the breakthrough. Bonnyman and six others scrambled onto the summit.

Sergeant Alfred E. "Pappy" Coleman, an 18th Marines pioneer, threw fused explosive charges as fast as he could, blowing open a camouflaged entrance to the bombproof. Other marines poured diesel fuel into air shafts of the shelter. As hundreds of marines watched, pinned down by enormous enemy fire, several dozen Japanese darted from the blown entrance. They threw grenades and charged up the summit, some with swords drawn.

As Corporal Niehoff and Sgt. Elmo J. Ferretti threw explosive charges, Sandy Bonnyman faced the enemy onslaught. Grabbing a rifle, he ran toward the edge of the summit and began firing rapidly on the Japanese. One vaulted over the crest toward the pioneers. Bonnyman shot him down. Another ran straight up the face and Bonnyman killed him too. Firing off his entire ammunition clip, the gallant assault engineer felled several more of the enemy. Bonnyman jammed another clip into the chamber load, just as marines from Companies F and G stormed up the back side of the bombproof. As the marines rushed uphill, film was rolling. Sergeant Hatch with his 35mm movie camera stood in the open at the base of the mound, calmly filming the charge. Nearby Sgt. Obie Newcomb photographed the attack with still footage.

"They ought to have medals for photographers," said Major Chamberlin. In fact, Newcomb won the Pulitzer Prize for one of his photographs of the charge, and Hatch received praise for his film, which was used in an award-winning news documentary on the battle. The film, *With the Marines at Tarawa,* received much play on the home front, and was the most graphic visual depiction of the war yet released for public viewing.

But the added firepower was too late and too little for Bonnyman. He was shot down, and his body rolled down the face of the bombproof. For his heroic fighting, the marine assault engineer was posthumously awarded the Medal of Honor, the third to be bestowed on former enlisted men at Tarawa. The Japanese surged again and again, and before they were driven off the summit, thirteen of the twenty-one marines who had reached the top were dead or wounded. When their counterattack failed, perhaps fifty of the Japanese who were still able burst from the bombproof. They were annihilated as they tried to escape. Marine artillerymen and tanks firing canister shot the enemy down as fast as gunners could reload their weapons. A bulldozer came in and closed the openings while engineers dropped explosives down the air shafts. When the bombproof erupted, the earth leapt for dozens of yards in all directions.

But the fighting did not stop just because the bombproof had fallen. The final obstacle to the advance from Red 3 was the massive three-story blockhouse that was the enemy command center in the Gilberts. Engineers blew open the two huge steel doors, then a marine with a flamethrower ran forward and sprayed a stream of fire through the opening. This was the culmination of the action that broke the back of the Japanese defenders. All over the shambles that was Red 3, marines cheered and whistled and pounded each other on the back. So great was the inspiration provided by the bold action against the complex of enemy positions that Major Crowe's understrength units swept forward, gaining four hundred yards before nightfall without further casualties.

In the center, the 2d Battalion, 2d Marines, and 1st Battalion, 8th Marines, also ground forward from Red 2, gradually enveloping The Pocket from the east. The fighting was grim, the enemy resistance deadly. Machine-gun fire flayed all across the front and casualties were heavy. Gunnery Sergeant William R. Jay, of Oklahoma City, ventured forth several times into the storm of fire sweeping the airfield in order to spot for his mortar squad. On one occasion a 5-inch naval shell barreled down the runway in front of him but failed to explode. On another daring foray, one of his men fell wounded while knocking out a pillbox. Jay rushed forward and picked the man up. While carrying him across the airfield, a sniper's round struck Jay in the head and killed him instantly.

In the afternoon a very anxious Maj. Gen. Julian Smith, having just inspected Green Beach, approached Red 2 in an LVT. With him were Brig. Gen. James Underhill, the senior 4th Division observer, and Brig. Gen. Thomas Bourke, the 10th Marines CO. On the way in the driver was wounded and the LVT was disabled and went out of control when it was struck by furious fire from The Pocket. The three generals and their aides transferred to a second LVT and landed on Red 2 in the early afternoon. Smith immediately took control, at last able to assume command ashore of the bloodiest battle the marines had ever fought. In the afternoon he and Edson met at Shoup's command post, and the three officers assayed the situation.

After three days of fighting, the landing force was finally firmly ashore, the heaviest enemy positions on Red 3 had fallen, and resistance in the west had ceased. Only The Pocket on the north shore and the Japanese forces in the east remained. All forces, the equivalent of nearly eight battalions on paper, could now concentrate on finishing off the Japanese garrison. Off to the east, the 2d Battalion, 6th Marines, started their forced march up the rest of Tarawa Atoll, pursuing an enemy force estimated at two hundred men. The rest of the 6th Marines would press straight down to the tail end of Betio Island. The 8th Marines on the southern coast would go into reserve, while the 2d Marines tackled The Pocket. The full weight of naval guns, aircraft, and marine artillery and tanks would be laid onto the narrow Japanese-held area for support of the main thrust.

It seemed that with such firepower arrayed against them, the Japanese must soon be wiped out, but the marines knew from the experience of the three previous days that there was probably no hope of enemy capitulation. They would fight to the bitter end. A message from Rear Admiral Hill came through, asking Julian Smith how long he expected the battle to last. Despite the substantial gains that had been made, the general's reply was disappointing. "At least five days of heavy fighting remain before the atoll will be completely subdued," he responded.

Thus, when night began to close in, it seemed that the marines were not a lot closer to the reduction of "Fortress Tarawa" than they had been in the morning. The day's toll was five hundred casualties, and the 2d Division's combat strength on Betio was estimated at 65 percent. In three days of fierce battle the marines and navy and coast guard shore parties had paid three thousand casualties for a two-thirds share of one tiny coral rock in the Central Pacific.

Marine intelligence officers, working with information gleaned from the few prisoners who had been captured, estimated that the Japanese had fifteen hundred men left. These had been pressed into two groups— the stubborn force in the notorious area called The Pocket and the remnants on the tail end of the island.

Rear Admiral Shibasaki had continued to report to Tokyo right up until his end. On November 20 he had radioed in great detail about how the Americans had attacked the island from the lagoon in their "little boats with wheels" and how naval gunfire had knocked out his communications. The next day, he reported, the officers and men of his command were still fighting, although overwhelming numbers of American marines were attacking in endless waves. The Japanese sent their last message to Imperial General Headquarters on D day plus one, November 21. It may have been from Shibasaki himself. It said simply: "All our weapons have been destroyed. From now on everyone who has survived is attempting a final charge. May Japan exist for ten thousand years." A few hours later the confident admiral was dead.

The circumstances of his death were never determined, but most accounts of the battle for Tarawa agree that he was killed when the marines finally succeeded in burning out his massive concrete blockhouse behind Red 3 on November 22. Other sources indicate that he may have died during the night of November 21. When the marines cleaned out the bombproof shelter, they discovered the ghastly charred remains of three hundred Japanese. Almost certainly Shibasaki was among them, but so awful was the carnage that his body was never identified. The only survivor of the shelter, as it turned out, was a mongrel dog, which marines found whimpering and badly burned when they opened up the place. Said one marine, "Any mutt that could live through an inferno like that has to be charmed." The 8th Marines took the animal with them to Hawaii and made it their mascot.

Ensign Kiyoshi Ota was captured on the third day. When the battle was over he would find himself the only Japanese officer to have survived. Other Japanese were captured in spurts. On the third day the marine policemen under the command of Lt. Douglas R. Key, of Port Arthur, Texas, cleared a four-hundred-yard stretch of Green Beach of 150 land mines—all the while under sniper fire. Looking for the source of the fire, they moved to the rear of a squat emplacement they presumed had been neutralized and set off an explosive charge. Eight Japanese ran out and raised their arms. A talkative one who spoke a little English—and whom the marines quickly dubbed "Tojo the Earbanger"—told them that four other men were in the dugout. Another charge was set off and three more Japanese emerged with their hands up. A fourth man apparently reconsidered. He came out firing and was killed instantly.

Tojo the Earbanger said that there were other Japanese and Koreans up and down Green Beach who wished to surrender. He offered to act as an intermediary for the marines. Lieutenant Key thought it was worth a try. Japanese rarely surrendered, but the main fighting had bypassed the area to such an extent that any defenders still there might agree to give up without further needless slaughter. Throughout the day, then, the marine policemen worked their way along the southern half of Green Beach. Tojo passed through the secret portals of numerous emplacements in which enemy were hiding. He carried to his comrades the proposal of surrender, explaining that dynamite was about to be used against them and inviting them to follow him out.

Tojo was so convincing in his mission that nine positions—all of which the marines had thought were cleaned out—were swiftly neutralized. At one bunker twenty-two Japanese and Koreans came out. Expecting to be summarily executed, some emerged with handkerchiefs tied over their eyes. In other instances, Tojo warned the marines when defenders intended to come out shooting. These the marines killed as they showed themselves. That night Key and his men stood guard around a makeshift stockade crowded with enemy prisoners. In all, Tojo the Earbanger and the marine policemen ended up with eighty-one Japanese and Korean prisoners, the largest haul taken by any one unit at Tarawa.

Some Japanese had been able to move about once the battle had passed over them and infiltrate through the American-held zones back to their own lines. Chief Petty Officer Tadeo Oonuki slipped away from his hiding place in the first-aid dugout on the second night, about the time the last message to Tokyo was being sent. He and his crew had abandoned their ruined tank on the afternoon of D day. During the night he stripped down to his G-string and crept through the enemy lines. He knew that the movement he saw among the wreckage on the island was American. He was challenged several times and was fired at, but he was not hit.

Oonuki went all the way to the tail end of the island and did not stop. He stepped off into the sea and waded across the reef to Bairiki. Halfway across he encountered another man heading in the same direction. Neither man stopped or called out, but continued wading toward the island. Expecting to find comrades, Oonuki entered the single bunker on Bairiki. As he looked over the burned remains of the defenders who had died when the fuel supply in the bunker exploded during the strafing attack on D day plus two, he felt sick. He guessed that they had been caught by a marine flamethrower.

Oonuki abandoned all hope. There was no escaping the fire and flames of the Americans, he reasoned, and he decided to commit suicide. Though he did not know it, as many as five hundred other Japanese already had, or soon would, choose the same option before Tarawa had fallen.

But how was he to do it? Oonuki wondered. He was unarmed. Looking around, he could find only a seashell. With this he tried to cut his wrists. But his desperate effort was to no avail—the seashell was not sharp enough. He lay down, crying, and was soon asleep.

The next day, November 22, four Japanese civilian construction workers came upon Oonuki in his hiding place on Bairiki. When the Americans attacked Betio, these men had been laboring on other islands of the atoll. Only with tremendous luck had they succeeded in avoiding the enemy force that had overrun Bairiki and was even now working up the island chain. There was heavy American activity on Bairiki by this time, and the Japanese survivors feared they would encounter a marine patrol in the darkness. Oonuki led them out into the surf, in water up to their waists, far enough that they could not be seen from the island. They remained there all night long, holding hands to keep from being swept away by the waves. What they saw while they stood huddled on the reef was the action that, more than anything else, affirmed the end for the defenders still resisting on Betio.

Chapter Thirty-four

At the end of the third day, November 22, the 27th Infantry Division had been pushed too far. By the time the halt was called just before dark, the forward elements had advanced three and a half miles at Makin through thick tropical bush in the equatorial heat. Their poor condition, said Lt. Col. S. L. A. Marshall, who accompanied them, "could be read in the sagging knees, the lack-luster eyes, the drooping jaws, the slavering lips." Most had discarded their packs and entrenching tools during the forced march.

"When we bivouacked at sundown," Marshall recalled, "men were too exhausted to eat, and the officers didn't bother to inspect our defense lines to make sure that the heavy weapons were set properly so that their fire bands would overlock. In fact, not one thing was done correctly. None of us dug in. We couldn't dig. Even had the loose soil not been laced with thick sub-surface roots, we were too far spent. I shunted two battered palm logs close together and lay down between them. This was to be my only cover if we became engaged. I remember telling myself before I dozed off that if I had to die for failure to dig, then it was time to die."

Men of the 3d Battalion, 165th Infantry, observed movement in front of their loosely held positions at about 1900. The Japanese still able to fight had gathered at the eastern command post. Perhaps two hundred men showed up, survivors from the combat troops and civilian construction corps. They were well armed. The officers brandished swords, and nearly all the others had rifles and grenades. In addition, there were at least two machine guns and one knee-mortar in their arsenal. Knowing that their fight for Butaritari was over and their retreat into the rest of Makin Atoll blocked, they were determined to take out as many American soldiers as they could.

Aided by the diversion of two dozen or more Gilbertese natives passing through the American lines, the first Japanese snipers infiltrated the army perimeter. Ten minutes later the soldiers held their fire as another group of figures approached their lines. Among them a baby was heard crying. The group came within thirty feet of the front before an engineer detachment saw through the charade. The 27th Division soldiers fired a machine gun, raising the alarm and killing ten Japanese. The rest of the enemy group scattered and from then on the fighting was constant. "Many of us had the idea there were no Japs left," said Lt. Robert Wilson. "When the firing began, I didn't believe it was the real thing."

The band of Japanese engaged the soldiers, not as a disorganized mob, but by crawling slowly and quietly through the underbrush and attacking in small units, sometimes singly. One group got to within twenty yards of an AT gun that Cpl. Louis Lula manned on the right side of the old plantation road. Some of the enemy ran back and forth and others threw firecrackers, trying to draw fire that would reveal the American positions in the darkness. Here and there the Rigosentai lobbed grenades and charged, shrieking, "Banzai!" Some shouted "*Heil* Hitler!" and "Blood for the Emperor!" A few even called individual soldiers by name, or yelled "Corpsman, corpsman" in slurred English. Soon chaos again reigned supreme.

Machine-gun and rifle fire, as well as grenades, cut into small knots of Japanese, but another group was always close behind or moving in from another direction. Private First Class George Graham scattered three enemy with a grenade. In quick succession, Sgt. Edward Pasdertz killed two of them. He shot the first from six feet away. The other leapt clear over Pasdertz and took off for the beach. The soldier shot him from twenty-five feet away. A half-dozen enemy charged with fixed bayonets, but the rapid fire of Pvt. Randolph Slatner with his BAR and a nearby machine gun killed them. Corporal Lula loaded his AT gun with canister and bowled over twenty onrushing Japanese at a range of just twenty-five yards.

The Japanese onrush faltered for an hour and the enemy fire slackened. From across the no-man's-land, American soldiers listened, amazed, as the enemy chanted and sang and beat their prayer sticks. They drank vast quantities of sake and worked themselves into a wild frenzy. Some crawled forward and retrieved wounded. Others taunted the soldiers. In between the thump of incoming mortar rounds one drunk Japanese shouted over and over, "Come on in, you Yankee bastards, and we will treat you right." Snipers who had infiltrated the American lines harassed the crews of the AT and machine guns.

Near the lagoon, a saber-wielding Japanese officer suddenly appeared over a foxhole in which Pfc. Elio Bizzari crouched. The intruder jumped in with the stunned soldier, shouting "I've got you, Joe!" He stabbed Bizzari with the sword. Private First Class Gerard L. Heck, who was with Bizzari, shot the Japanese officer but failed to kill him. The enraged Bizzari pulled the sword from the area just above his heart, leapt on the wounded enemy officer, and finished him off with his trench knife.

Twice more before dawn the Japanese charged. However, the combined fire of the BARs, machine guns, and AT guns kept them at bay. "They came on in a series of wild charges that lasted the night," remembered Lieutenant Colonel Marshall. "Eleven times they hit and each time our forward line was bloodied and lost some weapons. Two of our guys were run through with samurai swords. The position finally dangled on only one machine gun that held up the center. Hour after hour the melee continued. When dawn came the heat against our front was still so intense that it took two tanks and one rifle platoon to cover the pull-back of the one gunner who had saved the battalion. Suddenly everything quieted."

In the morning, the soldiers counted sixty badly mangled Japanese bodies in front of and behind their lines. Another hundred, who had been wounded and dragged themselves or were carried into the jungle, were later found on the eastern end of the island. The 27th Division soldiers lost three men killed and twenty-five wounded, but the fiercest Japanese action on Makin had been turned back.

One hundred miles to the south, it was a similar story—albeit on a far greater scale of violence. As at Makin, the American line at Tarawa on this third night was merely a few hundred yards long and was thinly held. Only three understrength rifle companies of the 1st Battalion, 6th Marines, were deployed forward. Behind them no reinforcements were immediately available.

The last pitched battle on Betio began strangely. As darkness closed in on the island at about 1900, the sounds of a menagerie of wild animals—none of which could be found anywhere in the Central Pacific—were heard among the wrecked and ruined landscape. The marines watched with a heightened wariness. From the beginning, the veterans of Guadalcanal understood intuitively that the weird cacophony of imitated baboons, monkeys, wolves, and birds was a prelude to something unusual.

Thirty minutes later the enemy made their first rush in a probing raid intended to appraise the marine strength. Word was passed down the line to "stand fast." Although they failed to surprise the Americans, the Japanese estimated the situation along the front with uncanny accuracy. Fifty of them narrowed their probe to the weakest link in the line—the junction of A and B companies. Here, on the right flank of the line, Company B manned a position that ran for 250 yards—a frontage normally defended by about 100 men. Company B, however, was down to perhaps 85 men out of an original reinforced landing strength of 200. They were commanded by Lt. Norman K. Thomas, of Long Beach, Mississippi, known to his men as "Hard Tom." He had taken over when Capt. George D. Krueger, the company commander, had been wounded earlier in the day during the sweep up the southern coast. The men, dug in east of the airfield, were organized in small islands of resistance to cover the areas in their immediate vicinities.

A rifleman in the center of Company B's sector heard men moving about—something marines did not do at night when they could help it. The stirring in the darkness made him uneasy, and he peered into the drifting smoke but was unable to see anything. Then, as he continued to listen, a barrage of grenades flew through the air and exploded among the network of foxholes in the center of the sector. A horde of screaming forms rose suddenly into view and charged. They had infiltrated the forward marine positions and already were in and among the foxholes. Japanese seemed to be everywhere, rising from the ground, firing rifles and throwing grenades. At least four foxholes were overrun. The marines threw up flares. Star shells lighted the sky. With bayonets and swords gleaming in the eerie, flickering light of burning fires and exploding grenades, the Japanese rushed any marine they could find, howling "Ban-zai-ai!"

The fighting was confused and intense. Lieutenant Thomas directed the firing of the men in foxholes near him. On the right and left the

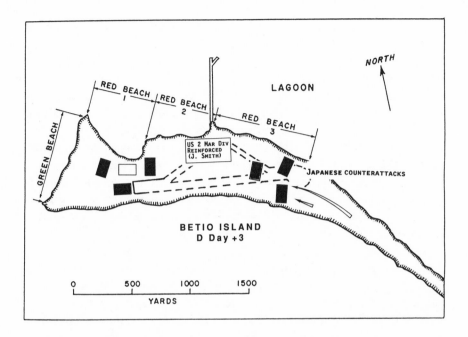

RED BEACH 1

RED BEACH 2

RED BEACH 3

GREEN BEACH

LAGOON

NORTH

US 2 MAR DIV
REINFORCED
(J. SMITH)

JAPANESE COUNTERATTACKS

BETIO ISLAND
D Day +3

0   500   1000   1500

YARDS

probe was checked, and the action gradually became concentrated on the center where the Japanese had established a pocket. From here they put light machine guns into action and continued hurling grenades against the marines. The Japanese pocket was eliminated by rifles and grenades during the next hour of close-quarters combat. Thomas grabbed his field phone and called up the command post a hundred yards to the rear. "We need help!" he shouted above the din of battle and the screams of dying and wounded men. "Another attack like that and the line may break."

Major William Jones, the battalion CO, said that he had no help to send. He told Thomas: "You've got to hold!" Jones then turned to his staff. "If they don't hold we may lose the entire battalion." Captain Lyle Specht, of Silverton, Georgia, organized a fire team in the rear. The men were from a mortar platoon and were not intended to fight as riflemen, but they had fought as such since they reached the front and waded into the Japanese. "We pitched everything we had at them," said Specht, "and when the melee of grenade-throwing, machine-gunning and bayoneting was finished, we moved across piles of dead Japs."

The action around the marine heavy machine guns was typical of what occurred on this night. Two of the weapons had just been sited in a foxhole when the Japanese struck. The crew chief of one gun got off only a short burst before he was killed. Private First Class Horace C. Warfield, of Houston, ran forward and took over. In the same instant a wave of Japanese swept over the position. One jumped into the foxhole with Warfield and ran a bayonet through his thigh. The wounded marine, his sidearm out of ammunition, pistol-whipped the man to the ground. Corporal Glasco W. Rector, of Detroit, and Pfc. Lowell H. Koci, of Kensett, Iowa—both of them also out of ammunition—rushed over to help Warfield subdue the Japanese. In their hysteria, "they just about beat his brains out," said their platoon leader, Lt. Alexander S. Walker, of Leander, Texas.

Meanwhile, Pfc. Daniel W. Ness, of Black Hills, South Dakota, manning a second heavy machine gun, also was wounded in action. Hit in the leg during the first few minutes of fighting, he said nothing about it and continued firing his weapon into knots of Japanese as fast as they appeared. Private First Class James L. Edwards, of Thayer, Missouri, no sooner had taken over the third heavy machine gun from a dead marine than he too was hit. Like dozens of others, Edwards stayed in the fierce fight until it was over. Battling for their lives, the marines had managed to forestall any full-scale enemy counterattack, at least for the moment.

When the enemy attack was renewed at 2300, the Japanese again probed the marine ranks. One group made a violent feint toward Company A with a shower of grenades and a storm of machine-gun fire, while a second band of fifty skirmishers, double-timing in assault formation, drove head on into Company B. Artillery from marine guns emplaced on Bairiki and naval gunfire from two destroyers on station three thousand yards offshore were called in, and soon a curtain of shells was impacting a mere seventy-five yards in front of the marines. "I had the field phone in my hands when I was rushed by the biggest Jap I've ever seen," recalled Lieutenant Thomas. "He yelled something I couldn't understand and charged me with his bayonet. We grappled for a few seconds, and I managed to kick him off me and throw him to the ground. Then I picked up a .45 and finished him off."

The combat was so close that Cpl. William H. Miles, Jr., of Livonia, Louisiana, a 60mm mortarman, lobbed HE rounds a mere thirty-five to forty yards into enemy groups. He aimed by dead reckoning in the darkness, and in one instance dropped two shells onto an enemy machine-gun position. Second Lieutenant Norman Milner, a forward artillery observer, called in 75mm fire from a dozen 10th Marines pack howitzers, laying an impenetrable screen between the marines and the Japanese lines. Navy Lieutenant Charles S. Corbin, of New York City, the naval gunfire liaison officer attached to the 6th Marines, called in 5-inch destroyer fire. The combination of naval gunfire, mortars, and field artillery allowed the marines to finish off the enemy who had crossed the no-man's-land in this second probe.

The front was quiet for the next few hours, with the exception of the ubiquitous "Washing Machine Charlie." The lone enemy raider came over after midnight and dropped a stick of fragmentation bombs on the airfield revetments. Then at about 0400, eight hours after the action had begun, an immense wave of the enemy suddenly surged from their lines and crashed into the American positions. It was the strongest, most terrifying attack of all. A horde of Japanese came on, moving in a mass, screaming, brandishing swords, bayonets, and knives. Some were already wounded and wrapped in bloody bandages. Others were naked or wore only loincloths or G-strings. In a moment they were upon the marines.

Exactly how many Japanese participated in the mad suicidal rush, no one could ever be sure. Men at the point of contact estimated that about three hundred to four hundred reasonably well organized troops made the charge. Like the crest of an enormous wave, they slammed head on into the depleted ranks of Companies A and B of the 1st Battalion, 6th Marines. They swept aside the forward pickets and moved swiftly into the midst of the marine foxholes. All along the line American red, pink, and white and Japanese yellow tracers flashed through the night, silhouetting the onrushing enemy. Artillery and mortar shells exploded all over the area from which the attack developed, and rolled back until the explosions were almost upon the American positions.

"We're killing them as fast as they come at us," Lieutenant Thomas reported to the battalion command post, "but we can't hold out much longer." Savage fighting, of the most primitive kind, swirled about the few dozen isolated pockets of marine resistance as the Japanese drove on. Some American positions were overrun; most, however, held out. Trying not to be killed in his first battle since joining the 2d Division in New Zealand, Pvt. Jack Stambaugh—the green replacement from Texas who suspected that he would become a "fighting fool" in combat—fought off a group of shadowy figures until his rifle jammed. Then he heard Pfc. Harold L. Carstens, of Kankakee, Illinois, shouting in a nearby foxhole. In the wavering light of flares and explosions, Stambaugh saw several Japanese emerge out of the darkness, running headlong for the man.

When Stambaugh reached the foxhole, he found his way blocked by a naked Japanese swinging a fixed bayonet. The two men engaged in a classic "thrust and parry" before Stambaugh ran him through and killed him. The Texan worked his way forward, killing three more Japanese with his bayonet. As he was withdrawing his blade from the third, a Japanese officer ran a sword through his back. Stambaugh fell dead, but his action rallied the marines and scattered the enemy around them. "It was one of the finest and bravest acts ever performed by a Marine," said Lieutenant Thomas. Private First Class Carstens, who had shouted the alarm, shot the enemy officer dead.

Immediately behind the hard-pressed 6th Marines line, assault engineers, mortar crews, and 2d Battalion reserves formed a secondary line of defense. Beyond the front, groups of Japanese armed with grenades and machine guns roamed the wooded areas behind their own line, in a determined attempt to support the attack of their raging comrades. What happened around the marine heavy machine guns, where the heaviest weight of the Japanese attack fell, occurred also around other squads and platoons.

Marines all along the line had equally serious moments during the night. Technical Sergeant Samuel Shaffer, a combat correspondent, formerly of the *Washington Times-Herald,* narrowly escaped being killed when a Japanese threw a grenade at him, but missed. The grenade landed in a nearby foxhole and exploded in a blinding flash. The marines were inspired by Lieutenant Thomas, one of the most popular officers in the 6th Marine Regiment. As wave after wave of Japanese rushed Company B's lines, only to be met by withering machine-gun and rifle fire, Thomas worked his way among his men, exhorting them to hold out. "If we go," he urged them to remember, "the whole battalion goes too. Stand fast. It's up to us."

The marines held, and averted a potentially serious situation.

The tenuous organization of the attacking enemy, many under the influence of sake, evaporated once they encountered the curtain of artillery and mortar fire. Their formation splintered into a hodgepodge of bands and individuals without leadership, communications, or purpose. Nevertheless, their furious, pell-mell attacks caused grievous damage. One inebriated mob stumbled into a trench where an 18th Marines detachment lay. Two marine flamethrower men were killed. Other Japanese died before they could cause much damage, like the man killed by marines while he was trying to gnaw through the wire of a field phone with his teeth. By dawn the Americans had wiped out most of them. The surviving attackers—leaderless, bewildered, battle-shocked—took to pillboxes and bunkers on the tail end of the island to hide out, and to wait for the inevitable end.

The furious Japanese counterattack, although few marines recognized it at the time, was a last gasp. However, the action had not ended at Tarawa. There was still fighting ahead for the marines on Betio and the rest of the atoll.

Chapter Thirty-five

With the coming of daylight on the fourth day at Tarawa, the marines were able to see in all too graphic terms how fierce the banzai attack had been. Only then could the terrible action be assessed. There was no question that the night had been a brutal one. The gruesome vista belied description. One man was reminded "of those strange, screwball pictures you see of a desert with a lot of wrecked watches and melted telephones, and nothing but just utterly weird ruins. It was something on that order—only much stranger." When Capt. Lyle Specht surveyed the carnage, he was shocked. "In some spots," he said, "dead bodies"—marines and Japanese alike—"were stacked four and five deep."

In fact, as the marine units re-formed their lines, it was found that Company B had been greatly reduced. Only 45 men remained capable of continuing the fight effectively out of the 85 or so who had dug in the evening before. These survivors were merged with Company A, which also had suffered heavy losses. Company B, in effect, ceased to exist. Perhaps 800 men were left in the 1st Battalion, 6th Marines, which had taken the full force of the Japanese counterattack. It had gone into action the previous morning reinforced to 1,100 men; in the night fighting, it had lost 45 men killed and 128 wounded and missing. The battalion was pulled out of action and moved back to the beaches at dawn. The destroyers *Sigsby* and *Schroeder,* which had supported the marine defense with naval gunfire, had fired their coffers dry. The 1st Battalion, 10th Marines, had shot off fifteen hundred rounds of 75mm ammunition, hundreds of which had been hand-carried directly from the Burns-Philp pier even as the guns were firing.

A total of 325 Japanese lay dead inside and beyond the American lines. The remainder of the enemy still on the island, perhaps 500, many wounded, most without weapons or ammunition, had withdrawn into the heavy fortifications on the bird's tail. Here they waited listlessly for the marines to come at them again.

When Lt. Norman Thomas reported to the battalion command post in the morning to check on his wounded, a marine combat correspondent approached him and asked about the night of horrors. "The boys stood up to it, slugging it out with the Japs," he said weakly, leaning against a coconut tree and staring at the torn bodies that lay around him, unburied in the hot sand. "They stood up to it by sheer guts alone." Thomas said that it had been touch and go, from the beginning of the first attack to the last. All that time, he said, his company had been in grave danger of being overwhelmed. Of his men, he concluded, "Every damn one of them is a champion." He then closed his eyes and fell asleep, his back resting against a splintered palm tree.

The battle also was nearly over for the marines of the units still in the front lines. Even as the Japanese had been counterattacking during the night, behind the American lines the embattled island of Betio was being transformed. Working all through the previous day and night, several hundred Seabees had been toiling on the airfield—filling in shell holes, smoothing the main runway. Bulldozers buried the island in crushed coral, then packed it down, spread it out, and graded it. The beaches, too, were soon unrecognizable. Trucks and jeeps appeared, towing electrical generators, water and fuel caissons, and AA guns. Before the battle was finished, then, Tarawa was already becoming what the marines had been told it would be—an advanced toehold in the Central Pacific far more powerful offensively than the Japanese had ever dreamed of making it defensively.

At 0800 the fresh 3d Battalion, 6th Marines, under Lt. Col. Kenneth F. McLeod, having replaced its bloodied sister battalion in the line, jumped off in what quickly had all the earmarks of a rout. By this time, Rear Admiral Shibasaki had been killed and the Japanese who remained were severely demoralized. They were now pressed into a few hundred square yards of heavily cratered ground, from the east end of the airfield to the tail end of the island. Deep trenches ran diagonally through the area from coast to coast, interspersed with thick but lightly manned fortifications. The most formidable of these, a concentration of bombproofs and trenches, became the locus of the final Japanese resistance. Here the last stand would be made.

McLeod's Company I moved up the center against light opposition for a distance of 350 yards until it was blocked by the enemy stronghold. There it was ordered to stop and deal with the resistance. The defenders were holed up in three enormous bombproof shelters, each mutually supporting with lateral trenches and wide fields of fire overlaying the system. One or two sprouted machine guns, and all were manned by riflemen. The marines here were aided by the presence of "Colorado," the seemingly indestructible Sherman tank commanded by its equally intrepid crew chief, Lt. Louis Largey. "Colorado" was the last fully operational Sherman on the island. "China Gal," commanded by Lt. Edward Bale, had lost its main gun in the D-day fighting and had only its machine guns still working. It was now being used as an armored supply carrier.

Two of the enemy strongpoints and all their covering positions were reduced to rubble by flamethrowers and demolitions trained down their air shafts. The third, however, proved more difficult to subdue. As flamethrower teams closed in on it and began unleashing their jets of fire, the massive steel doors burst open and the Japanese charged out. Largey had just maneuvered "Colorado" into position to cover the attack when the defenders surged forward. He cut loose with an HE round at point-blank range and fifty Japanese were eviscerated instantly. The dazed survivors were shot to death as they wandered about in the open.

Meanwhile, the bulk of the rest of the battalion fought up the southern coast and around the right. They made astounding gains all morning, forcing the fight with naval gunfire, tanks, flamethrowers, and demolitions. The toll on the listless defenders was terrible. By 1030, one of the two advancing assault companies was pinched out of the shrinking front—now only two hundred yards wide—and fell back in a supporting role. Japanese resistance from here on was so feeble that this reserve company hardly fought again.

The navy fighters and bombers had flown their last missions. The 2d Division artillery, which now had 75mm and 105mm howitzer battalions emplaced on Bairiki as well as Betio, was not used at all, much to the disappointment of the gun crews. The opposing forces were simply too close for such devastating support, and there were more marines on the tail of the island than Japanese. Now that the

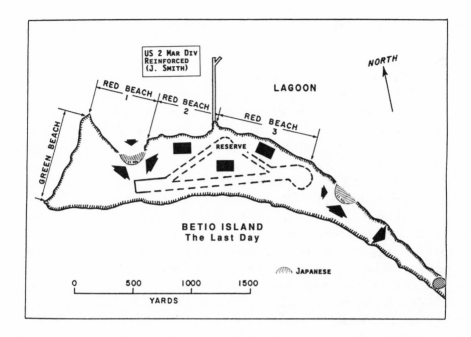

BETIO ISLAND
The Last Day

lines had straightened out, anything that moved ahead of the marines was fair game and was fired at. Though some pockets of resistance were encountered, in most places the enemy was wiped out with quick and ruthless dispatch.

Gunnery Sergeant L. L. Lucas and the men under his command watched several Japanese stumble from a shell hole, trying to reach a pillbox farther back. They threw grenades, and one or two of the enemy went down. Lucas and his men ran up the beach and discovered the Japanese huddled in their hole, unarmed, "convulsive and obviously nearly out of their minds." The marines tossed in grenades and "arms and legs just flew out the entrance." One Japanese somehow survived the blast but he was swiftly bayoneted to death. "By now we had quit even trying to take prisoners," recalled Lucas. In their drive to the tail end of the island, the marines had found evidence that wounded Americans had been captured and killed during the battle.

By 1310 enemy resistance to the front of the marines was down to twenty square yards at the tip of the island. A band of marines, from Company K and Company L, swept over the last position in a mere fifteen minutes. The battle for Betio was nearly finished. In the sweep to the tail end of the island 475 Japanese were killed and 14 prisoners—all but one were Korean laborers—were captured. Nine marines had been killed or were missing and 25 were wounded.

All that remained was to finish off the Japanese still holding on grimly in The Pocket. This stubborn complex of pillboxes and bunkers at the junction of Red 1 and Red 2, which had defied the 2d Division since D day and had inflicted the heaviest casualties on the marines, would be the last enemy bastion to fall on Betio.

At the same time, the battle for Makin—the operation that Maj. Gen. Holland Smith four days earlier had hoped would end quickly—also proceeded inexorably toward its elusive end. In Lt. Col. Joe Hart's front lines, the soldiers had repelled one fierce attack after another during the night, while fending off drunken enemy troops in numbers that had long been written off. Gone was the fear of the night before, that the battle would never be finished. The Japanese, their remaining strength expended during the night, were now reeling and in complete collapse. The American soldiers, who were bolstered by more than twenty tanks to spearhead their final attack, sensed this.

At precisely 0715 they jumped off smartly. For five miles, all the way to the end of Butaritari, as many soldiers as possible hung to the sides of the tanks as they roared eastward down the single-lane road. By 1030 advanced elements of this armored fist had reached the tip of the island and all organized resistance at Makin was declared to be over. Only a handful of Japanese had been encountered along the way and these were silenced swiftly. An hour later Maj. Gen. Ralph Smith radioed to Rear Admiral Turner: "Makin taken!" Except for minor mopping-up action, the battle for Makin was history.

So ended the last day of combat for the first American soldiers to fight in the Central Pacific in World War II. In a sense the victory was a Pyrrhic one. In some ways it was a bitter disappointment: for the officers of the 27th Division, whose untried troops had marched forward through unimaginable heat and dust and had been held up for days by an infinitely inferior enemy force, and even more for the weary troops themselves. These soldiers, who knew little of the kind of fighting necessary on small islands, and who were poorly trained and led by their officers from start to finish, still felt proud of their showing in their first action against a formidable enemy.

The battle for Makin, before the last Japanese and Koreans were killed or captured, had lasted four days. It had engaged a reinforced regimental combat team—about 6,500 soldiers backed by enormously strong naval and air forces—cost a total of 245 casualties, and held up the departure of the most vulnerable elements of the Fifth Fleet, as it would turn out, at least one day too long. They had been opposed by only about 280 Japanese combat troops, who were in action at different times and places over the period of four days on an island eleven miles long and no more than a few hundred yards wide. Casualties among enemy combat and support troops during those four days, including Korean laborers, amounted to 550 killed, or nearly the entire garrison. One hundred four prisoners were taken, all but one of whom were Korean laborers.

But the full price for the capture of Makin was yet to be paid.

At Tarawa the marines had surrounded the last bastion of Japanese resistance on Betio, the notorious redoubt they had dubbed The Pocket. The seemingly indestructible Japanese had suffered heavy losses and were beginning to lose ground. By midmorning at a conference at Maj. Gen. Julian Smith's command post, the idea was voiced that it was time to mount an all-out attack led by the remnants of the 2d Marines. Colonels Edson and Shoup pointed out that the Japanese tactics had been successful up to now in that the marines were continuing to suffer terribly in their piecemeal efforts; in their view a massive knockout blow could not possibly prove more costly. Such an undertaking was bound to succeed given the numerical and material superiority of the marines.

Surrounded though they were, with no hope of ultimate survival, the Japanese would not surrender. The marines had to take this complex of fortifications, the strongest on the island, before Betio could be declared secured. The 1st Battalion, 8th Marines, and 3d Battalion, 2d Marines, moved against it from all sides, including a hastily organized frontal amphibious assault from the lagoon. Supported by tanks, flamethrowers, LVTs, demolitions, and half-tracks mounting 75mm howitzers, they swarmed into and over individual pillboxes and bunkers. With grenades, and angry determination to finish the job, they succeeded in gradually winnowing down the area held by the enemy. The furious action, in which two dozen marines were killed or wounded, was completed in the afternoon. No Japanese offered themselves as prisoners—and none were taken. Finally, at 1330, Smith notified Rear Admiral Hill: "Betio has fallen."

At the end of the day, after four full days of practically nonstop combat, the cost to the marines and attached naval and coast guard personnel was an astonishing total of three thousand casualties. For this the 2d Division had bought only the most important of all the incredibly small islands that make up Tarawa Atoll. The 2d Battalion, 6th Marines, was even now still working its way up the rest of the tiny chain in pursuit of a fleeing enemy force that numbered close to two hundred in size. The battle for Tarawa would not be entirely over until this group of Japanese was eliminated.

Chapter Thirty-six

As dawn came up at Abemama on November 23, a native slipped across the channel dividing the V Amphibious Corps Reconnaissance Company and the small Japanese garrison. He was immediately taken to the command post for questioning, and surprised the company commander, Capt. James Jones, with his information.

"The Saps," he told his interrogators with excitement—to the great amusement of the Americans, the Gilbertese alphabet did not include the letter J—"are all dead."

It was welcome news to Jones, who had been contemplating how to rush the bothersome enemy stronghold after sunrise. Up to now he had not been certain how to do it. Now, it seemed, he would not have to try after all, though he had prepared diligently for the event.

Two days earlier, on the afternoon of November 21, after two marines had been wounded trying to eliminate the enemy strongpoint, Jones had radioed the submarine *Nautilus*. "Our weapons are too light to knock out the Japanese guns," he told navy Lt. Comdr. Bill Irvin.

"I'll surface at daybreak and we'll shell the hell out of them," said Irvin.

The marine explained that the strength of the entrenchments was such that the angle of the submarine's 3-inch deck gun would have to be flat. He doubted that the shells would have any effect. He was also worried about the natives. They had proved exceedingly friendly. Many were on the island where the Japanese had dug themselves in, and there was no way to alert them to find shelter. One stray shot into the midst of the helpless natives could prove seriously damaging to their future cooperation with the American garrison forces, due to arrive at Abemama within days. Then there was the question of the marines themselves, who were dug in very close to the Japanese positions.

Irvin was not deterred. "You just bring me a chart of the Japanese position."

Jones personally paddled out to the submarine that night with a chart that pinpointed the Japanese position. He brought with him Pfc. Harold Marek, who had been badly wounded on the first day, and another less seriously injured marine. Jones transferred these men to *Nautilus*. To some of the crew it was a grimly familiar affair. *Nautilus* had taken on dozens of marine casualties off Makin in 1942 during the famous action by Carlson's Raiders. Jones and Irvin worked out the parameters of the bombardment so that the marines and natives would be at minimum risk. Jones would display a large white banner—as it turned out, a mattress cover hastily hung from a coconut tree—to mark the northern limit of the marine positions.

The next day *Nautilus* surfaced, and at daybreak commenced a furious shelling of the Japanese position. For the better part of the morning, Irvin directed the firing of seventy-five rounds of 3-inch ammunition. Meanwhile, after learning that the reconnaissance scouts had encountered opposition, Rear Admiral Hill had dispatched a destroyer to the scene. It had arrived in the afternoon of November 22, and also briefly lent its guns to the bombardment.

And that was all it took, explained the native now standing before Jones. As his interrogators pressed him to be explicit, the native went on. When the Japanese learned that the Americans had landed, the enemy troops had taken as much food and supplies from the natives as they could carry back to their entrenchments—apparently preparing for a siege. Their commander told Father Mehl that it was his intention to fight it out and then kill his men before the Americans overwhelmed them. But four Japanese were killed by the shelling of the submarine, and when the destroyer arrived, the rest lost all hope. They believed that an all-out assault was imminent and they had no chance of withstanding such overwhelming firepower.

However, the lieutenant commanding the garrison objected strongly to the demoralization around him. While exhorting his troops to new heights of resolve—brandishing a sword in one hand and defiantly waving his pistol with the other—he accidentally shot himself in the head and died. Without hope, the rest of the now leaderless garrison calmly dug their own graves, laid down in them, and committed suicide with their rifles.

Shortly thereafter Jones and the marine scouts pushed across the fordable channel against no opposition and found the strange story to be true. Thus all three of the primary objectives of Galvanic—Tarawa, Makin, and Abemama—fell on November 23, the fourth day of action.

While Jones was investigating the ritual suicides on Abemama, aboard *Nautilus* a different kind of ceremony was completed. The submarine surfaced at dawn, and its crew buried Private First Class Marek at sea. He had died of his wounds during the night.

Although a marine battalion was on a forced march up the rest of Tarawa Atoll, the principal island of Betio was firmly in American hands. The first plane, a navy Hellcat fighter with Ens. William W. Kelly, of Castlewood, Pennsylvania, behind the stick, landed on the airfield before the battle was officially finished and before the Seabees had completed smoothing the runways. Flying in, he had seen dozens of bodies floating at sea as far as ten miles from Tarawa. Naively, he thought they were Japanese; in fact, they were marines who had been killed on D day and the day after, whose bodies had been carried out to sea by the tides and currents. Climbing down from the cockpit, Kelly asked sheepishly, "Is it over?" The mob of cheering marines who surged around him was answer enough.

At Makin the 27th Division had begun loading out. In the morning the 2d Battalion boarded a transport from Red 2 on the hammerhead end of the island. Throughout the rest of the day other battalions boarded ships at different points around the lagoon. The soldiers released their LVTs to the island garrison, and the convoy sailed for Hawaii at 1400. An infantry battalion and most of the heavy equipment also were left behind to defend the island. The escort carriers and some of the larger warships stayed behind in order to cover the buildup. The fighter squadron from the carrier *Lexington* intercepted a flight of Japanese Zeros headed for the Gilberts this same day, shooting down seventeen of twenty-one "bandits" without the loss of a man.

In the afternoon army detachments were sent to scout Little Makin and other islands in the atoll. Few Japanese were encountered on the outlying islands, and resistance amounted only to small groups of stragglers who were easily killed or captured. Five enemy seeking to cross the reef from Butaritari to Kuma were killed over the next few days. Much later, on December 13, another nine would be killed on the eastern end of Butaritari in a fierce firefight with thirteen soldiers. Among these last enemy dead was the Japanese executive officer of Makin.

At Tarawa a port director was put in charge of the anchorage, which quickly began to fill with transports and cargo ships. Destroyers on active ASW patrol covered the naval movement into the lagoon. The first navy and marine combat elements went aboard transports the afternoon of November 23. For three days thereafter the Burns-Philp pier and the beaches of Betio would be jammed with the process of loading and unloading. Rear Admiral Hill and his entourage came ashore to inspect the island that had been so difficult to seize.

Japanese snipers were still much in evidence, and the marines dug in for the night. During the hours of darkness three men were killed and a half dozen wounded in brief skirmishes, as Japanese survivors came out of their holes looking for food and water. The next day, November 24, the corps commander, Maj. Gen. Holland Smith, arrived by plane to make his own tour. When he was informed that casualties—after an estimate was hastily calculated—would likely exceed three thousand, "Howlin' Mad" Smith was shaken deeply.

The official victory ceremony took place precisely at noon on the fifth day, November 24.

The sun on Betio was hotter than it had been on any previous day of the battle, and the stench of six thousand Japanese and American unburied dead was overpowering. Men often stopped what they were doing and dropped to their knees, wretching. The explosions of demolitions work continued, and occasional firing still occurred as marines and Seabees found the hiding places of persistent snipers. The noise sometimes interrupted the solemn service. The splintered trunks of two palm trees served as poles for the flag-raising ceremony.

Private First Class James L. Williams, of Birmingham, Alabama, a member of a tank crew, stepped forward and prepared to sound "Colors" for the first time at Tarawa. Julian Smith stopped him when he saw that the marine was wearing the clean white uniform of a Japanese sailor. Numerous marines had discarded their own filth-encrusted uniforms for whatever Japanese clothing they could scrounge. At least one was seen working on the beach in nothing but a kimono. For this event, however, the general was adamant that the uniform of the day—certainly for the color bearer and honor guard—would comprise the dungarees, helmets, and arms they had fought with. "Get those damn things off and keep them off!" Julian Smith demanded of Private Williams. The man traded his outerwear with a nearby marine, and the ritual proceeded.

Technical Sergeant Vito Millione, of Philadelphia, walked to one of the poles. With him went Cpl. Mickey M. Frankenstein, of Los Angeles, one of the walking wounded among the marine ranks. Williams raised the bugle to his parched lips and "Colors" was heard all across the island. Millione held the flag while Frankenstein attached it to the shrouds and raised the Stars and Stripes to the top of the blasted trunk.

The area around the headquarters fell silent. A combat correspondent watched: "Men turned from digging foxholes, from unloading boats, from burying the dead. They stood at attention, with their dirty, tired young hands held at salute. Some of the wounded managed to stand up, too, while the more seriously hurt could only turn their heads as they lay on their litters. The assault troops paused in their shuffling toward the end of the pier." As the flag unfurled and snapped to the top, the marines "lost a little of their weariness and a little of their sorrow." A diminutive Union Jack was raised a few moments later on the other trunk. Major Frank Holland, the former director of education in the Gilberts, had produced the British flag from his pack. He had brought it from New Zealand. When the ceremony was over, the men got on with the work of disembarkation.

Also on the afternoon of November 24, Capt. William W. Lumpkin, of Charleston, South Carolina, the division chaplain, dedicated the 2d Marine Division cemetery in a cleared area behind Red 2. Small burial grounds had appeared all over the island where men had buried their buddies in groups. Such areas were marked by simple crosses made from wooden slats torn from packing crates. One Methodist chaplain, Lt. Norman Darling, of Jacksonville, New York, held more than two hundred burial services in one hour. An 8th Marines chaplain, Wyeth W. Willard, of Scituate, Massachusetts, by chance found the body of the man who formerly had been his clerical assistant on Guadalcanal and whom he had recommended for combat duty as a platoon leader.

Fewer and fewer Japanese were being captured or killed. Chief Petty Officer Tadeo Oonuki and the four civilian construction workers with him had watched the fireworks of the ill-fated banzai attack on the third night from their vantage point on the reef. They had not been sure of the results until the next morning when they saw the American fighter plane piloted by Ensign Kelly land. That night the forlorn group waded across the reef to Betio in order to steal a boat and escape. Oonuki was delirious with hunger and thirst, and along the way he became separated from the group when he stopped to claw some shellfish off the reef. He ate them voraciously. They made him violently ill, and upon reaching Betio he collapsed by the nearest bunker and fell asleep. It was here that he was found the next day and taken prisoner.

Up the island chain, the 2d Battalion, 6th Marines, continued their forced march until they cornered the elusive Japanese force on Buariki on November 26. That night and into the next morning a fierce battle was fought in which 156 heavily entrenched Japanese, supported by two mortars and ten machine guns, were killed at a cost of 32 American dead and 59 wounded. On November 29 Abaiang, Maiana, and Marakei atolls, lying north, south, and northeast, respectively, of Tarawa, were scouted. There were no Japanese on the latter two, but on Abaiang five of the enemy escaped the marines by fleeing in a motor launch, presumably for the Marshalls. Abemama was occupied in force on November 25, and Seabees quickly went about clearing an area for an airfield.

Rear Admiral Spruance came ashore at Tarawa on November 27 to prepare for the arrival of Admiral Nimitz, who had flown to the Ellice Islands from Hawaii and was now flying in from Funafuti aboard a troop carrier and cargo plane. As they inspected the Japanese fortifications, Spruance said little. His impassive face hid whatever thoughts came into his mind as he saw firsthand the utter devastation his forces had wrought. When Nimitz arrived he was outwardly deeply affected. He would later say that he had never in his life seen such desolation as at Tarawa. Lieutenant General Richardson, who accompanied Nimitz from Hawaii, had seen the Ypres battlefield in World War I. Tarawa, he told Nimitz, was comparable.

The high army and navy brass and main elements of the Southern Attack Force departed the Gilberts on November 30. The first naval aircraft had arrived and were based on the airfield at Tarawa, and the army air force garrison had landed. By the first week of December American aircraft, flying from the Gilberts, would be conducting bombing and photoreconnaissance missions over the Marshalls, the next objective in the amphibious war in the Central Pacific.

Once back at Pearl Harbor, Admiral Nimitz announced the official end of combat in the Gilberts and declared the campaign complete. He told the press that Makin had been "a pushover," but he revealed that the preliminary estimate the marines at Tarawa had suffered was 1,026 killed in action out of a total of 3,600 casualties, making it the bloodiest battle in the 167 years of U.S. Marine Corps history. Publication of the figures, which would be adjusted downward slightly as the full cost of the battle was learned, created a firestorm of accusation and recrimination in Washington.

When Holland Smith got back to Hawaii he was shocked by the stir the long casualty lists had caused on the mainland. Unjustly pushed to the wall to account for the loss of life and limb, the old warhorse could only counter, "No way yet has been found to make war safe and easy."

Assistant Secretary of the Navy Ralph A. Bard issued the navy view: "The Marines who took Tarawa knew that a beachhead would cost them many men, but they did not stop to count the cost in their own lives."

Lieutenant General Alexander A. Vandegrift, the victor of Guadalcanal, who had recently been named the U.S. Marine Corps commandant, delivered the final postmortem on Tarawa in Washington. "No one regrets the losses more than the Marine Corps itself," he said. "No one realizes more than does the Marine Corps that there is no Royal Road to Tokyo. We must steel our people to the same realization."

Vice Admiral Harold R. Stark, commander in chief of U.S. naval forces in Europe, "saw in the American action at Tarawa evidence of gallantry of the sort that should be commemorated." This former chief of naval operations observed, "In the selfless valor of the young marines who fought that action against such terrible odds, and of the sailors who supported them, was sacrifice of which not only Americans, but free men everywhere, can rightly be proud. Tarawa was not a large action, but the human mind can perhaps more readily comprehend it because of its dimensions." Finally, he concluded, the battle was "one of the epics of the war in the Pacific."

Chapter Thirty-seven

Even as the last fighting went on at Tarawa and the first admirals and generals had gone ashore to examine their handiwork, the final cost of Operation Galvanic in men and material was yet to be paid. One of the overwhelming lessons of World War II was that, even with the advent of the carrier battle group, the submarine was the most deadly naval weapon. This was proved decisively in the darkness of November 24 off Makin.

Since entering the Central Pacific a week before, the Americans had been expecting the Japanese navy to come by air and by sea. Yet while the Fifth Fleet carrier crews were preoccupied with preparations for the next day's air operations, the major concern of the air admirals and carrier captains was Japanese submarines. Numerous sightings of periscopes had been made in the Makin area since November 20. And ever since CINCPAC had issued its general alert about enemy submarines on D day plus one, ASW had been an all-consuming worry of the naval commanders.

The escort carrier group left behind to cover the army garrison at Makin was steaming at a leisurely fifteen knots through a gentle swell some twenty miles southwest of Butaritari. Rear Admiral Henry M. Mullinix, of Indiana, the top graduate of the Naval Academy in 1916, was in command of the group of "jeep" carriers, including *Liscome Bay, Coral Sea,* and *Corregidor.* These were traveling in company with the battleship *New Mexico,* flagship of the fire support group and its commander, RAdm. Robert M. Griffin, and a screen composed of four destroyers and a minesweeper. The sonar of these escorts blasted the deep black water all around without surfeit. Mullinix was flying his flag aboard *Liscome Bay,* commanded by Capt. Irving D. Wiltsie.

The little flotilla spent the hours of darkness uneventfully, preparing for the next day's operations. Beneath a moon obscured by thick clouds, the carrier crews readied planes for Dawn Launch. Aboard *Liscome Bay* thirteen planes had been spotted on the flight deck—armed, fueled, and ready to launch at sunrise. Seven more were below, armed but not yet fueled. Meanwhile, "bogies"—unidentified aircraft—were registering on radar. During the night one of the destroyers was dispatched to Makin, and the rest of the escort screen redeployed, adjusting their positions to cover a larger area.

At 0435 Comdr. Nicholas A. Lidstone, commanding the destroyer *Franks,* made an urgent report to Griffin: His lookouts had sighted a dim, flashing light. Despite the possibility that an enemy submarine might be lurking about, Griffin detached *Franks* from the escort screen in order to investigate the light. The departure of a second destroyer further thinned the already slim screen. As *Franks* darted out of formation, the remaining "tin cans" moved up to cover the gap.

Shortly thereafter, *New Mexico's* powerful radar established a surface contact to the northeast. It did not seem to belong to an American formation, but the technicians were at a loss to explain it. They watched the contact for four minutes—until it faded and disappeared. False radar contacts were common at this time in the war, and since no sound contact had been made, the carrier group executed a predetermined turn in a northerly direction.

In preparation for Dawn Launch, Wiltsie took *Liscome Bay* to General Quarters at 0505. Three minutes later *Franks* reported that it had found a float light dropped by an enemy plane. These were used as signals to any Japanese aircraft that might be in the area that American targets were also around. At 0507 the formation of ships turned again in order to face the carriers into the light southeasterly breeze. This time they turned in a northeasterly direction—right into the submerged periscope sights of Lt. Comdr. Sunao Tabata aboard the Japanese submarine I-175. It had been I-175 running on the surface which *New Mexico's* radar had picked up.

The 1,785-ton Type KD6B oceangoing submarine had been on patrol with its crew of sixty men northeast of the Marshalls when Rear Admiral Takagi at Truk ordered Tabata to rush to the Gilberts and do what he could to impede the invasion. I-175 arrived on November 23, but that day four patrolling destroyers had prohibited Tabata from engaging any of the numerous fat targets moving about off Makin. Now, however, Tabata attacked. He fired a spread of torpedoes from fifteen hundred yards, then wheeled around to vacate the area.

The "fish" ran straight and true. *Liscome Bay* never had a chance. Survivors from the bridge believed that she was hit by two torpedoes. Others, including a man who had been stationed below the forward fireroom, said that possibly as many as three torpedoes had struck amidships. Whatever the number, at 0516 the doomed carrier suddenly seemed to explode. At least one torpedo had hit the main bomb storage compartment, and every warhead therein detonated instantaneously. Perhaps as much as 135,000 pounds of HE bombs— nine 2,000-pound bombs, seventy-eight 1,000-pound bombs, and ninety-six 500-pound bombs—went up all at once. "One second she was there solid and untroubled," recalled an observer who had been idly watching the baby flattop from another ship about half a mile away. "The next she was only a sheet of flame shooting skyward, smoke billowing, and a few moments later my ear caught the report."

Lieutenant Commander Oliver Ames, the senior surviving officer, reported the explosion as a "huge column of bright orange-colored flames, with incandescent spots streaking through it, like white-hot metal." Men aboard the ships in the escort screen, through which I-175 had maneuvered and attacked, saw a column of fire and molten metal flare a thousand feet high. Some ships reported a single large roaring explosion; others reported multiple explosions that occurred simultaneously. So great was the unearthly force that burst the carrier apart that *New Mexico,* fifteen hundred yards away, and the destroyer *Maury,* five thousand yards distant, were showered with burning oil and fragments of steel, clothing, and human limbs as the entire after third of *Liscome Bay* was destroyed. Commander F. T. Williamson, captain of the destroyer *Morris,* had witnessed the deaths of the carriers *Lexington, Yorktown,* and *Hornet,* but reported that even he had never seen anything like the fiery end of *Liscome Bay.*

The gunnery officer, Lt. Comdr. John R. Bodler, and the navigator, Lt. Comdr. Delancey Nicoll, saw that even with the most efficient damage control there was no hope of saving the carrier. They gave the order to abandon ship. Fire swiftly raced throughout the interior and rose through the timbers of the flight deck. As ammunition and fuel supplies caught fire and exploded, the flight deck collapsed and flames reached up to engulf the superstructure.

An unusual holder of the Navy Cross was among the hundreds of men pushing their way to the upper deck from darkened, smoke-filled, and rapidly flooding compartments below. During the attack on Pearl Harbor, Seaman Doris "Dorie" Miller, of Waco, Texas, then a mess attendant aboard the battleship *West Virginia,* had shot down two, and perhaps as many as five, of the twenty-nine Japanese aircraft downed that day. For his action at Pearl Harbor, Miller became the first African-American to receive the Navy Cross. He died in the *Liscome Bay* inferno.

Lieutenant Commander John B. Rowe, the ship's surgeon, was huddled in the sick bay with three corpsmen and a patient when the first explosion knocked them down. As they scrambled back to their feet, another detonation threw them to the deck again. Somehow all of them made it topside and into the water. Rowe soon was working from the sick bay aboard *Morris.* Lieutenant Commander Wells W. Carroll, though badly wounded, led a damage control team to restore pressure to the ruptured fire main, but to no avail. Admiral Mullinix, Captain Wiltsie, and the executive officer, Comdr. Finley E. Hall, were last seen sliding down a line into the fire-swept sea.

Crewmen who survived, especially those who were burned, suffered terribly. They struggled in the oil and wreckage to free life rafts, but only a pitiful few craft were actually launched. At 0535 *Liscome Bay* flared up for one last time and sank stern first, settling into a two-thousand-fathom trench. She went down in less than five minutes.

The escort ships decided to pick up survivors rather than make good their own escape from danger or look for the enemy submarine. The rescue work was complicated by the fires burning on the surface of the sea. One man on the stricken carrier, operated on for appendicitis a mere two days earlier, climbed into the whaleboat launched from *Morris.* He asked for a rubber boat so he might return to the sea and try to rescue more of his shipmates. It was all too familiar to Seaman T. R. Furnas, an electrician's mate from *Morris,* who went into the water numerous times to rescue men. He had done the same in October 1942 after the *Hornet* had been fatally damaged by a torpedo launched by a Japanese submarine. In that action Furnas had won the Silver Star for his gallantry. Lieutenant Loren H. Killion and Ensign Joseph R. Guerrant located a rubber raft aboard *Morris* and paddled through the burning oil to pick up wounded men clinging to a piece of floating wreckage.

It was a stunning blow to the U.S. Navy—the loss of one of its new escort carriers. The sinking of *Liscome Bay* claimed the lives of 644 of the 959 American seamen who had been aboard her. The disaster accounted for the greatest loss of life from the sinking of a single warship at sea in the history of the U.S. Navy—until, significantly, a Japanese submarine put a torpedo into the cruiser *Indianapolis* in the last month of the war and 883 men died.

Soldiers of the 165th RCT aboard the transport *Leonard Wood,* one of the ships closest to the carrier when it blew up, had helped rescue many survivors. Lieutenant Colonel S. L. A. Marshall was among those on the transport. "All of the postbattle happiness was gone as we steamed back to Pearl," he remembered. "The survivors sat in the wardroom day after day, shocked men who would respond to a question if asked but were otherwise lost in their brooding. They stared into space. Games were not for them. They would not even communicate with one another. It was my first and only experience with group shock."

Yet, as devastating as the loss of *Liscome Bay* had been, it was a question of too little too late. The Combined Fleet lay impotently at anchor at Truk. The reinforcements that had left for Tarawa aboard the cruisers *Isuzu* and *Naka* ended up on Mili, where the war eventually passed them by. Four more cruisers— *Jumano, Chokai, Noshiro,* and *Suzuya,* practically all that remained from the debacle at Rabaul— and a dozen destroyers sortied from the Carolines, but the battle was over before they reached Kwajalein. Admiral Koga recalled them when they had been gone from Truk for just a few days.

Of the other Japanese naval forces available for action, only the Sixth Fleet submarines were dispatched to the Gilberts. I-35, commanded by Lieutenant Commander Yamamoto, had been sunk off Tarawa. Five other submarines also failed to return. I-19, the submarine that had sunk the American carrier *Wasp* in 1942, was also lost to enemy action. The destroyer *Radford* cornered her on November 25 about sixty miles west of Makin and depth-charged her to the bottom with four attacks spanning several hours. *Radford* also accounted for the destruction of I-40. Three other Japanese submarines—I-39, I-21, and RO-38— failed to return to the Marshalls, fate unknown. Of nine submarines that had been sent to the Gilberts, only three returned from their patrols.

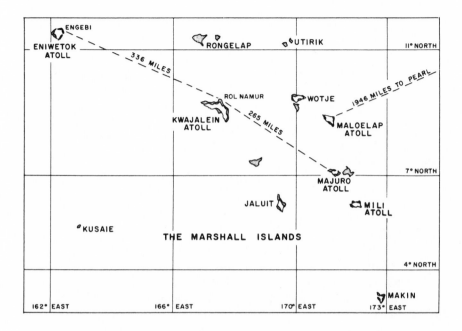

The other dimension of the Japanese defense—air power—could not be brought fully into play until November 27. On this night, however, one hundred aircraft flew off the airfields in the Marshalls in search of the American carriers. Thirty torpedo bombers found the carrier battle group comprising *Enterprise, Belleau Wood,* and *Monterey* north of the Gilberts and attacked just after nightfall. The night CAP of *Enterprise* succeeded in breaking up the attack, but at a cost. Lieutenant Commander Edward H. "Butch" O'Hare, one of the first heroes of the war, was shot down and killed. O'Hare had won the Medal of Honor in February 1942 after single-handedly shooting down six enemy bombers that were attacking *Lexington* off Rabaul. His loss was a demoralizing blow to the navy. Another Japanese air attack was beaten off the next day by the destroyer screen.

On December 4 Rear Admiral Pownall took his fast carrier forces deep into the Marshalls for one last strike at the Japanese before retiring back to Hawaii. An enormous flight of Hellcats, Dauntlesses, and Avengers swept over Kwajalein on this day and inflicted serious damage to the enemy base. Eighteen Japanese fighters were shot down in wild melees, and a dozen bombers were destroyed on the ground. Several ships, including a cruiser, were left burning in the large blue lagoon.

Not willing to expose the carriers to further risk, Pownall elected to disengage before the Japanese could regroup and come at the exhausted American carrier crews again. Although the carrier captains objected strongly to fleeing the area—they wanted to hit the Japanese airfields again—Pownall was in command and his orders stood. He granted the airmen one final mission against Wotje, where a dozen bombers were found and burned out. Task Force 50 then collected its far-ranging aircraft and headed for Hawaii. That night, however, before they were beyond enemy air space, a Japanese air attack achieved a measure of success when a bomber put a torpedo into the stern of *Lexington*. The enemy warhead killed nine men and wounded thirty-five, and left the rudder jammed. With the rest of the marauding American carriers, "*Lady Lex*" limped back to Pearl Harbor.

A final sequel to the battle for the Gilberts was as bitter, if less momentous. On December 8 the carriers *Bunker Hill* and *Monterey,* five battleships, and a dozen destroyers struck Nauru on their way back to join Admiral Halsey's Third Fleet in the South Pacific. The warships bombarded the island from a range of only fifteen hundred yards, while the planes of the carriers wrecked the airfield. Perhaps ten Japanese planes were destroyed on the ground.

When the destroyer *Boyd* came within two miles of the island in order to investigate a life raft, the Japanese retaliated. A large-caliber shore battery opened up and in quick succession put two shells into the ship—one into the engine room and another into the forward stack. *Boyd* soon controlled her fires, but ten men had been killed and twenty or more wounded. The stricken ship retired as swiftly as possible, zigzagging, and managed to reach Efate under her own steam. Only then were the books closed on Operation Galvanic—nearly a month after the B-24s of the Seventh Air Force had commenced the furious campaign to seize from the Japanese their gains in the Gilbert Islands.

That was it. The time for naiveté had passed. There had been plenty of glory—and plenty of gore. After the dramatic twenty-six days of Operation Galvanic, there was a general belief among American soldiers, sailors, coast guardsmen, marines, and airmen, if not also their political, naval, and military leaders, that too little of the glory and too much of the gore lay ahead in the war in the Pacific.

Afterword

The battle for the Gilberts, as was clearly apparent at the time, was a stunning American victory. In the four days of fighting on Tarawa and Makin atolls, the Japanese lost their bid once and for all for a limited victory—if, in fact, they had not already done so at Midway and Guadalcanal. For the United States, the bloodletting was convincing evidence that winning the war against Japan would not be easy.

The hit-and-run raids against Rabaul and other targets by the American fast carrier forces, in which the core of Japanese naval air power was irrevocably lost, opened a strategic gap between the opposing sides, which the Imperial Combined Fleet could never hope to overcome. The issue of battle in the Gilberts had depended on air power. Victory and defeat had turned on whether the Japanese could succeed in crushing either or both the American amphibious forces and fast carriers before Rear Admiral Spruance could exploit the gap created at Rabaul and gain a forward foothold in the Central Pacific. The American fast carrier forces established air supremacy over the Gilberts and held it from start to finish. What remained of Japanese air power entered the battle too slowly and utterly failed to influence the outcome.

Yet so close had the Japanese come to victory on the incomparably small island of Betio—despite having written off the Gilberts many months before—so near had the U.S. Navy and Marine Corps come to disaster, that the battle by which Operation Galvanic came to be best known is today still commonly referred to as "Terrible Tarawa" or "the Tarawa killing ground." For decades thereafter, mere mention of Tarawa at a reunion of marines was enough to engender deep remorse. Among naval and military historians, even today the debate continues over whether the costs were worth it.

Major General Holland Smith, who knew something of the mystique of Marine esprit de corps, understood Tarawa in a way few others were willing then or now to admit. His verdict, which he revealed to a group of correspondents while touring the Japanese fortifications after the battle: "Gentlemen, it was their will to die." The Japanese—suddenly encountering Americans who, with total disregard for the risks, threw themselves into the fury of heavy automatic weapons and artillery firing at point-blank range—understood it too. More than anything else, said the few Japanese prisoners captured, it had been the sight of wave upon wave of green-clad infantry climbing over the seawall and over their own dead to secure the beachhead that had broken the enemy's resolve to resist. Said a Japanese officer after the war, "Such driven American courage and bravery was something we had not expected to see when the war began."

But Marine valor at Tarawa notwithstanding, it was the resurgence of American sea power after Pearl Harbor that determined the issue in the Gilberts. And beyond sea power, the errors and shortcomings of Japanese planning contributed as much as the heroism of the American fighting forces to final victory. If the Japanese had not sent the cream of their remaining naval air strength to Rabaul and had kept it based at Truk instead, these assets would have been available from the start of Galvanic and might have seriously impeded the American amphibious assault; the meager land-based air forces already in the Marshalls might then have provided the extra strength to pierce the overstretched and immobile American air umbrella and overwhelm one or more of the beachheads or their supporting naval forces. Yet Rear Admiral Spruance's unnatural disposition of his available air strength at least shielded the battle zone from mass air attacks. The importance of this element was underscored indirectly by Maj. Rathvon M. Tompkins, the 2d Marine Division assistant operations officer. "Tarawa," he said ten years after the fact, "was the only landing in the Pacific that the Japanese could have defeated."

In its grand gamble in the Gilberts the United States accomplished overwhelming numerical and material superiority over a broader front and to a degree it had not been able to achieve at any one time in the South Pacific—except at the end of the long, drawn-out struggle for Guadalcanal. The enfeeblement of Japanese naval and air forces was partly responsible, but the balance was tipped by the warships and fast carriers borrowed from the embattled Third Fleet of Vice Admiral Halsey in the South Pacific. All during Galvanic, while the carriers of Rear Admirals Pownall and Radford isolated the Marshalls, Rear Admiral Montgomery held shut the back door to the Gilberts with carriers borrowed from Halsey. For more than a month, some carriers fought an almost continuous series of air actions until, fearing Japanese retaliation on a scale not possible, Pownall pulled them back too soon. If the Fifth Fleet carriers had given way at any point before that—assuming that the Japanese had been able to launch a swift and determined counter-attack—the end in the Gilberts might have been different. At the least, American losses would have been much greater. If there was an in-dispensable feature to Galvanic, ironically it was the strategic weapon used least efficiently—the fast carrier forces. Misused and poorly led though they were at this time in the war, the fast carrier forces still provided the ultimate margin of victory.

Similarly, without Colonel Shoup no marine beachhead would have been established at Tarawa. It was his determination and coolness under fire during the tragic and terrible first two days of stalemate that pre-vented the marines from fully disintegrating. With the exception of Colonel Edson, it is difficult to imagine a more quick-thinking, con-fident commander who could have led the marines out of chaos against such awful odds. "The brainiest, finest soldiering marine I ever knew," said one of the men who remained closest to Shoup during the battle. "Without him the bastards would have pushed us off that damn rock," said another.

Besides the grievous casualties to their ranks, the marines rued the battle because of the LVTs. Seventy-five of them that were judged combat capable were already in the Table of Organization and Equipment (TO/E) of the 2d Division in New Zealand. With a hundred more, each carrying 20 riflemen and making the eight-hundred- to twelve-hundred-yard round-trip to shore once, Maj. Gen. Julian Smith fig-ured that he could transport about 3,000 assault troops—three rein-forced rifle battalions—across the deadly barrier reef and into the beach-head. Only fifty more LVTs were provided, however, enough to land only 2,000 marines rather than 3,000.

In the end, the LVT battalion was the hardest hit of any unit com-mitted to battle at Tarawa. Julian Smith later estimated that thirty-five of the tracked vehicles filled with water and sank on their own or were destroyed in deep water by gunfire, twenty-six sank or were knocked out on the reef, nine burned when their fuel tanks ignited as a result of hits, two were blown up by underwater mines, ten were wrecked on the beaches and seawall, and eight were lost to mechanical failures. Of the 651 sailors and marines attached to the battalion, 323 were killed or wounded, including both the commander and deputy commander. Perhaps no other special services unit in any branch of the American armed forces lost a greater proportion of its personnel killed and wounded in a single battle of the war than the 2d LVT Battalion at Tarawa.

After the Gilberts there followed the American thrust into the Marshalls; the envelopments of Truk and Rabaul; the fall of Saipan, Tinian, and Guam; and the battle for Iwo Jima. After this, with the end of combat on small islands, came the slow deadly siege of Okinawa. In each brutal encounter over the next eighteen months after Tarawa, the tactics of amphibious assault that were proved in the Gilberts carried the day. The "recommendations made and acted upon as a result of the Gilberts offensive," said Holland Smith after the Marshalls, "proved sound."

For the Japanese, the Yogaki plan, or "waylaying attack," had failed to slow the Americans in the Gilberts—as it later would in the Marshalls, at Truk, and in the Marianas. But the failure of Yogaki was the by-product of the risky RO operation. This more than anything else was responsible for the loss of the Gilberts and later the entire Central Pacific—more so even than the Japanese decision not to fight for the islands to the finish. It ultimately allowed the Americans to arrive and concentrate relatively unopposed in the Central Pacific—permitting them to finish the job of assault, siege, and seizure on islands long before the Japanese were able to gather even token forces from their scattered and grossly weakened naval and air strength. When Admiral Fukudome called "the almost complete loss of carrier planes at Rabaul a mortal blow to Japan" he had not been exaggerating.

In fact, before the end of the war such developments led to a strategic situation that could be countered, on successively greater scales, only by a degree of attrition that was to make Tarawa the progenitor of the battle for Okinawa in 1945. The RO operation was an error of commission by the Imperial General Headquarters that could never be repaired. In many ways the failure of the RO operation was as fatal as the failure at Midway, and together they affirmed the inevitable defeat of Japan before the war was fully two years old. The air losses at Rabaul in the autumn of 1943 ate up Japanese air strength at a rate that predetermined the failure of other later similar efforts such as that of Operation A-Go, which the world came to call "The Great Marianas Turkey Shoot," which might otherwise have hurt the Allied war effort badly. Thus, no matter where one looks for cause and effect, it was the attrition in the air that determined the future course of the great Pacific conflict and, as a result, the means of Allied victory.

After the battle for the Gilberts the war increased exponentially in scale and intensity until at Okinawa it would inflict a ghastly 150,000 casualties in three months. Operation Galvanic was one of the turning points of the war in the Pacific not because it demonstrated that Japan would go down in defeat or that the Allies would win the war— this had been determined on December 7, 1941, when Pearl Harbor was attacked and the American carriers escaped destruction.

Rather, Tarawa and the battle for the Gilberts demonstrated graphically that in some ways the Pacific war would be nearly as costly to the United States as the conflict in Europe, and that the Japanese would fight for what they had taken, if necessary to the last man on both sides. As it was, Galvanic became the key from which the most important part of the subsequent campaign in the Pacific theater of operations developed. After Tarawa, in particular, it was truly as Admiral Nimitz had said to Admiral King: "It'll only become worse."

A Note on Casualties

In Operation Galvanic, the battle for the Gilberts, American land, sea, and air forces suffered casualties comparable to losses in the much longer and more publicized Guadalcanal campaign.

In the six months of battle that raged on, over, and around Guadalcanal from August 1942 until February 1943, American losses among soldiers, sailors, marines, and airmen reached an estimated 6,960 killed or missing. Of these, 1,207 marines and 562 soldiers were killed and another 2,600 troops wounded out of 60,000 men committed to action on the notorious "Island of Death" itself. The Americans lost about three times as many dead at sea as they did on land. In comparison, Japanese losses may have been as high as 26,000 on the ground and 5,000 in the air and at sea.

In the twenty-six days of Galvanic, from November 13 through December 8, 1943, combined casualties of Spruance's Central Pacific Force—in killed, wounded, captured, and missing on land, at sea, and in the air—amounted to about 5,100. Of these, at least 2,000 were killed. Total losses among marine and supporting personnel at Tarawa were a harrowing 3,500, divided between 1,147 dead and 2,353 wounded. The conquest of Tarawa alone cost three times as many American lives as had the landings in North Africa, twice as many as in seizing the beachhead on Sicily, and only about 500 less than the awesome two-week struggle for a foothold on the European continent at Salerno, Italy.

With losses totaling 20 percent of their forces committed to the battle for the Gilberts, U.S. Marine Corps casualties were by far the greatest. They reached 3,429. Julian Smith's magnificent 2d Marine Division was all but shattered and, after rebuilding and retraining itself, would not see action again until seven months later at Saipan. Among the 15,700 troops who fought only on tiny Betio—not including 1,400 sailors and coast guardsmen who also landed—losses totaled 3,333. Of these, 1,085 were killed, later died of wounds, or were missing and presumed dead. The wounded numbered 2,248.

The 2d Battalion, 6th Marines, which did not fight on Betio but secured the rest of Tarawa Atoll, lost 32 killed and 61 wounded in the march up the atoll and in the final action at Buariki and Lone Tree Islet. In addition, 3 marines were killed or wounded at Abemama, making a total of 1,118 marines killed and 2,311 wounded in the battle for the Gilberts.

The U.S. Navy and Coast Guard sustained approximately 1,400 casualties of all types, of which more than 850 were killed. These figures include combat casualties among corpsmen, coxswains, shore parties, Seabees, and aircrews, as well as losses related to the battle. These latter include the seamen lost in the tragic sinking of the escort carrier *Liscome Bay*, the mishap aboard the battleship *Mississippi*, the torpedoing of both the fleet carrier *Lexington* off Kwajalein and the light carrier *Independence* off Tarawa, the sinking of the submarines *Corvina* and *Sculpin*, the shelling of the destroyer *Boyd* off Nauru, and the seamen who fell during the Japanese shelling of the transports at Tarawa on D day.

United States Army casualties are put at about 305. This figure is based primarily on the official military history of the battle for Makin, which gives the following breakdown: 58 killed in action, 8 who died of wounds, 152 wounded in action, and 35 injured in noncombat incidents. Included in the overall compilation are the Seventh Air Force losses, which amounted to about 50 killed and wounded among aircrews and air service support ground personnel.

What were Japanese losses? Over the decades a variety of vague and misleading figures have been given on the casualties suffered by Japanese forces during the battle for the Gilberts. None of them of course can be said to be accurate. At best they must remain estimates, for by the very nature of the war in the Pacific and the tremendous destruction wrought upon Japanese garrisons it was always impossible for anyone—friend or foe—to arrive at an exact figure after any battle. However, a compilation of the most reliable official sources reveals that the Japanese and Korean casualties in the Marshalls and Gilberts during Galvanic may have reached 7,000—possibly only a third more than overall American losses.

Although no exact breakdown is available for the total number of enemy killed, wounded, and captured—including the battles for Tarawa and Makin, the losses on other islands in the Gilberts, and losses in the air and at sea—I conservatively estimate that the Japanese lost at least 6,000 men, practically all of whom were killed. Without question, the casualties at Tarawa Atoll were by far the worst. They reached almost 4,900, of whom all but 17 Japanese and 129 Koreans were killed. Of the 650 to 800 men who defended Makin—only 280 of whom were combat troops—at least 550 died. Losses suffered as a result of naval and air action in the Gilberts and Marshalls reached 500 to 1,000.

Whatever the true count, which we will never know, by the end of the year commanders were to report to the Naval General Staff in Tokyo that personnel losses in the Central Pacific since the attack on the Gilberts were two admirals, a half-dozen senior officers, two thousand laborers, and eighty-five hundred naval infantry, airmen, and sailors. Numerous naval losses, such as the six submarines that failed to return after the Gilberts debacle and the shipping losses inflicted in Pownall's raids on the Marshalls, must have contributed to these figures.

Casualties among the noncombatant native population in the Gilberts were never reported. They were suggested to have been low, but no one could know with any certainty. Taking into account the forced relocation of residents from most garrison islands in the Gilberts and Marshalls and figures from after-action reports and historical surveys, I would estimate that fewer than 25 were killed and wounded. Most of these occurred at Makin, and were the result of naval shelling and the use of civilians as human shields by the defenders.

A Note on Honors

In honor of their achievement in capturing Tarawa Atoll, the 2d Marine Division (Reinforced) was awarded the Presidential Unit Citation. A list of the units that shared in this citation follows.

PRESIDENTIAL UNIT CITATION
******

The 2ND MARINE DIVISION (REINFORCED), V AMPHIBIOUS CORPS, composed of the following units:

HEADQUARTERS AND HEADQUARTERS BATTALION;
2ND TANK BATTALION;
COMPANY C, I AMPHIBIOUS CORPS MEDIUM TANK BATTALION (ATTACHED);
2ND MARINE REGIMENT (INFANTRY);
6TH MARINE REGIMENT (INFANTRY);
8TH MARINE REGIMENT (INFANTRY);
10TH MARINE REGIMENT (ARTILLERY);
1ST BATTALION, 18TH MARINE REGIMENT (ENGINEERS);
2ND BATTALION, 18TH MARINE REGIMENT (PIONEERS);
3RD BATTALION, 18TH MARINE REGIMENT (SEABEES);
2ND SPECIAL WEAPONS BATTALION;
2ND AMPHIBIOUS TRACTOR BATTALION;
2ND MEDICAL BATTALION;
2ND SPECIAL WEAPONS DEFENSE BATTALION (ATTACHED);
AIR LIAISON GROUP & FIRE CONTROL PARTY, V AMPHIBIOUS CORPS (ATTACHED);

is cited for outstanding performance in combat during the seizure and occupation of the Japanese-held Atoll of Tarawa, Gilbert Islands, November 20 to 24, 1943. Forced by treacherous coral reefs to disembark from their landing craft hundreds of yards off the beach, the 2nd Marine Division (Reinforced) became a highly vulnerable target for devastating Japanese fire. Dauntlessly advancing in spite of rapidly mounting losses, the marines fought a gallant battle against crushing odds, clearing the limited beach-heads of snipers and machine guns, reducing powerfully fortified enemy positions, and completely annihilating the fanatically determined and strongly entrenched Japanese forces. By the successful occupation of Tarawa, the 2nd Marine Division (Reinforced) has provided our forces with highly strategic and important air and land bases from which to continue future operations against the enemy; by the valiant fighting spirit of these men, their heroic fortitude under punishing fire, and their relentless perseverance in waging this epic battle in the Central Pacific, they have upheld the finest traditions of the United States Naval Forces.

> For the President,
> James Forrestal
> Acting Secretary of the Navy
> Washington, D.C.

INDIVIDUAL HONORS

Exclusive of the Purple Heart, which a man receives when he is wounded, numerous citations and decorations for meritorious service were awarded to participants in the battle for the Gilbert Islands. Chief among them, of course, was the Congressional Medal of Honor, the highest award that is conferred on members of the U.S. Armed Forces.

Medal of Honor
The following officers and men were awarded the Medal of Honor for their contribution above and beyond the call of duty in Operation Galvanic:

Navy Captain John P. Cromwell, of Henry, Illinois, commanding Submarine Division 42, in the submarine *Sculpin*. For heroism and self-sacrifice. With his boat mortally damaged by a depth charge attack on November 19, Cromwell, entrusted with the knowledge that the Japanese naval communication codes were being deciphered by the U.S. Navy, went down with *Sculpin* and gave up his life rather than risk capture and torture, which might have caused him to divulge this astonishing military secret.

Staff Sergeant William James Bordelon, of San Antonio, Texas, platoon leader, 2d Platoon, Company A, 1st Battalion, 18th Marines. For selflessness and gallantry. As a member of the shore party supporting the 2d Battalion, 2d Marines, Bordelon was one of the first assault engineers to cross the Tarawa seawall. Although severely wounded, he returned to the water and carried injured comrades to safety. He used demolitions to personally destroy four bunkers. He was killed in action on November 20.

First Lieutenant William Deane Hawkins, of El Paso, Texas, commanding the Scout & Sniper Platoon, Headquarters Company, 2d Marines. For extraordinary heroism and uncommon valor. Hawkins cleaned out machine-gun nests along the Burns-Philp pier, led several destructive forays into enemy lines, and, although wounded three times, single-handedly destroyed numerous bunkers along the seawall and inland of the beachhead. He died of wounds on November 21.

First Lieutenant Alexander Bonnyman, Jr., of Santa Fe, New Mexico, platoon leader, 3d Platoon, Company C, 1st Battalion, 18th Marines. For extraordinary heroism and courage. As executive officer of the shore party supporting the 2d Battalion, 8th Marines, Bonnyman destroyed numerous pillboxes with a flamethrower and demolitions and led the capture of a large enemy bombproof. He was killed in action on November 22.

Colonel David M. Shoup, of Covington, Indiana, commanding officer, 2d Marines. For conspicuous gallantry and intrepidity. Although wounded in trying to reach the shore on D day, Shoup, at the risk of his life above and beyond the call of duty and aware that the amphibious assault was in jeopardy, quickly established and thereafter maintained command and control of the assault forces until he was relieved on November 22.

Navy Cross

The Navy Cross is the highest award that is conferred exclusively on members of the U.S. Navy. It is second only to the Medal of Honor, which is awarded to members of all branches of service. Several officers and men were awarded the Navy Cross for their heroism during Galvanic. The following is a sampling of those so honored at Tarawa:

Major Michael P. Ryan, of Osage City, Kansas, company commander, Company L, 3d Battalion, 2d Marines. For extraordinary heroism, great determination and leadership, conspicuous fighting spirit, great personal bravery, and tactical skill. When his battalion commander failed to reach shore, as senior officer Ryan assumed command of the badly disorganized and isolated survivors of three battalions. He organized and directed critical operations of these elements throughout the battle until he was relieved, leading assaults on enemy positions, retaining initiative in his sector, and clearing his isolated beachhead into which reinforcements could be moved. (Ryan also received the British Distinguished Service Order.)

Major Henry Pierson Crowe, of Boston, Kentucky, commanding officer, 2d Battalion, 8th Marines. For extraordinary heroism, the greatest of personal and unflinching valor, great military skill, inspirational and outstanding leadership, and ceaseless energy. Despite the fiercest resistance, Crowe was the first battalion commander to reach shore. Braving intense machine-gun and shell fire, constantly with his men at the most violent points of fighting, he organized the establishment of a beachhead and directed the elimination of hostile snipers and gun crews from along the seawall and inland of the beachhead. Without rest and at great personal risk, he maintained continuous aggressive pressure against heavily reinforced enemy emplacements. Crowe was personally largely responsible for winning and maintaining the beachhead at Tarawa.

Major William C. Chamberlin, of Seattle, Washington, executive officer, 2d Battalion, 8th Marines. For outstanding leadership and uncommon valor, and disregarding personal safety. Chamberlin cleaned out machine-gun nests along the seawall and, although wounded, directed operations on the extreme left of the beachhead. He led attacks against numerous bunkers and commanded the destruction of an important enemy bombproof.

Colonel Merrit A. Edson, of Washington, D.C., chief of staff, 2d Marine Division. For exceptionally meritorious conduct and outstanding service. Under his direction, the division staff made a complete intelligence study of the chief objective and a situation estimate from which the decision to invade Tarawa across the lagoon beaches was made. During the operation he presented sound solutions to many difficult problems, established the division's advance command post under heavy fire, and prepared plans for the final attack and mopping-up operations against enemy positions.

Corporal John J. Spillane, crew chief, 2d Amphibian Tractor Battalion. For great personal bravery and heroic conduct. During the H-hour assault, several enemy grenades on separate occasions were thrown into the troop compartment of his vehicle. Spillane began throwing the grenades out of the vehicle with absolute disregard for his own safety until one exploded in his throwing hand, mutilating it and causing severe multiple wounds elsewhere on his body. His dauntless courage and quick thinking saved the lives of the assault troops in his vehicle.

Private Jack R. Stambaugh, of Bowie, Texas, rifleman, Company B, 1st Battalion, 6th Marines. For extraordinary heroism, self-sacrifice, and devotion to duty while repulsing an enemy counterattack at night and giving his life gallantly for a comrade. He observed four enemy attacking a wounded and isolated marine. On his own initiative and without regard for his own safety, he went to the aid of his comrade and killed all four enemy with his rifle and bayonet, suffering a sword wound which caused his death before aid could reach him.

Navy Lieutenant Wayne A. Parker, engineer officer, destroyer *Ringgold.* For extraordinary heroism, bravery, and intrepidity. When an enemy shell penetrated the after engine room below the waterline of his ship, he plugged the underwater hole with his body, preventing flooding until emergency repairs could be made. Then with total disregard for personal safety he cleared the room of all personnel and disposed of the live shell by carrying it topside and disposing of it overboard.

Distinguished Service Medal

The Distinguished Service Medal (DSM) is awarded for exceptionally meritorious service, most commonly to members of the U.S. Army. It is also conferred on members of other branches of service.

Rear Admiral Harry W. Hill, of Oakland, California, commanding officer, Southern Attack Force, 5th Amphibious Force. For exceptionally meritorious service in duty of great responsibility, outstanding leadership, skill in planning and operations, and personal courage. His efforts contributed materially to the success of Operation Galvanic. (Hill was also awarded the Russian Order of Kutuzov, second degree, by the Soviet government.)

Major General Julian C. Smith, of Elkton, Maryland, commanding general, 2d Marine Division. For outstanding professional ability, tireless energy, and brilliant leadership. Despite immense communication and amphibious transport difficulties, through personal leadership qualities, resourcefulness, determination, courage, endurance, and tenacity, Smith's handling of this major amphibious assault operation was in the highest quality manner.

Silver Star

The Silver Star is awarded by all branches of service for personal valor and exceptionally heroic service.

Gunnery Sergeant Jared J. Hooper, of Milford, New Jersey, Scout & Sniper Platoon, Headquarters Company, 2d Marines. For conspicuous gallantry and intrepidity, inspiring leadership, and devotion to duty that contributed immeasurably to final victory. Hooper greatly aided his platoon leader by his personal valor and courage. Many times he led sections of the platoon against enemy positions, always at great personal risk and under heavy fire. When the platoon leader was mortally wounded, Hooper took command and, without rest, led the platoon successfully in mission after mission.

Lieutenant Colonel Walter I. Jordan, observer, 4th Marine Division. For conspicuous gallantry and intrepidity. Although only an observer, upon seeing the commander of the assault battalion to which he was attached killed and all his staff either isolated, killed, or wounded, Jordan assumed command and with tireless energy and at great personal risk directed the critical action which resulted in the winning of the limited and hard-pressed beachhead in his sector.

Second Lieutenant Louis R. Largey, of Hollywood, California, platoon leader, 2d Assault Tank Platoon, Company C, I Amphibious Corps Medium Tank Battalion. For conspicuous gallantry and intrepidity. Largey fought his tanks well within enemy lines until three were destroyed and the fourth caught fire. He organized the crews of his destroyed tanks and led them back to his unit through enemy lines, exhibiting outstanding leadership and courage. While under heavy fire he salvaged ammunition from a disabled tank on the reef, giving small-arms ammunition to an infantry unit and rearming his one remaining tank with heavy shells. Largey maintained conspicuous gallantry, intrepidity, and conscientious devotion to duty with utter disregard for his own personal safety.

First Lieutenant Alan G. Leslie, of Milwaukee, Oregon, platoon leader, 1st Assault Engineer Platoon, Company A, 1st Battalion, 18th Marines. For conspicuous gallantry and intrepidity, devotion to duty, coolness under fire, initiative, and utter disregard for his personal safety. Leslie landed under intense fire with a scout-sniper group before the initial assault waves, and used his flamethrower to neutralize several dangerous enemy positions along the Burns-Philp pier. His exceptional daring was a source of inspiration to his men and to the assault waves advancing through the water behind him.

Lieutenant Colonel Presley M. Rixey, of Virginia Beach, Virginia, commanding officer, 1st Battalion, 10th Marines. For conspicuous gallantry and intrepidity, technical skill, personal valor, and inspiring leadership. He landed under heavy fire and tirelessly, and often at risk of his life, directed the night landing and employment of his 75mm pack howitzer artillery battalion. Throughout the battle, Rixey effectively coordinated and directed artillery barrages, enabling infantry to overcome almost impassable defenses, breaking up an enemy counterattack, and contributing greatly to ultimate victory.

First Lieutenant Norman K. Thomas, of Long Beach, Mississippi, executive officer, Company B, 1st Battalion, 6th Marines. For conspicuous gallantry and intrepidity, leadership, and fearless devotion to duty. After assuming control of his company when the commanding officer was wounded, he repeatedly exposed himself to heavy enemy fire while moving up and down his lines during three successive enemy counterattacks at night and encouraging his troops to hold on against nearly overwhelming resistance. His direction of his troops turned back the hostile attacks with severe losses to the enemy.

Corporal Leonce Olivier, of Eunice, Louisiana, squad leader, Scout & Sniper Platoon, Headquarters Company, 2d Marines. For gallantry and intrepidity, personal valor, military skill, absolute coolness, tireless energy, fearless devotion to duty, and extraordinary example. For three days without sleep Olivier destroyed numerous enemy positions, exposing himself to heavy fire by crawling up to gunports and destroying emplacements with grenades and demolitions. In other instances, although wounded, he exposed himself to provide fire support to comrades who were advancing upon the entrances of enemy emplacements. An inspiration to his comrades, he contributed greatly to the success of his regiment.

Bronze Star

The Bronze Star is awarded by all branches of service for exceptional meritorious service. Numerous Bronze Stars were awarded to the marines at Tarawa. A sample follows:

First Lieutenant Stacy C. Davis, platoon leader, 1st Platoon, Company F, 2d Battalion, 8th Marines. For meritorious service in connection with operations against the enemy during which he was wounded but continued to courageously and effectively lead his infantry unit as a company officer. His leadership and perseverance were an inspiration to his comrades and contributed greatly to the success of troops in his sector of the beachhead.

U.S. ARMY HONORS

Curiously, the army awarded at least twice as many decorations for gallantry and meritorious service to soldiers and airmen as were awarded to naval and marine personnel for Galvanic. This caused more than a little anger in naval circles. The army honors presented for the Gilberts ranged from the Legion of Merit (for example, to Maj. Gen. Ralph Smith, for the "massive planning" of the Makin operation), Silver and Bronze Stars, to the Air Medal. In addition, one marine officer at Makin, Lt. Col. James Roosevelt, President Franklin Roosevelt's son, received the Silver Star.

Notes & References

In the bibliographic notes that follow, only those sources that were of most critical importance in the reconstruction of this story have been cited. (All protected sources are cited.) The absence of a particular source does not reflect a lack of overall value to history; rather, it is only that a full discussion of all the official and unofficial sources consulted would fill a book. Those interested in a more extensive accounting of the material pertaining to Galvanic should begin by turning to the official naval, military, and air force histories.

All passages or information in the text based on the author's conversations with individuals are given specific references on the subject's first mention, but usually not thereafter unless there may be the possibility for confusion with other material. Publication information on books is provided in the bibliography.

PART ONE—THE PRELUDE

Page

3   The basis for the discussion of the strategic background of the Central Pacific drive in the first and second chapters is based primarily on Morison, *History of U.S. Naval Operations in World War II*, Vol. VII, *Aleutians, Gilberts and Marshalls, June 1942–April 1944*, 79–85.

3   F6F Hellcat fighter specifications: Fitzsimons, *The Illustrated Encyclopedia of Twentieth Century Weapons and Warfare*, Vol. 12, 1289–90. Although the F6F and its predecessor the F4F Wildcat both had six .50-caliber machine guns, the F6F carried twice as much ammunition.

3   The Mitsubishi A6M model naval fighter, originally code-named Zero and later Zeke, turned tighter than any other plane of the war. Its armament was dual 20mm cannon and two machine guns. The cockpit was not armored and the fuel tanks were not self-sealing, so that the A6M flamed easily when hit (Fitzsimons, *Ibid.*, Vol. 1, 7–9).

3   "We have to start somewhere": Based on Notes, COMINCH-CINCPAC Meeting, February 22, 1943; Strategic Plan for the Defeat of Japan, May 14, 1943. (The year for dated documents cited hereafter, unless otherwise indicated, is 1943.)

4   Nimitz, Spruance, and call for action: Dyer, *The Amphibians Came to Conquer: The Story of Admiral Richmond Kelly Turner*, Vol. II, 611–12. See also Potter, *Nimitz*, 239–43; Hoyt, *Storm over the*

Gilberts: War in the Central Pacific, 1943, 10–16; Spector, *Eagle against the Sun: The American War with Japan,* 255–56.

6 "With our paucity of carriers": From complete and original statements of Galvanic participants, provided by *Time-Life* correspondent Robert Sherrod to Historical Branch, Headquarters, U.S. Marine Corps, official historical archives, excerpts of which quoted in Sherrod, *Tarawa: The Story of a Battle,* 181–92. Hereafter referred to as Sherrod Papers.

6 Target date for invasion: Strategy in the Pacific (JCS 386/1), July 19; Notes, JCS Meeting, July 20; JCS dispatch to CINCPAC (CM-IN 14465), July 20.

6 Composition of Spruance forces: TF 54 Report on Galvanic, December 4. In comparison, elements of the Guadalcanal invasion consisted of only three carriers, one battleship, eleven heavy cruisers, three light cruisers, thirty-three destroyers, twenty-two transports and cargo ships, five minesweepers, and nineteen thousand troops (Dyer, 642–43).

6 Landing craft: The Pacific war gave rise to a variety of specialized amphibious landing craft and ships with cumbersome acronyms and nicknames. Some of the most common types mentioned herein are:

Acronym	Definition
DUKW	Amphibious Truck
LCI	Landing Craft, Infantry
LCM	Landing Craft, Medium
LCP	Landing Craft, Personnel
LCT	Landing Craft, Tank
LCVP	Landing Craft, Vehicle and Personnel
LST	Landing Ship, Tank
LSD	Landing Ship, Dock
LVT	Landing Vehicle, Tracked
LCS	Landing Craft, Support
LCS (R)	Landing Craft, Support (Rockets)
LCS (A)	Landing Craft, Support (Artillery)

6 "Without them we held no positions": Sherrod Papers.

6 Pownall and Marcus raid: Miller, *The Complete History of World War II,* 490–93; Morison, *Aleutians, Gilberts and Marshalls,* 92.

8 "Island Raid Gives Japs Jitters": *The Stars and Stripes,* Middle East edition, September 3.

9 "Americans could have raided the mainland": *Ibid.*

10   "Paradoxical as it may sound": Miller, 488.

10   "Our enemy is preparing to seek final victory": d'Albas, *Death of a Navy: Japanese Naval Action in World War II*, 254–55.

11   Allied strength in South Pacific: Department of the Army, *United States Army in World War II*, Vol. VI, Crowl and Love, *The War in the Pacific: Seizure of the Gilberts and Marshalls*, 11–12.

12   Koga, subordinates and strategy: Narrative on Japanese discussions about developments in 1943 is based primarily on various U.S. Strategic Bombing Survey (hereafter USSBS) naval, air, and military analyses, affidavits, and interrogation/testimony of events during the period April–October.

13   Carlson's raid on Makin: Morison, *History of U.S. Naval Operations in World War II*, Vol. IV, *Coral Sea, Midway and Submarine Actions, May 1942–August 1942*, 235–41. For discussion regarding relative merits of this action, see Morison, *Aleutians, Gilberts and Marshalls*, 76–77, and H. M. Smith, *Coral and Brass*, 124. Morale boosting though it was, a later commentator observed: "The victory-starved American public inflated the minor incident on that distant coral island to the proportions and importance of a second Gettysburg." (Werstein, *Tarawa: A Battle Report*, 13–14).

13   Japanese construction in Gilberts: Fourth Fleet HQ, Construction of Fortifications at Tarawa, Nauru, and Ocean Islands (JICPOA 5085); Office of Naval History, Japanese Bases in the Mandated Islands and Gilberts; Crowl and Love, 64–66.

14   New Operational Policy: USSBS, *Campaigns of the Pacific War*, 6–7; USSBS, *Interrogations of Japanese Officials*, Vol. II, 516; Crowl and Love, 65.

16   Fukudome on Koga plan: USSBS, *Interrogations*, 512.

17   "We have to decrease enemy pressure": CINCPAC-CINCPOA Operations in Pacific Ocean Areas, September 1943, 7–10; Crowl and Love, 53.

19   "The Gun Club" discussion: Hoyt, *How They Won the War in the Pacific: Nimitz and His Admirals*, 286–92. For all his prolific writing about the Pacific campaign, this magnificent volume stands as Hoyt's greatest contribution to the study of the American war with Japan.

20   Sources for air raids on the Gilberts, unless otherwise noted, are Craven and Cate, *The Army Air Forces in World War II*, Vol. IV, *The Pacific: Guadalcanal to Saipan, August 1942–July 1944*, 284–87; Morison, *Aleutians, Gilberts and Marshalls*, 82–99; Crowl and Love, 52–54; R. Boyden, Notes on Carrier Raids, Operational Information Section,

COMAIRPAC; CTF 15 (Pownall) and *Princeton* action reports; captured diaries (JICPOA 3872, 4991).

24 Coleman: Karig, *Battle Report,* Vol. IV, *Pacific War: The End of an Empire,* Plate XXII photographs and captions.

25 Allied POWs executed at Tarawa: Hammel and Lane, *76 Hours: The Invasion of Tarawa,* 27–28.

25 Japanese autumn naval movements: CINCPAC Command Summary, October 26; Morison, *Aleutians, Gilberts and Marshalls,* 136; Crowl and Love, 68–69; USSBS, *Interrogations,* 411, and *Campaigns,* 191, 200–03.

26 Sources for air raid on Wake, unless otherwise noted, are Morison, *Aleutians, Gilberts and Marshalls,* 92–93; CINCPAC-CINCPOA, Operations in Pacific Ocean Areas, October, 5–8; USSBS, *Interrogations,* 133; Miller, 493; Crowl and Love, 54; Boyden; CTF 14 (Montgomery) Action Report.

26 Sherrod: Sherrod, *Tarawa,* 3.

27 "Lifeguard" submarine *Skate:* Lockwood, *Sink 'Em All,* 107–08; Roscoe, *Pig Boats,* 269–70.

29 "Whittling-down campaign": Japanese Studies in World War II, No. 50, Vol. III, 5; Crowl and Love, 69–70.

30 Bougainville: Defended by 35,000 Japanese, invaded November 1 by 3d Marine Division, marine Maj. Gen. Alexander Vandegrift commanding. In the first two months of fighting, the marines suffered 1,841 casualties—423 killed, 1,418 wounded. There were 2,500 Japanese dead and 20 prisoners taken.

30 American POWs executed at Wake: R. Wheeler, *A Special Valor: The U.S. Marines and the Pacific War,* 446.

31 "This will only be the beginning": Based on Notes, COMINCH-CINCPAC Meeting, February 22.

31 Guadalcanal, over which desperate battle raged: Griffith, *The Battle for Guadalcanal,* 273–75. For comparative American losses at Guadalcanal, see the section of this book entitled "A Note on Casualties." Recent publication of Richard Frank, *Guadalcanal: A Definitive History of the Landmark Battle,* Random House (1990), has added immeasurably to the study of this interesting campaign and its influence on the war.

31 New Guinea: MacArthur's forces had taken eastern New Guinea "after a campaign which—contrary to his press releases—'had been neither cheaply won nor conducted on the supposition that there was necessity of a hurry attack.'" It had cost 3,085 Allied dead. The Japanese lost about three-fourths of their 16,000 men (Ropp, *War in the Modern World,* 372–73).

31   American submarines: Roscoe, 447–49.

32   The official reasons given for seizing the Gilberts were "(1) to [prepare to] capture, occupy and control the Marshalls; (2) to improve Allied lines of communication; and (3) to support other operations in the Pacific, but primarily to open through Micronesia a second road to Tokyo" (Morison, *Aleutians, Gilberts and Marshalls,* 83–84).

32   "Spruance, you are lucky": Buell, *The Quiet Warrior: A Biography of Admiral Raymond A. Spruance,* 182.

32   Japan should be defeated quickly: JCS, Operations in the Pacific and Far East in 1943–44, May 23.

32   Competing army and navy plans: Crowl and Love, 10–17; Spector, 220–51; Dyer, 613–16.

33   King advocates two-pronged attack: JCS, Strategic Plan for the Defeat of Japan; Ropp, 375.

33   "Operations in the Central Pacific": MacArthur dispatch to General Marshall, June 20; Crowl and Love, 21.

34   Galvanic plan issued: Operation Plan 13-43, CINCPAC, October 5.

35   Planning difficulties: Crowl and Love, 18–34; Stockman, *The Battle for Tarawa,* 3–5; H. M. Smith, *Coral and Brass,* 103–06; Holmes, *Double-Edged Secrets: U.S. Naval Intelligence Operations in the Pacific during World War II,* 139–43.

35   American command structure: Stockman, 2–4; Crowl and Love, 34–39; Dyer, 629–36; Hoyt, *How They Won the War in the Pacific,* 262–85.

36   Holland Smith and planning: H. M. Smith, *Coral and Brass,* 21–23, 98, 101–02. Turner had recommended Smith to Nimitz. Of the general and the job, Turner later said, "[Smith] was the best man I knew for it. He was a marvelous offensively minded and capable fighting man. It was no mistake, and I would do it again." (Dyer, 600).

37   "Giant toy factory": Richardson, *The Epic of Tarawa,* 40.

37   2d Marine Division ordered to prepare for Tarawa: Curiously, "No formal orders were issued. . . . Admiral Spruance assigned the capture of Tarawa Atoll verbally to the 2d Marine Division." (Stockman, 3).

37   Julian Smith: *Maryland in World War II* (Baltimore, MD: War Records Division, Maryland Historical Society), 285.

37   "The guy next door": Werstein, 33–34.

37   Ralph Smith and 27th Infantry Division: Crowl and Love, 44; Gailey, *"Howlin' Mad" Vs the Army: Conflict in Command, Saipan 1944,* 35–52. Gailey presents the most complete picture of Ralph Smith yet published.

39   Cumulative Japanese air losses: In the battle for the Coral Sea, May

1942, Japan lost 75 percent of 121 carrier aircraft and aircrews (Preston, *Decisive Battles of the Pacific War,* 42); at Midway, June 1942, 322 planes and crews (Ito, *The End of the Imperial Japanese Navy,* 83–85); and at Guadalcanal, between August 1942 and February 1943, 683 planes and 1,200 aircrewmen (Frank, 614). In the half year that ended with the withdrawal from Guadalcanal, total Japanese losses everywhere were 893 planes and 2,362 airmen (Ito, 83–85).

39   Japanese Rabaul reinforcements: Morison, *History of U.S. Naval Operations in World War II,* Vol. VI, *Breaking the Bismarcks Barrier, July 1942–May 1944,* 323–36; d'Albas, 262; Crowl and Love, 69–70.

40   Fifth Air Force attacks on Rabaul: Craven and Cates, 325–27.

40   Empress Augusta Bay action: d'Albas, 263–64.

41   Sources for naval air campaign against Rabaul, unless otherwise noted, are Karig, 37–49; Morison, *Breaking the Bismarcks Barrier,* 323–36; Japanese Studies, 26; USSBS, *Campaigns,* 152–53.

42   Japanese cruisers devastated: d'Albas, 264–65.

44   "We have located the Yankee navy": For this anecdote, I am grateful to my late grandfather, Denver D. Roush, a navy veteran of the war who served in landing craft in the Pacific and remembered hearing shipmates (possibly in jest) speak of it or a variation thereof. To be sure, however, some later improved models of the Kawanishi H6K actually were capable of absorbing considerable battle damage (Fitzsimons, 1185–86).

44   Kates: Nakajima B5N2 Type 97 Model 12 carrier-based torpedo bomber. At the time of the attack on Pearl Harbor, the Kate was the most advanced torpedo bomber in the world, but by the time of the Gilberts campaign it was severely outclassed by American models. By the end of the war advances in aviation design of other aircraft relegated the Kate to aerial reconnaissance and ASW duty (Victor Cross, *Battlehawks 1942,* Lucasfilm, San Rafael, CA, 1989, 108–09).

45   Vals: Aichi D3A2 Type 99 Model 12 carrier-based bomber. The D3A1 was so maneuverable it was sometimes used as a fighter, though with its fixed landing gear, it had a slow airspeed. Despite the fact that it could carry only a light bomb load, it was considered one of the best dive bombers of the war (*Ibid.,* 106–07).

46   Bettys: Mitsubishi G4M OB-01 medium bomber. The backbone of Japan's long-range land-based air forces, the Betty was more highly combustible when hit by bullets than any other Japanese aircraft, which earned it the sobriquet "the one shot lighter" (Fitzsimons, 1070–71).

54   Japanese strength in Gilberts: Crowl and Love, 60–66, 70–72; Morison, *Aleutians, Gilberts and Marshalls,* 122, 146–50; JICPOA, Japanese Forces in the Gilbert Islands.

55   Sinking of *Bangkok Maru:* Holmes, 144–45; Morison, *Aleutians, Gilberts and Marshalls,* 78.

56   Japanese fortifications: Morison, *Ibid.*; Crowl and Love, 73–74; Stockman, 7–8; Dyer, 626–29.

57   *Sculpin* departs Pearl Harbor: Chambliss, *The Silent Service,* 73–75.

59   Edson: Griffith, 141–42, 144–46.

59   Shoup: Sherrod, 27.

60   Tarawa plan: Dyer, 688–91; Morison, *Aleutians, Gilberts and Marshalls,* 149–51; Crowl and Love, 43; Stockman, 5.

60   Hereafter in order to avoid unnecessary repetition, official military abbreviations for unit designations may be used in some cases. For example, 2/8 is short for 2d Battalion, 8th Marines; 1/105 means 1st Battalion, 105th Infantry.

61   Makin plan: Morison, *Aleutians, Gilberts and Marshalls,* 121–27; Crowl and Love, 40–43.

62   LVT controversy: Reconstructed from Dyer, 655–56; Crowl and Love, 41, 47–48; Stockman, 4–5; H. M. Smith, *Coral and Brass,* 91, 111–12; Shaw, Nalty, and Turnbladh, *History of U.S. Marine Corps Operations in World War II,* Vol. III, *Central Pacific Drive,* 38–39; Werstein, 33–36.

62   Morison on LVTs: Morison, *Aleutians, Gilberts and Marshalls,* 89–90.

66   Naval support plan: Operations Plan 1-43, October 13, 1; Crowl and Love, 35, 40, 42; Buell, 201–02.

67   "Twiddling my thumbs at Pearl Harbor": H. M. Smith, *Coral and Brass,* 109.

68   ASSRONs: Craven and Cate, 295–96.

68   Shipping and provisioning: Crowl and Love, 49–51; Morison, *Aleutians, Gilberts and Marshalls,* 100–02, 106–07, 112.

68   Rehearsals: Crowl and Love, 47; Stockman 9–10.

69   "My Darling—Australia"; quoted in S. E. Smith, *The United States Marine Corps in World War II,* Vol. II, *Battering the Empire,* 591.

70   Sources for preliminary naval and air action in the Marshalls and Gilberts, unless otherwise noted: TF 57 (Hoover) Report on Air Strike Operations, December 16; CINCPAC-CINCPOA, Operations in the Pacific Ocean Areas, November, Annex E, 20; Craven and Cate, 298–310; Morison, *Aleutians, Gilberts and Marshalls,* 98, 114–18; Crowl and Love, 54–59, 193–99; Dyer, 644–48.

71   Japanese strength at Mili: Crowl and Love, 208–10.
71   "These attacks did little damage": COMAIRPAC Report on Gilberts Operations, November.
75   "Mili is a Jap cemetery": Karig, 95–96.
76   "Gilberts theater of decisive war": *Asahi Shimbun*, November 28.

PART TWO—THE ATTACK

Page
79   Ota: Hoyt, *Storm over the Gilberts*, 21, 32.
80   "Work was started immediately": From 755th Naval Air Group, Report of Present Conditions at Tarawa Air Base, September 29 (JICPOA 4051), quoted in Crowl and Love, 67.
80   *Nautilus* reconnaissance: Morison, *Aleutians, Gilberts and Marshalls*, 97–98.
81   Oonuki and Tanikaze: Russ, *Line of Departure: Tarawa*, 17–19.
82   Ota: Hoyt, *Storm over the Gilberts*, 72–73.
83   Japanese air reconnaissance: Crowl and Love, 58–59; Dyer, 653–54.
83   "Enemy contact report": Karig, 78.
83   Japanese air attacks: CTG 54.4, November 18–19 Action Report. See also Love, *The Twenty-seventh Infantry Division in World War II*, 29, and Dyer, 653–54.
84   "We must replenish ammo": CINCPAC-CINCPOA translation 10018; Crowl and Love, 56.
85   Scouting submarines: Morison, *Aleutians, Gilberts and Marshalls*, 187–88.
86   *Sculpin* vs. Japanese destroyer: Chambliss, 78–92.
89   "Jarred holy hell out of us": Karig, 100.
90   "After strafing us in the water": *Ibid.*, 101.
91   Cromwell self-sacrifice: Holmes, 148–49.
92   "Units attached to this force": CTF 52 (Turner) to his combined forces, letter, November 19, quoted in Morison, *Aleutians, Gilberts and Marshalls*, 120.
93   "A great offensive to destroy": CG SECMARDIV (J. C. Smith) to his marines, letter, November 19, quoted in Stockman, 86.
93   Amey briefing: Sherrod, 36–38.
94   "Japanese will be punch–drunk": *Ibid.*, 38–39.
94   "I don't give a damn": *Ibid.*, 39–40, 41.
95   "There won't be a damned Jap": *Ibid.*, 42.
95   Guadalcanal and poor morale: Griffith, 90.
96   Galvanic press corps: Sherrod, 4; Hannah, *Tarawa: The Toughest Battle in Marine Corps History*, 75–77, 97–99; Buell, 210–12.

96   "The Japs are probably out there": Hannah, 16.

96   "Just six days from now": S. E. Smith, *Battering the Empire,* 531–32.

96   "It is not our intention": H. M. Smith, *Coral and Brass,* 122. In *Combat Correspondent* (p. 170), Lucas attributes this boast to a public relations major. However, Russ (p. 35) is correct in pinning it on Kingman, who uttered the words at a predeparture staff briefing at Efate. Later, en route to Tarawa, Kingman used it again in a press conference and it was flashed throughout the fleet, presumably to reinforce confidence among the troops. Thereafter numerous officers and correspondents repeated it, until it became only the most memorable of many embarrassingly arrogant predictions about Tarawa. It was quoted so many times, in fact, that it has even been attributed mistakenly to Hill.

96   "When marines meet the enemy": S. E. Smith, 531.

97   Hayward: Hannah, 12, 97–99, 103–04.

98   Shibasaki alerts Truk: IGH, Summary of American Army Counterattack in the Gilbert Area, January 1944; Karig, 78.

98   Japanese reaction to threat: Morison, *Aleutians, Gilberts and Marshalls,* 137–38.

98   Mars the red planet: Karig, 86.

99   *Ringgold* in action: *Ibid.,* 79–82; CTG 53.4 (Kingman) Galvanic Action Report, 25 December; *Ringgold* Action Report, 5 December, and ship's log.

100   *Nautilus* under friendly fire: Karig, 82–83; Roscoe, 274–76; Lockwood, 119; Morison, *Aleutians, Gilberts and Marshalls,* 154; *Nautilus* War Patrol Report; CINCPAC Report on Shelling of *Nautilus,* 24 December.

102   Naval organization and approach: TF 52 (Turner) Report on Galvanic, December 16; Dyer, 689–92; Morison, *Aleutians, Gilberts and Marshalls,* 114–20.

103   *Zeilin:* Sherrod, 53.

104   "You felt the muscle": McCardle, quoted in Hoyt, *How They Won the War in the Pacific,* 298.

104   "Men knelt in the dripping room": Sherrod, 51–52.

104   "The younger guys": As related by Lucas in conversations with author.

104   "Are you scared": Sherrod, 32.

105   "This kid with a Bronx accent": As related by Carl Thomas in conversations with the author.

105   "Hey, Bill, I just remembered": Sherrod, 50.

105   "Only a few even whistled": *Ibid.,* 54.

105   "I don't know how I'll feel": Wilson, Lucas, Shaffer, and Zurlinden, *Betio Beachhead: U.S. Marines' Own Story of the Battle for Tarawa,* 116.

105   Seventh wedding anniversary: Karig, 87.

105   "Coral Kiska": Kiska, in the Aleutian Islands off Alaska, was invaded August 15 by 34,500 American and Canadian troops, army Maj. Gen. Charles H. Cortlett commanding. Unknown to the attackers, the Japanese had evacuated the island some days before the Allied attack.

105   Breakfast aboard ships: Morison, *Aleutians, Gilberts and Marshalls,* 120, 154; Sherrod, 52–53.

106   "Tokyo Rose": Hammel and Lane, 36.

106   Onorio and natives: TF 53 (Hill) Special Action Report of Tarawa Operation, 13 December. Onorio is identified as one of the natives in Manchester, *Goodbye, Darkness: A Memoir of the Pacific War,* 258–59.

107   Ota: Hoyt, *Storm over the Gilberts,* 72–73.

108   Sasaki: *Ibid.,* 85–86.

109   Sources for general movement and activities of defenders and attackers at Tarawa, unless otherwise indicated, are Morison, *Aleutians, Gilberts and Marshalls,* 153–63; Stockman, 7–15; Crowl and Love, 127–55; TF 52 (Turner) and 53 (Hill) reports; IGH, Military Action in the Gilbert Islands Area, November.

110   "When you have a good target": Werstein, 60.

110   "In a few minutes": Morison, *Aleutians, Gilberts and Marshalls,* 155.

110   "Spiritual Ration for D-Day": Johnston, *Follow Me! The Story of the Second Marine Division in World War II,* 109–10.

110   "Bring glory to our Corps": Richardson, 74.

110   "God have mercy on the Japanese": *Ibid.,* 78.

111   Bonnyman and Clerou: Hammel and Lane, 36–37.

111   Welte: Sherrod, 55–56.

112   "Let the bastards keep it": As related by WO David Fitzsimmons in conversations with the author.

112   Davis: Berry, *Semper Fi, Mac: Living Memories of the United States Marines in World War II,* 148–49.

112   Typical marine combat load: Hannah, 81.

113   Mishap aboard *Heywood:* Hammel and Lane, 38.

114   Japanese open fire: Morison, *Aleutians, Gilberts and Marshalls,* 156; Stockman, 11; TF 53 (Hill); individual ships' logs.

114   "The curtain was up": Sherrod, 56.

115   "Shall we go ahead, sir": McCardle, quoted in Hoyt, *How They Won the War in the Pacific,* 302.

115   "The big ship flinched": *Ibid.*

116   "We weren't used to the quiet": Werstein, 62.

117   "Suddenly about 100 yards off": Karig, 86.

117   "My God, what wide shooting": Sherrod, 59.

118   "They splattered steel": TG 53.1 (Knowles) Action Report on Tarawa Operation, 1 December; Dyer, 692–94.

118   "Without warning": Hannah, 29.

118   "Behind our boats strung out": Karig, 86–87.

119   "Of four 8-inch and eight 5-inch guns": TF 53 (Hill) Report of Observers' Comments on Galvanic Operation, December 23.

119   "Wall of naval gunfire": Later in the war, experience proved that this was not a problem. Aircraft bombed and strafed from heights far above the arc of naval gunfire. At this time, however, it was a great concern to aviators.

120   LST-34: LST-34 ship's log; CTG 53.14 (McGovern), Report on Galvanic, December 4.

121   "I recalled pictures of Union gunboats": As related by Seaman Myron Karl in conversations with the author.

121   Departure of transports: CTG 53.1 (Knowles) Galvanic Report.

121   "The ship opposite us": Karig, 87.

121   "Fat mother ducks": *Maryland* air observer's log, quoted in Werstein, 63.

122   "Boat-race day at New London": Karig, 87.

124   "It was still dark enough": *Independence* Galvanic Action Report, December 4.

124   "One moment there was a plane": McCardle, quoted in Hoyt, *How They Won the War in the Pacific,* 302.

125   "One could see coconut palms": Narrative by Morison, December 15, Operational Sound Recording OFR-36, quoted in Dyer, 661.

125   *Pennsylvania* marksmanship: Smith, *Keystone Battlewagon,* 30; TF 52 (Turner) Report.

125   Makin fortifications: Crowl and Love, 71–73.

126   Sasaki: In part Hoyt, *Storm over the Gilberts,* 85–86.

128   "We had a fine training period": TF 53 (Hill), signal, November 19, to COMCENPAC, quoted in Buell, 215–16.

128   "Tougher than anyone has said": Sherrod, 40.

129   *Ringgold:* Karig, 87; *Ringgold* Action Report.

133   B-24s at Funafuti: Russ, 58.

136   "Within five minutes": Sherrod, 60.

137   "Numbed a man's senses": Werstein, 65.

137   "Island fall apart and sink": Richardson, 82.

137   "Couldn't see anything": Werstein, 62.

137   "It seemed almost impossible": CTG 53.4 (Kingman), Special Action Report, 17–22 November, 2.

137   "The whole island was ablaze": Werstein, 65.

138   "Voice of doom": *Ibid.*

139   "I jumped down": S. L. A. Marshall, Makin Notes, quoted in Crowl and Love, 77.

140   "Fires were burning everywhere": Buell, 217–18.

143   "The thirty-four men in my platoon": Sherrod, 45.

143   Commando assault on pier: There are as many versions of what actually occurred during this dramatic event as there have been books about Tarawa. This conservative reconstruction, after studying the battle for a decade or more, is probably as accurate as one dares try to be these almost fifty years after the fact. Unless otherwise noted, this account relies only on official sources, such as the 2d and 18th Marines' action reports.

143   "On ship they were giving odds": Richardson, 91.

144   "Fifteen hundred yards from shore": *Ibid.,* 90.

144   Olivier: Hammel and Lane, 49; Olivier Silver Star citation.

144   Hawkins' personal determination: Sherrod, 45–48.

145   Spruance observes landing: Buell, 217–18.

148   Japanese deaths in bombardment: V Amphibious Corps (Smith) Report on Gilbert Islands Operation, 11 January 1944, 2.

148   "The earth shook": Captured diary, quoted in Werstein, 67.

149   *Hachimaki* and *Sennimbari:* R. Wheeler, 172.

PART THREE—THE HORROR

Page
155   The sources for the capture of Tarawa, unless otherwise indicated, are Stockman; Crowl and Love, 127–55; TF 53 (Hill) War Diary (November) and Galvanic Report; 2d Marine Division Special Action Report, including regimental operations reports; and individual ships' logs and reports.

155   When the 1st Marine Division invaded Guadalcanal in August 1942, it was reinforced primarily by the 2d Marines of the 2d Marine Division. This regiment landed on and captured neighboring Florida, Gavutu, and Tulagi islands and fought on Guadalcanal, remaining in action until relieved in January 1943. From beginning to end, the 2d Division sustained casualties of 278 killed and missing and 932 wounded in the campaign. Fifty percent of these occurred among the 2d Marine Regiment.

155   Marine regiments were designated by the generic "Marines" following their regimental number. Infantry regiments were numbered 1 through 9, and 21 through 29; artillery regiments 10 through 15; engineer regiments 16 through 20. In contrast, army regiments were desig-

nated by branch of service—9th Infantry, 25th Field Artillery, 5th Engineers, et cetera. It is a mistake, then, to refer to the 2d Marine Division as the 2d Marines, although the latter term refers to a component of that division.

155   As late as autumn 1943, the 2d Marine Division continued to suffer from chronic poor health. On October 10, for example, the division had 1,387 combat ineffectives among its ranks as a result of illness. Admissions for malaria alone at this time averaged forty reported cases per day. But on the eve of battle at Tarawa only seventeen men were not among the ranks; this speaks more to high morale than to the miracles of U.S. Navy medicine.

155   Tarawa "gave the nation a name": *Time,* December 6, 1943.

156   "I had a panoramic view": R. Wheeler, 176.

157   "An anti-boat gun stopped our craft": *Ibid.*

158   Baird: J. Campbell Bruce, "One Square Mile of Hell," *Sea Power,* April 1944, quoted in Morison, *Aleutians, Gilberts and Marshalls,* 162–63. Baird's account has become the classic participant description of H hour at Tarawa. No history of the battle would be (or ever has been) complete without returning to it in some way.

158   Company K platoon leaders: 3d Battalion, 2d Marines, Action Report; 2d Marines Report of Operations on Betio Island, 20–23 November; Hammel and Lane, 51–54.

159   Tatom: Hammel and Lane, 55–56.

159   "He had been standing": There were numerous instances of officers and men who tried to sneak a peek at the shore on their way in and came to similar tragic ends. This testifies to the volume of Japanese small-arms fire against the assault waves.

160   "Most if not all": Russ, 74.

160   Bale: In part Wilson, Lucas, *et al.,* 61; Hannah, 47.

161   "Have landed": Werstein, 81. See also Lucas, *Combat Correspondent,* 177, for the wartime censored variation of this communique: "Have landed. Heavy opposition. Casualties 70 percent. Can't hold." Interestingly, it is this latter abridged version reported by Lucas that has continued to be used since the battle.

161   Bayer: Richardson, 90.

161   "We realized with a shock": R. Wheeler, 179.

162   "It was too damn bad": Richardson, 91.

162   "We swore everybody was dead": *Ibid.,* 93.

164   Hawkins and Leslie: In part Hammel and Lane, 48–50; Werstein, 70–71.

165   Hawkins "was a madman": Sherrod, 89.

165   Morgan "was shot in the throat": *Ibid.*

166   Bordelon: Moskin, *The U.S. Marine Corps Story,* 296–97; Bordelon Medal of Honor citation.

166   Drewes "died with a grin": Wilson, Lucas, *et al.,* 46.

166   Lawrence: Sherrod, 191–92.

167   Spillane: Steinberg, *Island Fighting,* 111; Spillane Silver Star citation.

167   Beckwith: Russ, 66–68.

167   Newcomb: Hannah, 113–14.

168   Doyle: Sherrod, 87.

169   Ivary: Richardson, 91.

169   Amey and Hipple: Hannah, 24–25.

170   "It was like being suspended": Richardson, 89.

170   Swenceski: Morison, *Aleutians, Gilberts and Marshalls,* 164.

170   Bundy: Wilson, Lucas, *et al.,* 45–46; Hannah, 122–26; Sherrod, 192.

171   Sherrod: Sherrod, 64–65.

171   The Russells: Island group thirty-five miles from Cape Esperance. Invaded February 21 by 43d Infantry Division and attached marine units, under overall command of army Maj. Gen. Millard Harmon, as an intermediate step in Halsey's capture of New Georgia.

174   Spooner: Berry, 149.

174   Libby: Russ, 89–90.

175   Crowe landing: *Ibid.,* 77–78.

176   "You'll never get the purple heart": Griffith, 272.

176   "His men spoke about him": Wilson, Lucas, *et al.,* 60.

176   "The fire was heavy as hell": Berry, 89.

177   "I wasn't about to try and swim": *Ibid.,* 150.

177   Oonuki: Russ, 71–72.

180   Shoup landing: In part Russ, 84–86, 90–95.

182   "OK, let's get going": Hannah, 24–25.

184   "They've done it": Hoyt, *How They Won the War in the Pacific,* 305.

185   "Can't something be done": *Maryland* air observer's log, quoted in Wilson, Lucas, *et al.,* 38.

185   "The water seemed never clear": *Ibid.*

186   "Like fighting in the middle of a pool table": Richardson, 14.

187   "A steel girder": Johnston, 120.

187   "Pierced the ears": *Ibid.*

188   Hospodar: Wilson, Lucas, *et al.,* 64.

189   "They were pulverized": Berry, 152.

190   Spruance and "issue in doubt": Buell, 218–19.

191   Smith and "issue in doubt": H. M. Smith, *Coral and Brass,* 114–15.

192   Oonuki: Russ, 104–07.

196   "A disaster is developing": Based on Buell, 219.

197   The sources for the capture of Makin, unless otherwise indicated, are Crowl and Love, 75–125; TF 52 (Turner) Report; 165th RCT Journal; 27th Infantry Division Operations Report; and logs and reports of individual ships.

197   "Some of the men read": War Department Report, "Makin Operation," quoted in Morison, *Aleutians, Gilberts and Marshalls*, 129–30.

197   "The bullets were dropping all around": *Ibid.*

199   "We went forward": 193d Tank Battalion After Action Report of Makin Operation, 56; Crowl and Love, 85.

200   Campbell: Love, 32.

203   Bale: In part Johnston, 120; Wilson, Lucas, *et al.*, 62.

204   "She lit up": *Ibid.*

205   Nimitz: Potter, 257.

206   Bordelon: Moskin, 296–97; Bordelon Medal of Honor citation.

209   Largey and Sherman tanks: Wilson, Lucas, *et al.*, 61–62.

210   Duplessie: *Ibid.*

211   "I never had much use": *Ibid.*

211   Japanese air attack west of Tarawa: TF 50 (Pownall), TG 50.3 (Montgomery), *Independence* Galvanic action reports; Japanese Fourth Fleet War Diary; Morison, *Aleutians, Gilberts and Marshalls*, 138.

214   "I was quite certain": Sherrod, 77–78.

215   Brukardt: Wilson, Lucas, *et al.*, 86–87; Hannah, 40–44.

216   Vincent: Although this grim event is much reported in the Tarawa literature, to the best of the author's knowledge, this is the first time the dead navy doctor whose shot-up landing craft floated alongside *Biddle* is reported to have been Lieutenant Vincent. The basis for this assumption is that two doctors were killed at Tarawa—Vincent and "Doc" Welte. The latter was a member of Lieutenant Colonel Amey's party and died wading ashore with that unfortunate battalion commander on Red Beach 2.

216   Barnhill: Hannah, 35.

217   Marine losses in historical context: Sherrod, 94.

218   "An untried doctrine": Sherrod Papers.

220   "This is the damndest crap game": *Ibid.*

224   Matthews: Lucas, *Combat Correspondent,* 185–90; Hannah, 110.

225   Flak mistaken for naval battle: Sherrod, 78.

226   *Nautilus* and scouts at Abemama: *Nautilus* War Patrol Report; Karig, 82–83.

229   Cook: Russ, 113–15, 120; TF 53 (Hill) Action Report.

229   "We were so seasick": Werstein, 91–92.

231   "Within five minutes": Sherrod, 82.

232   Carlson: *Ibid.*, 99.

232   "The water was red": *Ibid.*, 110.

233   "I wormed along": S. E. Smith, 554–55.

233   Heimberger: Morison, *Aleutians, Gilberts and Marshalls,* 171.

234   "They can't hit me": Wilson, Lucas, *et al.*, 86.

236   "Cheering as we would at a football game": Lucas, *Combat Correspondent,* 192.

237   "Psst! Hey, Sarge!": Love, 45.

237   "Reveille, fellows!": *Ibid.*

239   "Don't worry about me": Lucas conversations.

239   "I came here to kill Japs": Sherrod, 89.

239   Death of "Hawk": Hannah, 38–40.

240   "His relentless fighting": Hawkins Medal of Honor citation.

240   Towers and loss of *Independence:* Potter, 259; Hoyt, 310–11.

241   "The use of surface craft": Potter, *Ibid.*

242   "We had to stay there": Morison, *Aleutians, Gilberts and Marshalls,* 181.

243   Holland Smith at Makin: Unless otherwise indicated, H. M. Smith, *Coral and Brass,* 117–20; Marshall, *Bringing Up the Rear,* 61–71, *Battle at Best,* 141–51; Gailey, 20–82. Many sources have noted that H. M. Smith's account is biased. Nevertheless, the version of Smith at Makin given here is but a pale reflection of his acerbating description of this operation in his writings. It is impossible to reconcile conflicting accounts of Smith at Makin.

　　　The chief source available for checking up on Smith is the famous soldier-historian S. L. A. Marshall, who was there. However, Marshall's work on Makin, though wonderfully written, is often specious. It does not always jibe with the official army history, which, although largely based on Marshall's notes, is implicitly critical of the 27th Division and was co-written by another soldier who was also there (Love). In addition, to put it mildly, Marshall was not one of Holland Smith's most enthusiastic admirers.

　　　Gailey's detailed *"Howlin' Mad" Vs the Army* is the latest and best attempt to atone for the 27th Division's encounters with the enemy. Relying on oral evidence against H. M. Smith, it is an interesting revisionist condemnation of the general's controversial memoirs. Although Gailey obscures occasional facts in excoriating Smith and his disagreeable personality, the truth about Makin probably lies closer to Gailey's admirable effort than to Smith's self-aggrandizing memoirs.

Because of the abstract issue—whether Ralph Smith and his green troops moved fast enough—it is difficult to separate personal opinion from pure reporting on Makin. Love's various writings on Makin, which are measured and dispassionate, remain the only overall reliable popular sources about that battle.

246   "This is worse": Sherrod, 83.

246   Strange: *Ibid.,* 87–88.

246   "As long as we have boys": Werstein, 109–10.

246   "Mighty tough spot": Sherrod, 85.

247   "Situation ashore doesn't look good": *Ibid.*

250   Japanese submarine I-35: Hoyt, *Storm over the Gilberts,* 120–23; CINCPAC, *A/S Bulletin,* January 1944, 26; JICPOA, Interrogation of Japanese POWs from the Gilberts; Sixth Fleet War Diary.

251   *Meade* and *Frazier* ASW action: Karig, 91–92; Morison, *Aleutians, Gilberts and Marshalls,* 139; *Meade* and *Frazier* action reports; COMDESDIV 14 to CINCPAC, 16 December; *Frazier* report to CINCPAC, 30 November.

258   "Touch and go": Sherrod, 94.

258   "Smile of grinning marine": *Maryland* air observer's log, quoted in Wilson, Lucas, *et al.,* 82.

258   "Reflected in everyone's face": Sherrod, 90.

258   "It has been my privilege": Hannah, 47.

260   "We were not all heroes": Morison, 171–72.

PART FOUR—THE END

Page
265   "Shots whizzed": H. M. Smith, *Coral and Brass,* 119–20.

266   "Get your men out": From a combination of Marshall, *Bringing Up the Rear,* 69, and *Battle at Best,* 147–48, which give slightly different accounts of this episode.

266   "General, that plain isn't so": Marshall, *Bringing Up the Rear,* 69.

266   "All of the main enemy works": *Ibid.,* 70.

267   "We three sat there together": *Ibid.,* 69.

267   "Those infantrymen were terrific": Hannah, 47.

268   "All right, you bastards": Wilson, Lucas, *et al.,* 96–97.

268   Kranc: *Ibid.,* 98.

270   Chamberlin and Hatch: Hannah, 115–17.

270   Bonnyman: Bonnyman Medal of Honor citation; Hammel and Lane, 232–34; Russ, 154–55; Johnston, 143.

271   "They ought to have medals": Hannah, 116. So graphic was the film *With the Marines at Tarawa,* there followed an alarming drop in marine enlistments (Sherrod, quoted in R. Wheeler, *A Special Valor,* 210).

272   Jay: Wilson, Lucas, *et al.*, 86.

274   Marine policemen: Wilson, Lucas, *et al.*, 100–02.

275   Oonuki: Russ, 147.

277   "Sagging knees": Marshall, *Battle at Best*, 154.

277   "When we bivouacked at sundown": Marshall, *Bringing Up the Rear*, 71.

278   "Many of us had the idea": Crowl and Love, 123.

278   Graham, Pasdertz, Slatner: Marshall, *Battle at Best*, 157–59.

279   "Come on in": *Ibid.*, 160.

279   Bizzari: *Ibid.*

279   "They came on in a series": Marshall, *Bringing Up the Rear*, 71–72.

281   "We need help": Wilson, Lucas, *et al.*, 110.

281   "We pitched everything": Hannah, 51–52.

282   Warfield: Wilson, Lucas, *et al.*, 118–19.

282   Rector and Koci: *Ibid.*, 120.

282   Ness and Edwards: *Ibid.*

282   "I had the field phone": Hannah, 51–52.

282   Miles: Wilson, Lucas, *et al.*, 120.

283   Milner: Hammel and Lane, 253–55.

283   Corbin: Wilson, Lucas, *et al.*, 110.

283   "We're killing them": Sherrod, 113.

283   Stambaugh, Carstens: Wilson, Lucas, *et al.*, 114–15.

284   Shaffer: Lucas, *Combat Correspondent*, 198.

284   "Stand fast": Wilson, Lucas, *et al.*, 108–10. For his inspiring leadership, Lieutenant Thomas was awarded the Silver Star. He was later killed at Saipan.

286   "Strange screwball pictures": Richardson, 17.

286   "In some spots": Hannah, 50–51.

287   "The boys stood up": Wilson, Lucas, *et al.*, 118.

289   Japanese "convulsive and obviously nearly out of their minds": Though it has been noted in connection with other Pacific battles, most notably Iwo Jima, this is the first time that atrocities committed by the marines and Japanese against one another at Tarawa have been acknowledged or even hinted at. As Lucas told the author: "It's not something we were proud of, but what choice did we have. The Japanese nearly always refused to surrender, or they would act like they were surrendering and then come at you firing."

293   "The Saps": Steinberg, 113.

293   "Our weapons are too light": Karig, 183.

294   Father Mehl and Japanese: Lucas, *Combat Correspondent*, 204–05.

295   Kelly: Wilson, Lucas, *et al.*, 144.

296   Williams, Millione, Frankenstein: *Ibid.*, 154.

297   "Men turned from digging": *Ibid.*

297   Lumpkin: Wilson, Lucas, *et al.*, 146.

297   Darling: Lucas, *Combat Correspondent*, 198–99.

297   Willard: Willard, *The Leathernecks Come Through*, quoted in S. E. Smith, 589–93.

298   Oonuki: Russ, 173–75.

298   Nimitz and Richardson: Potter, 260–61.

299   "No way to make war safe": Hannah, 72.

299   "The Marines who took Tarawa": *Ibid.*, 74.

299   "No one regrets the losses": *Ibid.*

299   "Saw in the American action": Richardson, 4.

301   End of *Liscome Bay:* TG 52.13 (Griffin), Report on Loss of *Liscome Bay,* December 11. See also Karig, 92–94; Hoyt, *Storm over the Gilberts,* 152–57; Morison, *Aleutians, Gilberts and Marshalls,* 140; Dyer, 677–80.

306   Glory—and plenty of gore: Dyer, in his section entitled "The Gory Glory" (p. 731), notes: "To many who fought through the campaigns of the Central Pacific and on north to Japan, Galvanic was the foundation and the portend of the future. Others thought of the masterly way the blow was struck, the grimness of the task, and the incomparable courage of the men who struck it."

308   "Their will to die": Hannah, 72.

308   "Driven American courage": USSBS, *Interrogations.*

308   "Tarawa was the only landing": Sherrod, 186.

309   "Brainiest, finest soldiering marine": Wilson, Lucas, *et al.*, 54.

309   LVT losses: Morison, *Aleutians, Gilberts and Marshalls,* 186.

310   "Recommendations made and acted upon": Crowl and Love, 370.

311   "It'll only become worse": Based on Notes, COMINCH-CINCPAC Meetings, September 25–October 4. Reader should know that this is author's extrapolation. Inasmuch as this sentiment could relate to the forthcoming Central Pacific campaign, the case probably could also be made for its application to Nimitz's views on something as mundane as logistics, which were heavily discussed during these meetings. Nevertheless, the record is clear that Nimitz viewed the Central Pacific campaign with some measure of trepidation. In addition, several veterans have told me of an occasion (or occasions) when they overheard him say this or other words to this effect, after the Gilberts campaign. For the record, however, the statement is an implied one here.

A NOTE ON CASUALTIES

Page

312   Guadalcanal casualties: Frank, 614.

312   Overall American losses in Galvanic: With the exception of army noncombat injuries, the total primarily reflects only losses from combat causes of all personnel employed in missions connected directly or indirectly to Galvanic. The figure is notably higher than anything reported heretofore, and not only compares closely to Guadalcanal but also ranks Galvanic among the costliest American campaigns in the Pacific. Proportionate to the forces engaged, however, Galvanic was the costliest. At the time, the casualties were the highest American losses for any three days of the war, Pacific or European (R. Wheeler, 209).

The data for Operation Galvanic were compiled from the records of all commands in which it is known from published sources that casualties occurred. Anything more exact was beyond the author's means.

312   North Africa, Sicily, Salerno: From "Army Battle Casualties and Nonbattle Deaths in World War II, Final Report, 7 December 1941– 31 December 1946."

312   Marine Corps casualties: The figures for Tarawa were revised several times between 1943 and 1952 as the full cost of the operation became known. The basic source used here is "Final Report on Tarawa Casualties," Casualty Division, Headquarters, USMC, 1952.

313   Navy and Coast Guard casualties: In part Dyer, 730, and Willoughby, *The U.S. Coast Guard in World War II,* 268–71. Dyer, apparently basing his comparison on the outdated tally given by Morison, *Aleutians, Gilberts and Marshalls* (p. 185), notes that "the shocking news to those in the Navy . . . was that the Naval officers [KIA] off Makin and Tarawa amounted to [more than] the Marine officers dead at Tarawa." In addition, "the Navy's enlisted [KIA] . . . were 74 percent of [the] total of marine enlisted dead at Tarawa." Overall, however, Dyer's accounting of 62 naval officers and 684 enlisted KIA is spotty and is of limited value for casualty analysis.

313   Army casualties: Crowl and Love, 125. Army Air Force losses are arrived at by adding the costs of the various actions between November 6 and December 4 in support of Galvanic, cited elsewhere herein.

313   Japanese losses: No two original sources agree on Japanese casualties. Data used here, for the period November 6–December 4, include Morison, *Aleutians Gilberts and Marshalls,* 148-49; Dyer 640–41; Stockman, 73; Crowl and Love, 125.

Estimates of Japanese land, sea, and air personnel losses caused by U.S. air and naval action in the Marshalls and Gilberts are based on USSBS, captured documents, and JICPOA intelligence summaries.

314 Native casualties: There are no sound figures for this topic. Author's estimate is an educated guess, based on the sum total of the Gilberts literature in which occasional references are made to injured natives.

315 Presidential Unit Citation: Stockman, 87.

316 Individual honors: Official record-keeping data, citations.

Bibliography

PRIMARY SOURCES
The year for dated documents, unless otherwise noted, is 1943.

Official Records

Board of Decorations and Medals, Department of the Navy, Alexandria, Virginia.
Official citations, individual navy and marine honors and awards, Galvanic.

U.S. Army Military History Institute, Department of the Army, Carlisle, Pennsylvania. Photographic Records.
World War II S.C. Coll.—Gilbert Islands—Tarawa.
World War II S.C. Coll.—Gilbert Islands—Makin.

U.S. Marine Corps Historical Archives, Washington, D.C.
18th Marines Special Action Report. The period covered by marine special action reports, unless otherwise noted, is November 20–24, 1943.
8th Marines Special Action Report.
2d Amphibious Tractor Battalion Special Action Report.
2d Marine Tank Battalion Special Action Report.
2d Marine Division Special Action Report, November.
2d Marine Division War Diary, September–November.
2d Marines Operations Journal, 19–24 November.
2d Marines Special Action Report.
6th Marines Special Action Report, 20–26 November.
V Amphibious Corps Operations Plan 1-43, 13 October.
V Amphibious Corps Reconnaissance Company Special Action Report, 20–28 November.
V Amphibious Corps Report on Gilbert Islands Operation.

National Archives, Washington, D.C.
Office of Military History, War Department, Japanese Studies in World War II, No. 50, Vol. III, 1946.
Office of Military History, Department of the Army, "Japanese Forces in the Gilberts Islands, 10 December 1942–November 1943," 1951.
165th Regimental Combat Team Journal.
193rd Tank Battalion After Action Report of Makin Operation.
Records of the Joint and Combined Chiefs of Staff, Record Group 218.

Record Group 242, Seized Enemy Records.

Photographic Record Groups 80, 111, 127, and 208.

27th Infantry Division Report on Makin Operation, 16–25 November.

U.S. Naval Historical Archives, Washington, D.C.

CINCPAC-CINCPOA Operations Plan 13-43 (Galvanic), 5 October.

CINCPAC-CINCPOA, Operations Report, Pacific Ocean Areas, September.

CINCPAC-CINCPOA, Operations Report, Pacific Ocean Areas, October.

CINCPAC-CINCPOA, Operations Report, Pacific Ocean Areas, November.

CINCPAC Galvanic Action Report, November-December.

COMAIRPAC Report on Gilberts Operations, November.

COMCARDIV 24 Action Report, 20–26 November.

Dahsiell Action Report, 20–22 November.

Frazier Action Report, November.

Independence Galvanic Report.

JCS Strategic Plan for the Defeat of Japan, 14 May 1943.

JICPOA Bulletin 11-43, "Air Target Bulletin of Tarawa Island [sic]."

JICPOA Bulletin 8-44, "Japanese Forces in the Gilbert Islands."

JICPOA Bulletin 11-44, "Study of Japanese Defenses of Betio Island, Tarawa Atoll," December.

LST-31 War Diary, November.

LST-34 Ship's Log, November.

Maryland Action Report, 20 November.

Meade Action Report, November.

Nautilus War Patrol Report, November.

Office of Naval History, "Japanese Bases in the Mandated Islands and Gilberts," October.

Office of Naval Intelligence, "The Gilbert Islands," October.

Papers of Admiral E. J. King.

Princeton Action Report, September.

Pursuit Action Report, 20–22 November.

Ringgold Action Report, 21 October–2 December.

TF 14 Action Report on Wake Operation, October.

TF 15 Action Report on Gilberts air raid, September.

TF 53 Report on Observers' Comments on Galvanic Operation.

TF 53 Special Action Report on Tarawa Operation, November.

TF 53 War Diary, November.

TF 53.4 (Fire Support Group) Special Action Report, 17–22 November.

TF 54 (5th Amphibious Force) Galvanic Operations Plan, A2-43, 23 October.

TF 54 (5th Amphibious Force) Report of Amphibious Operations for the Capture of the Gilbert Islands, 4 December.

TF 57 (Galvanic Air Forces) Report of Air Strike Operations, 16 December.
Task Group (TG) 52.13 (Makin Air Support Group) Report of Loss of USS *Liscome Bay.*
TG 53.1 (Transport Group) Action Report on Tarawa Operation, November-December.
TG 54.4 Action Report, 18–19 November.
U.S. Pacific Fleet War Diary, November.

Published Works

Craven, W. F., and J. L. Cate, eds. *The Army Air Forces in World War II,* Vol. IV, *The Pacific: Guadalcanal to Saipan, August 1942–July 1944.* Chicago: University of Chicago, 1953.

Department of the Army, Office of the Chief of Military History. *United States Army in World War II,* Vol. VI, Crowl, P. A., and E. G. Love. *The War in the Pacific: Seizure of the Gilberts and Marshalls.* Washington, D.C.: U.S. Government Printing Office, 1955.

Department of the Army, Office of the Chief of Military History. *United States Army in World War II,* Vol. X, Louis Morton. *The War in the Pacific, Strategy and Command: The First Two Years.* Washington, D.C.: U.S. Government Printing Office, 1962.

Department of the Navy, U.S. Naval History Division. *U.S. Naval History Sources in the United States.* Washington, D.C.: U.S. Government Printing Office, 1979.

Dyer, G. C. *The Amphibians Came to Conquer: The Story of Admiral Richmond Kelly Turner.* Washington, D.C.: U.S. Government Printing Office, 1970. Semi-official.

Morison, S. E. *History of United States Naval Operations in World War II,* Vol. IV, *Coral Sea, Midway and Submarine Actions, May 1942–August 1942.* Boston: Little, Brown, 1949. Semi-official.

——. *History of United States Naval Operations in World War II,* Vol. VI, *Breaking the Bismarcks Barrier, July 1942–May 1944.* Boston: Little, Brown, 1950. Semi-official.

——. *History of United States Naval Operations in World War II,* Vol. VII, *Aleutians, Gilberts and Marshalls, June 1942–April 1944.* Boston: Little, Brown, 1951. Semi-official.

Shaw, H., B. Nalty, and E. Turnbladh, Historical Branch, Operations Division, Headquarters, U.S. Marine Corps. *History of U.S. Marine Corps Operations in World War II,* Vol. III, *Central Pacific Drive.* Washington, D.C.: U.S. Marine Corps, 1966.

Stockman, J. R. Historical Section, Division of Public Information, Headquarters, U.S. Marine Corps. *The Battle for Tarawa*. Washington, D.C.: U.S. Marine Corps, 1947.

United States Strategic Bombing Survey (USSBS), Naval Analysis Division (Pacific). *The Campaigns of the Pacific War*. Washington, D.C.: U.S. Government Printing Office, 1946.

USSBS. *Interrogations of Japanese Officials,* 2 vols. Washington, D.C.: U.S. Government Printing Office, 1946.

War Department, Historical Division. *American Forces in Action* series, *The Capture of Makin, 20 November–24 November 1943*. Washington, D.C.: U.S. Government Printing Office, 1946.

BOOKS

Berry, H. *Semper Fi, Mac: Living Memories of the U.S. Marines in World War II*. New York: Arbor House, 1982.

Blankfort, M. *The Big Yankee: A Biography of Evans Carlson*. Boston: Little, Brown, 1947.

Buell, T. B. *The Quiet Warrior: A Biography of Admiral Raymond A. Spruance*. Annapolis, MD: U.S. Naval Institute, 1987 (Little, Brown, 1978).

Chambliss, W. C. *The Silent Service*. New York: New American Library, 1959.

d'Albas, A. *Death of a Navy: Japanese Naval Action in World War II*. New York: Devin-Adair, 1957.

Ewing, S. *USS Enterprise (CV-61): The Most Decorated Ship of World War II*. Missoula, MT: Pictorial Histories, 1982.

Fitzsimons, B. *The Illustrated Encyclopedia of Twentieth Century Weapons and Warfare*. New York: Columbia House, 1978.

Frank, R. B. *Guadalcanal: The Definitive Account of the Landmark Battle*. New York: Random House, 1990.

Gailey, H. A. *"Howlin' Mad" Vs the Army: Conflict in Command, Saipan 1944*. Novato, CA: Presidio Press, 1986.

Griffith, S. B. *The Battle for Guadalcanal*. New York: Ballantine, 1966 (Lippincott, 1963).

Hammel, E., and J. Lane. *76 Hours: The Invasion of Tarawa*. Pacifica, CA: Pacifica Press, 1985 (Belmont Tower, 1980).

Hannah, R. *Tarawa: The Toughest Battle in Marine Corps History*. New York: U.S. Camera, 1944.

Holmes, W. J. *Double-Edged Secrets: U.S. Naval Intelligence Operations in the Pacific during World War II*. Annapolis, MD: U.S. Naval Institute, 1979.

Hough, F. *The Island War: The United States Marine Corps in the Pacific*. New York: J. P. Lippincott, 1947.

Howard, C., and J. Whitley. *One Damned Island After Another: The Saga of the Seventh Air Force.* Chapel Hill, NC: University of North Carolina, 1946.

Hoyt, E. P. *Storm over the Gilberts: War in the Central Pacific, 1943.* New York: Avon, 1983 (Van Nostrand Reinhold, 1978).

———. *How They Won the War in the Pacific: Nimitz and His Admirals.* New York: Weybright and Talley, 1970.

———. *To the Marianas: War in the Central Pacific, 1944.* New York: Van Nostrand Reinhold, 1980.

———. *The Carrier War.* New York: Avon, 1987.

———. *Japan's War.* New York: De Capo, 1986.

Isley, J., and P. Crowl. *The U.S. Marines and Amphibious War.* Princeton, NJ: Princeton University Press, 1951.

Ito, M. with R. Pineau. *The End of the Imperial Japanese Navy.* New York: W. W. Norton, 1962.

Johnston, R. W. *Follow Me! The Story of the Second Marine Division in World War II.* New York: Random House, 1948.

Karig, W. *Battle Report,* Vol. IV, *Pacific War: The End of an Empire.* New York: Rinehart, 1947.

King, E. J. *Fleet Admiral King, A Naval Record.* New York: W. W. Norton, 1952.

Lockwood, C. A. *Sink 'Em All.* New York: Bantam, 1984.

Love, E. G. *The Twenty-seventh Infantry Division in World War II.* Nashville, TN: Battery Press, 1982 (Infantry Journal Press, 1949).

Lucas, J. G. *Combat Correspondent.* New York: Reynal & Hitchcock, 1944.

McCombs, D., and F. Worth. *World War II Super Facts.* New York: Warner, 1983.

Manchester, W. M. *Goodbye, Darkness: A Memoir of the Pacific War.* New York: Dell, 1979 (Little, Brown, 1978).

Marshall, S. L. A. *Battle at Best.* New York: Jove, 1989 (William Morrow, 1963).

———. *Bringing Up the Rear.* San Rafael, CA: Presidio Press, 1979.

Miller, F. T. *The Complete History of World War II.* Chicago: Readers' Service Bureau, 1947.

Morison, S. E. *The Two Ocean War.* Boston: Little, Brown, 1963.

Morrison, W. *Above and Beyond.* New York: St. Martins Press, 1983.

Moskin, J .R. *The U.S. Marine Corps Story.* New York: McGraw-Hill, 1987.

Potter, E. B. *Nimitz.* Annapolis, MD: U.S. Naval Institute, 1976.

Preston, A., ed. *Decisive Battles of the Pacific War.* Secaucus, NJ: Bison Books, 1979.

Richardson, W. *The Epic of Tarawa.* London: Odhams, 1944.

Robson, R. W. *The Pacific Islands Handbook.* New York: MacMillan, 1946.

Rooney, A. A. *The Fortunes of War: Four Great Battles of World War II*. Boston: Little, Brown, 1962.

Ropp, T. *War in the Modern World*. New York: Collier Books, 1962 (Durham, NC: Duke University Press, 1959).

Roscoe, T. *United States Destroyer Operations in World War II*. Annapolis, MD: U.S. Naval Institute, 1953.

————. *Pig Boats*. New York: Bantam, 1982. (Previously published as *United States Submarine Operations in World War II*. Annapolis, MD: U.S. Naval Institute, 1949.)

Russ, M. *Line of Departure: Tarawa*. Garden City, NY: Doubleday, 1975.

Shapiro, M. T. *Assault on Tarawa*. New York: McKay, 1981.

Shaw, H. I. *Tarawa: A Legend Is Born*. New York: Ballantine, 1969.

Sherrod, R. *Tarawa: The Story of a Battle*. New York: Bantam, 1983 (Duell, Sloan & Pearce, 1945).

Smith, H. M., and P. Finch. *Coral and Brass*. New York: Bantam, 1987 (Charles Scribner's Sons, 1949).

Smith, M. J. *Keystone Battlewagon*. Charleston, WV: Pictorial Histories, 1983.

Smith, S. E., ed. *The United States Marine Corps in World War II*, Vol. II, *Battering the Empire*. New York: Ace, 1973 (Random House, 1969).

Spector, R. H. *Eagle Against the Sun: The American War with Japan*. New York: The Free Press, 1985.

Stafford, E. P. *The Big E: The Story of the USS Enterprise*. New York: Dell, 1964 (Random House, 1962).

Steinberg, R. *Island Fighting*. Arlington, VA: Time-Life Books, 1978.

Werstein, I. *Tarawa: A Battle Report*. Binghamton, NY: Vail-Ballou, 1965.

Wheeler, K. *War under the Pacific*. Arlington, VA: Time-Life, 1980.

Wheeler, R. *A Special Valor: The U.S. Marines and the Pacific War*. New York: Harper & Row, 1983.

Willard, W. *The Leathernecks Come Through*. New York: Revell, 1944.

Willoughby, M. F. *The U.S. Coast Guard in World War II*. Annapolis, MD: U.S. Naval Institute, 1957.

Wilson, E. J., J. G. Lucas, S. Shaffer, and C. P. Zurlinden. *Betio Beachhead: U.S. Marines' Own Story of the Battle for Tarawa*. New York: Putnam, 1945.

Young, P. *The World Almanac of World War II*. New York: World Almanac, 1981.

PERIODICALS

Brown, R. G. "Tarawa: Lest We Forget," *Marine Corps Gazette,* November 1980, 46–50.

Bruce, J. C. "One Square Mile of Hell," *Sea Power,* April 1944.

Fleming, V. K., Jr. "Hurried Invasion's Grim Toll," *World War II,* January 1987, 16–25.

Haley, J. F. "Reconnaissance at Tarawa Atoll," *Marine Corps Gazette,* November 1980, 51–55.

Hammel, E., and J. Lane. "1st Battalion, 8th Marines Lands at Tarawa," *Marine Corps Gazette,* November 1983, 84–91.

Jones, W. K. "Tarawa: The Stinking Little Island," *Marine Corps Gazette,* November 1983, 30–41.

Ladd, D. "Reliving the Battle: A Return to Tarawa," *Marine Corps Gazette,* November 1983, 93–98.

Lillibridge, G. D. "Not Forgetting May Be the Only Heroism of the Survivor," *American Heritage,* October 1983, 27–35.

McKiernan, P. L. "Tarawa: The Tide That Failed," *U.S. Naval Institute Proceedings,* February 1962, 38–49.

Rixey, P. M., and W. H. Best. "Artillery at Tarawa," *Marine Corps Gazette,* November 1944.

Shaw, H. I. "That's My Beach," *Marine Corps Gazette,* November 1978, 26.

Sherrod, R. "Hawk," *Marine Corps Gazette,* November 1970, 27–29.

Smith, H. M. "Tarawa Was a Mistake," *Saturday Evening Post,* November 6, 1943.

Tolbert, F. X. "Abemama: A Model Operation in Miniature," *Leatherneck,* February 1945, 26.

Wukovits, J. F. "Even Hell Wouldn't Have It," *American History Illustrated,* February 1986, 38–48.

NEWSPAPERS

Asahi Shimbun, Tokyo, Japan, November 28, 1943.

The Stars and Stripes, Middle East Edition, Cairo, Egypt, September 3, 1943.

Index